D1094702

Robert Jordan's
the WHEEL of TIME®
the EYE of the WORLD

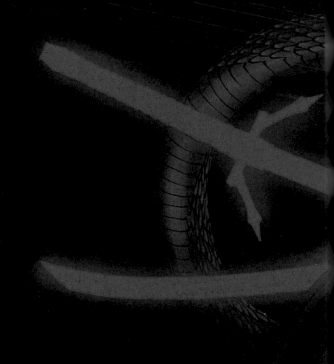

The Wheel of Time®
Graphic Novels

Based on the Novels by Robert Jordan

New Spring:
The Graphic Novel
Robert Jordan, Chuck Dixon, Mike Miller, Harvey Tolibao

The Eye of the World:
The Graphic Novel, Volume One
Robert Jordan, Chuck Dixon, Chase Conley

The Eye of the World:
The Graphic Novel, Volume Two
Robert Jordan, Chuck Dixon, Andie Tong

Robert Jordan's the WHEEL of TIME

the EYE of the WORLD

Volume Two

TOR

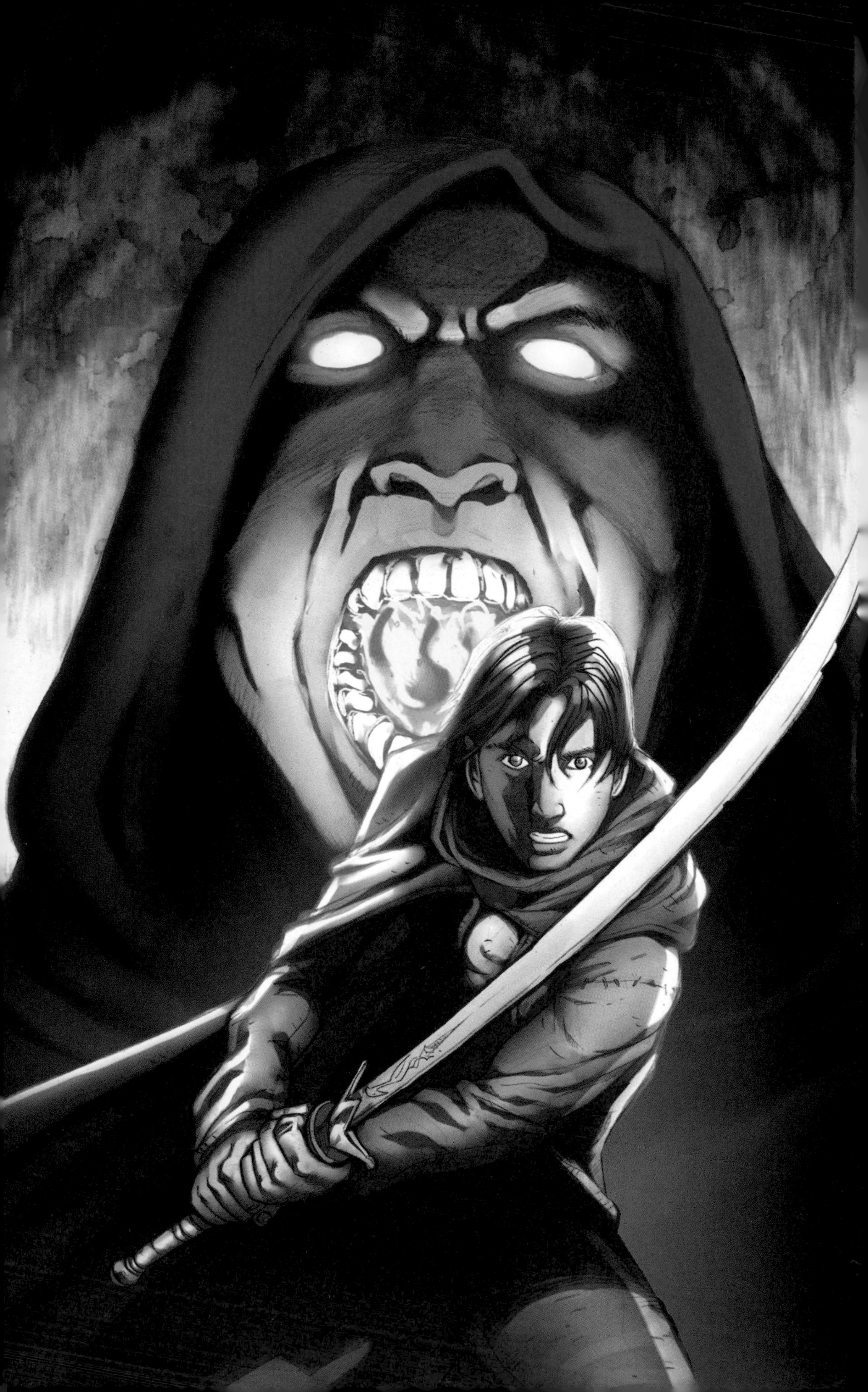

written by
ROBERT JORDAN

adapted by
CHUCK DIXON

artwork by
ANDIE TONG

colors by
NICOLAS CHAPUIS

lettered by
BILL TORTOLINI

original series edited by
ERNST DABEL
RICH YOUNG

consultation
ERNST DABEL
LES DABEL

thematic consultants
MARIA SIMONS
BOB KLUTTZ
ALAN ROMANCZUK

Covers by Andie Tong
Collection edits by Rich Young
Collection design by Bill Tortolini

DYNAMITE®
ENTERTAINMENT

Dynamite Entertainment:

NICK BARRUCCI · PRESIDENT
JUAN COLLADO · CHIEF OPERATING OFFICER
JOSEPH RYBANDT · EDITOR
JOSH JOHNSON · CREATIVE DIRECTOR
RICH YOUNG · BUSINESS DEVELOPMENT
JASON ULLMEYER · GRAPHIC DESIGNER

www.dynamiteentertainment.com

A Tor Book
Published by Tom Doherty Associates, LLC
175 Fifth Avenue
New York, NY 10010

www.tor-forge.com

Tor® is a registered trademark of Tom Doherty Associates, LLC
ISBN 978-0-7653-3162-5
First Edition: June 2012
Printed in the United States of America

Table of Contents

WHAT CAME BEFORE...

Springtime had not come to the world, but the towns-
folk of Emond's Field pushed ahead with their Bel Tine
Festival regardless--a gleeman had come to town, and
there were rumors of fireworks. They would celebrate
no matter what the portents whispered.

Padan Fain, a peddler, brought stories of a man with
the ability to wield the One Power. People were as
interested in these tales as they were in the items
Fain had to sell.

But the peddler was not the only visitor to Emond's
Field. There was also Moiraine, an Aes Sedai, and her
Warder, Lan; they came for reasons known only to
Moiraine. She showed a special interest in three boys
from the village: Rand al'Thor, Mat Cauthon, and
Perrin Aybara.

Sinister forces came to the town as well. A menacing
rider in a black cloak untouched by the wind was seen
by several young men. On Winternight, Trollocs
attacked Emond's Field and the outlying farms;
Rand barely escaped their clutches, fleeing through
the thick of the forest with his injured father.

Come the daylight, Moiraine revealed to Rand that this was no random raid. The Trollocs--and the eyeless Myrddraal that commanded them--were looking for him, Mat, and Perrin. In one of these boys, or all three, was an element of latent power that the Dark One feared. Moiraine suggested that the only safe haven for them, the only place they could perhaps learn why the Myrddraal were after them, was Tar Valon, the fabled city of the Aes Sedai.

Before they left Emond's Field they were joined by Thom Merillin, the gleeman, and Egwene, a young woman who had noticed the boys preparing to leave and insisted on joining them. Despite Lan's opposition, Moiraine accepted Egwene into the party.

The group was hardly beyond the Two Rivers when Rand spotted a Draghkar's silhouette against the moon ...

chapter one

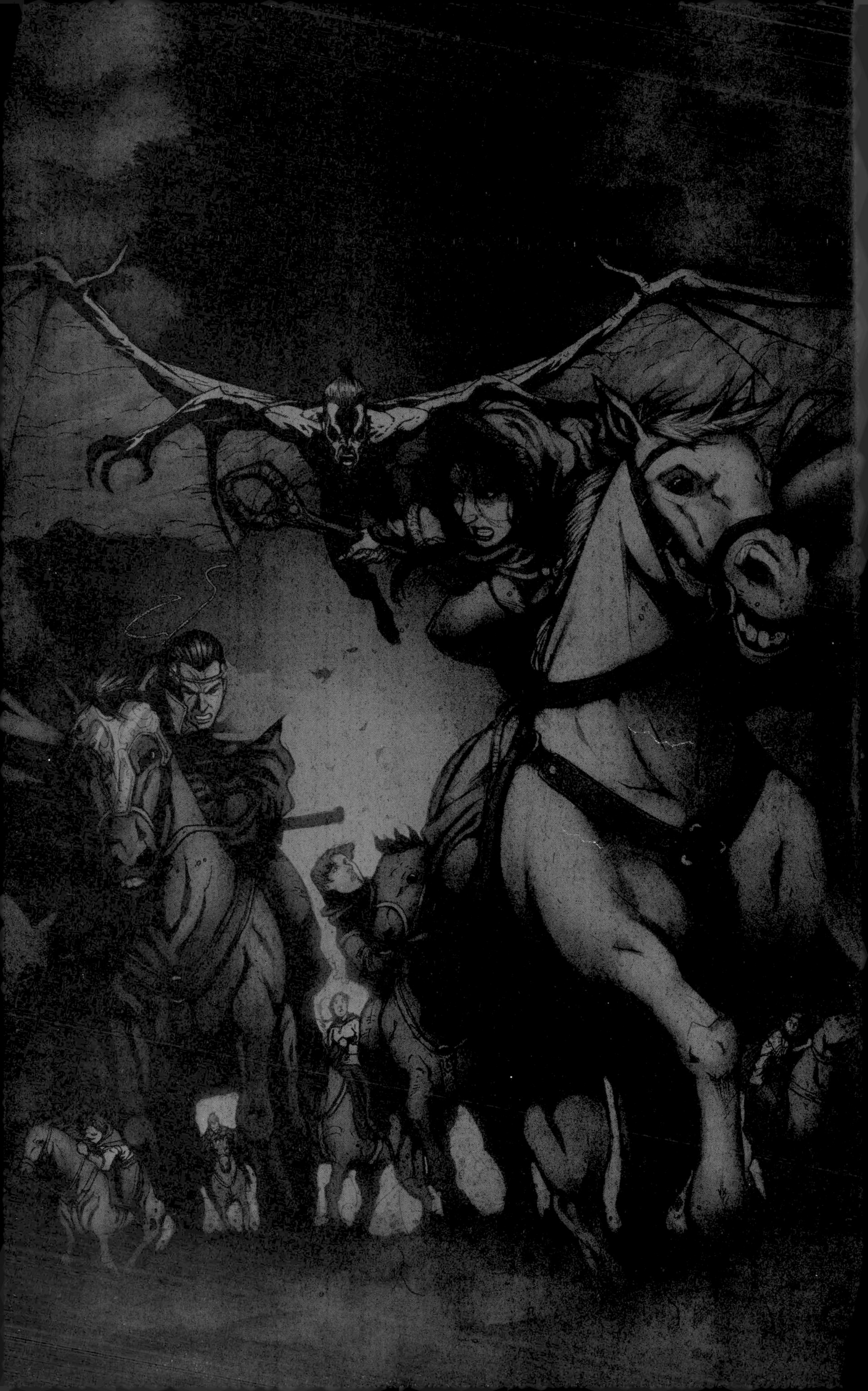

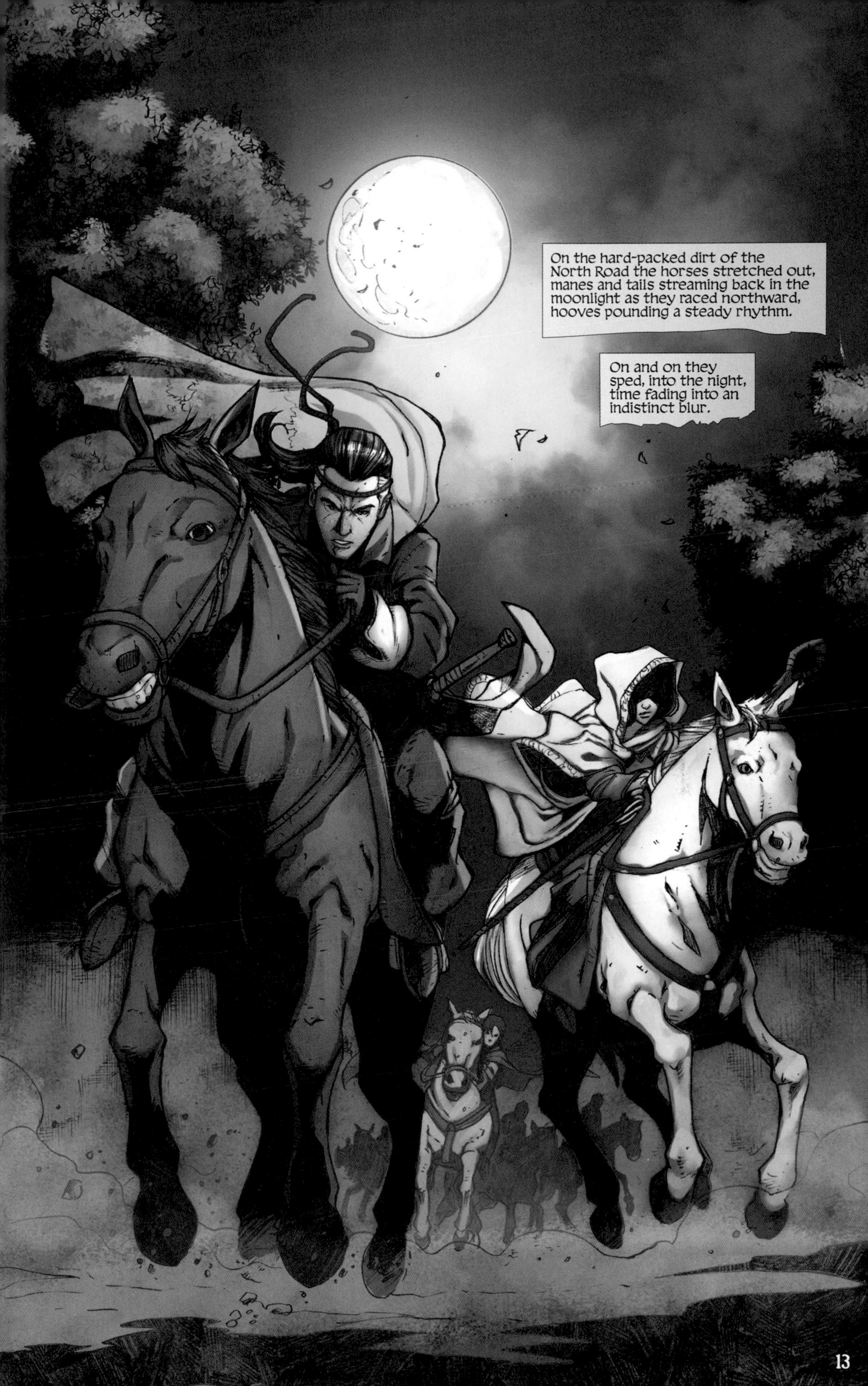
On the hard-packed dirt of the North Road the horses stretched out, manes and tails streaming back in the moonlight as they raced northward, hooves pounding a steady rhythm.
On and on they sped, into the night, time fading into an indistinct blur.

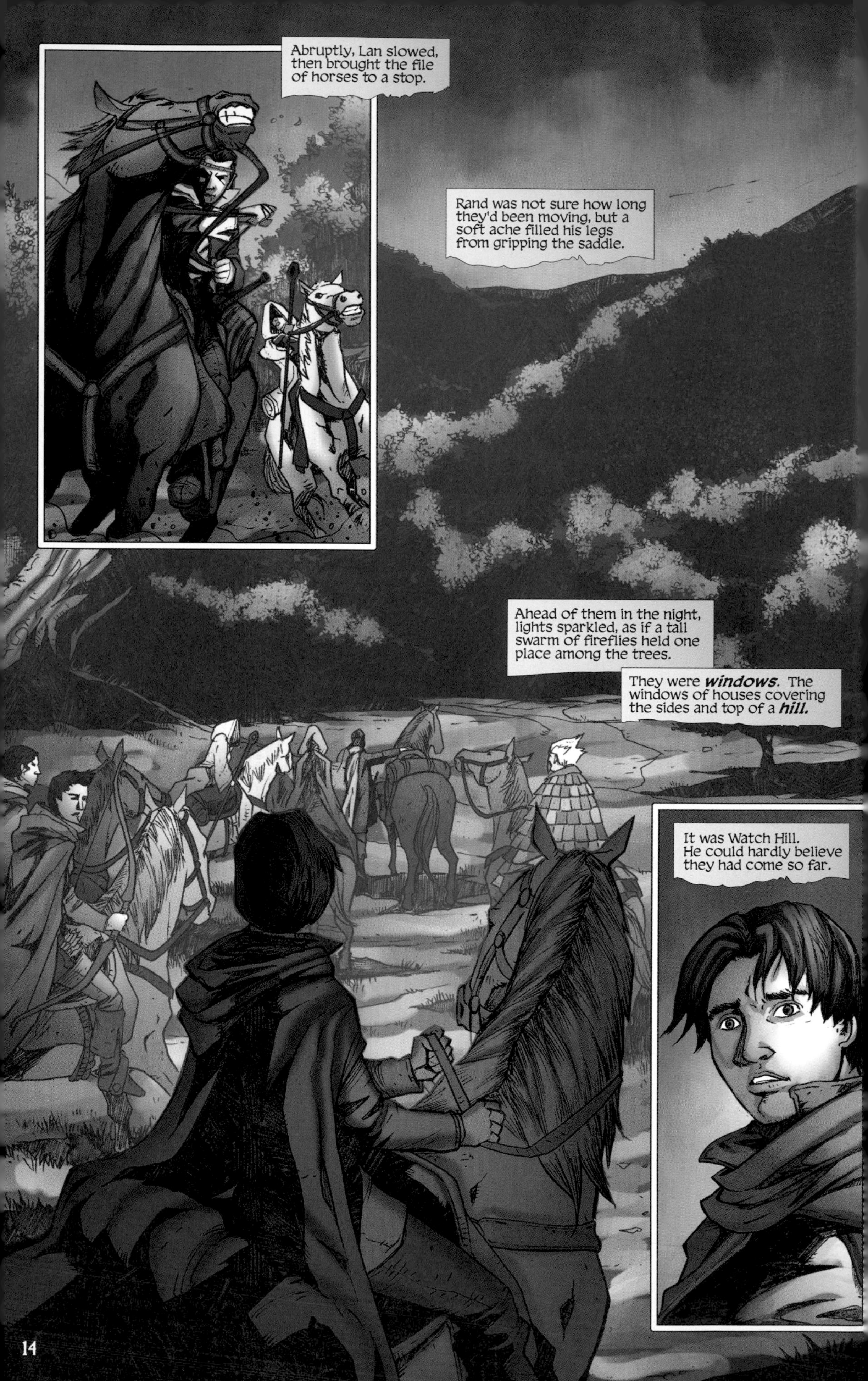
Abruptly, Lan slowed, then brought the file of horses to a stop.
Rand was not sure how long they'd been moving, but a soft ache filled his legs from gripping the saddle.
Ahead of them in the night, lights sparkled, as if a tall swarm of fireflies held one place among the trees.
They were ***windows***. The windows of houses covering the sides and top of a ***hill.***
It was Watch Hill. He could hardly believe they had come so far.

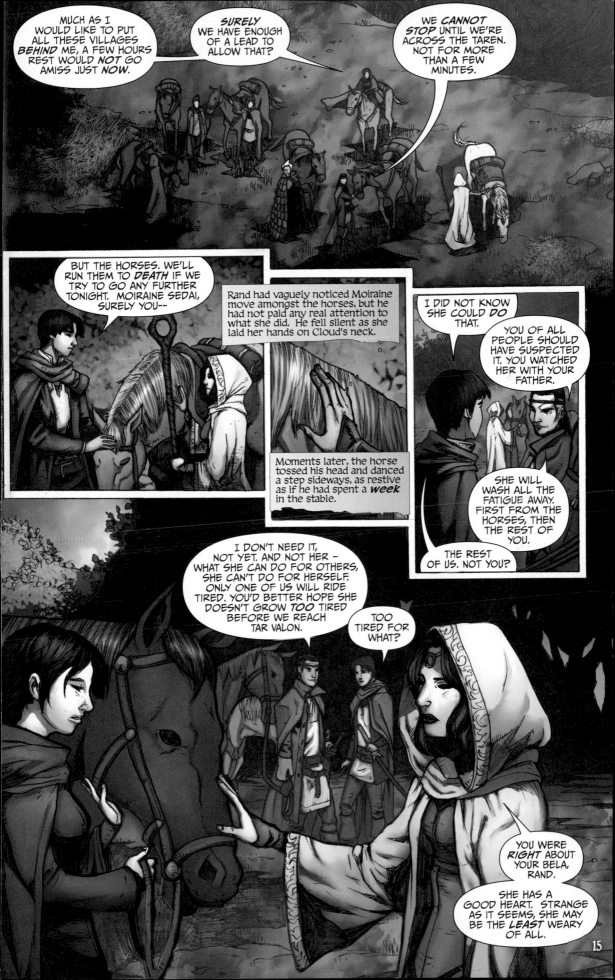

MUCH AS I WOULD LIKE TO PUT ALL THESE VILLAGES *BEHIND* ME, A FEW HOURS REST WOULD *NOT* GO AMISS JUST *NOW*.

SURELY WE HAVE ENOUGH OF A LEAD TO ALLOW THAT?

WE *CANNOT STOP* UNTIL WE'RE ACROSS THE TAREN. NOT FOR MORE THAN A FEW MINUTES.

BUT THE HORSES. WE'LL RUN THEM TO *DEATH* IF WE TRY TO GO ANY FURTHER TONIGHT. MOIRAINE SEDAI, SURELY YOU--

Rand had vaguely noticed Moiraine move amongst the horses, but he had not paid any real attention to what she did. He fell silent as she laid her hands on Cloud's neck.

Moments later, the horse tossed his head and danced a step sideways, as restive as if he had spent a *week* in the stable.

I DID NOT KNOW SHE COULD *DO* THAT.

YOU OF ALL PEOPLE SHOULD HAVE SUSPECTED IT. YOU WATCHED HER WITH YOUR FATHER.

SHE WILL WASH ALL THE FATIGUE AWAY. FIRST FROM THE HORSES, THEN THE REST OF YOU.

THE REST OF US. NOT YOU?

I DON'T NEED IT, NOT YET. AND NOT HER – WHAT SHE CAN DO FOR OTHERS, SHE CAN'T DO FOR HERSELF. ONLY ONE OF US WILL RIDE TIRED. YOU'D BETTER HOPE SHE DOESN'T GROW *TOO* TIRED BEFORE WE REACH TAR VALON.

TOO TIRED FOR WHAT?

YOU WERE *RIGHT* ABOUT YOUR BELA, RAND.

SHE HAS A GOOD HEART. STRANGE AS IT SEEMS, SHE MAY BE THE *LEAST* WEARY OF ALL.

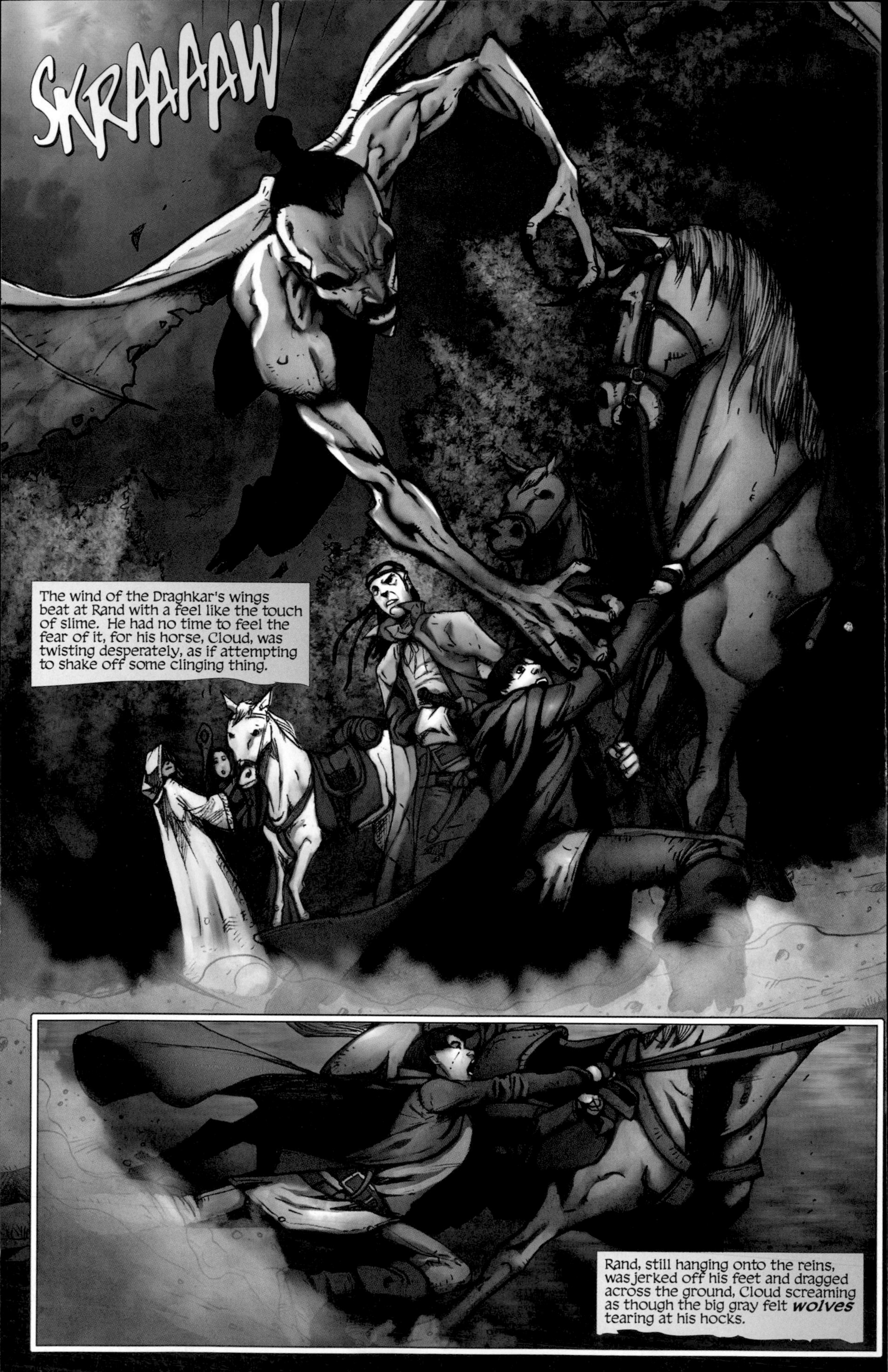
SKRAAAAW
The wind of the Draghkar's wings beat at Rand with a feel like the touch of slime. He had no time to feel the fear of it, for his horse, Cloud, was twisting desperately, as if attempting to shake off some clinging thing.
Rand, still hanging onto the reins, was jerked off his feet and dragged across the ground, Cloud screaming as though the big gray felt ***wolves*** tearing at his hocks.

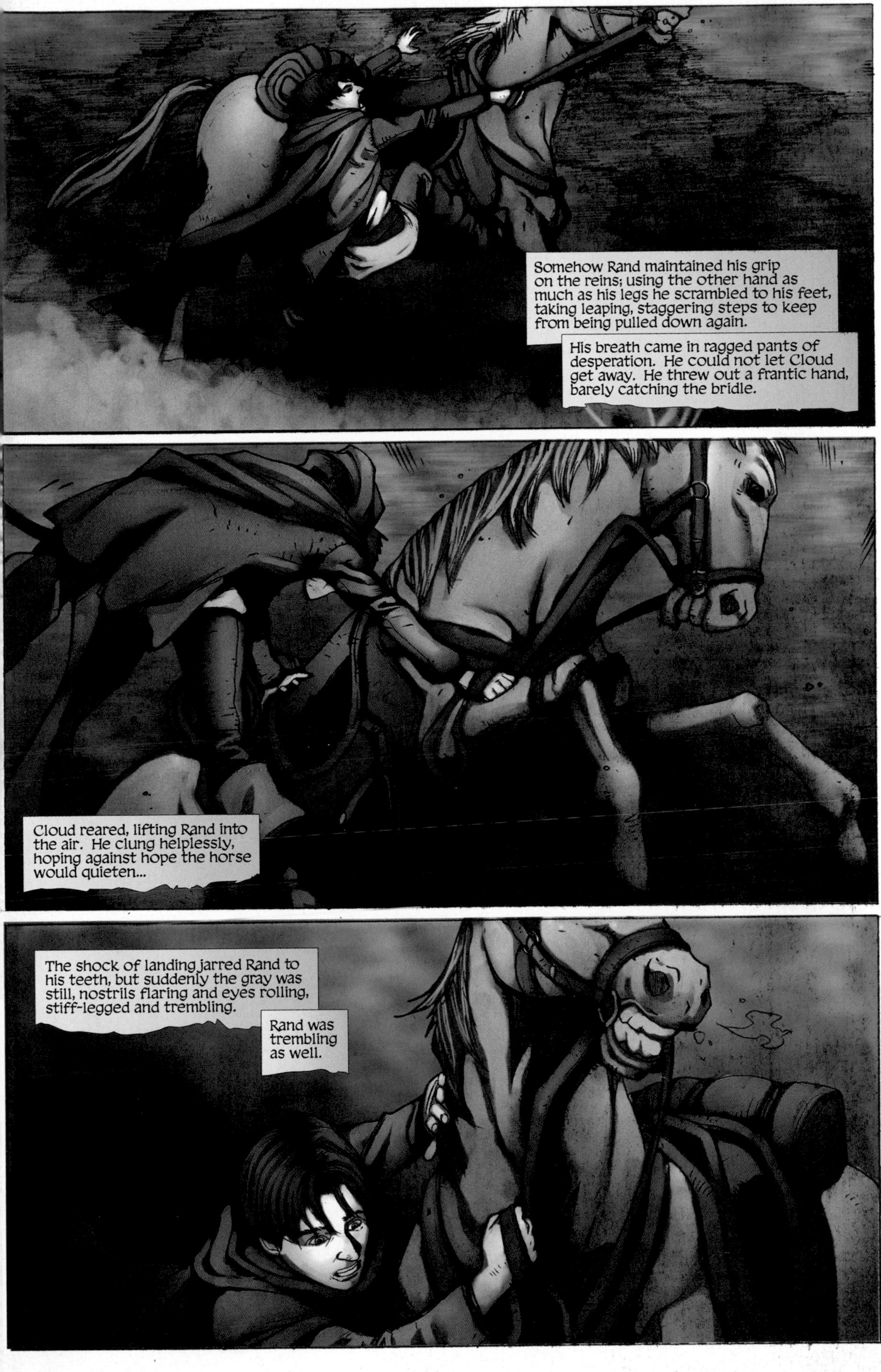
Somehow Rand maintained his grip on the reins; using the other hand as much as his legs he scrambled to his feet, taking leaping, staggering steps to keep from being pulled down again.
His breath came in ragged pants of desperation. He could not let Cloud get away. He threw out a frantic hand, barely catching the bridle.
Cloud reared, lifting Rand into the air. He clung helplessly, hoping against hope the horse would quieten...
The shock of landing jarred Rand to his teeth, but suddenly the gray was still, nostrils flaring and eyes rolling, stiff-legged and trembling.
Rand was trembling as well.

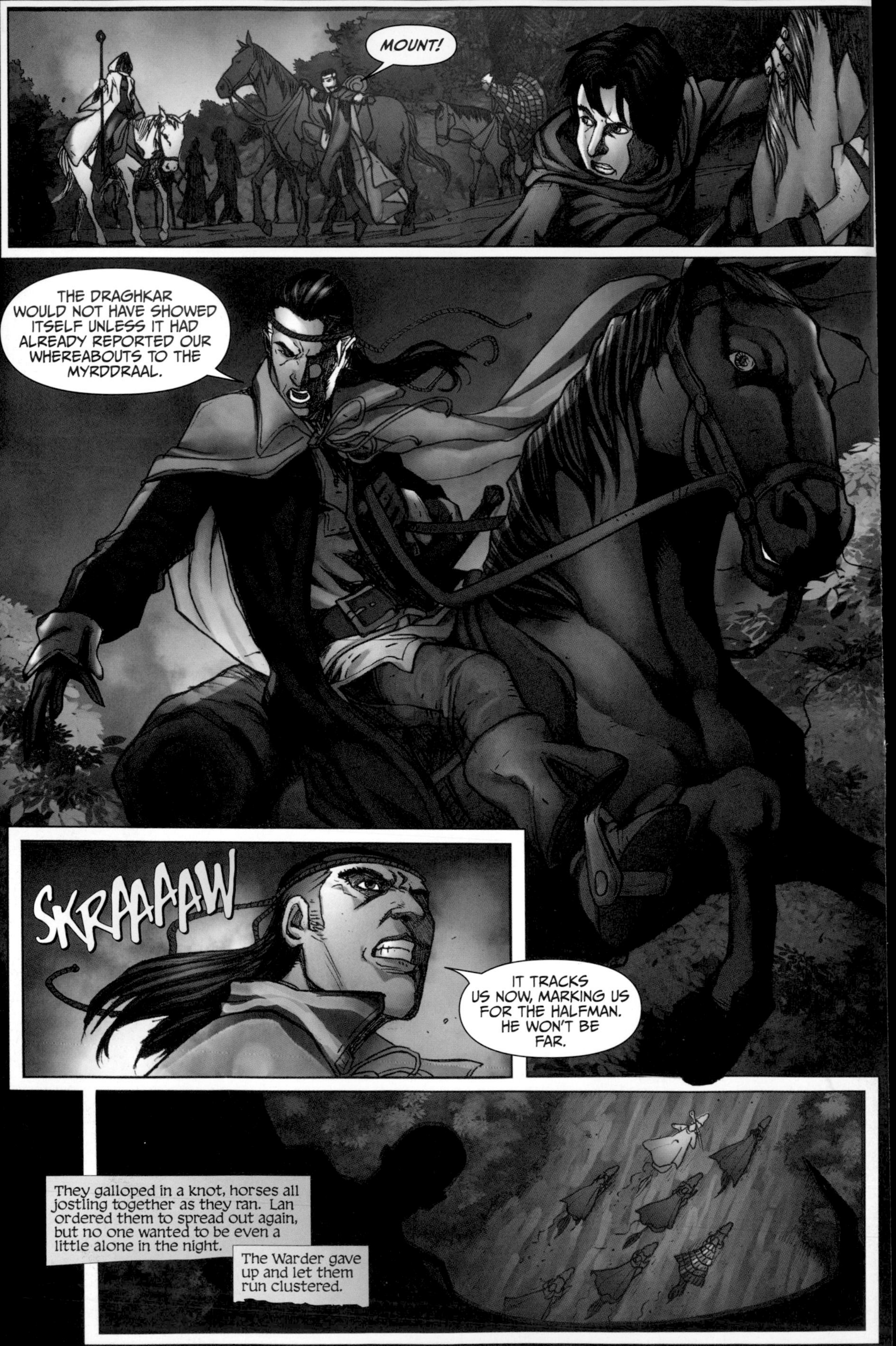
MOUNT!
THE DRAGHKAR WOULD NOT HAVE SHOWED ITSELF UNLESS IT HAD ALREADY REPORTED OUR WHEREABOUTS TO THE MYRDDRAAL.
SKRAAAAW
IT TRACKS US NOW, MARKING US FOR THE HALFMAN. HE WON'T BE FAR.
They galloped in a knot, horses all jostling together as they ran. Lan ordered them to spread out again, but no one wanted to be even a little alone in the night.
The Warder gave up and let them run clustered.

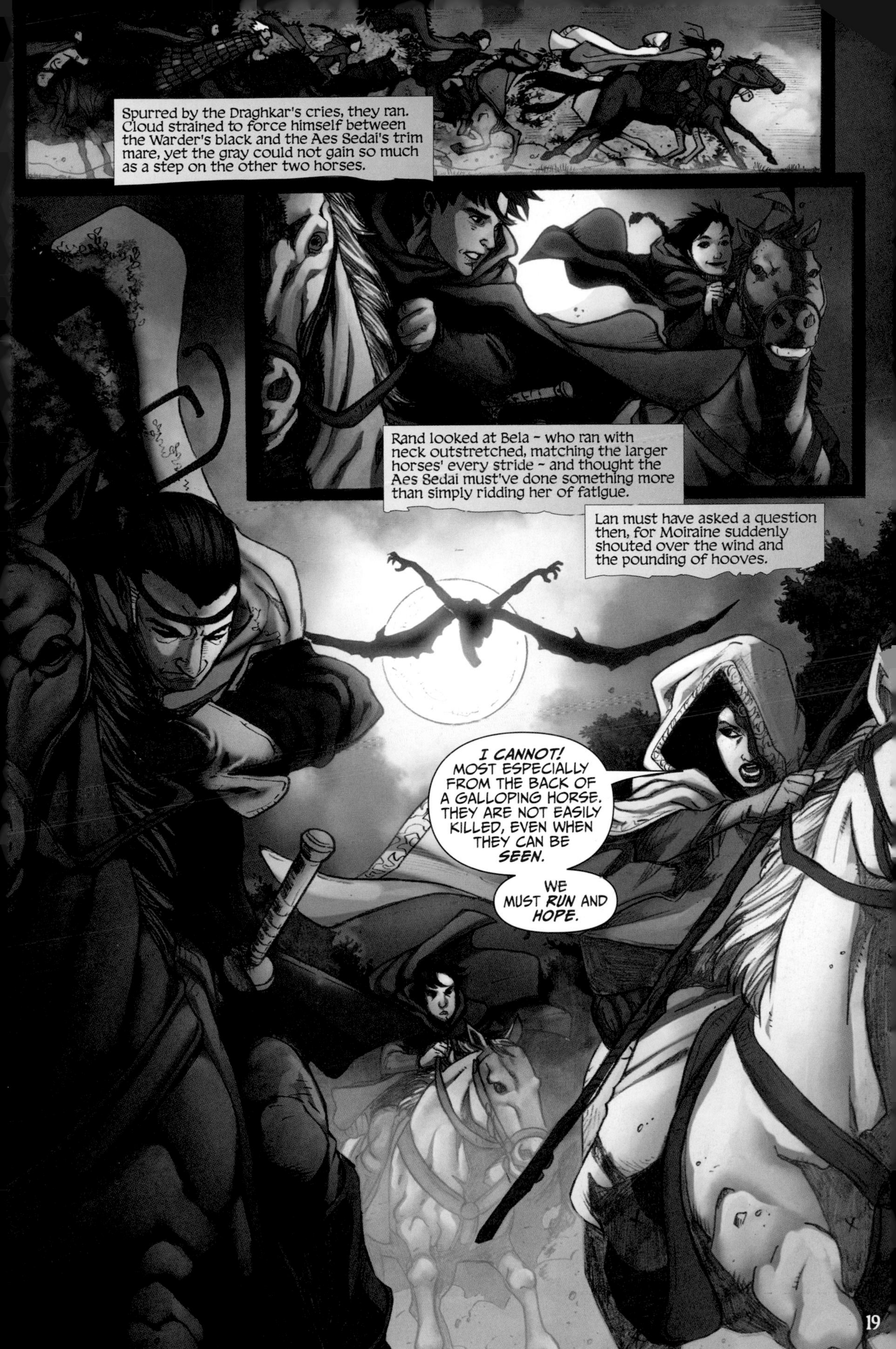

Spurred by the Draghkar's cries, they ran. Cloud strained to force himself between the Warder's black and the Aes Sedai's trim mare, yet the gray could not gain so much as a step on the other two horses.
Rand looked at Bela – who ran with neck outstretched, matching the larger horses' every stride – and thought the Aes Sedai must've done something more than simply ridding her of fatigue.
Lan must have asked a question then, for Moiraine suddenly shouted over the wind and the pounding of hooves.
I CANNOT! MOST ESPECIALLY FROM THE BACK OF A GALLOPING HORSE. THEY ARE NOT EASILY KILLED, EVEN WHEN THEY CAN BE SEEN.
WE MUST RUN AND HOPE.

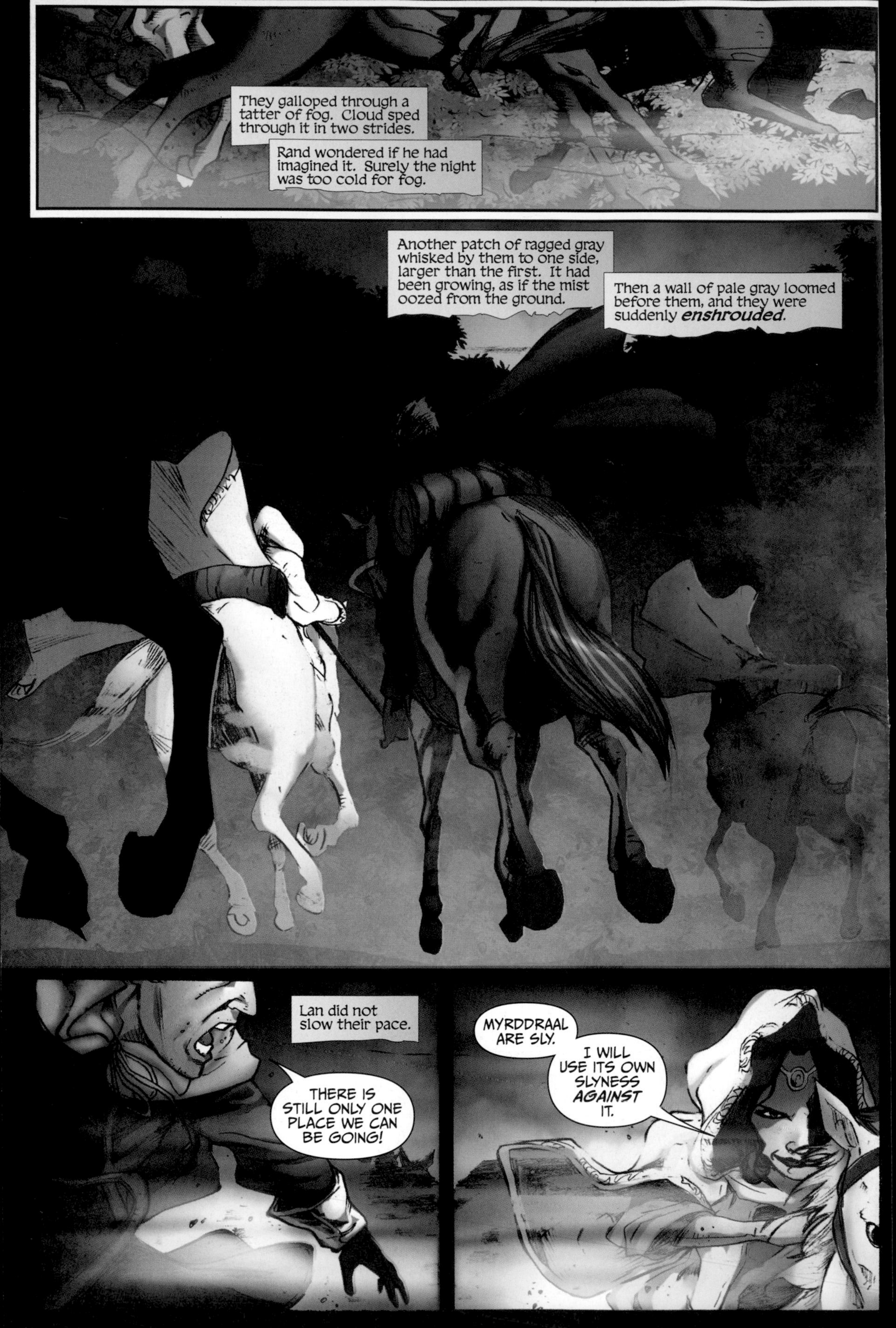
They galloped through a tatter of fog. Cloud sped through it in two strides.
Rand wondered if he had imagined it. Surely the night was too cold for fog.
Another patch of ragged gray whisked by them to one side, larger than the first. It had been growing, as if the mist oozed from the ground.
Then a wall of pale gray loomed before them, and they were suddenly enshrouded.
Lan did not slow their pace.
THERE IS STILL ONLY ONE PLACE WE CAN BE GOING!
MYRDDRAAL ARE SLY.
I WILL USE ITS OWN SLYNESS AGAINST IT.

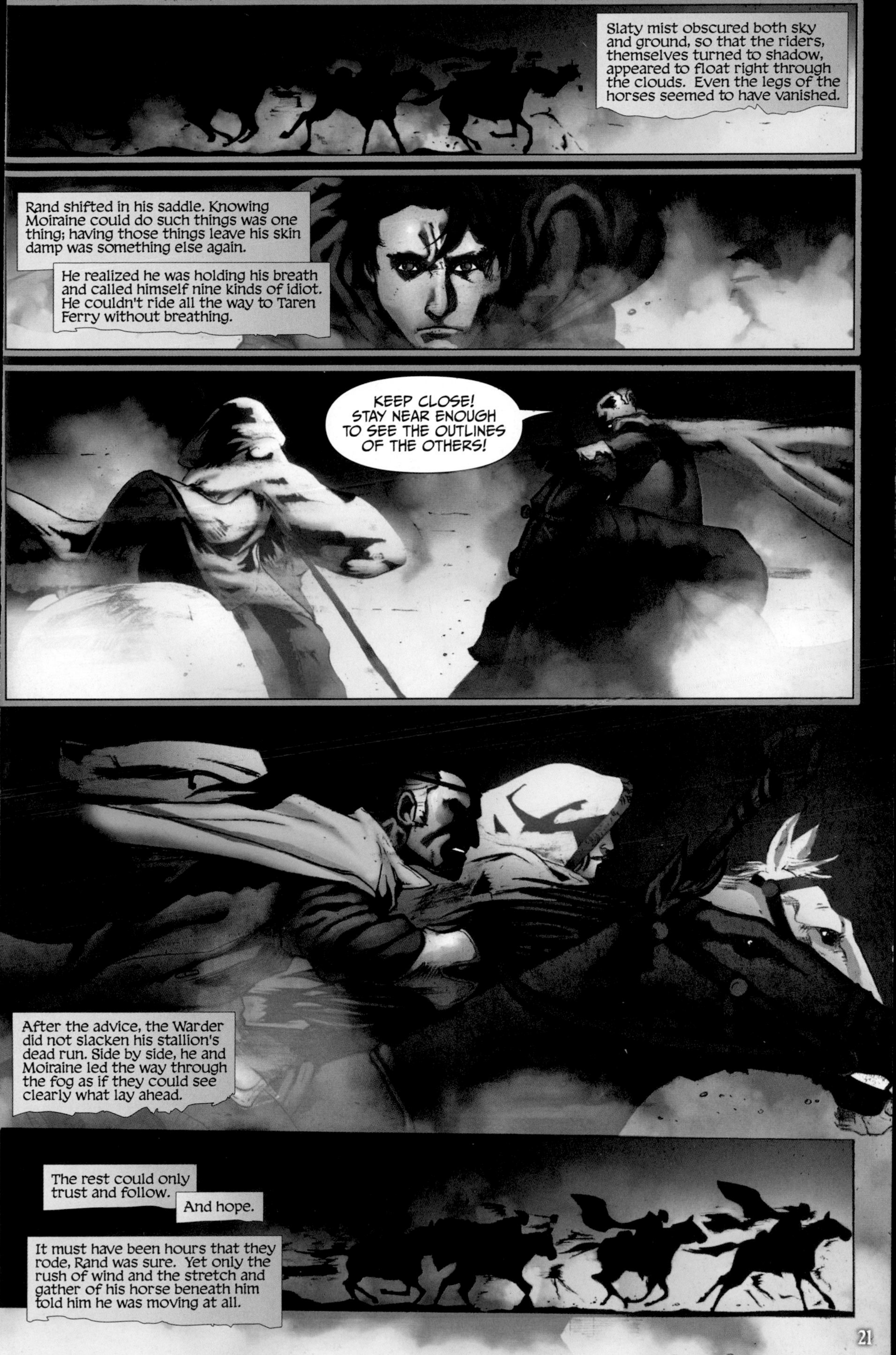
Slaty mist obscured both sky and ground, so that the riders, themselves turned to shadow, appeared to float right through the clouds. Even the legs of the horses seemed to have vanished.
Rand shifted in his saddle. Knowing Moiraine could do such things was one thing; having those things leave his skin damp was something else again.
He realized he was holding his breath and called himself nine kinds of idiot. He couldn't ride all the way to Taren Ferry without breathing.
KEEP CLOSE! STAY NEAR ENOUGH TO SEE THE OUTLINES OF THE OTHERS!
After the advice, the Warder did not slacken his stallion's dead run. Side by side, he and Moiraine led the way through the fog as if they could see clearly what lay ahead.
The rest could only trust and follow.
And hope.
It must have been hours that they rode, Rand was sure. Yet only the rush of wind and the stretch and gather of his horse beneath him told him he was moving at all.

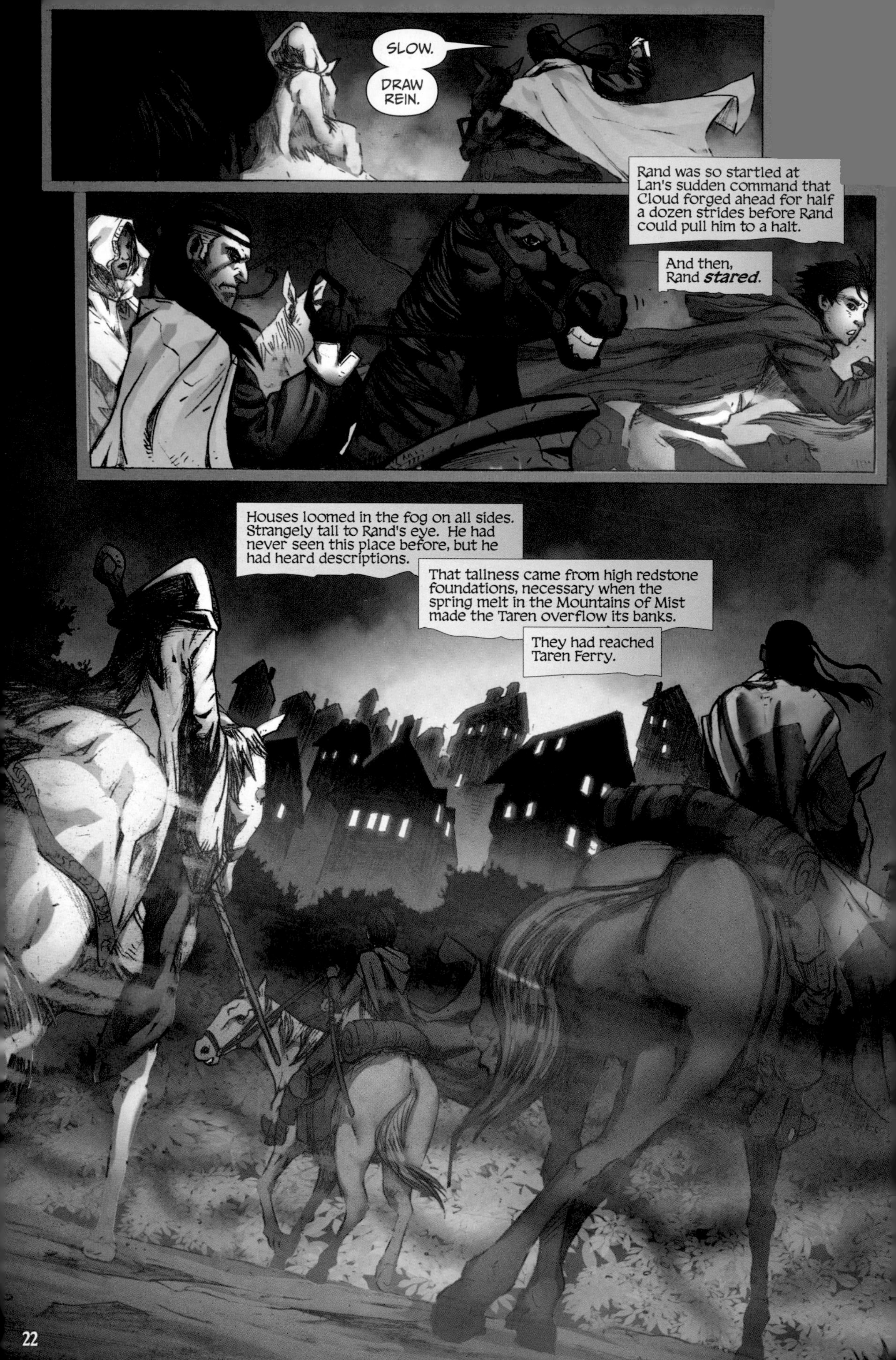
SLOW.
DRAW REIN.
Rand was so startled at Lan's sudden command that Cloud forged ahead for half a dozen strides before Rand could pull him to a halt.
And then, Rand *stared*.
Houses loomed in the fog on all sides. Strangely tall to Rand's eye. He had never seen this place before, but he had heard descriptions.
That tallness came from high redstone foundations, necessary when the spring melt in the Mountains of Mist made the Taren overflow its banks.
They had reached Taren Ferry.

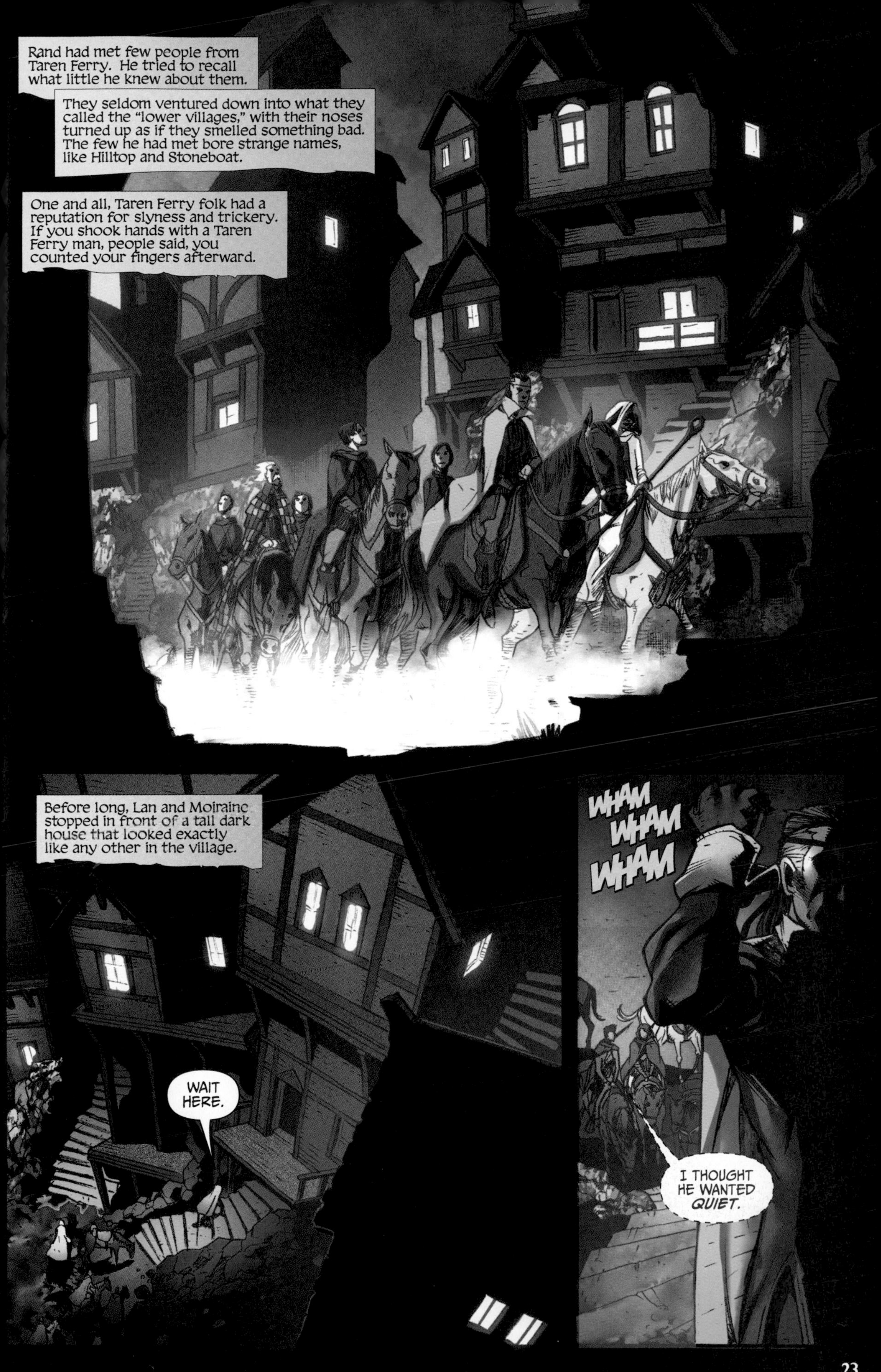
Rand had met few people from Taren Ferry. He tried to recall what little he knew about them.
They seldom ventured down into what they called the "lower villages," with their noses turned up as if they smelled something bad. The few he had met bore strange names, like Hilltop and Stoneboat.
One and all, Taren Ferry folk had a reputation for slyness and trickery. If you shook hands with a Taren Ferry man, people said, you counted your fingers afterward.
Before long, Lan and Moiraine stopped in front of a tall dark house that looked exactly like any other in the village.
WAIT HERE.
WHAM
WHAM
WHAM
I THOUGHT HE WANTED *QUIET.*

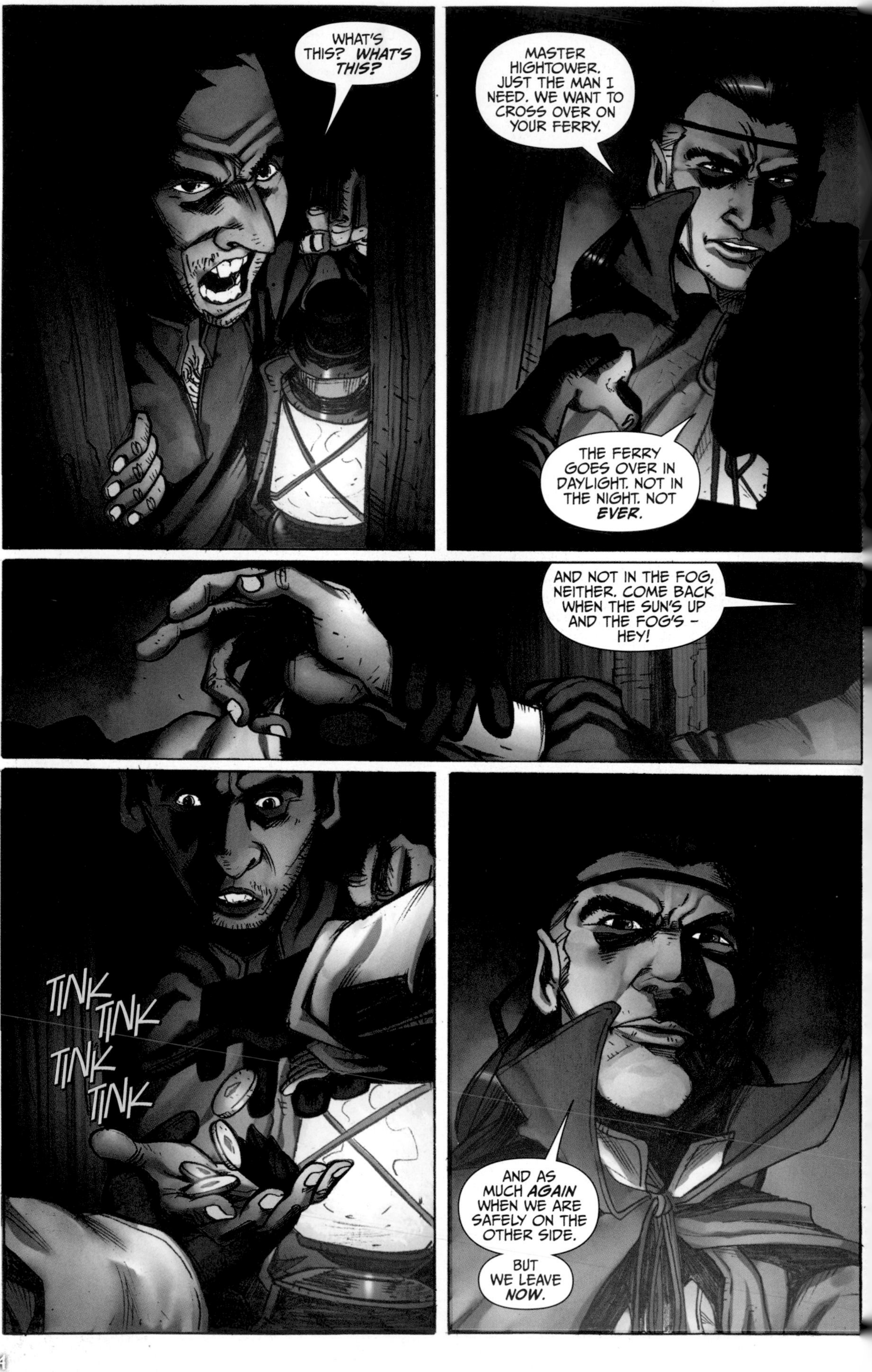
WHAT'S THIS? WHAT'S THIS?
MASTER HIGHTOWER. JUST THE MAN I NEED. WE WANT TO CROSS OVER ON YOUR FERRY.
THE FERRY GOES OVER IN DAYLIGHT. NOT IN THE NIGHT. NOT EVER.
AND NOT IN THE FOG, NEITHER. COME BACK WHEN THE SUN'S UP AND THE FOG'S – HEY!
TINK TINK TINK TINK
AND AS MUCH AGAIN WHEN WE ARE SAFELY ON THE OTHER SIDE.
BUT WE LEAVE NOW.

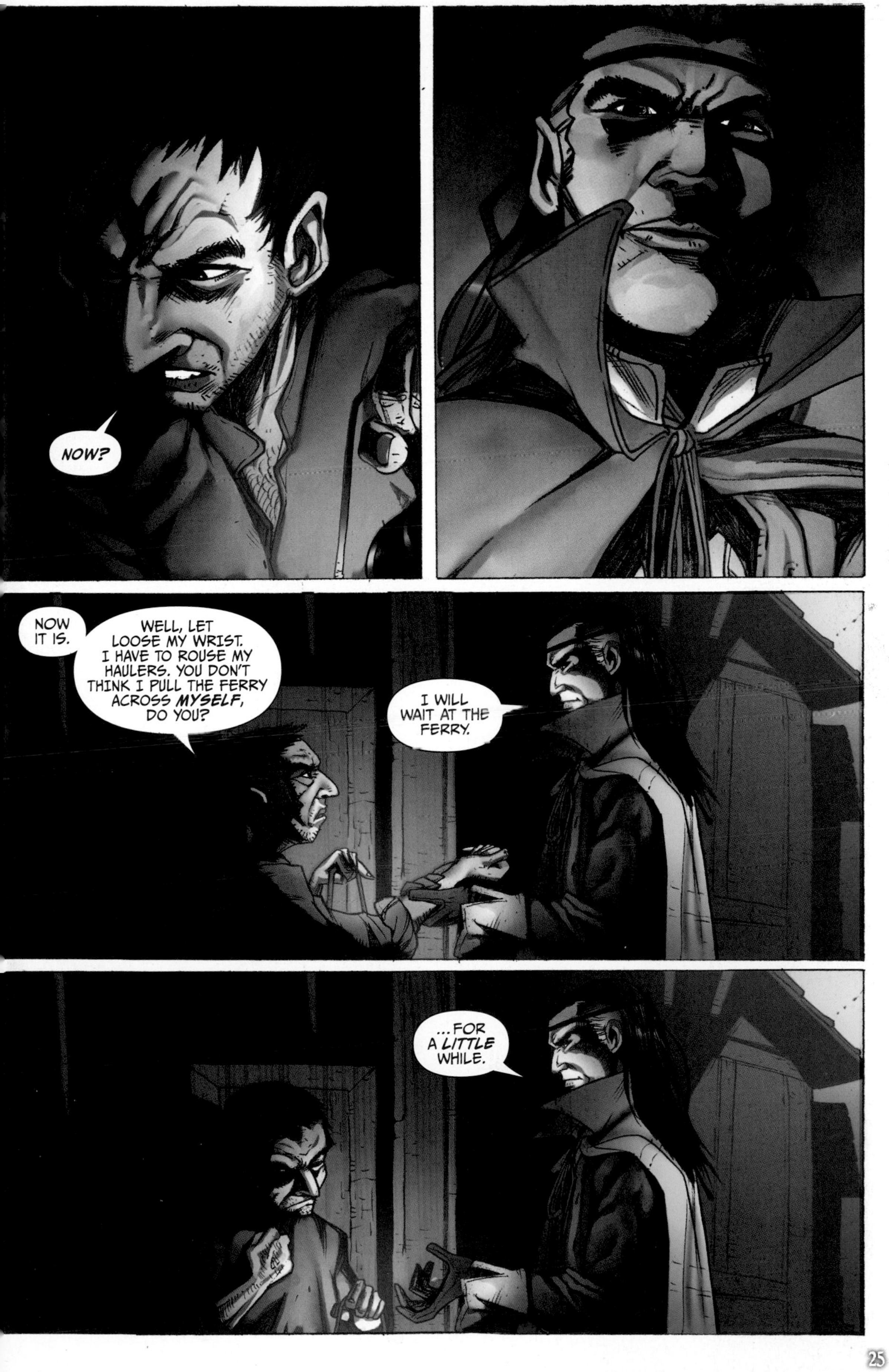
NOW?
NOW IT IS.
WELL, LET LOOSE MY WRIST. I HAVE TO ROUSE MY HAULERS. YOU DON'T THINK I PULL THE FERRY ACROSS *MYSELF*, DO YOU?
I WILL WAIT AT THE FERRY.
...FOR A *LITTLE* WHILE.

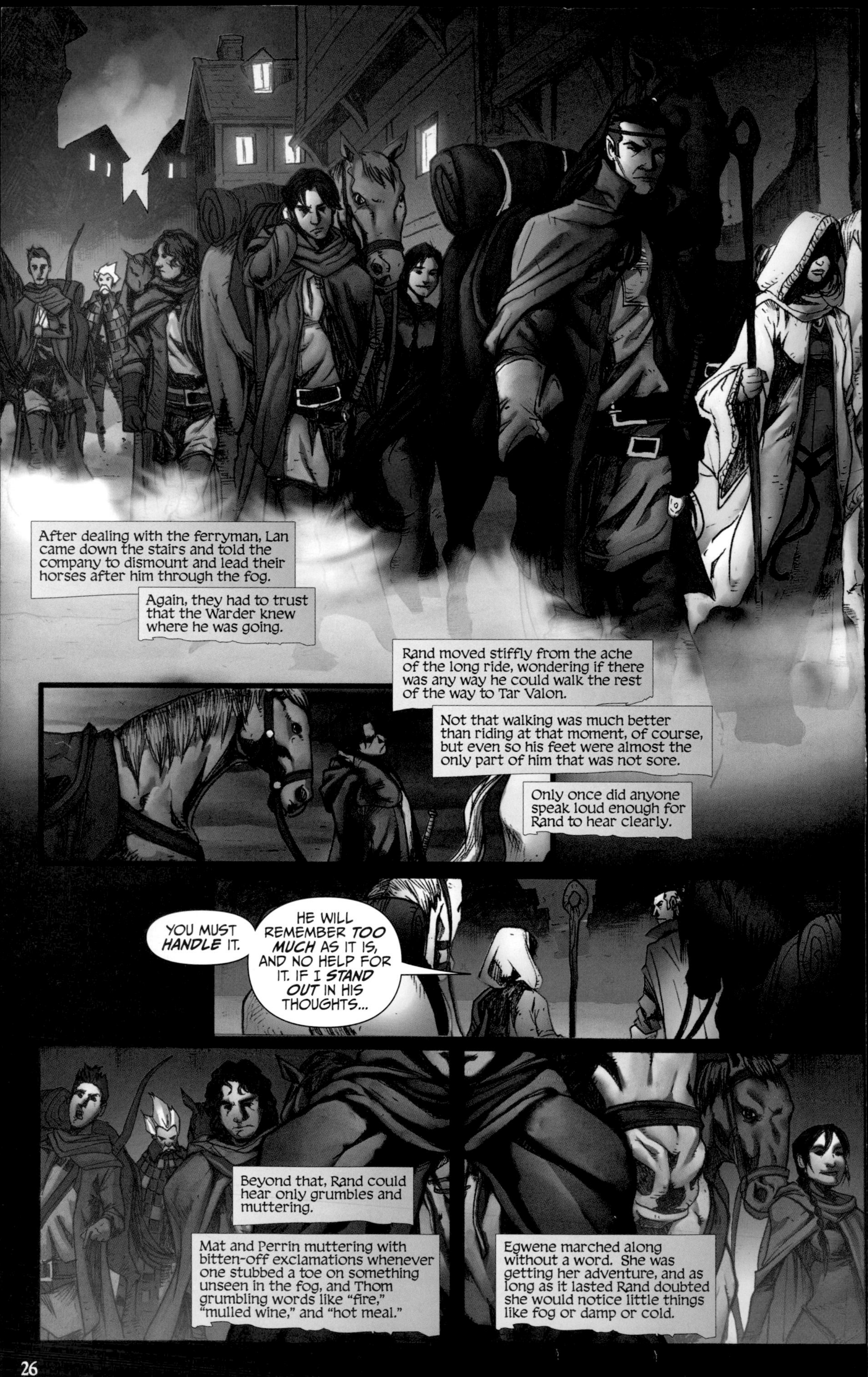
After dealing with the ferryman, Lan came down the stairs and told the company to dismount and lead their horses after him through the fog.
Again, they had to trust that the Warder knew where he was going.
Rand moved stiffly from the ache of the long ride, wondering if there was any way he could walk the rest of the way to Tar Valon.
Not that walking was much better than riding at that moment, of course, but even so his feet were almost the only part of him that was not sore.
Only once did anyone speak loud enough for Rand to hear clearly.
YOU MUST HANDLE IT.
HE WILL REMEMBER TOO MUCH AS IT IS, AND NO HELP FOR IT. IF I STAND OUT IN HIS THOUGHTS...
Beyond that, Rand could hear only grumbles and muttering.
Mat and Perrin muttering with bitten-off exclamations whenever one stubbed a toe on something unseen in the fog, and Thom grumbling words like "fire," "mulled wine," and "hot meal."
Egwene marched along without a word. She was getting her adventure, and as long as it lasted Rand doubted she would notice little things like fog or damp or cold.

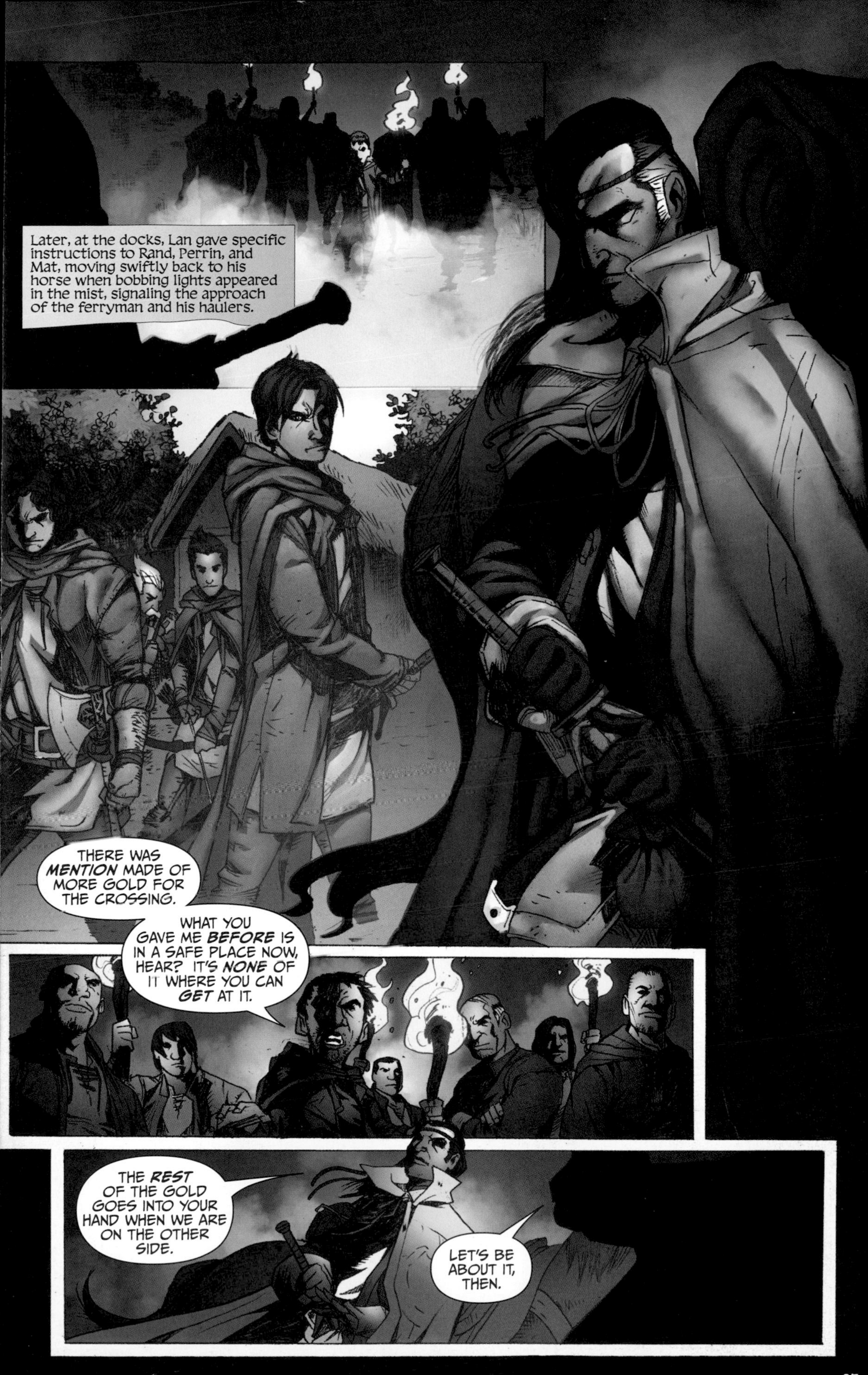
Later, at the docks, Lan gave specific instructions to Rand, Perrin, and Mat, moving swiftly back to his horse when bobbing lights appeared in the mist, signaling the approach of the ferryman and his haulers.
THERE WAS MENTION MADE OF MORE GOLD FOR THE CROSSING.
WHAT YOU GAVE ME BEFORE IS IN A SAFE PLACE NOW, HEAR? IT'S NONE OF IT WHERE YOU CAN GET AT IT.
THE REST OF THE GOLD GOES INTO YOUR HAND WHEN WE ARE ON THE OTHER SIDE.
LET'S BE ABOUT IT, THEN.

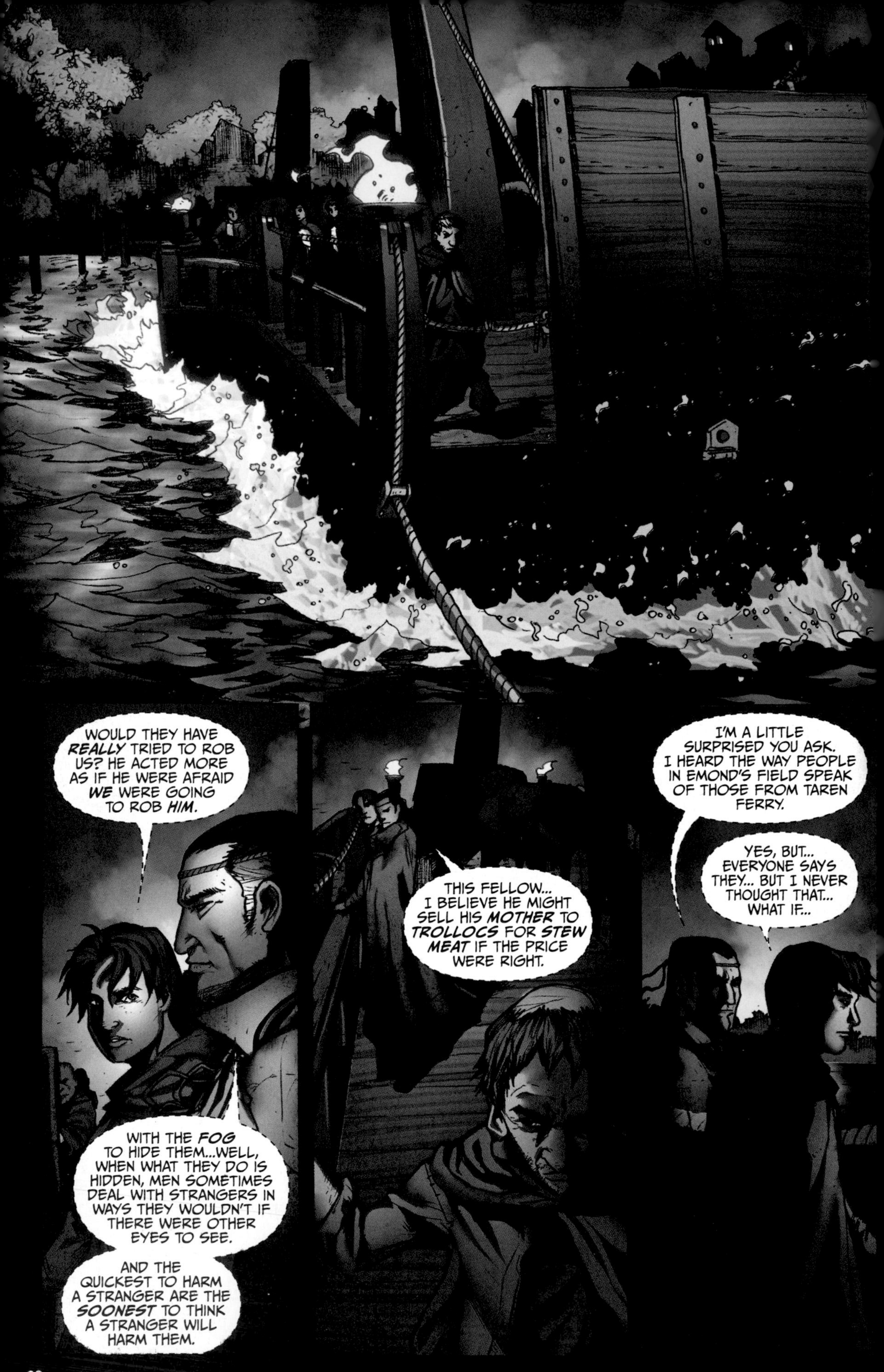
WOULD THEY HAVE REALLY TRIED TO ROB US? HE ACTED MORE AS IF HE WERE AFRAID WE WERE GOING TO ROB HIM.
THIS FELLOW... I BELIEVE HE MIGHT SELL HIS MOTHER TO TROLLOCS FOR STEW MEAT IF THE PRICE WERE RIGHT.
WITH THE FOG TO HIDE THEM...WELL, WHEN WHAT THEY DO IS HIDDEN, MEN SOMETIMES DEAL WITH STRANGERS IN WAYS THEY WOULDN'T IF THERE WERE OTHER EYES TO SEE.
AND THE QUICKEST TO HARM A STRANGER ARE THE SOONEST TO THINK A STRANGER WILL HARM THEM.
I'M A LITTLE SURPRISED YOU ASK. I HEARD THE WAY PEOPLE IN EMOND'S FIELD SPEAK OF THOSE FROM TAREN FERRY.
YES, BUT... EVERYONE SAYS THEY... BUT I NEVER THOUGHT THAT... WHAT IF...

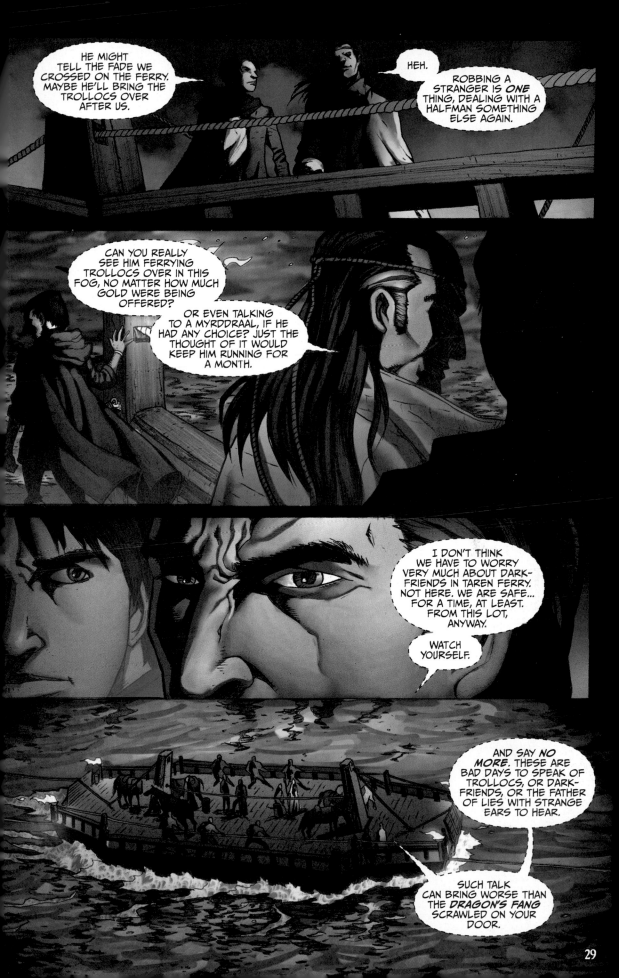

HE MIGHT TELL THE FADE WE CROSSED ON THE FERRY. MAYBE HE'LL BRING THE TROLLOCS OVER AFTER US.

HEH.

ROBBING A STRANGER IS *ONE* THING, DEALING WITH A HALFMAN SOMETHING ELSE AGAIN.

CAN YOU REALLY SEE HIM FERRYING TROLLOCS OVER IN THIS FOG, NO MATTER HOW MUCH GOLD WERE BEING OFFERED?

OR EVEN TALKING TO A MYRDDRAAL, IF HE HAD ANY CHOICE? JUST THE THOUGHT OF IT WOULD KEEP HIM RUNNING FOR A MONTH.

I DON'T THINK WE HAVE TO WORRY VERY MUCH ABOUT DARK-FRIENDS IN TAREN FERRY. NOT HERE. WE ARE SAFE... FOR A TIME, AT LEAST. FROM THIS LOT, ANYWAY.

WATCH YOURSELF.

AND SAY *NO MORE.* THESE ARE BAD DAYS TO SPEAK OF TROLLOCS, OR DARK-FRIENDS, OR THE FATHER OF LIES WITH STRANGE EARS TO HEAR.

SUCH TALK CAN BRING WORSE THAN THE *DRAGON'S FANG* SCRAWLED ON YOUR DOOR.

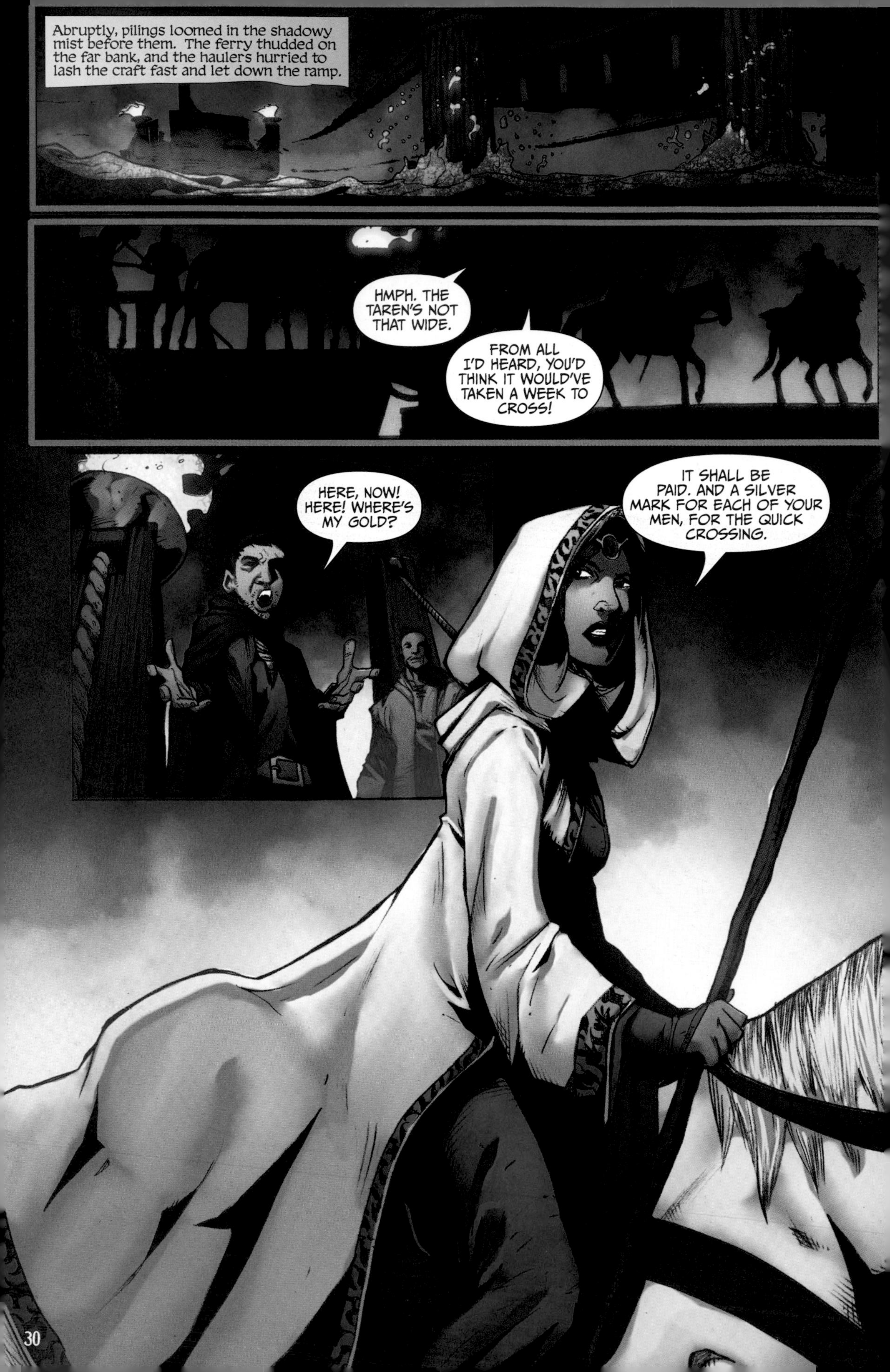
Abruptly, pilings loomed in the shadowy mist before them. The ferry thudded on the far bank, and the haulers hurried to lash the craft fast and let down the ramp.
HMPH. THE TAREN'S NOT THAT WIDE.
FROM ALL I'D HEARD, YOU'D THINK IT WOULD'VE TAKEN A WEEK TO CROSS!
HERE, NOW! HERE! WHERE'S MY GOLD?
IT SHALL BE PAID. AND A SILVER MARK FOR EACH OF YOUR MEN, FOR THE QUICK CROSSING.

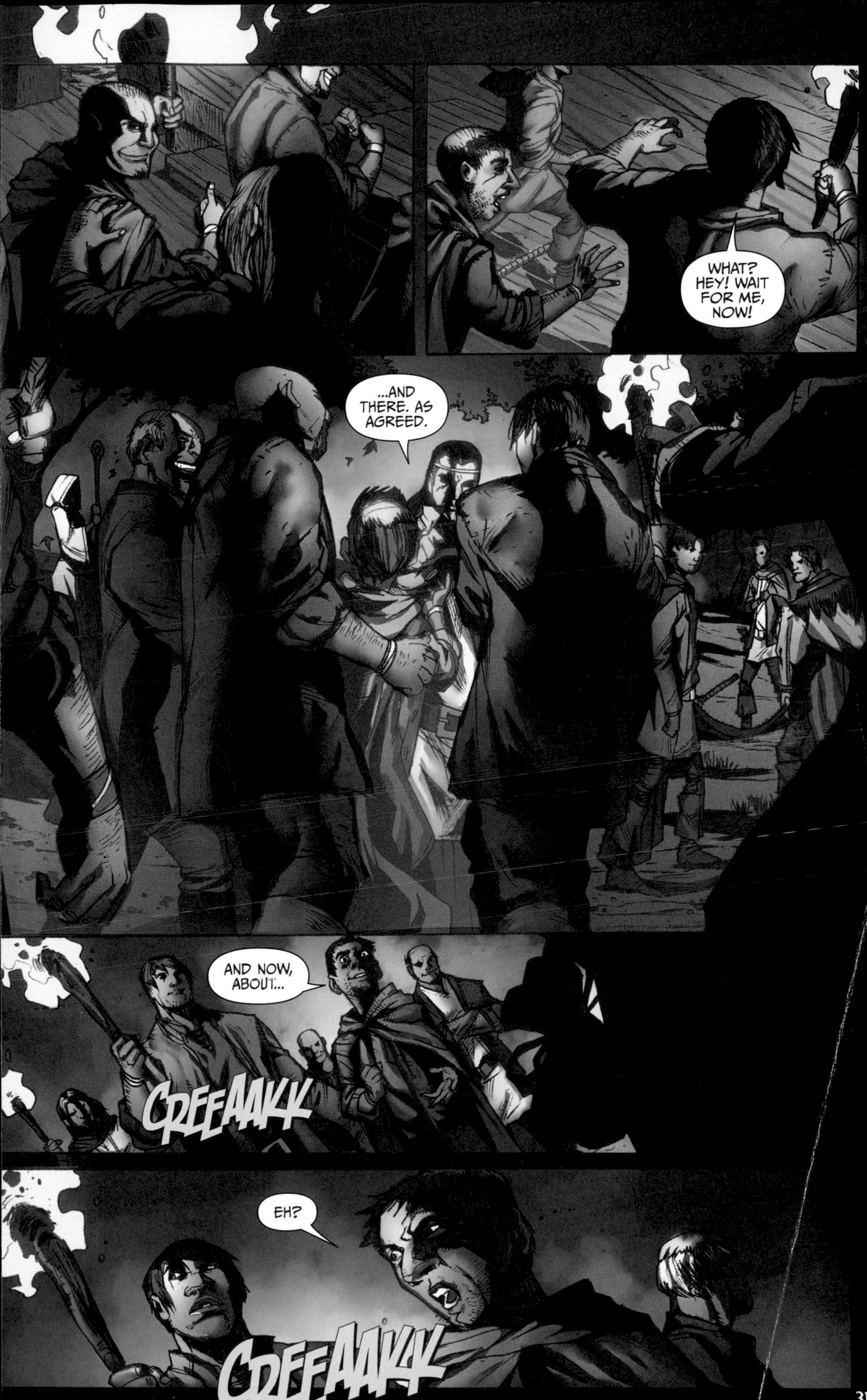
WHAT? HEY! WAIT FOR ME, NOW!
...AND THERE. AS AGREED.
AND NOW, ABOUT...
CREEAAKK
EH?
CREEAAKK

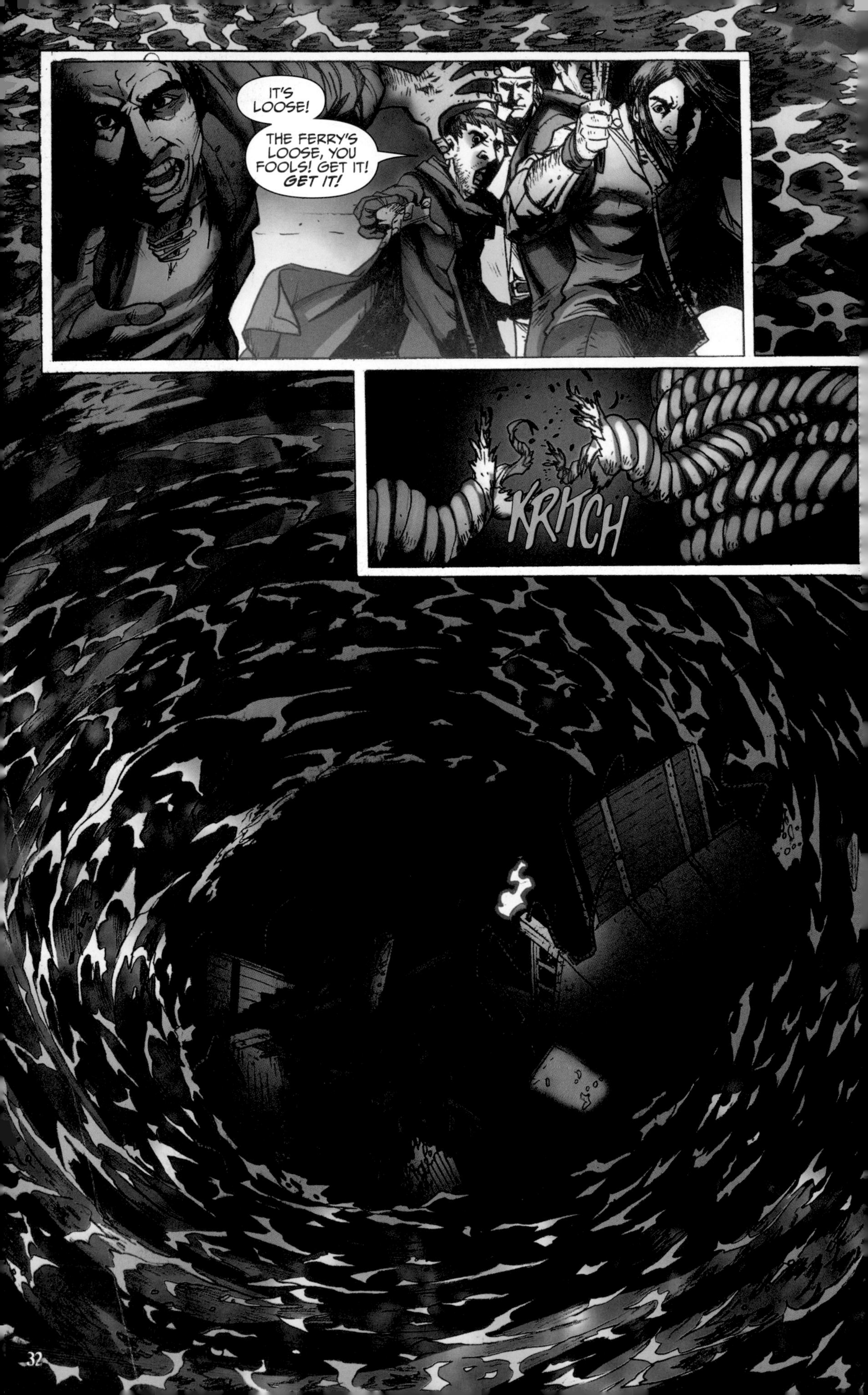
IT'S LOOSE!
THE FERRY'S LOOSE, YOU FOOLS! GET IT! *GET IT!*
KRITCH

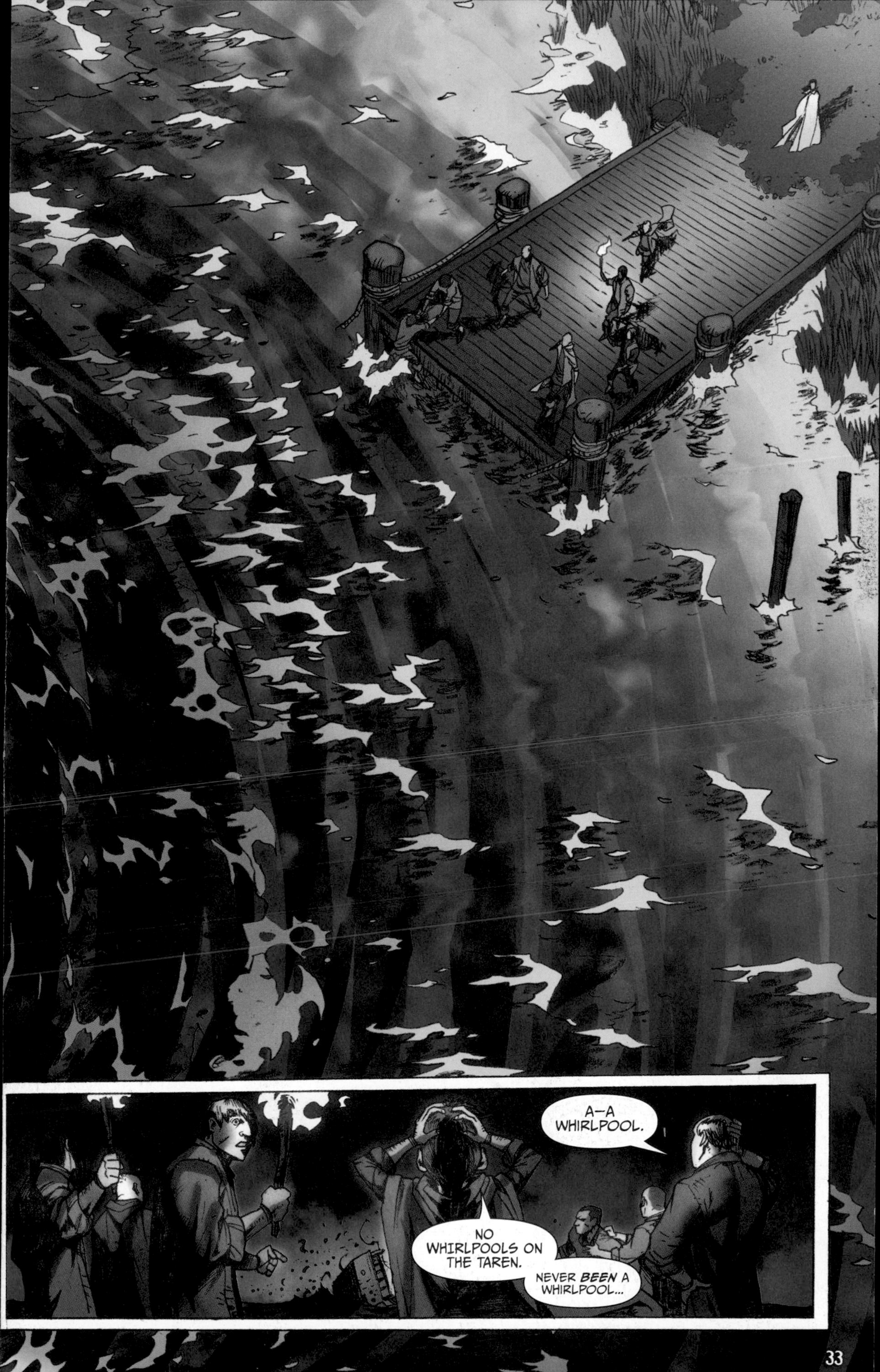
A—A WHIRLPOOL.
NO WHIRLPOOLS ON THE TAREN.
NEVER *BEEN* A WHIRLPOOL...

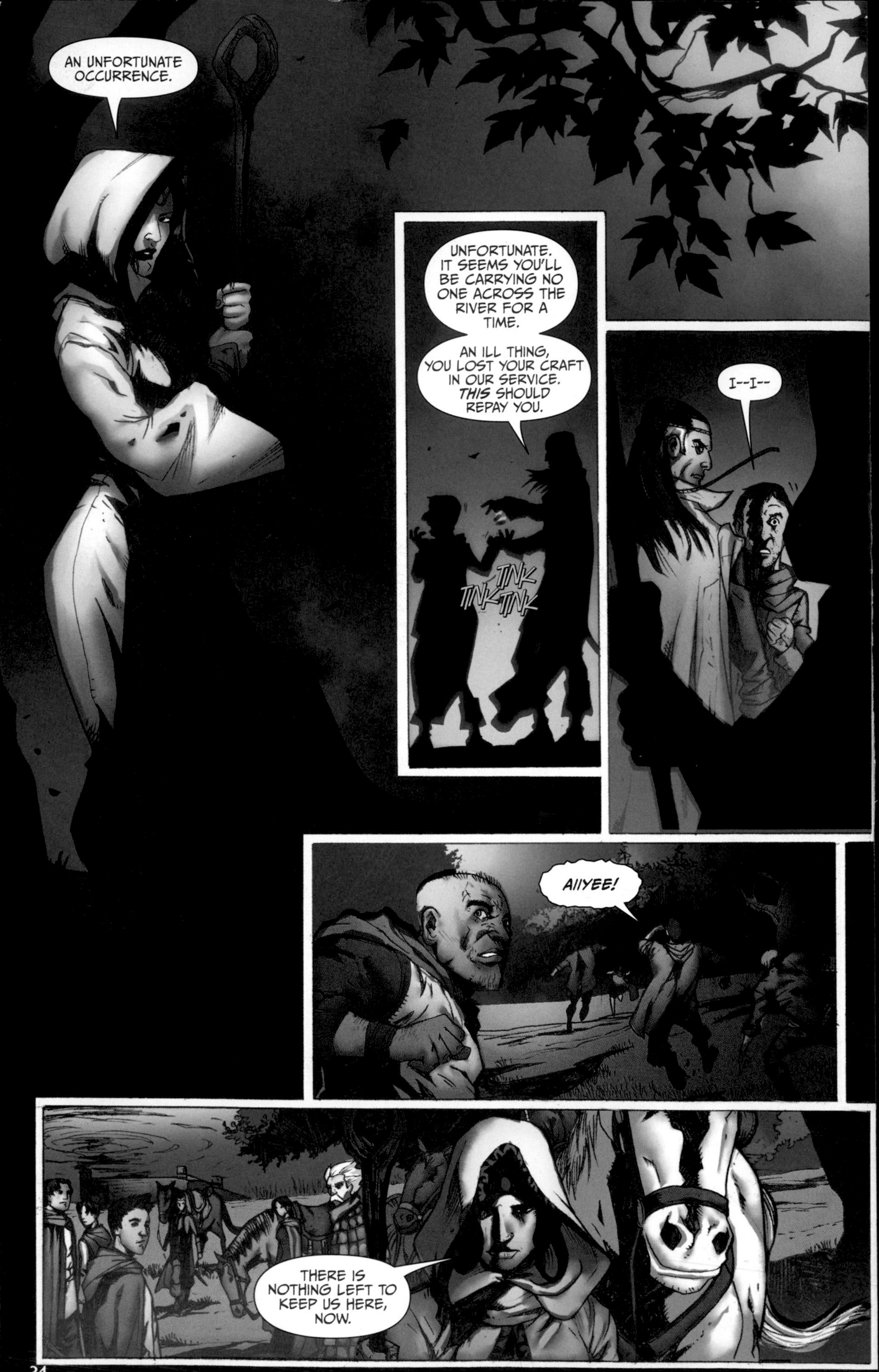
AN UNFORTUNATE OCCURRENCE.
UNFORTUNATE. IT SEEMS YOU'LL BE CARRYING NO ONE ACROSS THE RIVER FOR A TIME.
AN ILL THING, YOU LOST YOUR CRAFT IN OUR SERVICE. *THIS* SHOULD REPAY YOU.
TINK TINK TINK
I--I--
AIIYEE!
THERE IS NOTHING LEFT TO KEEP US HERE, NOW.

chapter two

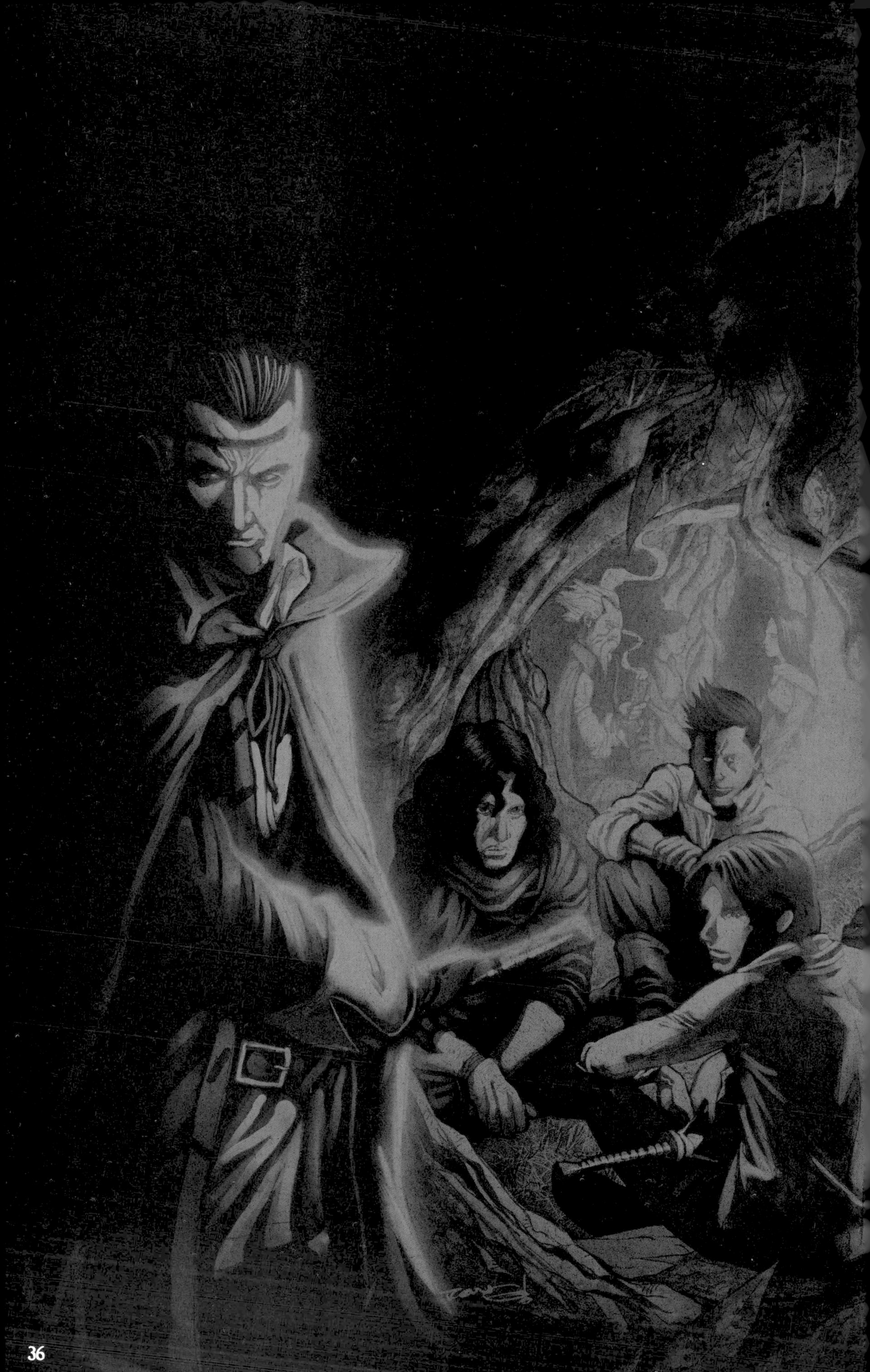

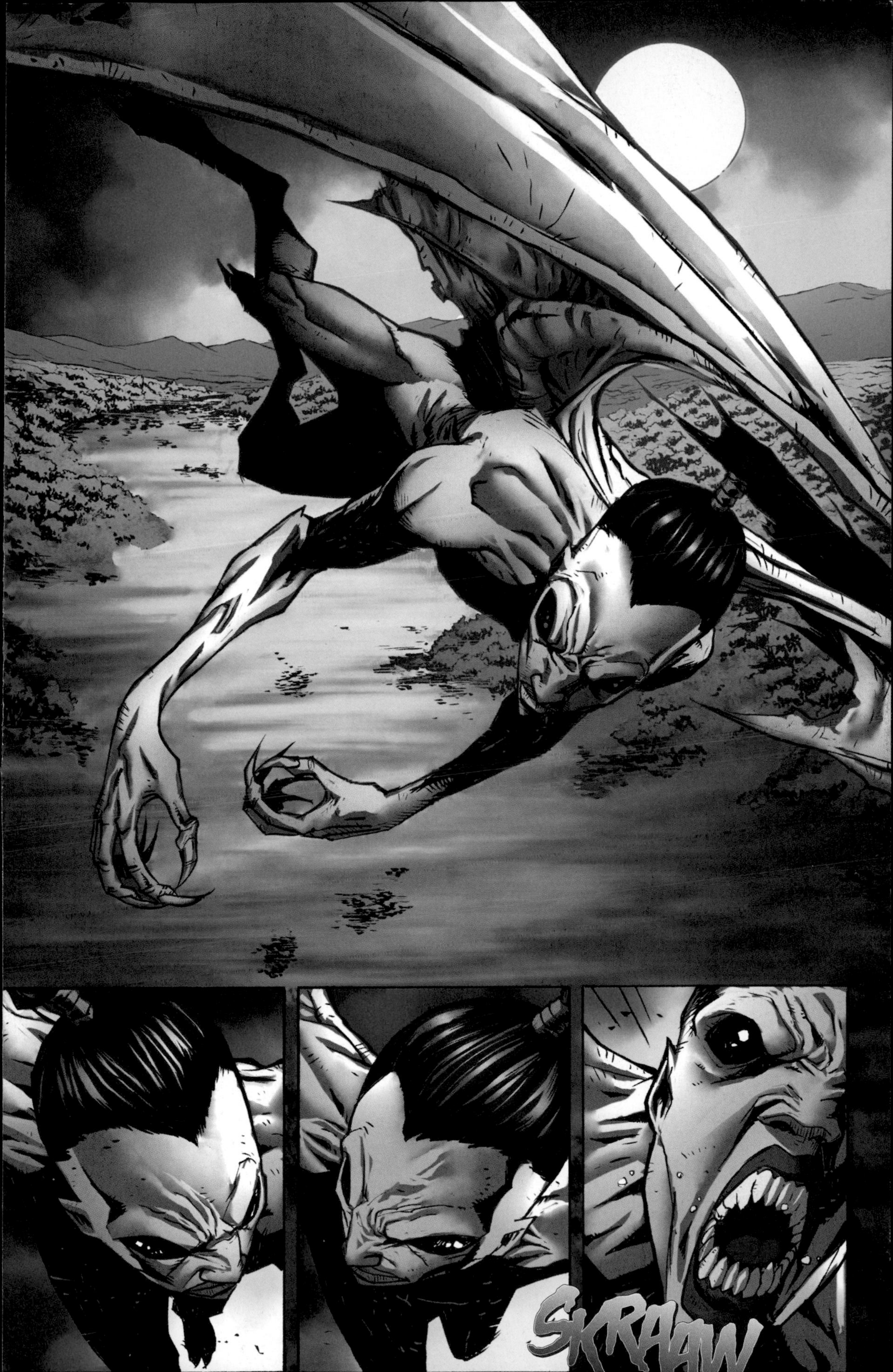
SKRAAW

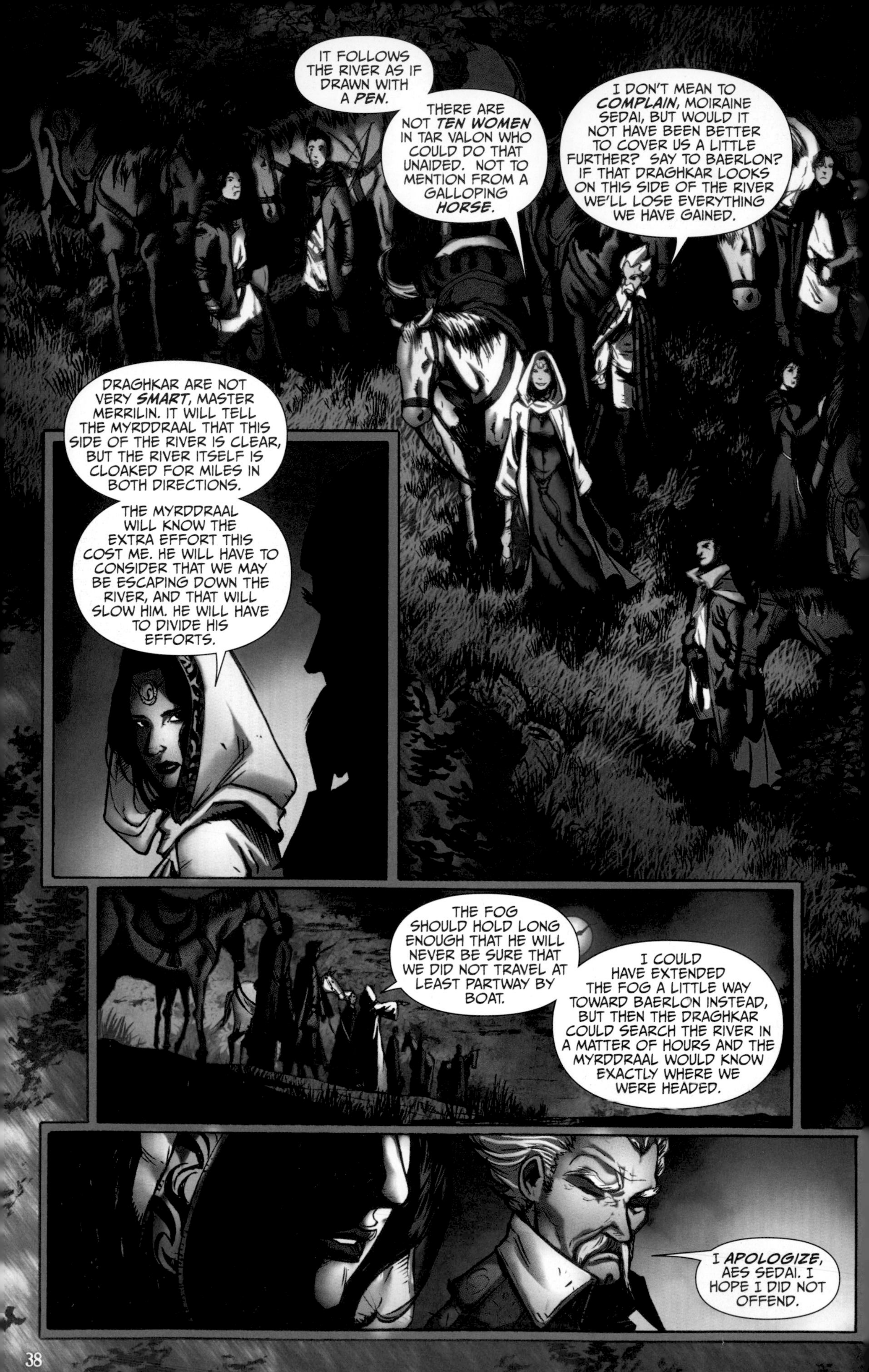
IT FOLLOWS THE RIVER AS IF DRAWN WITH A PEN.
THERE ARE NOT TEN WOMEN IN TAR VALON WHO COULD DO THAT UNAIDED. NOT TO MENTION FROM A GALLOPING HORSE.
I DON'T MEAN TO COMPLAIN, MOIRAINE SEDAI, BUT WOULD IT NOT HAVE BEEN BETTER TO COVER US A LITTLE FURTHER? SAY TO BAERLON? IF THAT DRAGHKAR LOOKS ON THIS SIDE OF THE RIVER WE'LL LOSE EVERYTHING WE HAVE GAINED.
DRAGHKAR ARE NOT VERY SMART, MASTER MERRILIN. IT WILL TELL THE MYRDDRAAL THAT THIS SIDE OF THE RIVER IS CLEAR, BUT THE RIVER ITSELF IS CLOAKED FOR MILES IN BOTH DIRECTIONS.
THE MYRDDRAAL WILL KNOW THE EXTRA EFFORT THIS COST ME. HE WILL HAVE TO CONSIDER THAT WE MAY BE ESCAPING DOWN THE RIVER, AND THAT WILL SLOW HIM. HE WILL HAVE TO DIVIDE HIS EFFORTS.
THE FOG SHOULD HOLD LONG ENOUGH THAT HE WILL NEVER BE SURE THAT WE DID NOT TRAVEL AT LEAST PARTWAY BY BOAT.
I COULD HAVE EXTENDED THE FOG A LITTLE WAY TOWARD BAERLON INSTEAD, BUT THEN THE DRAGHKAR COULD SEARCH THE RIVER IN A MATTER OF HOURS AND THE MYRDDRAAL WOULD KNOW EXACTLY WHERE WE WERE HEADED.
I APOLOGIZE, AES SEDAI. I HOPE I DID NOT OFFEND.

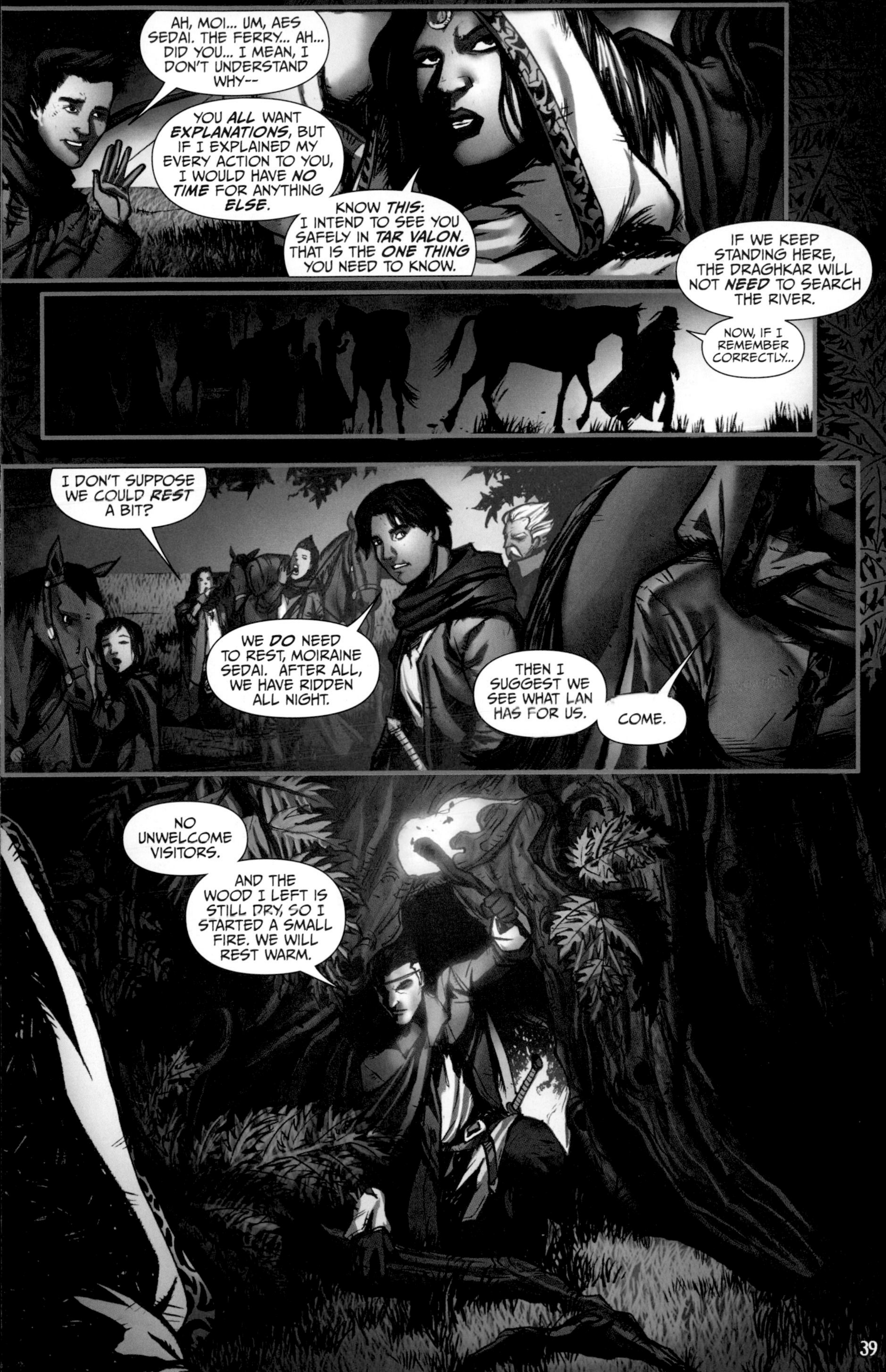

AH, MOI... UM, AES SEDAI. THE FERRY... AH... DID YOU... I MEAN, I DON'T UNDERSTAND WHY--
YOU ALL WANT EXPLANATIONS, BUT IF I EXPLAINED MY EVERY ACTION TO YOU, I WOULD HAVE NO TIME FOR ANYTHING ELSE.
KNOW THIS: I INTEND TO SEE YOU SAFELY IN TAR VALON. THAT IS THE ONE THING YOU NEED TO KNOW.
IF WE KEEP STANDING HERE, THE DRAGHKAR WILL NOT NEED TO SEARCH THE RIVER.
NOW, IF I REMEMBER CORRECTLY...
I DON'T SUPPOSE WE COULD REST A BIT?
WE DO NEED TO REST, MOIRAINE SEDAI. AFTER ALL, WE HAVE RIDDEN ALL NIGHT.
THEN I SUGGEST WE SEE WHAT LAN HAS FOR US.
COME.
NO UNWELCOME VISITORS.
AND THE WOOD I LEFT IS STILL DRY, SO I STARTED A SMALL FIRE. WE WILL REST WARM.

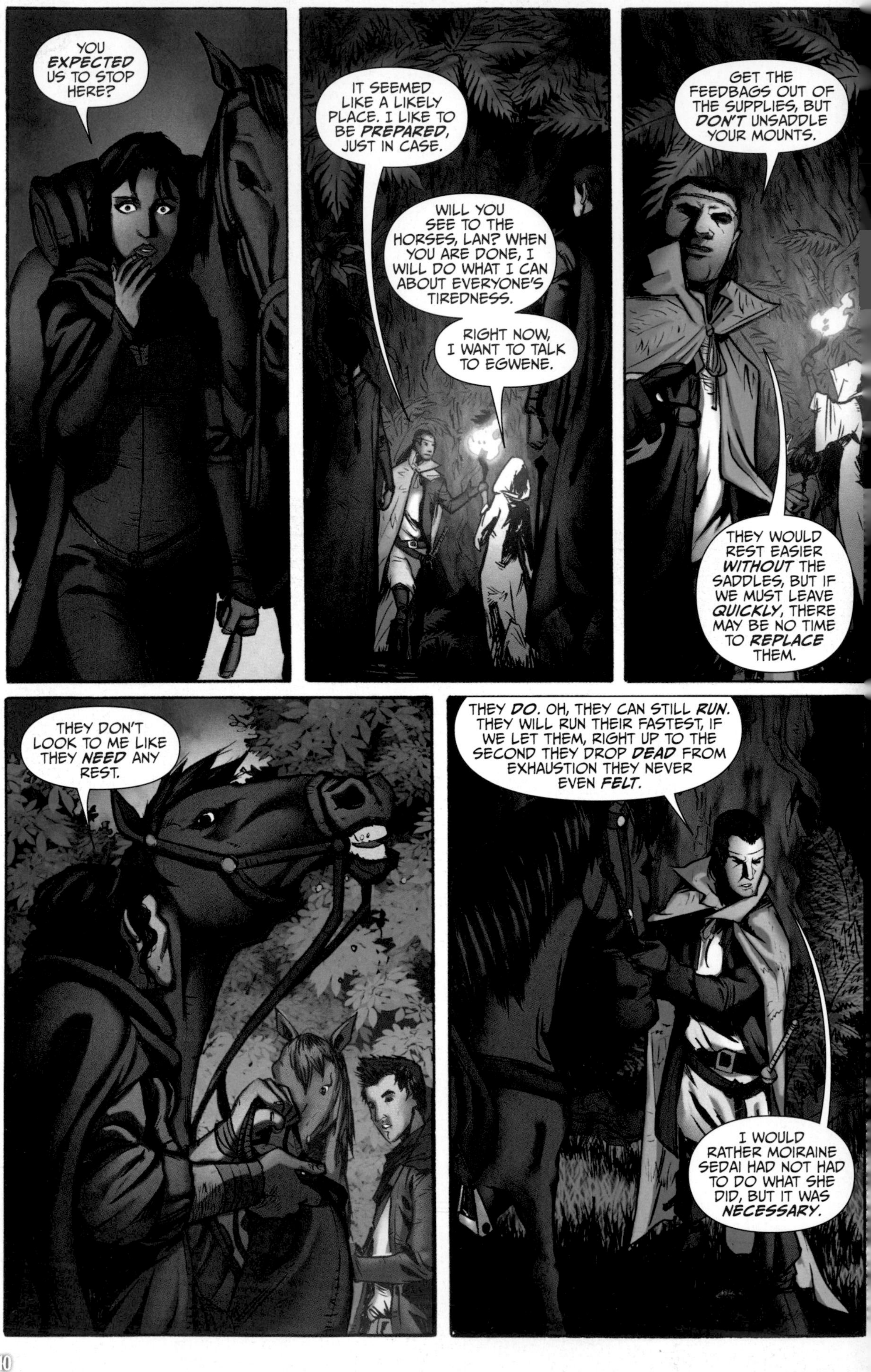
YOU EXPECTED US TO STOP HERE?
IT SEEMED LIKE A LIKELY PLACE. I LIKE TO BE PREPARED, JUST IN CASE.
WILL YOU SEE TO THE HORSES, LAN? WHEN YOU ARE DONE, I WILL DO WHAT I CAN ABOUT EVERYONE'S TIREDNESS.
RIGHT NOW, I WANT TO TALK TO EGWENE.
GET THE FEEDBAGS OUT OF THE SUPPLIES, BUT DON'T UNSADDLE YOUR MOUNTS.
THEY WOULD REST EASIER WITHOUT THE SADDLES, BUT IF WE MUST LEAVE QUICKLY, THERE MAY BE NO TIME TO REPLACE THEM.
THEY DON'T LOOK TO ME LIKE THEY NEED ANY REST.
THEY DO. OH, THEY CAN STILL RUN. THEY WILL RUN THEIR FASTEST, IF WE LET THEM, RIGHT UP TO THE SECOND THEY DROP DEAD FROM EXHAUSTION THEY NEVER EVEN FELT.
I WOULD RATHER MOIRAINE SEDAI HAD NOT HAD TO DO WHAT SHE DID, BUT IT WAS NECESSARY.

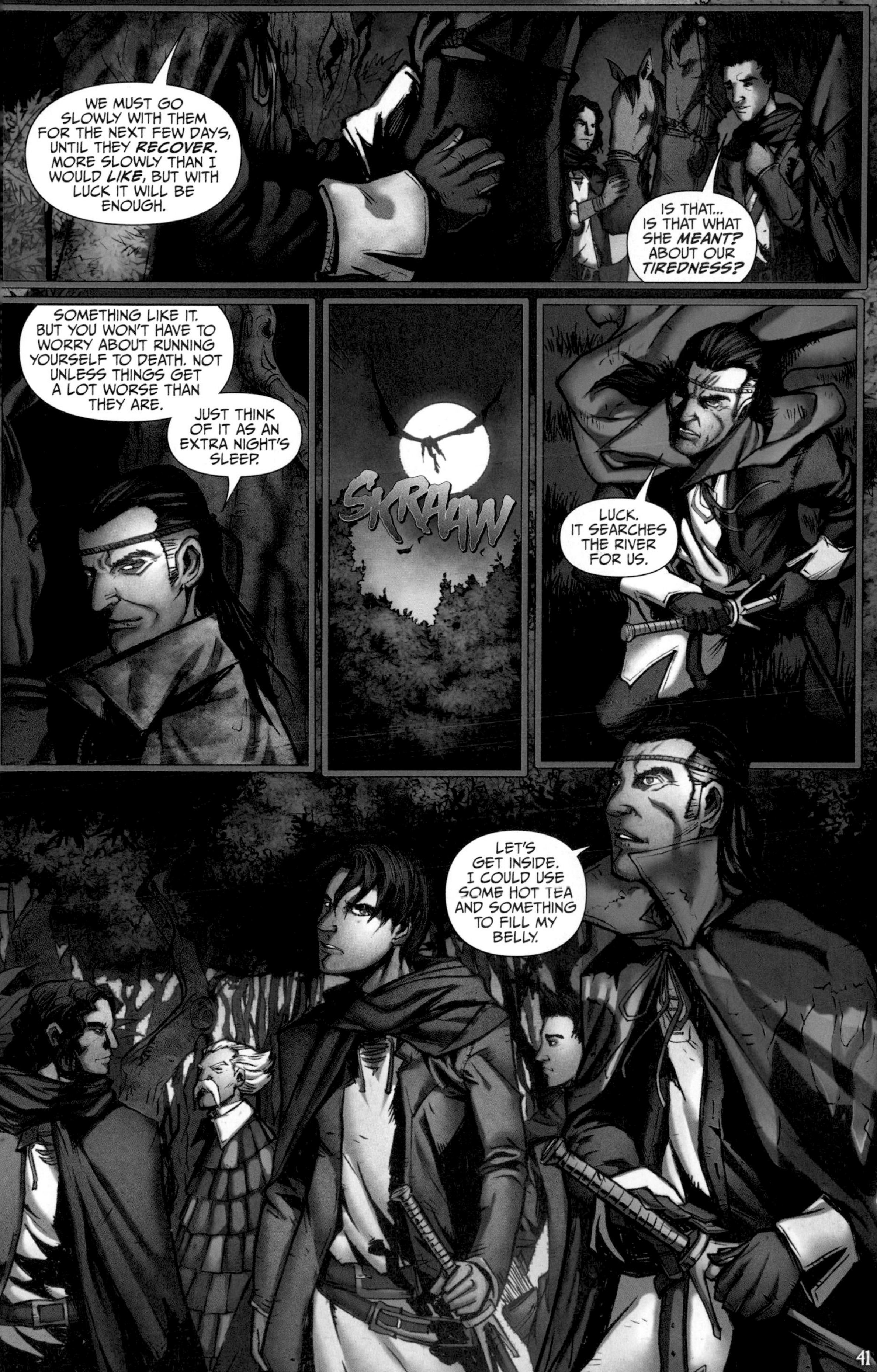
WE MUST GO SLOWLY WITH THEM FOR THE NEXT FEW DAYS, UNTIL THEY *RECOVER.* MORE SLOWLY THAN I WOULD *LIKE*, BUT WITH LUCK IT WILL BE ENOUGH.
IS THAT... IS THAT WHAT SHE *MEANT?* ABOUT OUR *TIREDNESS?*
SOMETHING LIKE IT. BUT YOU WON'T HAVE TO WORRY ABOUT RUNNING YOURSELF TO DEATH. NOT UNLESS THINGS GET A LOT WORSE THAN THEY ARE.
JUST THINK OF IT AS AN EXTRA NIGHT'S SLEEP.
SKRAAW
LUCK. IT SEARCHES THE RIVER FOR US.
LET'S GET INSIDE. I COULD USE SOME HOT TEA AND SOMETHING TO FILL MY BELLY.

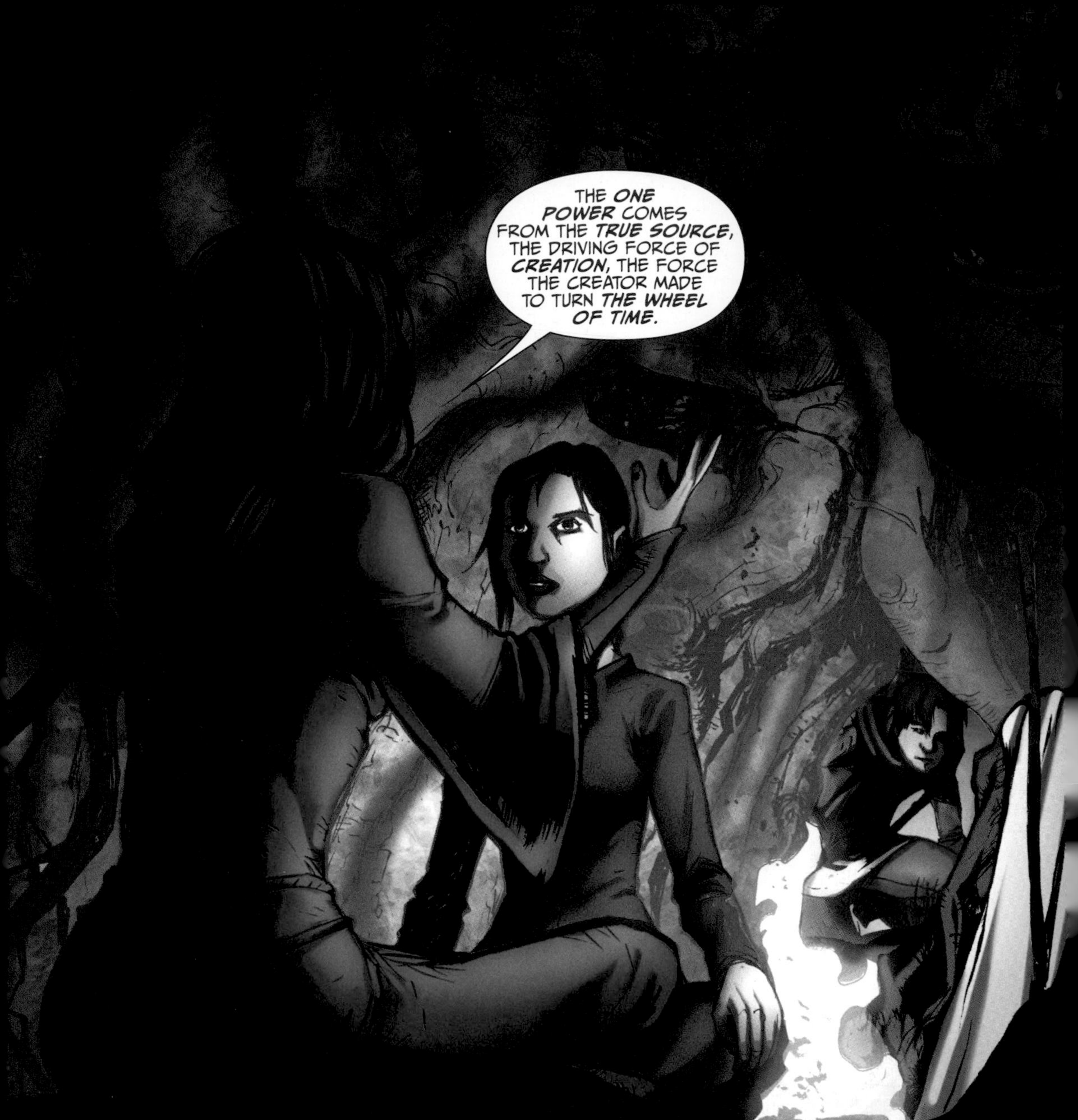
THE ONE POWER COMES FROM THE TRUE SOURCE, THE DRIVING FORCE OF CREATION, THE FORCE THE CREATOR MADE TO TURN THE WHEEL OF TIME.

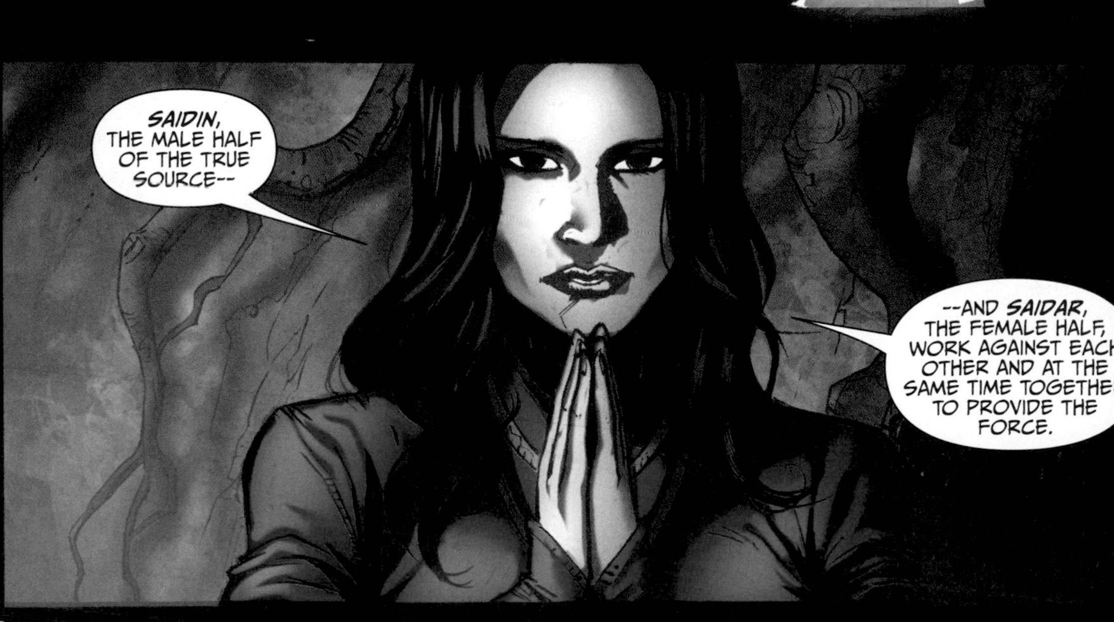
SAIDIN, THE MALE HALF OF THE TRUE SOURCE--
--AND SAIDAR, THE FEMALE HALF, WORK AGAINST EACH OTHER AND AT THE SAME TIME TOGETHER TO PROVIDE THE FORCE.

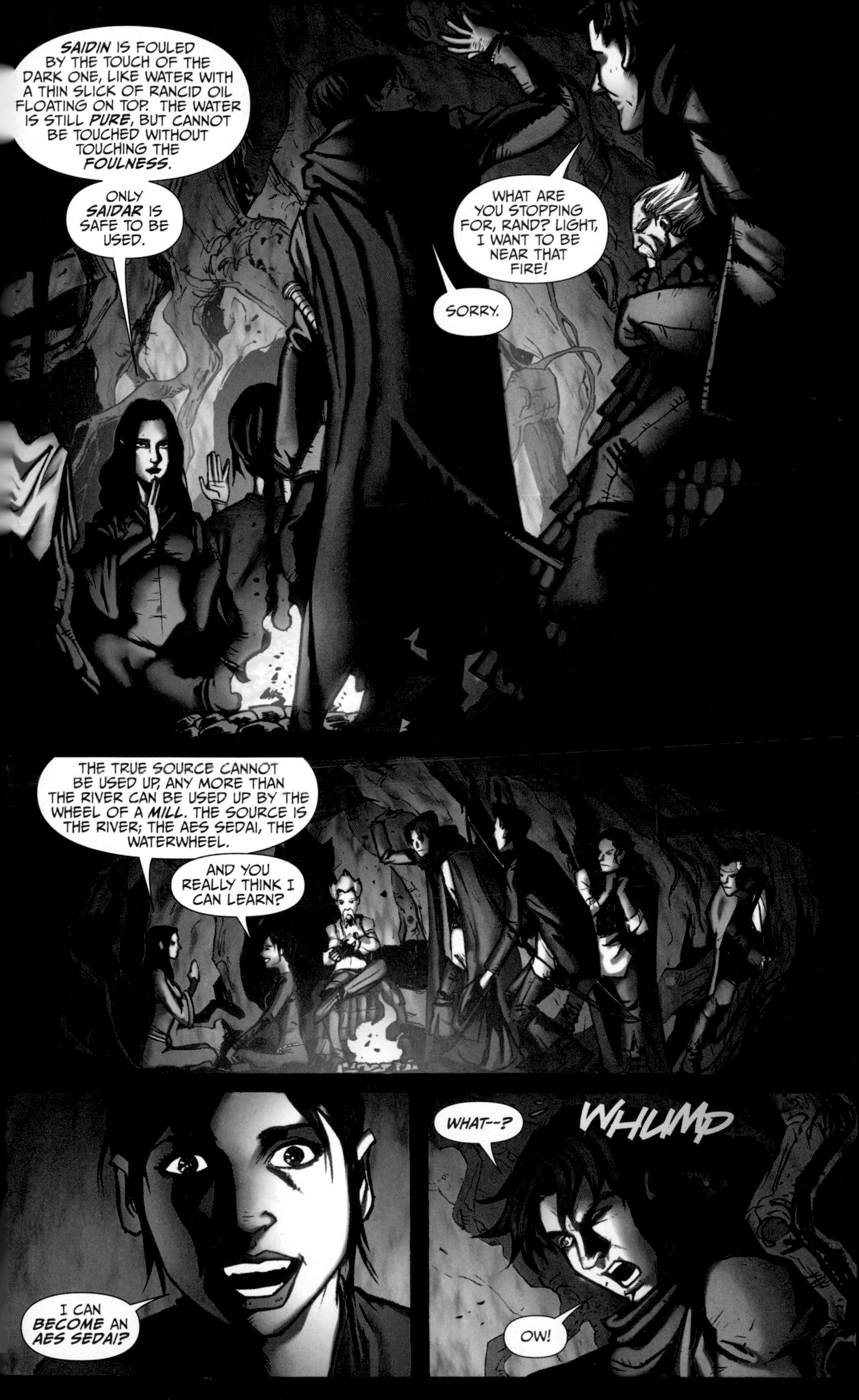
SAIDIN IS FOULED BY THE TOUCH OF THE DARK ONE, LIKE WATER WITH A THIN SLICK OF RANCID OIL FLOATING ON TOP. THE WATER IS STILL PURE, BUT CANNOT BE TOUCHED WITHOUT TOUCHING THE FOULNESS.
ONLY SAIDAR IS SAFE TO BE USED.
WHAT ARE YOU STOPPING FOR, RAND? LIGHT, I WANT TO BE NEAR THAT FIRE!
SORRY.
THE TRUE SOURCE CANNOT BE USED UP, ANY MORE THAN THE RIVER CAN BE USED UP BY THE WHEEL OF A MILL. THE SOURCE IS THE RIVER; THE AES SEDAI, THE WATERWHEEL.
AND YOU REALLY THINK I CAN LEARN?
I CAN BECOME AN AES SEDAI?
WHAT--?
WHUMP
OW!

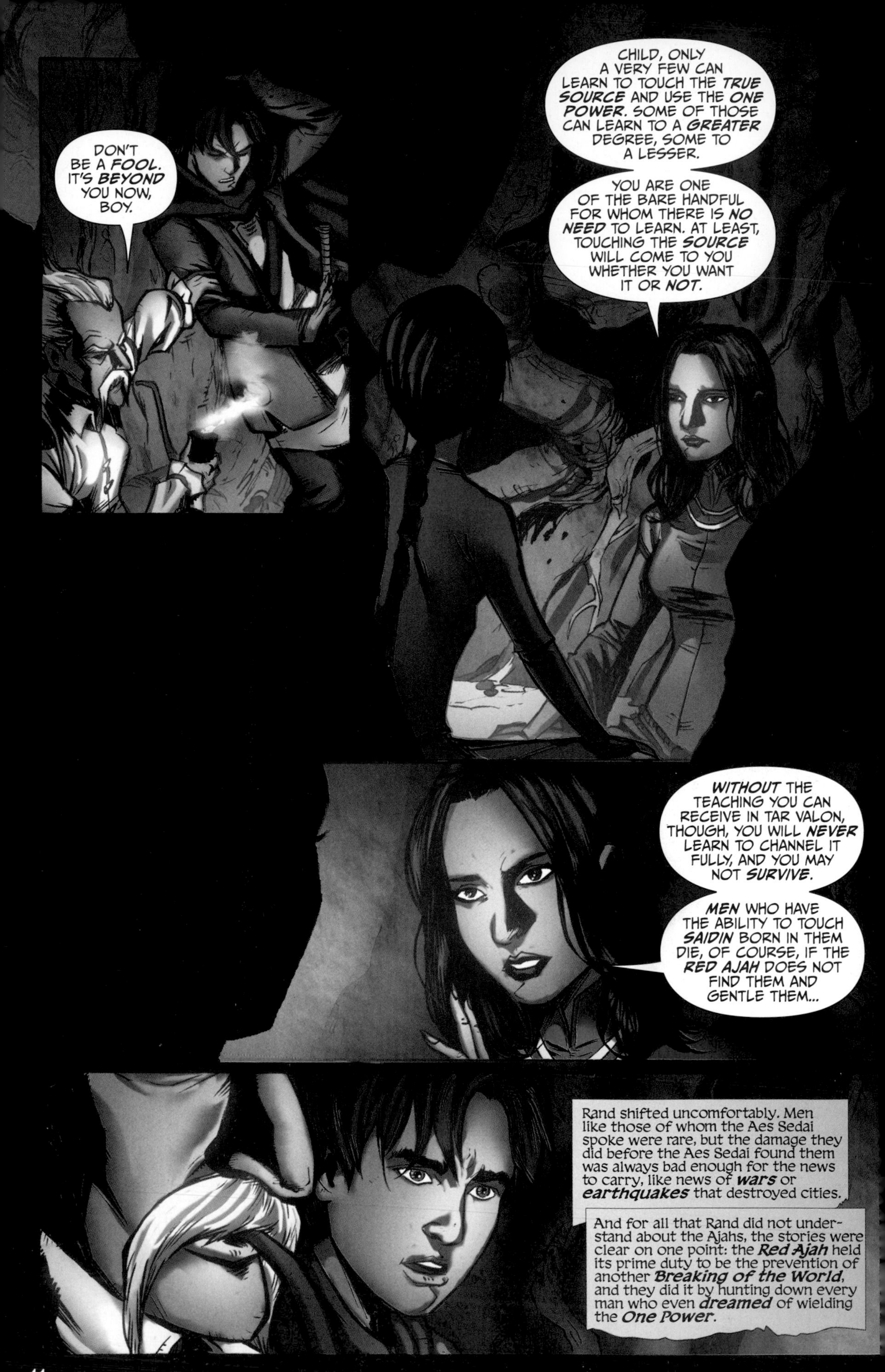
DON'T BE A FOOL. IT'S BEYOND YOU NOW, BOY.
CHILD, ONLY A VERY FEW CAN LEARN TO TOUCH THE TRUE SOURCE AND USE THE ONE POWER. SOME OF THOSE CAN LEARN TO A GREATER DEGREE, SOME TO A LESSER.
YOU ARE ONE OF THE BARE HANDFUL FOR WHOM THERE IS NO NEED TO LEARN. AT LEAST, TOUCHING THE SOURCE WILL COME TO YOU WHETHER YOU WANT IT OR NOT.
WITHOUT THE TEACHING YOU CAN RECEIVE IN TAR VALON, THOUGH, YOU WILL NEVER LEARN TO CHANNEL IT FULLY, AND YOU MAY NOT SURVIVE.
MEN WHO HAVE THE ABILITY TO TOUCH SAIDIN BORN IN THEM DIE, OF COURSE, IF THE RED AJAH DOES NOT FIND THEM AND GENTLE THEM...
Rand shifted uncomfortably. Men like those of whom the Aes Sedai spoke were rare, but the damage they did before the Aes Sedai found them was always bad enough for the news to carry, like news of wars or earthquakes that destroyed cities.
And for all that Rand did not understand about the Ajahs, the stories were clear on one point: the Red Ajah held its prime duty to be the prevention of another Breaking of the World, and they did it by hunting down every man who even dreamed of wielding the One Power.

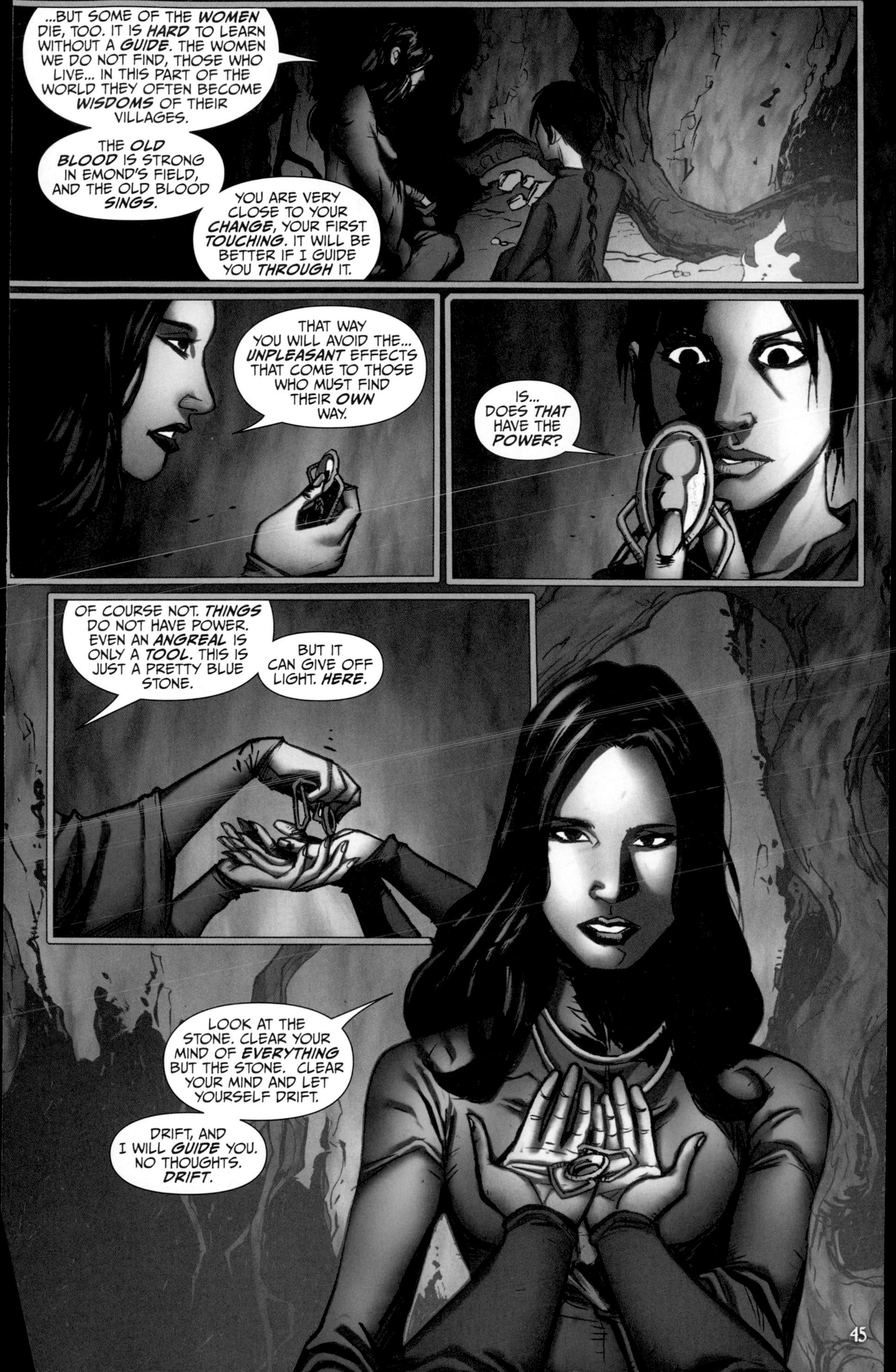
...BUT SOME OF THE WOMEN DIE, TOO. IT IS HARD TO LEARN WITHOUT A GUIDE. THE WOMEN WE DO NOT FIND, THOSE WHO LIVE... IN THIS PART OF THE WORLD THEY OFTEN BECOME WISDOMS OF THEIR VILLAGES.
THE OLD BLOOD IS STRONG IN EMOND'S FIELD, AND THE OLD BLOOD SINGS.
YOU ARE VERY CLOSE TO YOUR CHANGE, YOUR FIRST TOUCHING. IT WILL BE BETTER IF I GUIDE YOU THROUGH IT.
THAT WAY YOU WILL AVOID THE... UNPLEASANT EFFECTS THAT COME TO THOSE WHO MUST FIND THEIR OWN WAY.
IS... DOES THAT HAVE THE POWER?
OF COURSE NOT. THINGS DO NOT HAVE POWER. EVEN AN ANGREAL IS ONLY A TOOL. THIS IS JUST A PRETTY BLUE STONE.
BUT IT CAN GIVE OFF LIGHT. HERE.
LOOK AT THE STONE. CLEAR YOUR MIND OF EVERYTHING BUT THE STONE. CLEAR YOUR MIND AND LET YOURSELF DRIFT.
DRIFT, AND I WILL GUIDE YOU. NO THOUGHTS. DRIFT.

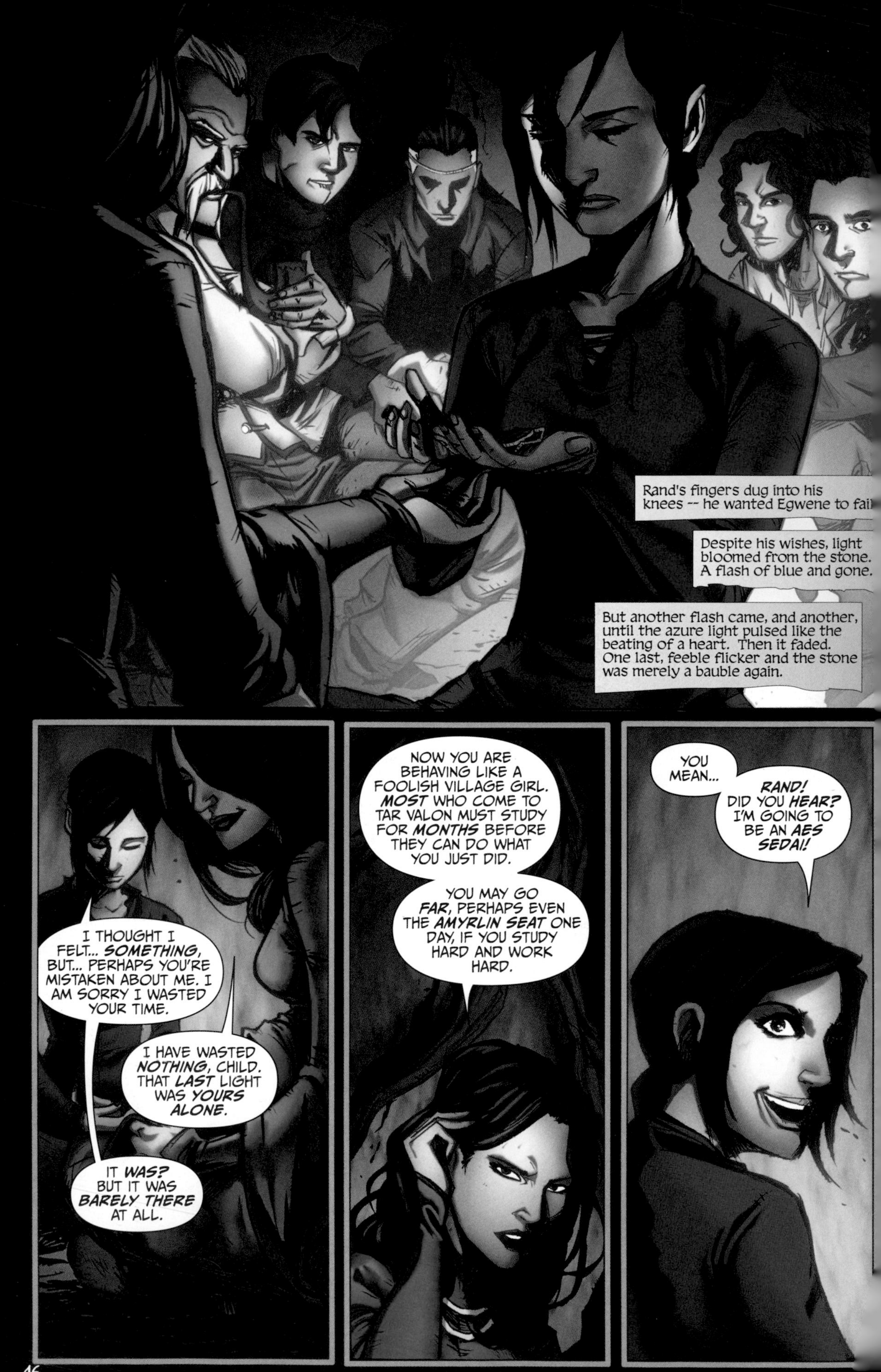
Rand's fingers dug into his knees -- he wanted Egwene to fai
Despite his wishes, light bloomed from the stone. A flash of blue and gone.
But another flash came, and another, until the azure light pulsed like the beating of a heart. Then it faded. One last, feeble flicker and the stone was merely a bauble again.
I THOUGHT I FELT... SOMETHING, BUT... PERHAPS YOU'RE MISTAKEN ABOUT ME. I AM SORRY I WASTED YOUR TIME.
I HAVE WASTED NOTHING, CHILD. THAT LAST LIGHT WAS YOURS ALONE.
IT WAS? BUT IT WAS BARELY THERE AT ALL.
NOW YOU ARE BEHAVING LIKE A FOOLISH VILLAGE GIRL. MOST WHO COME TO TAR VALON MUST STUDY FOR MONTHS BEFORE THEY CAN DO WHAT YOU JUST DID.
YOU MAY GO FAR, PERHAPS EVEN THE AMYRLIN SEAT ONE DAY, IF YOU STUDY HARD AND WORK HARD.
YOU MEAN...
RAND! DID YOU HEAR? I'M GOING TO BE AN AES SEDAI!

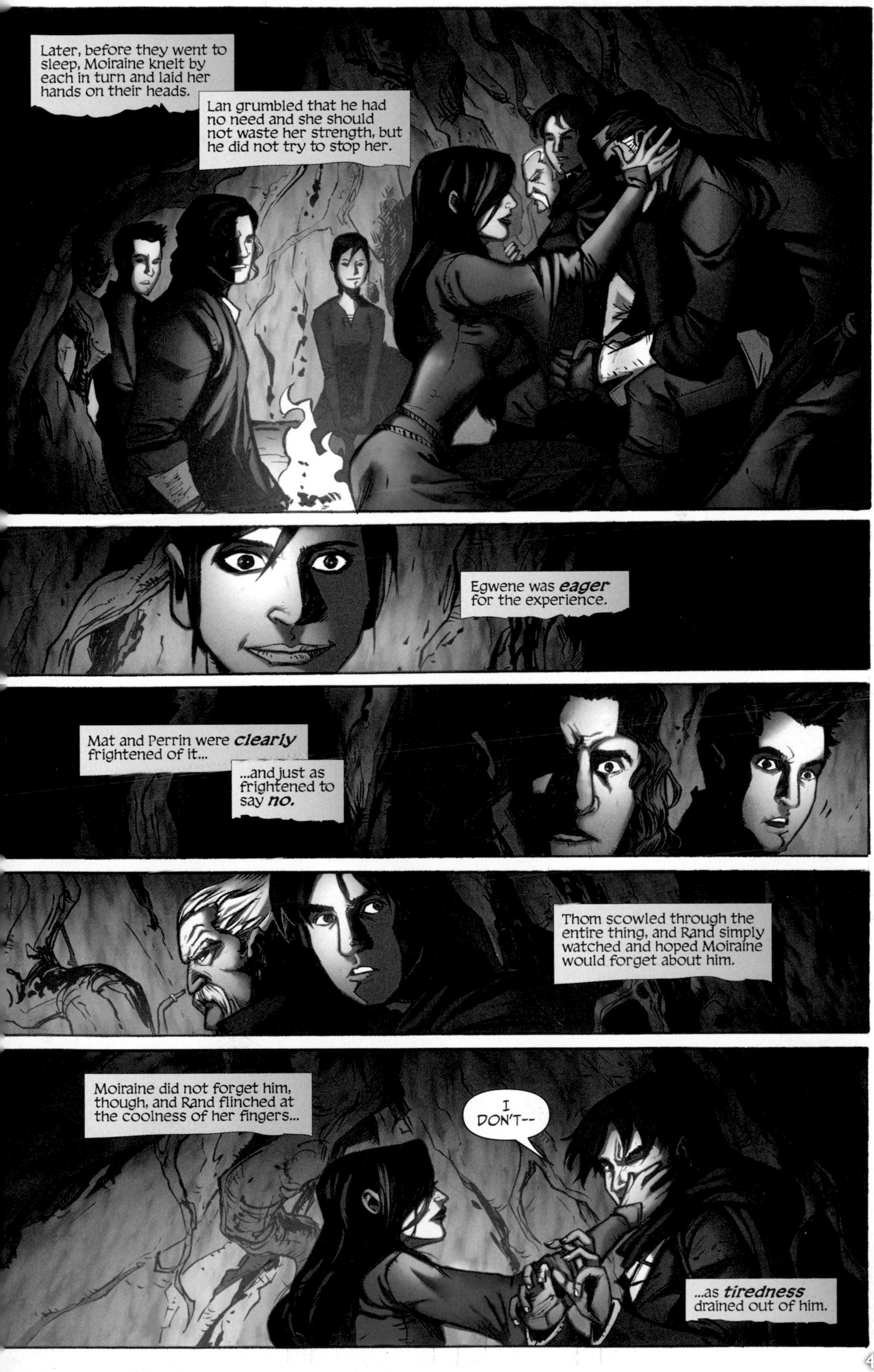
Later, before they went to sleep, Moiraine knelt by each in turn and laid her hands on their heads.
Lan grumbled that he had no need and she should not waste her strength, but he did not try to stop her.
Egwene was eager for the experience.
Mat and Perrin were clearly frightened of it...
...and just as frightened to say no.
Thom scowled through the entire thing, and Rand simply watched and hoped Moiraine would forget about him.
Moiraine did not forget him, though, and Rand flinched at the coolness of her fingers...
I DON'T--
...as tiredness drained out of him.

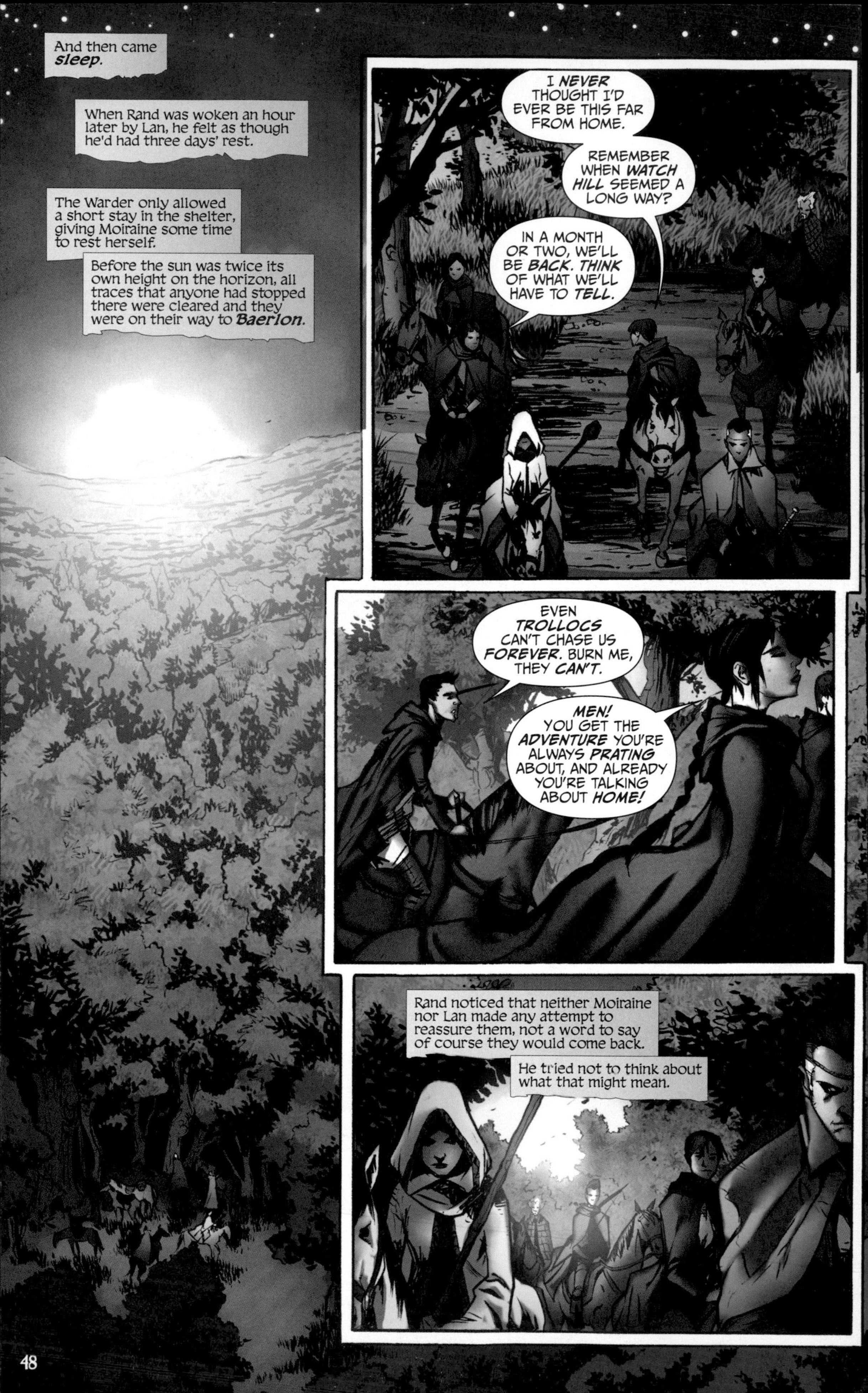

And then came *sleep*.
When Rand was woken an hour later by Lan, he felt as though he'd had three days' rest.
The Warder only allowed a short stay in the shelter, giving Moiraine some time to rest herself.
Before the sun was twice its own height on the horizon, all traces that anyone had stopped there were cleared and they were on their way to *Baerlon*.
I *NEVER* THOUGHT I'D EVER BE THIS FAR FROM HOME.
REMEMBER WHEN *WATCH HILL* SEEMED A LONG WAY?
IN A MONTH OR TWO, WE'LL BE *BACK*. *THINK* OF WHAT WE'LL HAVE TO *TELL*.
EVEN *TROLLOCS* CAN'T CHASE US *FOREVER*. BURN ME, THEY *CAN'T*.
MEN! YOU GET THE *ADVENTURE* YOU'RE ALWAYS *PRATING* ABOUT, AND ALREADY YOU'RE TALKING ABOUT *HOME!*
Rand noticed that neither Moiraine nor Lan made any attempt to reassure them, not a word to say of course they would come back.
He tried not to think about what that might mean.

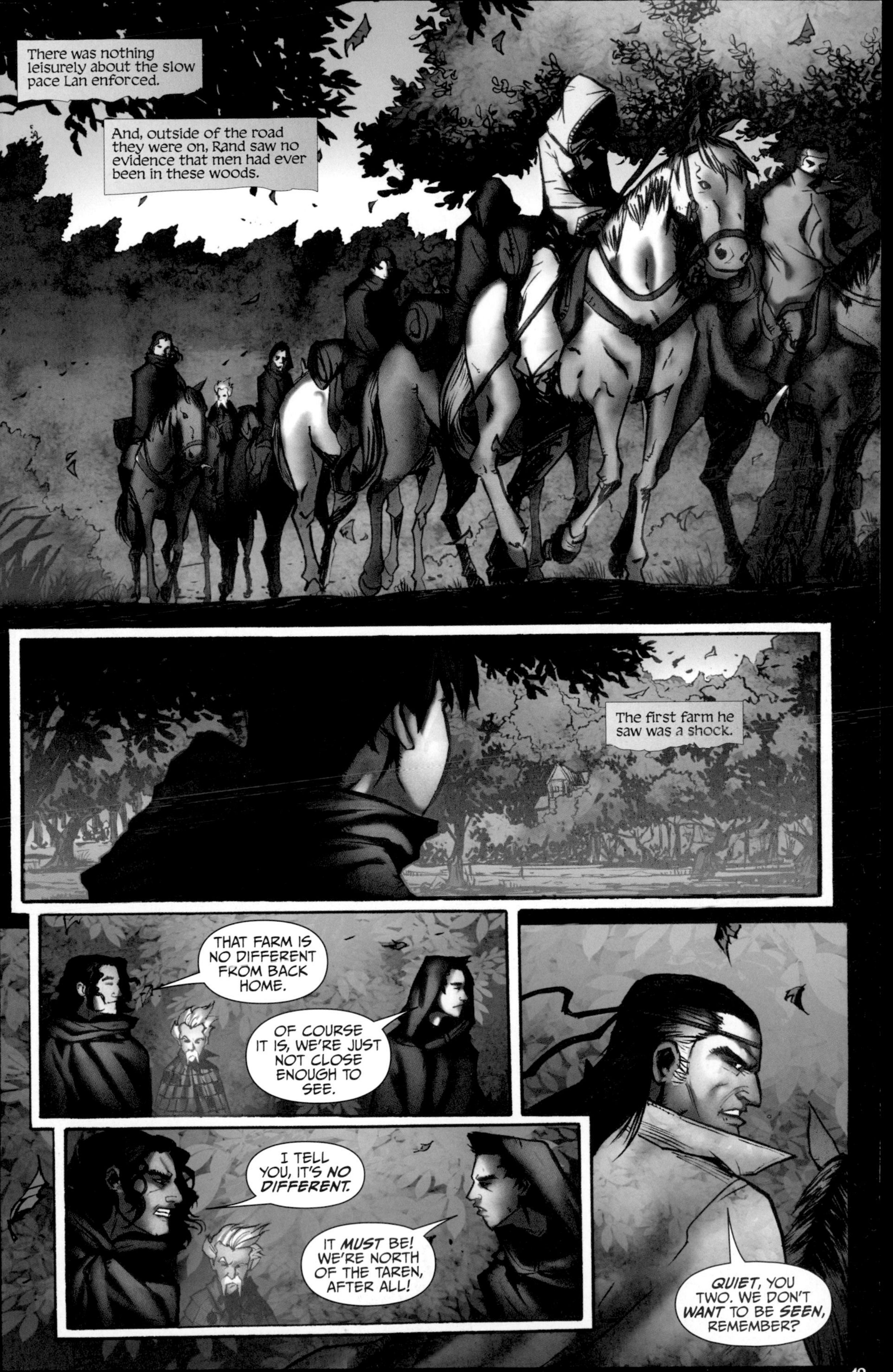
There was nothing leisurely about the slow pace Lan enforced.
And, outside of the road they were on, Rand saw no evidence that men had ever been in these woods.
The first farm he saw was a shock.
THAT FARM IS NO DIFFERENT FROM BACK HOME.
OF COURSE IT IS, WE'RE JUST NOT CLOSE ENOUGH TO SEE.
I TELL YOU, IT'S *NO DIFFERENT.*
IT *MUST* BE! WE'RE NORTH OF THE TAREN, AFTER ALL!
QUIET, YOU TWO. WE DON'T *WANT* TO BE *SEEN*, REMEMBER?

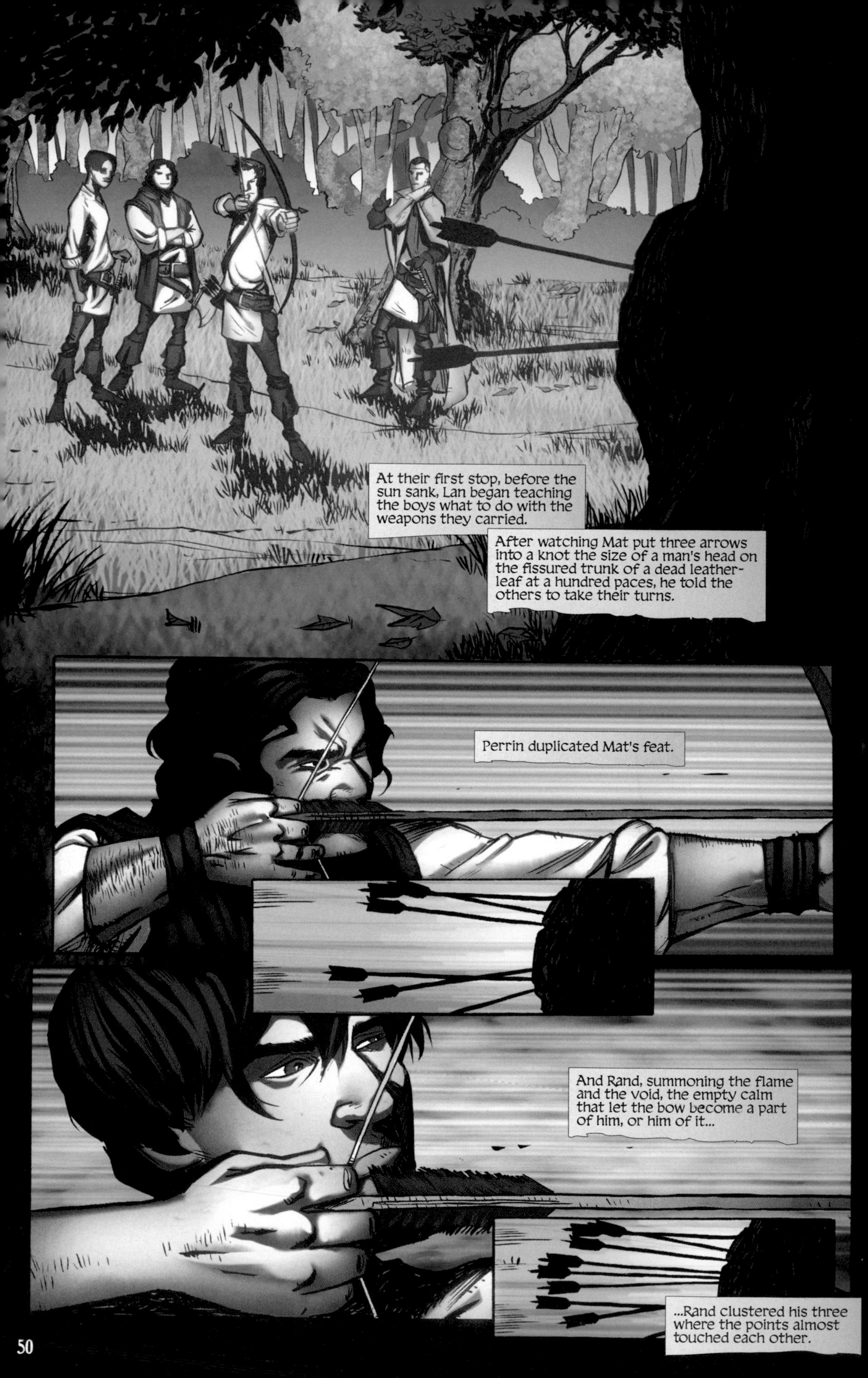
At their first stop, before the sun sank, Lan began teaching the boys what to do with the weapons they carried.
After watching Mat put three arrows into a knot the size of a man's head on the fissured trunk of a dead leather-leaf at a hundred paces, he told the others to take their turns.
Perrin duplicated Mat's feat.
And Rand, summoning the flame and the void, the empty calm that let the bow become a part of him, or him of it...
...Rand clustered his three where the points almost touched each other.

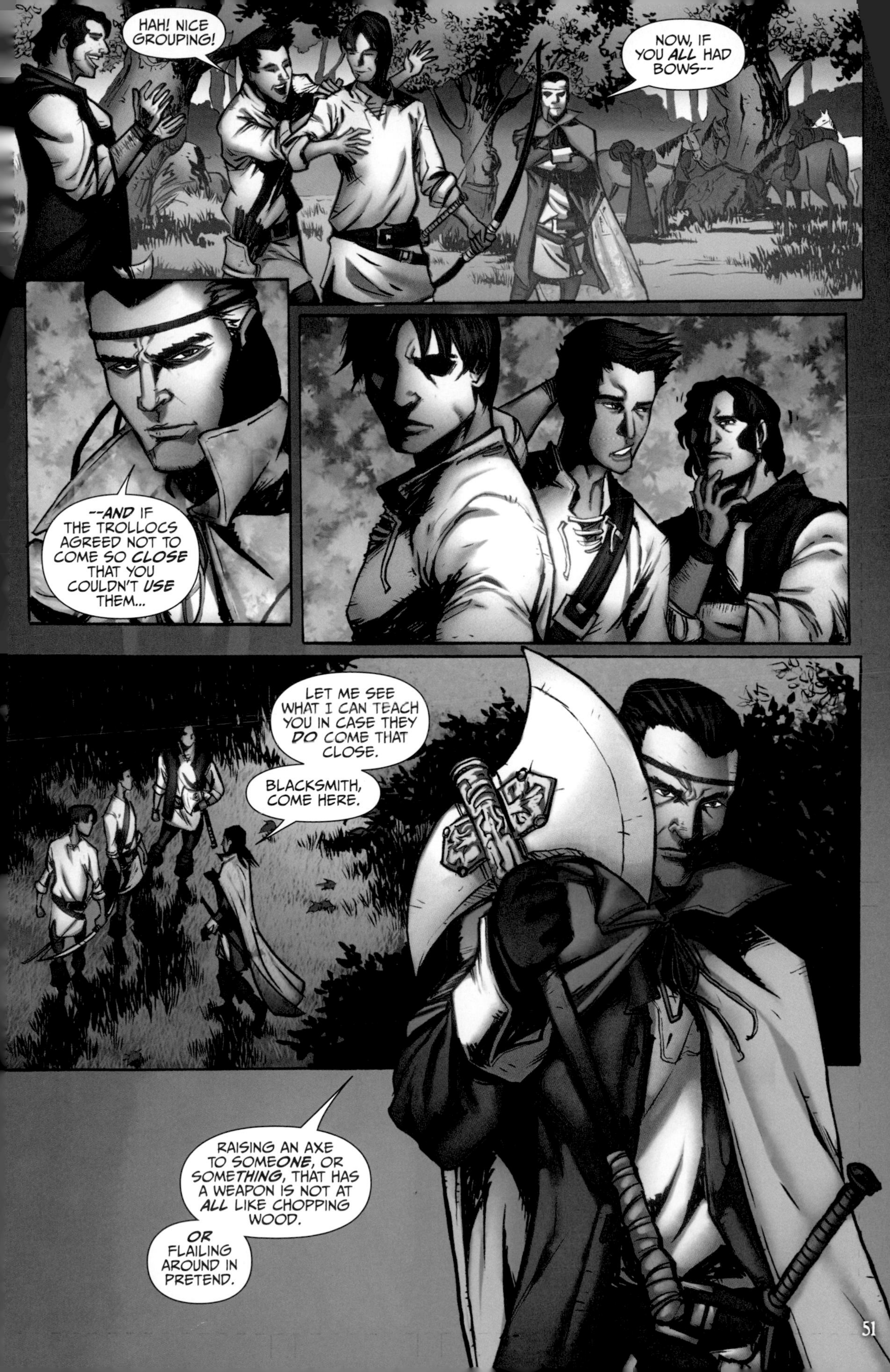
HAH! NICE GROUPING!
NOW, IF YOU ALL HAD BOWS--
--AND IF THE TROLLOCS AGREED NOT TO COME SO CLOSE THAT YOU COULDN'T USE THEM...
LET ME SEE WHAT I CAN TEACH YOU IN CASE THEY DO COME THAT CLOSE.
BLACKSMITH, COME HERE.
RAISING AN AXE TO SOMEONE, OR SOMETHING, THAT HAS A WEAPON IS NOT AT ALL LIKE CHOPPING WOOD.
OR FLAILING AROUND IN PRETEND.

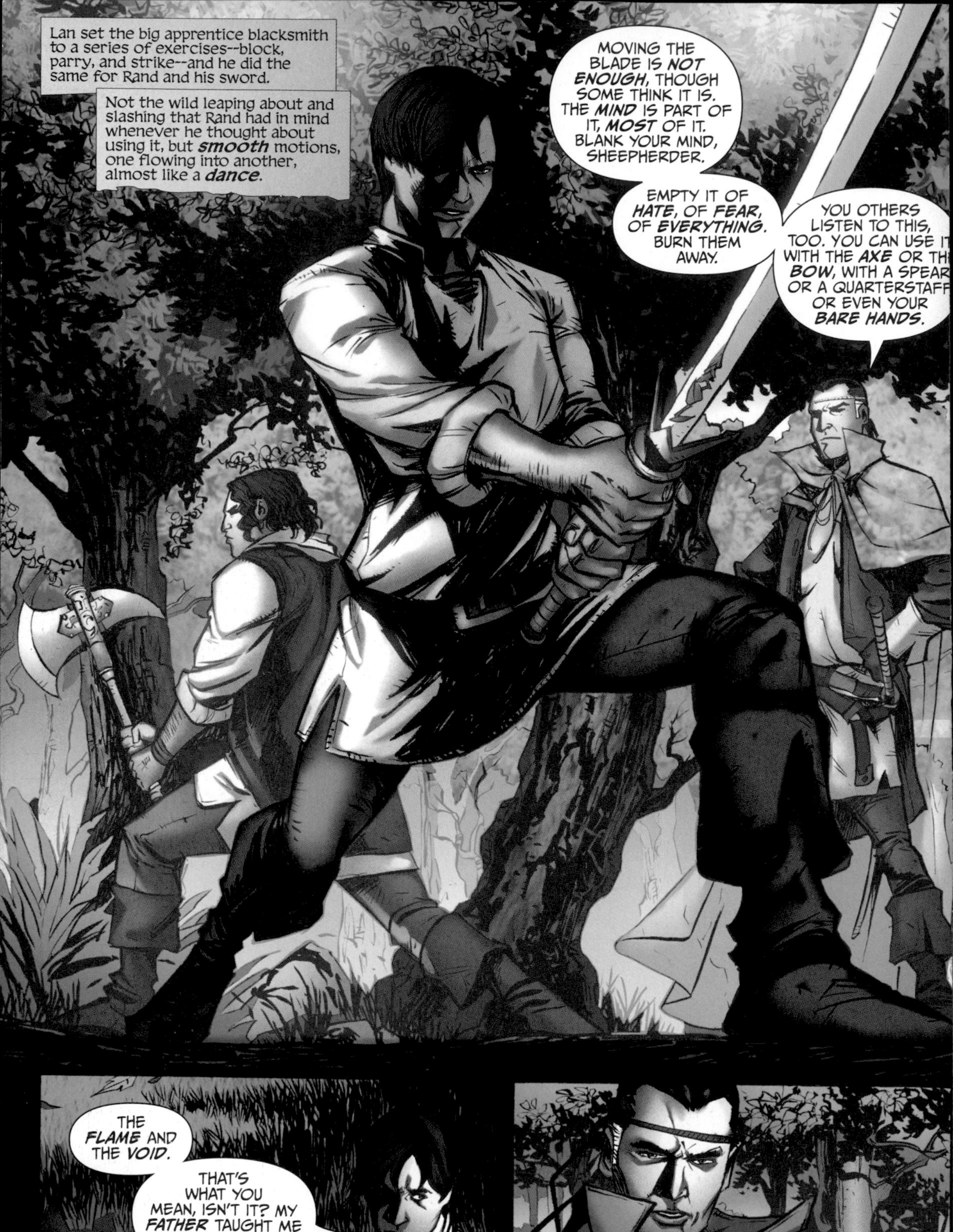

Lan set the big apprentice blacksmith to a series of exercises--block, parry, and strike--and he did the same for Rand and his sword.
Not the wild leaping about and slashing that Rand had in mind whenever he thought about using it, but *smooth* motions, one flowing into another, almost like a *dance*.
MOVING THE BLADE IS *NOT ENOUGH*, THOUGH SOME THINK IT IS. THE *MIND* IS PART OF IT, *MOST* OF IT. BLANK YOUR MIND, SHEEPHERDER.
EMPTY IT OF *HATE*, OF *FEAR*, OF *EVERYTHING*. BURN THEM AWAY.
YOU OTHERS LISTEN TO THIS, TOO. YOU CAN USE IT WITH THE *AXE* OR THE *BOW*, WITH A SPEAR OR A QUARTERSTAFF OR EVEN YOUR *BARE HANDS*.

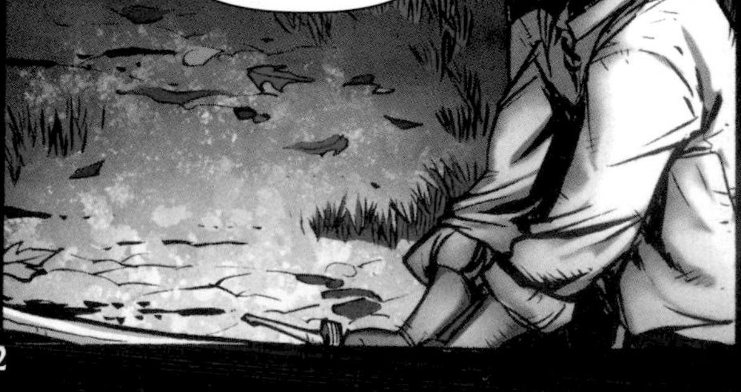

THE *FLAME* AND THE *VOID*.
THAT'S WHAT YOU MEAN, ISN'T IT? MY *FATHER* TAUGHT ME ABOUT THAT.

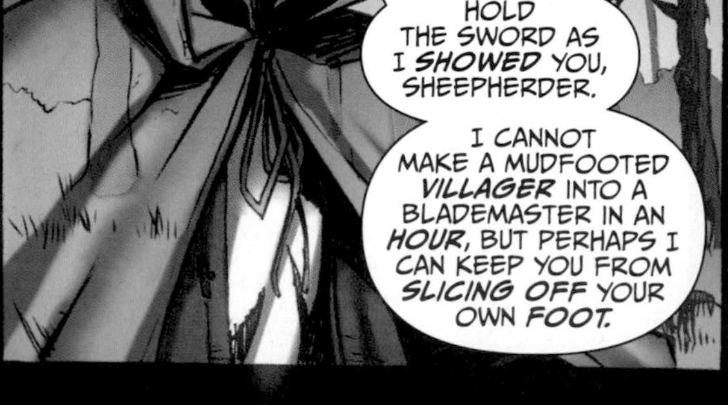

HOLD THE SWORD AS I *SHOWED* YOU, SHEEPHERDER.
I CANNOT MAKE A MUDFOOTED *VILLAGER* INTO A BLADEMASTER IN AN *HOUR*, BUT PERHAPS I CAN KEEP YOU FROM *SLICING OFF* YOUR OWN *FOOT*.

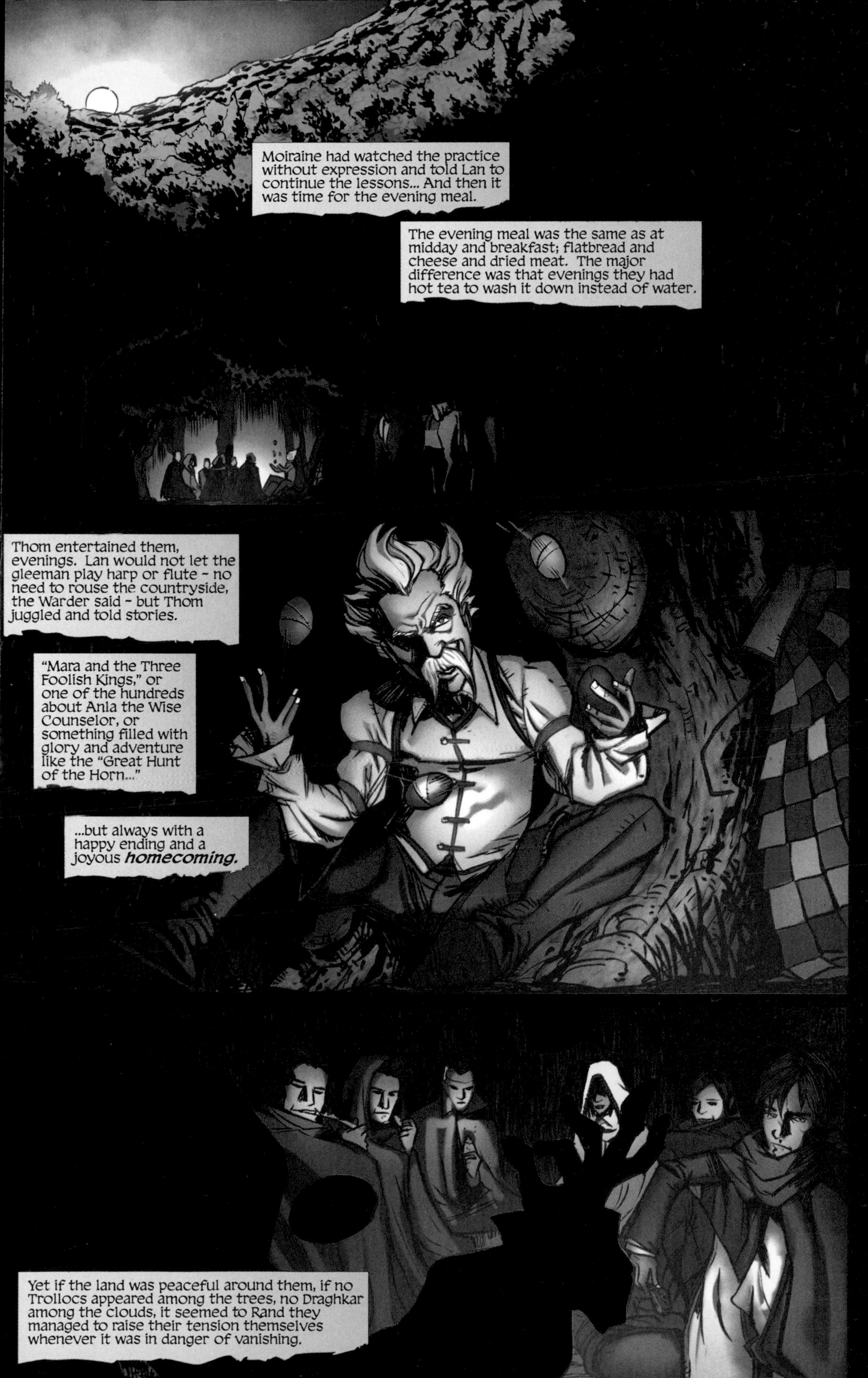
Moiraine had watched the practice without expression and told Lan to continue the lessons... And then it was time for the evening meal.
The evening meal was the same as at midday and breakfast; flatbread and cheese and dried meat. The major difference was that evenings they had hot tea to wash it down instead of water.
Thom entertained them, evenings. Lan would not let the gleeman play harp or flute - no need to rouse the countryside, the Warder said - but Thom juggled and told stories.
"Mara and the Three Foolish Kings," or one of the hundreds about Anla the Wise Counselor, or something filled with glory and adventure like the "Great Hunt of the Horn..."
...but always with a happy ending and a joyous *homecoming.*
Yet if the land was peaceful around them, if no Trollocs appeared among the trees, no Draghkar among the clouds, it seemed to Rand they managed to raise their tension themselves whenever it was in danger of vanishing.

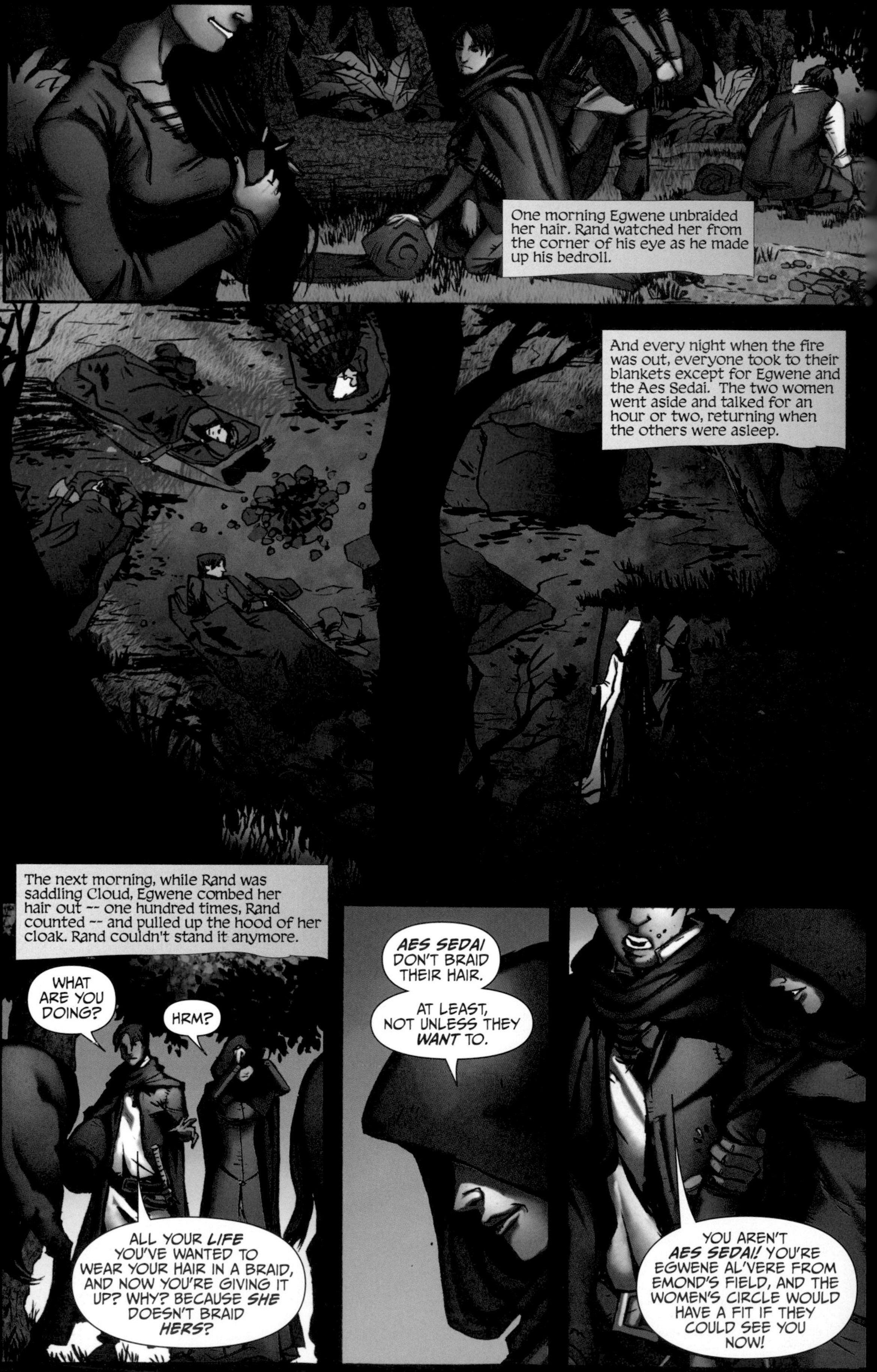
One morning Egwene unbraided her hair. Rand watched her from the corner of his eye as he made up his bedroll.
And every night when the fire was out, everyone took to their blankets except for Egwene and the Aes Sedai. The two women went aside and talked for an hour or two, returning when the others were asleep.
The next morning, while Rand was saddling Cloud, Egwene combed her hair out -- one hundred times, Rand counted -- and pulled up the hood of her cloak. Rand couldn't stand it anymore.
WHAT ARE YOU DOING?
HRM?
ALL YOUR *LIFE* YOU'VE WANTED TO WEAR YOUR HAIR IN A BRAID, AND NOW YOU'RE GIVING IT UP? WHY? BECAUSE *SHE* DOESN'T BRAID *HERS?*
AES SEDAI DON'T BRAID THEIR HAIR.
AT LEAST, NOT UNLESS THEY *WANT* TO.
YOU AREN'T *AES SEDAI!* YOU'RE EGWENE AL'VERE FROM EMOND'S FIELD, AND THE WOMEN'S CIRCLE WOULD HAVE A FIT IF THEY COULD SEE YOU NOW!

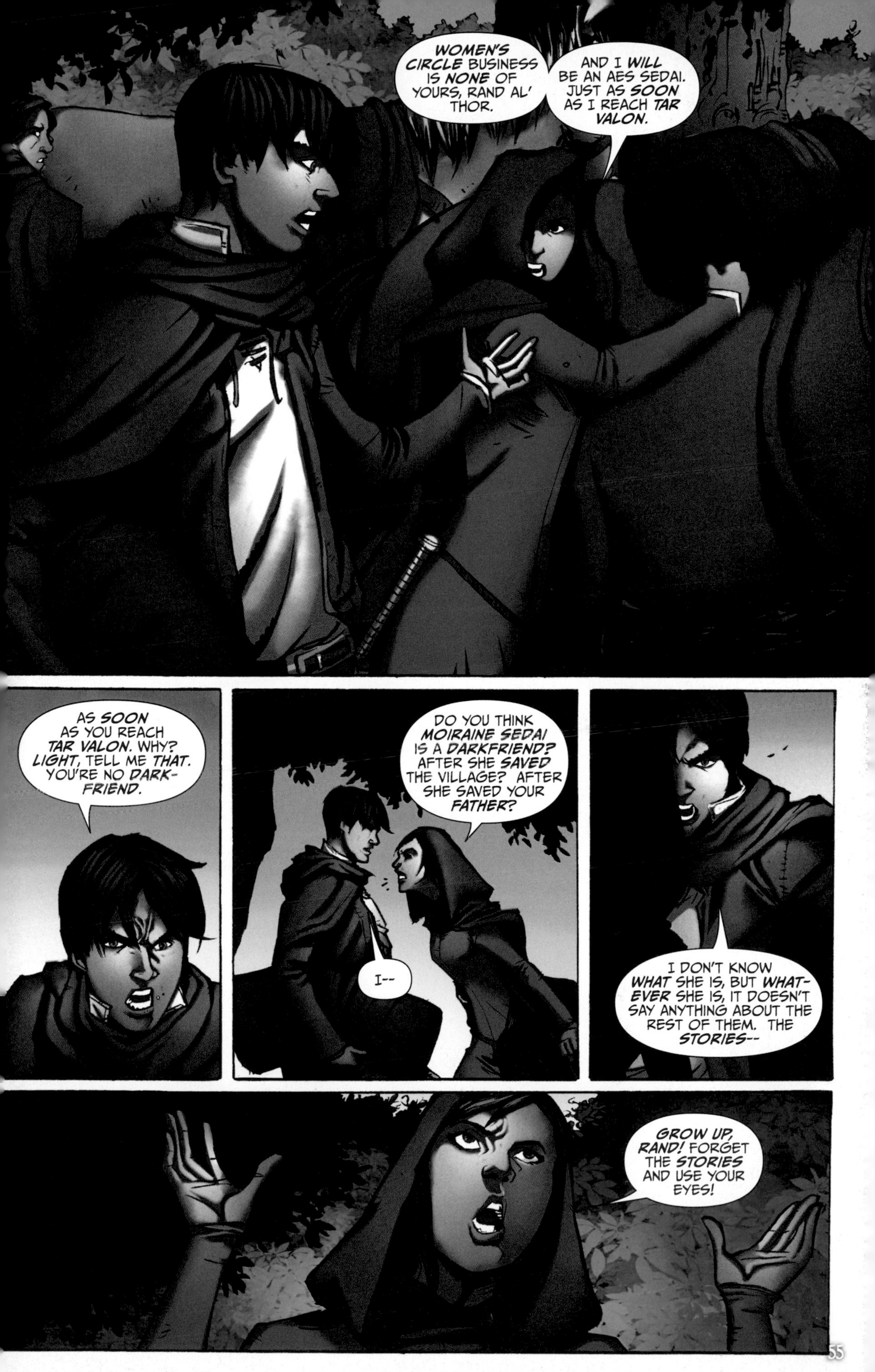
WOMEN'S CIRCLE BUSINESS IS NONE OF YOURS, RAND AL' THOR.
AND I WILL BE AN AES SEDAI. JUST AS SOON AS I REACH TAR VALON.
AS SOON AS YOU REACH TAR VALON. WHY? LIGHT, TELL ME THAT. YOU'RE NO DARK-FRIEND.
DO YOU THINK MOIRAINE SEDAI IS A DARKFRIEND? AFTER SHE SAVED THE VILLAGE? AFTER SHE SAVED YOUR FATHER?
I--
I DON'T KNOW WHAT SHE IS, BUT WHAT-EVER SHE IS, IT DOESN'T SAY ANYTHING ABOUT THE REST OF THEM. THE STORIES--
GROW UP, RAND! FORGET THE STORIES AND USE YOUR EYES!

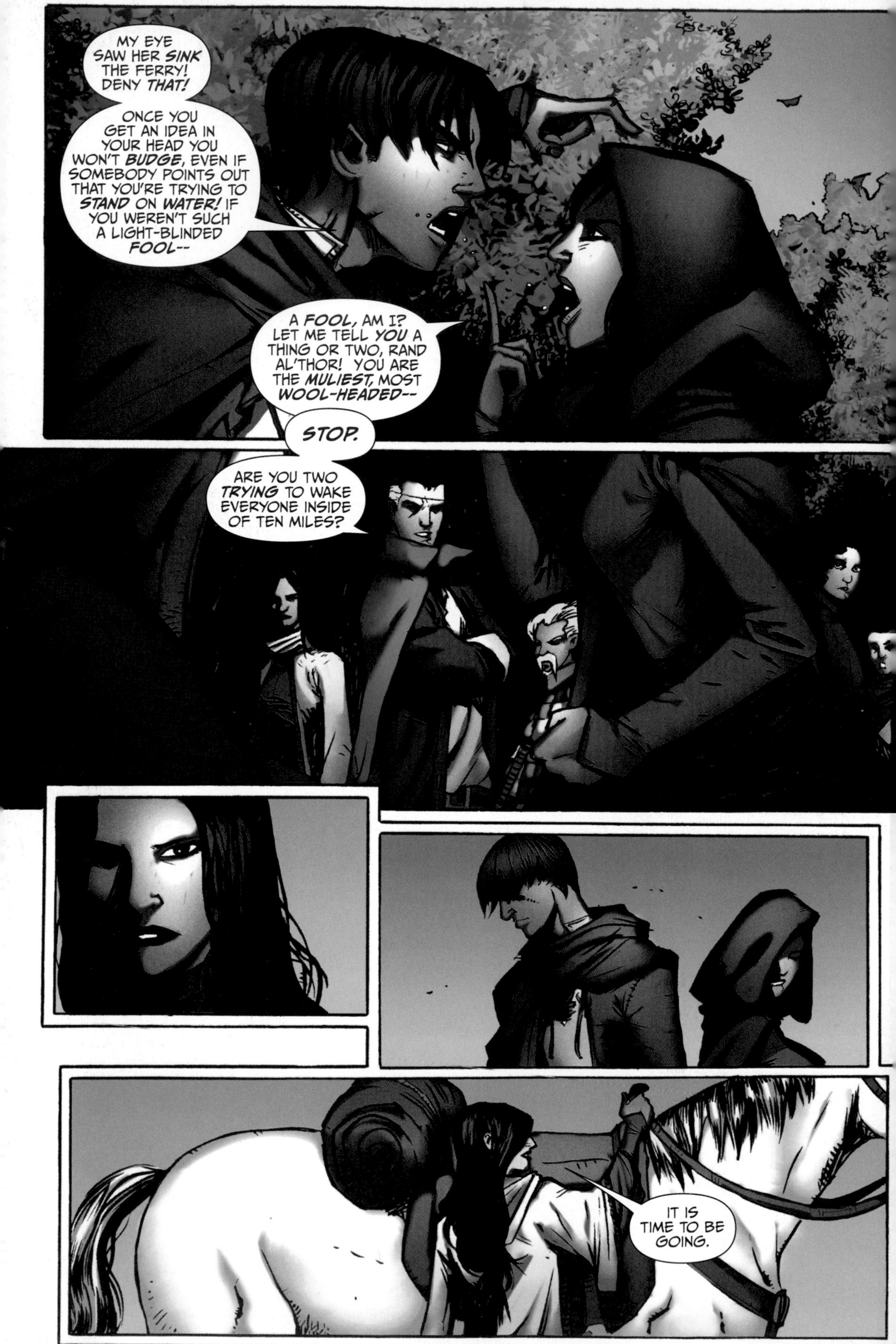
MY EYE SAW HER SINK THE FERRY! DENY THAT!
ONCE YOU GET AN IDEA IN YOUR HEAD YOU WON'T BUDGE, EVEN IF SOMEBODY POINTS OUT THAT YOU'RE TRYING TO STAND ON WATER! IF YOU WEREN'T SUCH A LIGHT-BLINDED FOOL--
A FOOL, AM I? LET ME TELL YOU A THING OR TWO, RAND AL'THOR! YOU ARE THE MULIEST, MOST WOOL-HEADED--
STOP.
ARE YOU TWO TRYING TO WAKE EVERYONE INSIDE OF TEN MILES?
IT IS TIME TO BE GOING.

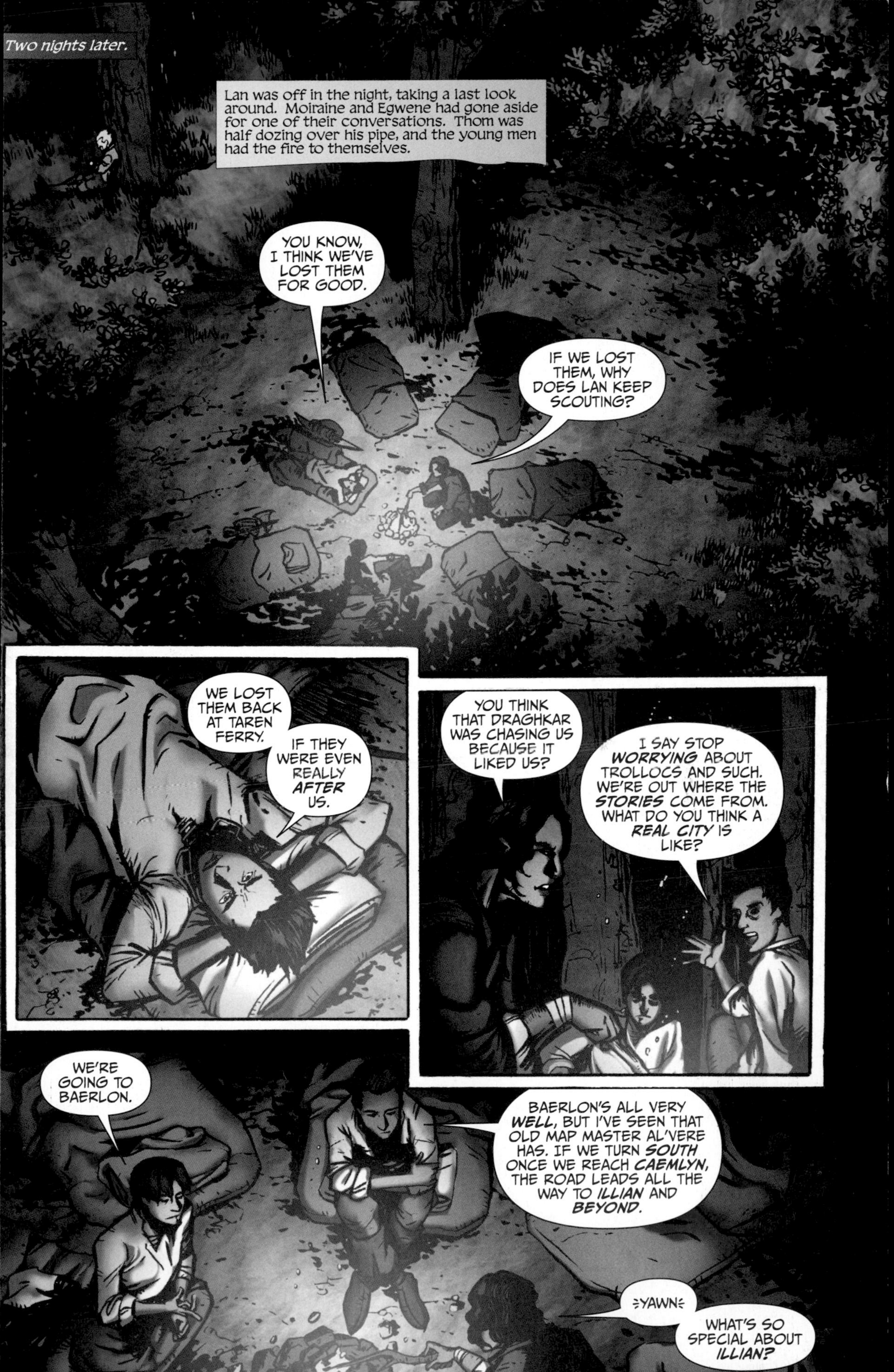
Two nights later.
Lan was off in the night, taking a last look around. Moiraine and Egwene had gone aside for one of their conversations. Thom was half dozing over his pipe, and the young men had the fire to themselves.
YOU KNOW, I THINK WE'VE LOST THEM FOR GOOD.
IF WE LOST THEM, WHY DOES LAN KEEP SCOUTING?
WE LOST THEM BACK AT TAREN FERRY.
IF THEY WERE EVEN REALLY AFTER US.
YOU THINK THAT DRAGHKAR WAS CHASING US BECAUSE IT LIKED US?
I SAY STOP WORRYING ABOUT TROLLOCS AND SUCH. WE'RE OUT WHERE THE STORIES COME FROM. WHAT DO YOU THINK A REAL CITY IS LIKE?
WE'RE GOING TO BAERLON.
BAERLON'S ALL VERY WELL, BUT I'VE SEEN THAT OLD MAP MASTER AL'VERE HAS. IF WE TURN SOUTH ONCE WE REACH CAEMLYN, THE ROAD LEADS ALL THE WAY TO ILLIAN AND BEYOND.
YAWN
WHAT'S SO SPECIAL ABOUT ILLIAN?

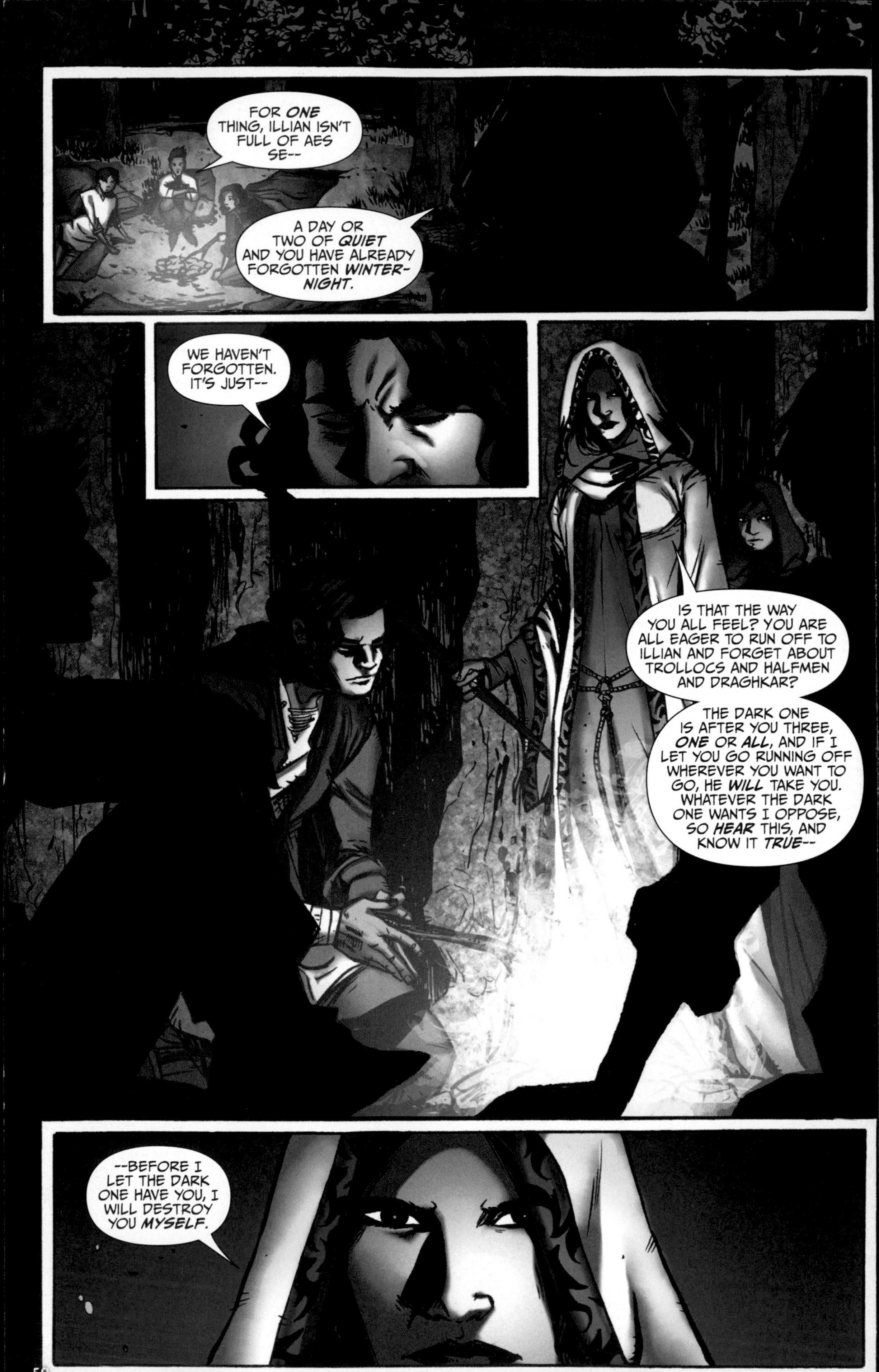
FOR ONE THING, ILLIAN ISN'T FULL OF AES SE--
A DAY OR TWO OF QUIET AND YOU HAVE ALREADY FORGOTTEN WINTER-NIGHT.
WE HAVEN'T FORGOTTEN. IT'S JUST--
IS THAT THE WAY YOU ALL FEEL? YOU ARE ALL EAGER TO RUN OFF TO ILLIAN AND FORGET ABOUT TROLLOCS AND HALFMEN AND DRAGHKAR?
THE DARK ONE IS AFTER YOU THREE, ONE OR ALL, AND IF I LET YOU GO RUNNING OFF WHEREVER YOU WANT TO GO, HE WILL TAKE YOU. WHATEVER THE DARK ONE WANTS I OPPOSE, SO HEAR THIS, AND KNOW IT TRUE--
--BEFORE I LET THE DARK ONE HAVE YOU, I WILL DESTROY YOU MYSELF.

chapter three

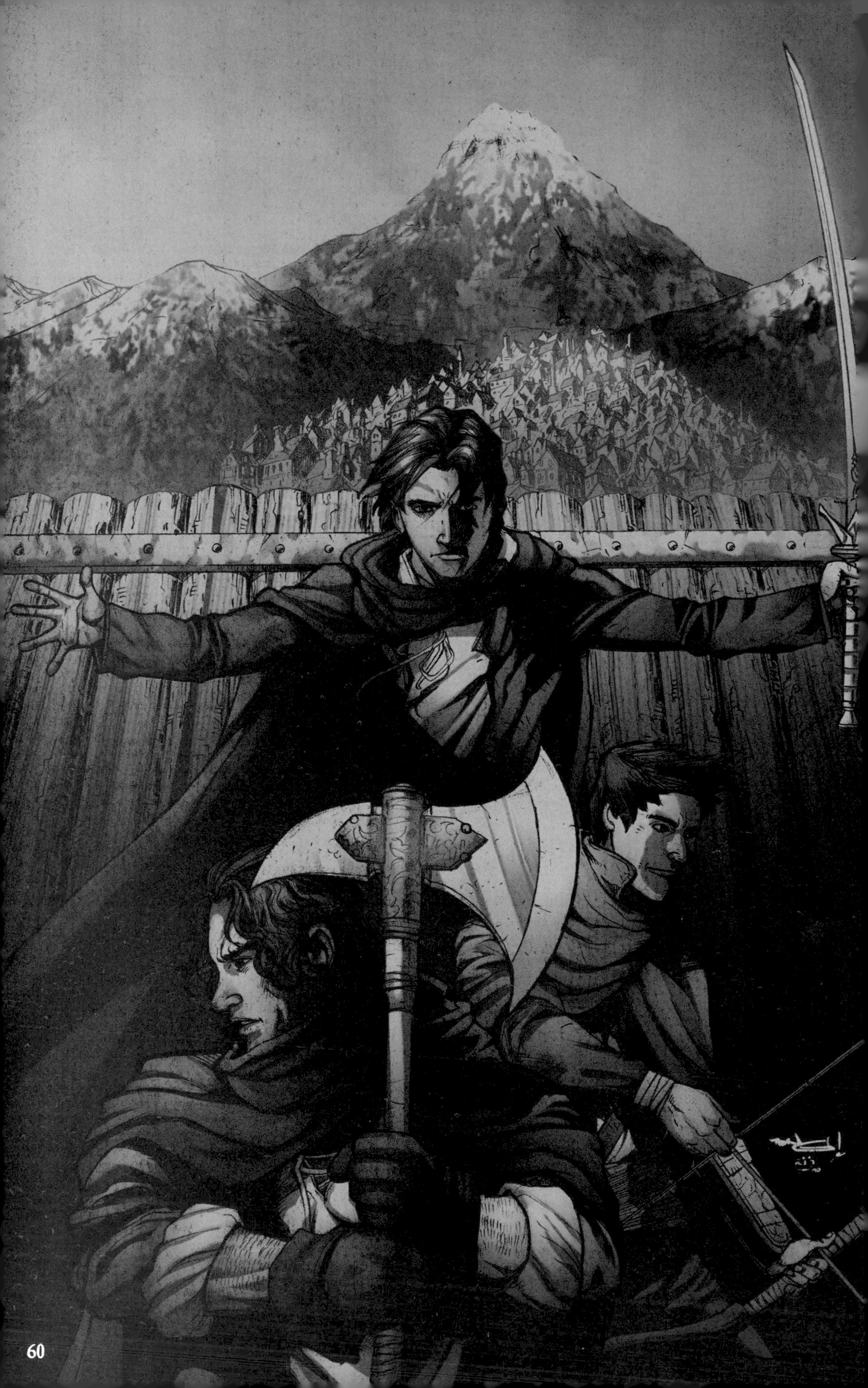

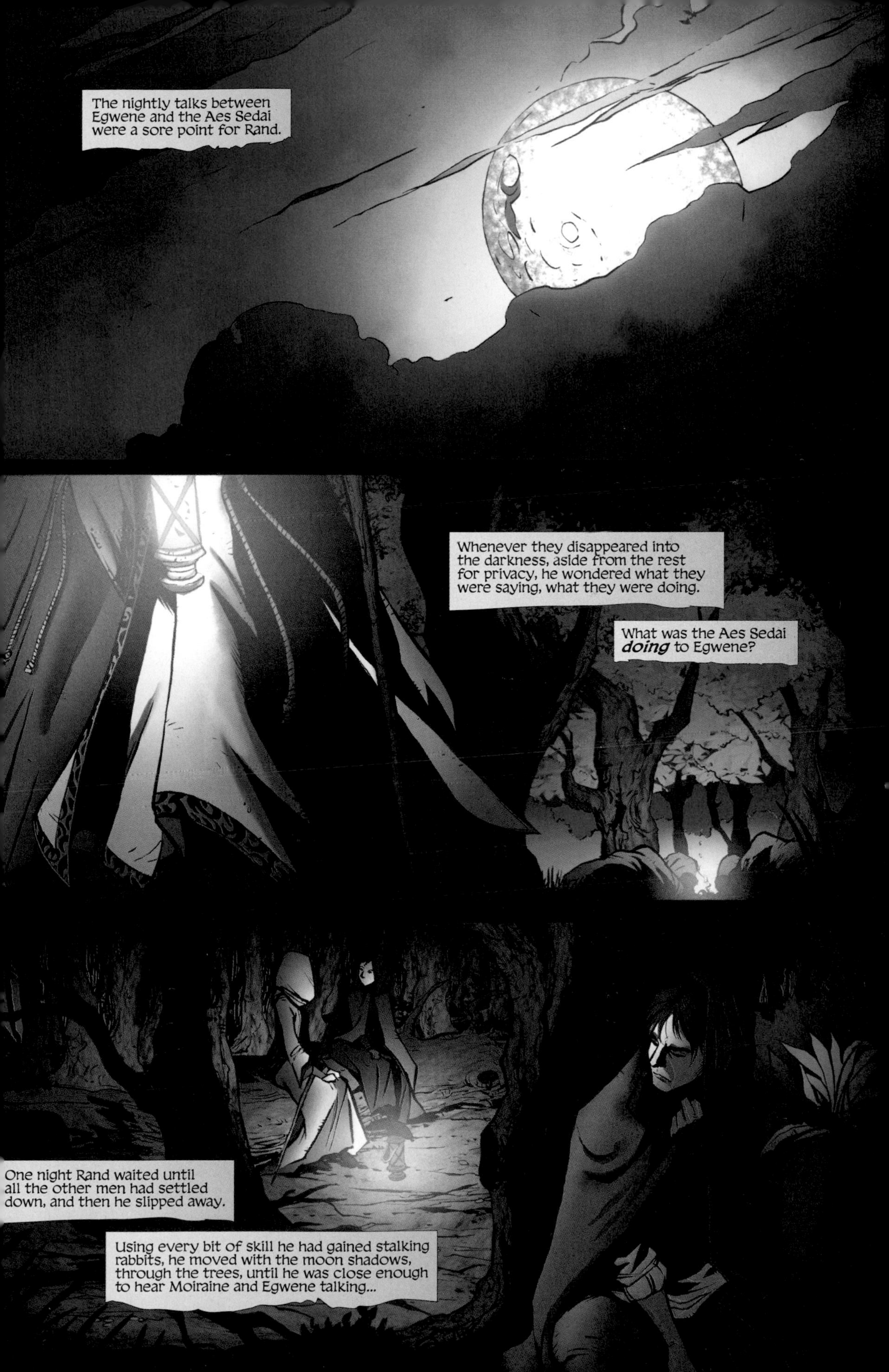
The nightly talks between Egwene and the Aes Sedai were a sore point for Rand.
Whenever they disappeared into the darkness, aside from the rest for privacy, he wondered what they were saying, what they were doing.
What was the Aes Sedai *doing* to Egwene?
One night Rand waited until all the other men had settled down, and then he slipped away.
Using every bit of skill he had gained stalking rabbits, he moved with the moon shadows, through the trees, until he was close enough to hear Moiraine and Egwene talking...

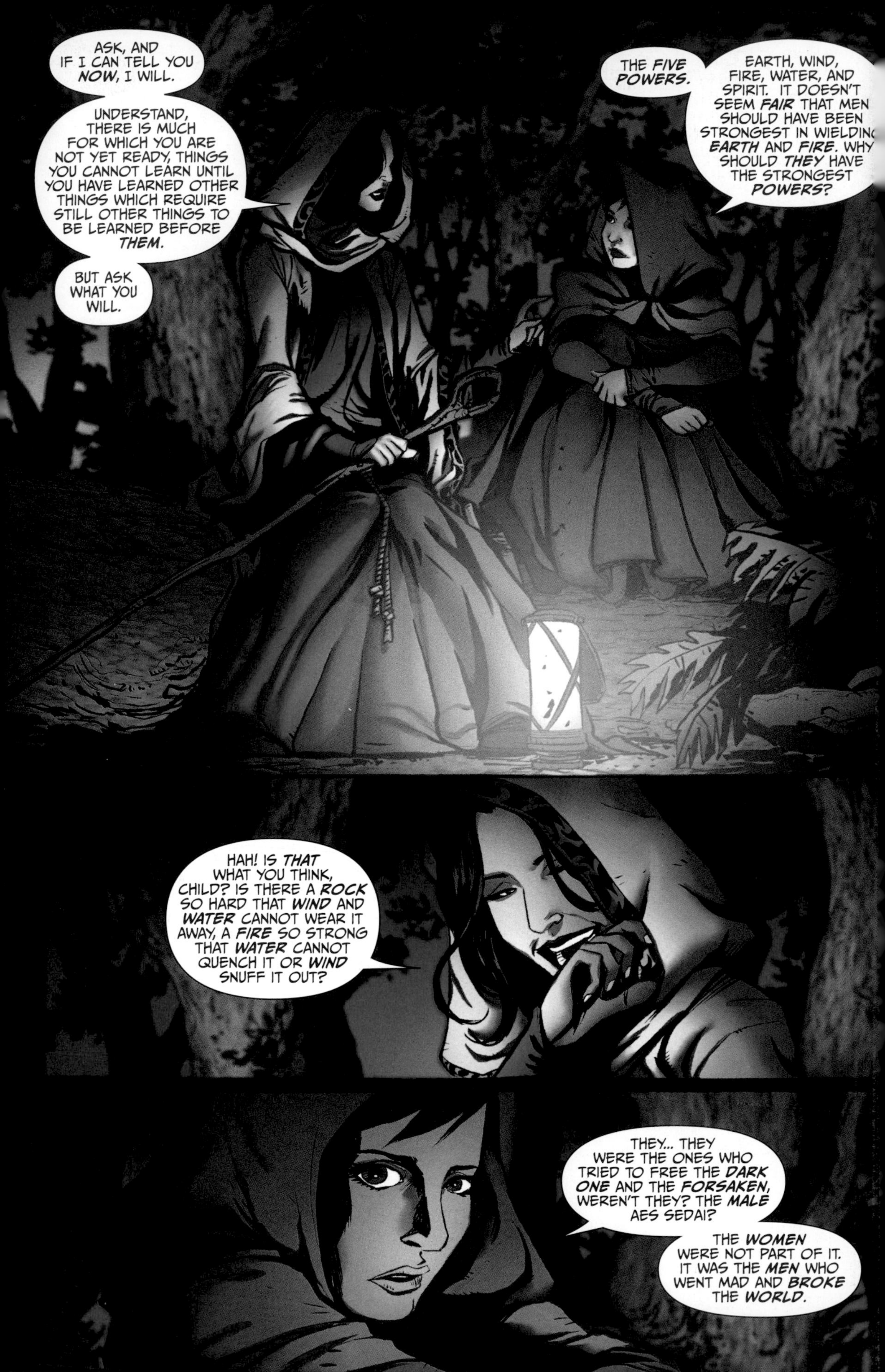

ASK, AND IF I CAN TELL YOU NOW, I WILL.
UNDERSTAND, THERE IS MUCH FOR WHICH YOU ARE NOT YET READY, THINGS YOU CANNOT LEARN UNTIL YOU HAVE LEARNED OTHER THINGS WHICH REQUIRE STILL OTHER THINGS TO BE LEARNED BEFORE THEM.
BUT ASK WHAT YOU WILL.
THE FIVE POWERS.
EARTH, WIND, FIRE, WATER, AND SPIRIT. IT DOESN'T SEEM FAIR THAT MEN SHOULD HAVE BEEN STRONGEST IN WIELDING EARTH AND FIRE. WHY SHOULD THEY HAVE THE STRONGEST POWERS?
HAH! IS THAT WHAT YOU THINK, CHILD? IS THERE A ROCK SO HARD THAT WIND AND WATER CANNOT WEAR IT AWAY, A FIRE SO STRONG THAT WATER CANNOT QUENCH IT OR WIND SNUFF IT OUT?
THEY... THEY WERE THE ONES WHO TRIED TO FREE THE DARK ONE AND THE FORSAKEN, WEREN'T THEY? THE MALE AES SEDAI?
THE WOMEN WERE NOT PART OF IT. IT WAS THE MEN WHO WENT MAD AND BROKE THE WORLD.

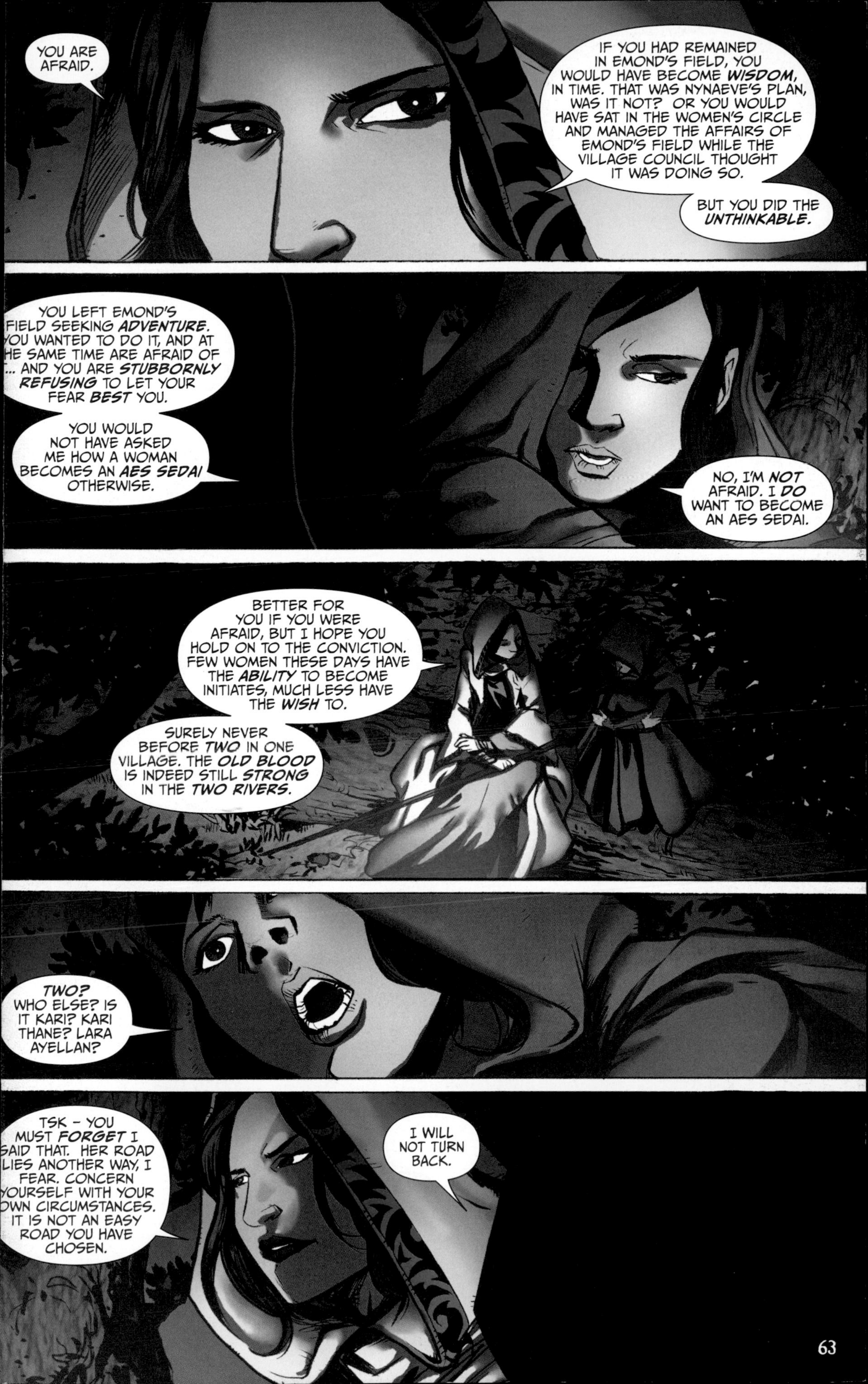
YOU ARE AFRAID.
IF YOU HAD REMAINED IN EMOND'S FIELD, YOU WOULD HAVE BECOME *WISDOM,* IN TIME. THAT WAS NYNAEVE'S PLAN, WAS IT NOT? OR YOU WOULD HAVE SAT IN THE WOMEN'S CIRCLE AND MANAGED THE AFFAIRS OF EMOND'S FIELD WHILE THE VILLAGE COUNCIL THOUGHT IT WAS DOING SO.
BUT YOU DID THE *UNTHINKABLE.*
YOU LEFT EMOND'S FIELD SEEKING *ADVENTURE.* YOU WANTED TO DO IT, AND AT HE SAME TIME ARE AFRAID OF ... AND YOU ARE *STUBBORNLY REFUSING* TO LET YOUR FEAR *BEST* YOU.
YOU WOULD NOT HAVE ASKED ME HOW A WOMAN BECOMES AN *AES SEDAI* OTHERWISE.
NO, I'M *NOT* AFRAID. I *DO* WANT TO BECOME AN AES SEDAI.
BETTER FOR YOU IF YOU WERE AFRAID, BUT I HOPE YOU HOLD ON TO THE CONVICTION. FEW WOMEN THESE DAYS HAVE THE *ABILITY* TO BECOME INITIATES, MUCH LESS HAVE THE *WISH* TO.
SURELY NEVER BEFORE *TWO* IN ONE VILLAGE. THE *OLD BLOOD* IS INDEED STILL *STRONG* IN THE *TWO RIVERS.*
TWO? WHO ELSE? IS IT KARI? KARI THANE? LARA AYELLAN?
TSK – YOU MUST *FORGET* I SAID THAT. HER ROAD LIES ANOTHER WAY, I FEAR. CONCERN YOURSELF WITH YOUR OWN CIRCUMSTANCES. IT IS NOT AN EASY ROAD YOU HAVE CHOSEN.
I WILL NOT TURN BACK.

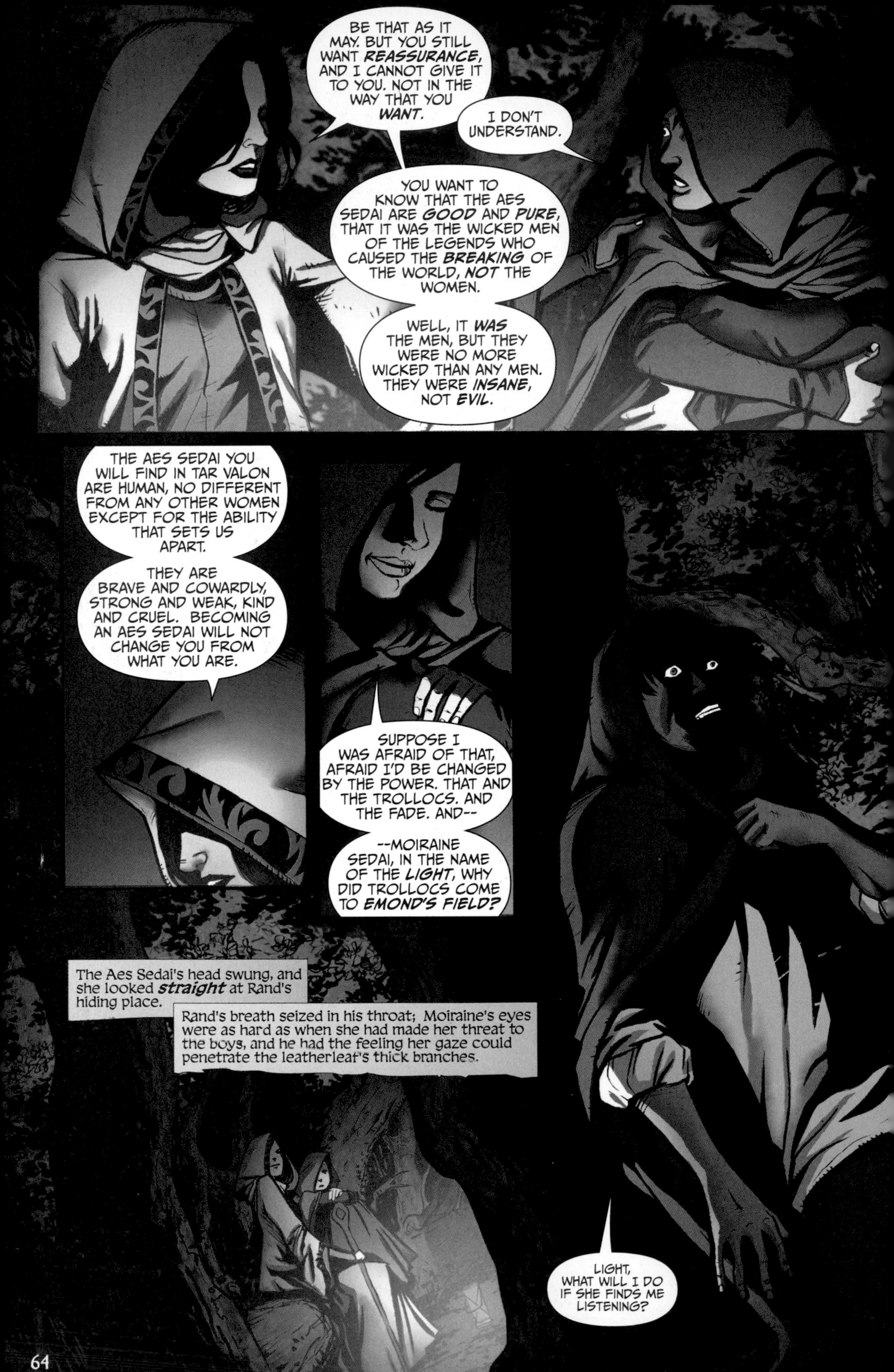
BE THAT AS IT MAY. BUT YOU STILL WANT REASSURANCE, AND I CANNOT GIVE IT TO YOU. NOT IN THE WAY THAT YOU WANT.
I DON'T UNDERSTAND.
YOU WANT TO KNOW THAT THE AES SEDAI ARE GOOD AND PURE, THAT IT WAS THE WICKED MEN OF THE LEGENDS WHO CAUSED THE BREAKING OF THE WORLD, NOT THE WOMEN.
WELL, IT WAS THE MEN, BUT THEY WERE NO MORE WICKED THAN ANY MEN. THEY WERE INSANE, NOT EVIL.
THE AES SEDAI YOU WILL FIND IN TAR VALON ARE HUMAN, NO DIFFERENT FROM ANY OTHER WOMEN EXCEPT FOR THE ABILITY THAT SETS US APART.
THEY ARE BRAVE AND COWARDLY, STRONG AND WEAK, KIND AND CRUEL. BECOMING AN AES SEDAI WILL NOT CHANGE YOU FROM WHAT YOU ARE.
SUPPOSE I WAS AFRAID OF THAT, AFRAID I'D BE CHANGED BY THE POWER. THAT AND THE TROLLOCS. AND THE FADE. AND--
--MOIRAINE SEDAI, IN THE NAME OF THE LIGHT, WHY DID TROLLOCS COME TO EMOND'S FIELD?
The Aes Sedai's head swung, and she looked straight at Rand's hiding place.
Rand's breath seized in his throat; Moiraine's eyes were as hard as when she had made her threat to the boys, and he had the feeling her gaze could penetrate the leatherleaf's thick branches.
LIGHT, WHAT WILL I DO IF SHE FINDS ME LISTENING?

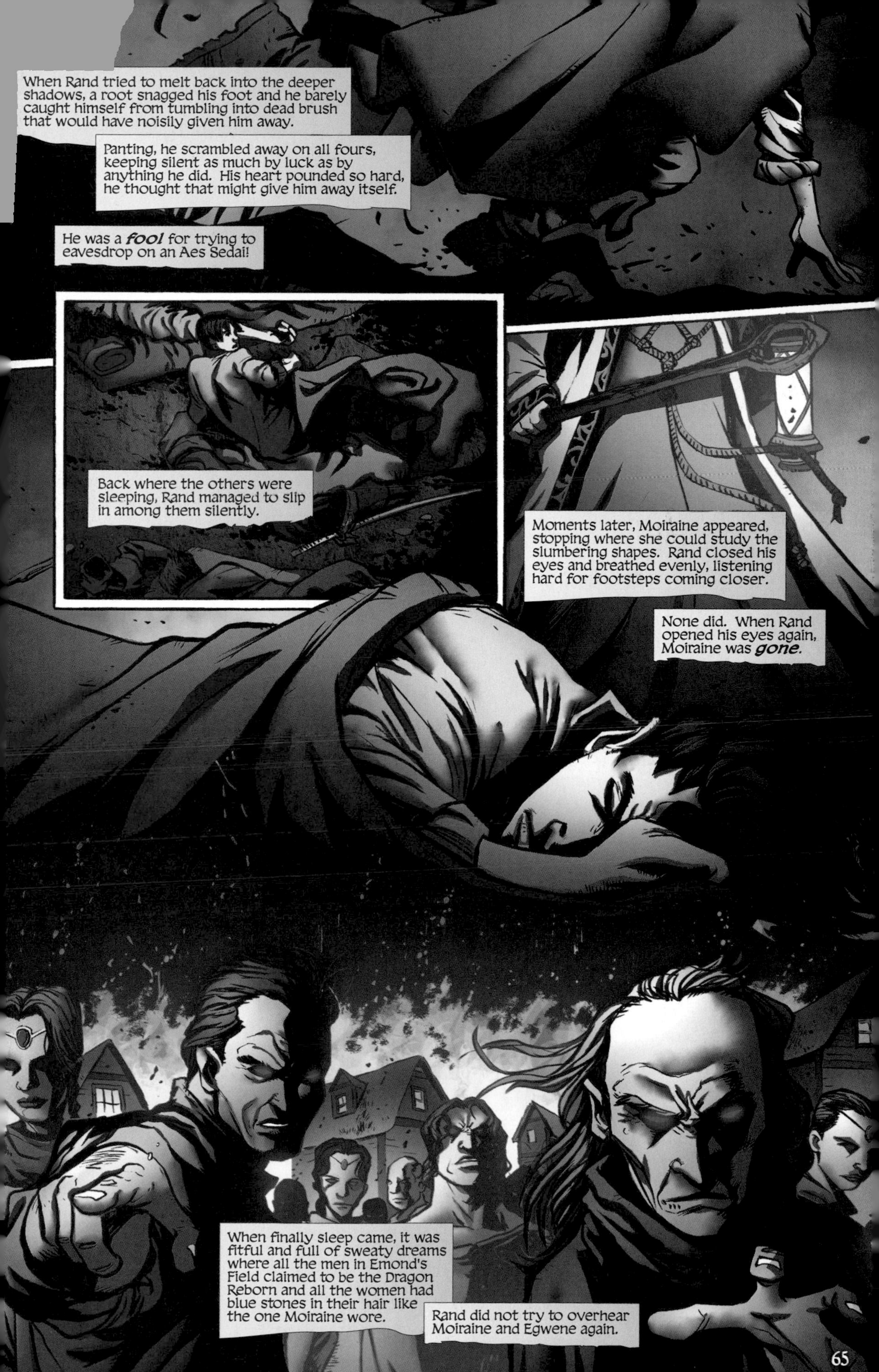
When Rand tried to melt back into the deeper shadows, a root snagged his foot and he barely caught himself from tumbling into dead brush that would have noisily given him away.
Panting, he scrambled away on all fours, keeping silent as much by luck as by anything he did. His heart pounded so hard, he thought that might give him away itself.
He was a *fool* for trying to eavesdrop on an Aes Sedai!
Back where the others were sleeping, Rand managed to slip in among them silently.
Moments later, Moiraine appeared, stopping where she could study the slumbering shapes. Rand closed his eyes and breathed evenly, listening hard for footsteps coming closer.
None did. When Rand opened his eyes again, Moiraine was *gone.*
When finally sleep came, it was fitful and full of sweaty dreams where all the men in Emond's Field claimed to be the Dragon Reborn and all the women had blue stones in their hair like the one Moiraine wore.
Rand did not try to overhear Moiraine and Egwene again.

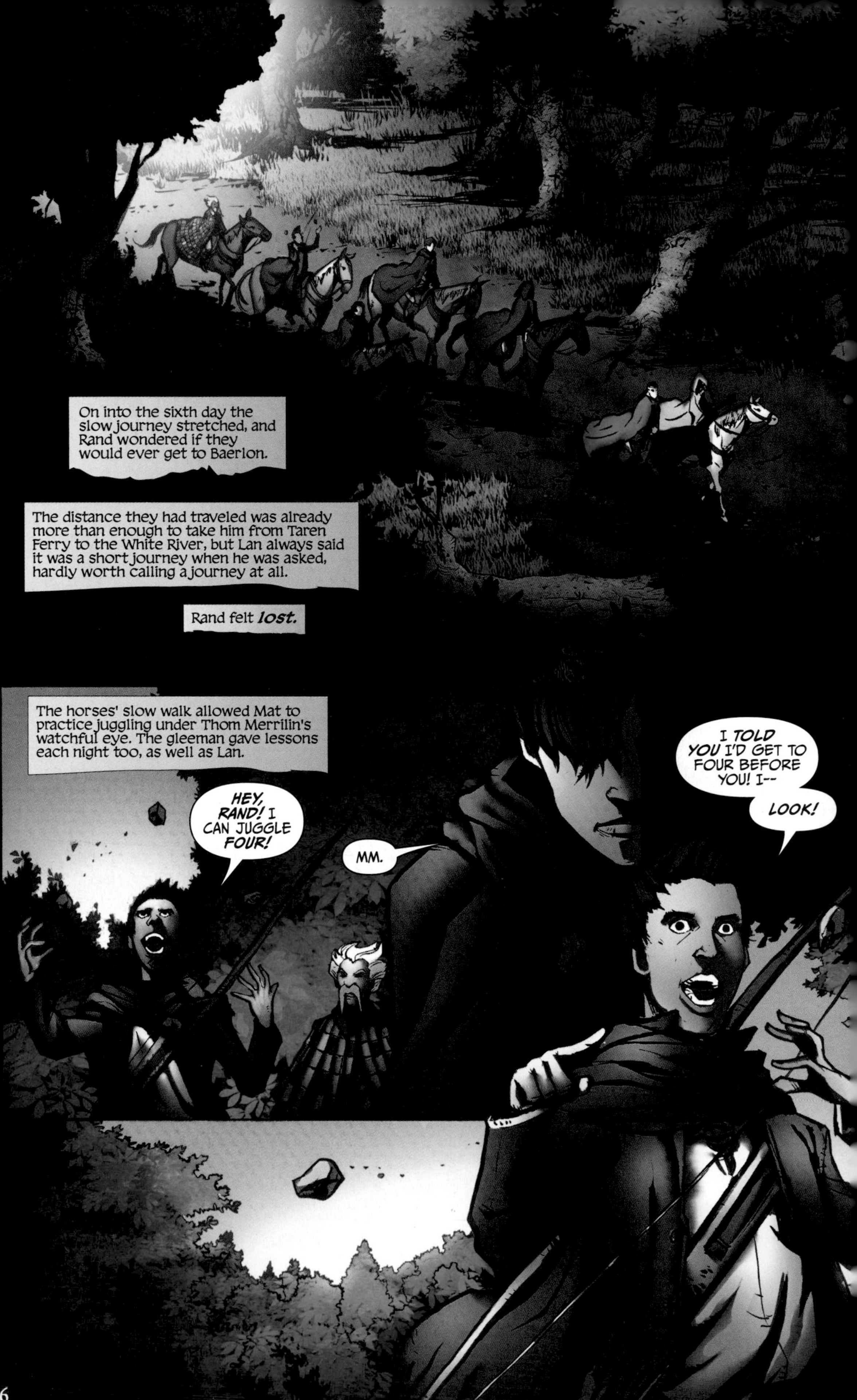
On into the sixth day the slow journey stretched, and Rand wondered if they would ever get to Baerlon.
The distance they had traveled was already more than enough to take him from Taren Ferry to the White River, but Lan always said it was a short journey when he was asked, hardly worth calling a journey at all.
Rand felt *lost.*
The horses' slow walk allowed Mat to practice juggling under Thom Merrilin's watchful eye. The gleeman gave lessons each night too, as well as Lan.
HEY, RAND! I CAN JUGGLE FOUR!
MM.
I TOLD YOU I'D GET TO FOUR BEFORE YOU! I--
LOOK!

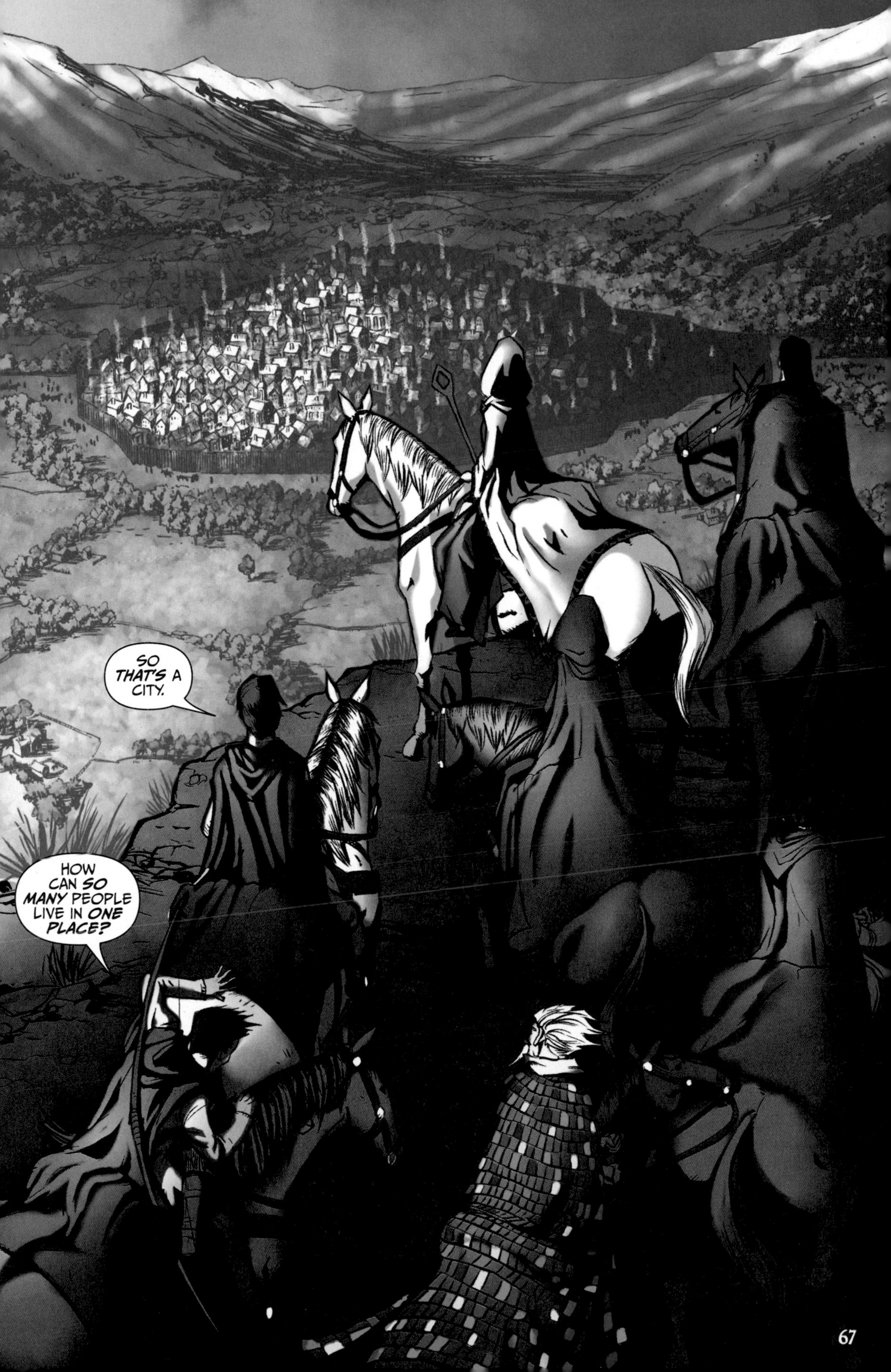
SO *THAT'S* A CITY.
HOW CAN *SO MANY* PEOPLE LIVE IN *ONE PLACE?*

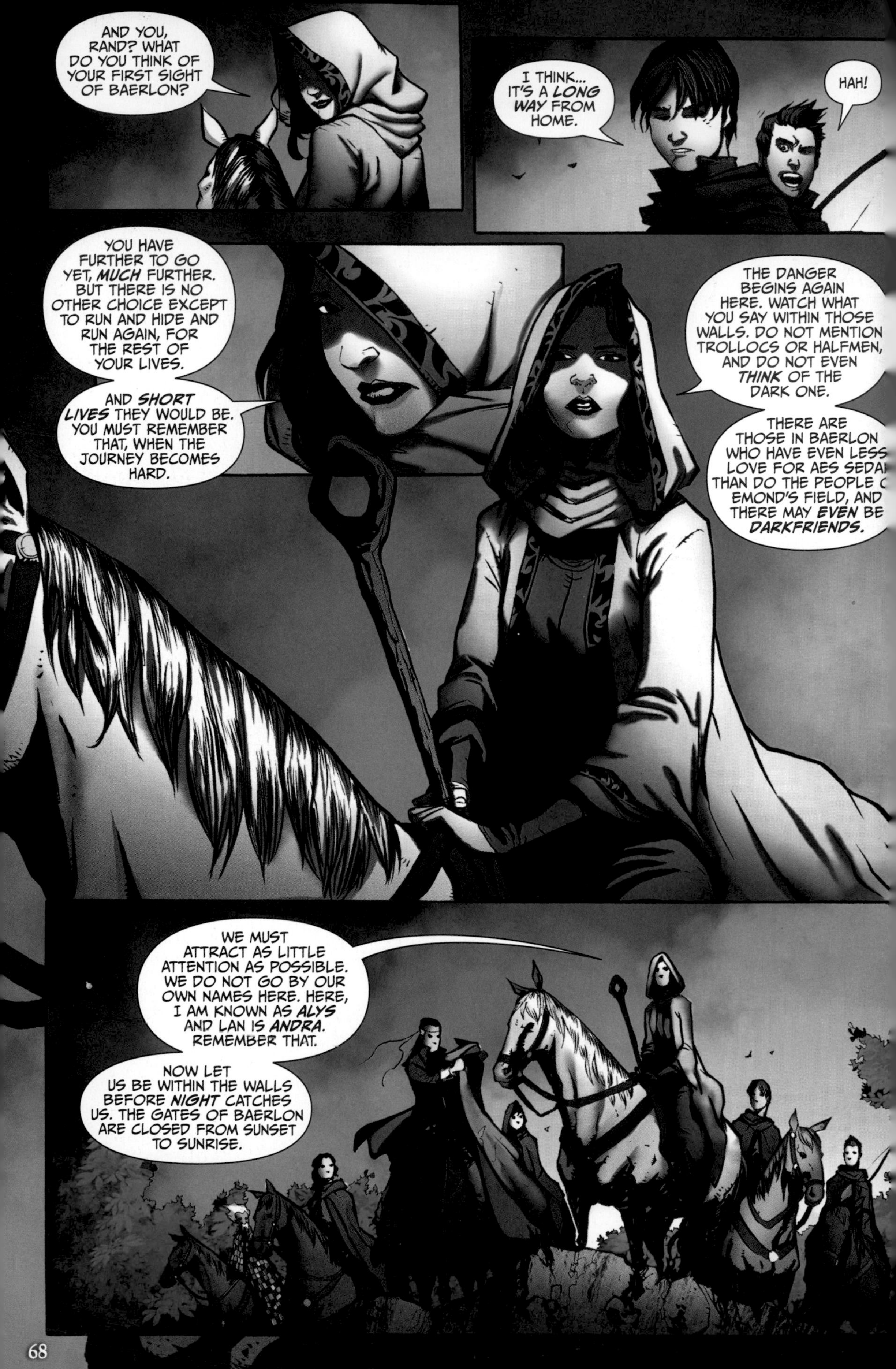

AND YOU, RAND? WHAT DO YOU THINK OF YOUR FIRST SIGHT OF BAERLON?
I THINK... IT'S A LONG WAY FROM HOME.
HAH!
YOU HAVE FURTHER TO GO YET, MUCH FURTHER. BUT THERE IS NO OTHER CHOICE EXCEPT TO RUN AND HIDE AND RUN AGAIN, FOR THE REST OF YOUR LIVES.
AND SHORT LIVES THEY WOULD BE. YOU MUST REMEMBER THAT, WHEN THE JOURNEY BECOMES HARD.
THE DANGER BEGINS AGAIN HERE. WATCH WHAT YOU SAY WITHIN THOSE WALLS. DO NOT MENTION TROLLOCS OR HALFMEN, AND DO NOT EVEN THINK OF THE DARK ONE.
THERE ARE THOSE IN BAERLON WHO HAVE EVEN LESS LOVE FOR AES SEDA THAN DO THE PEOPLE EMOND'S FIELD, AND THERE MAY EVEN BE DARKFRIENDS.
WE MUST ATTRACT AS LITTLE ATTENTION AS POSSIBLE. WE DO NOT GO BY OUR OWN NAMES HERE. HERE, I AM KNOWN AS ALYS AND LAN IS ANDRA. REMEMBER THAT.
NOW LET US BE WITHIN THE WALLS BEFORE NIGHT CATCHES US. THE GATES OF BAERLON ARE CLOSED FROM SUNSET TO SUNRISE.

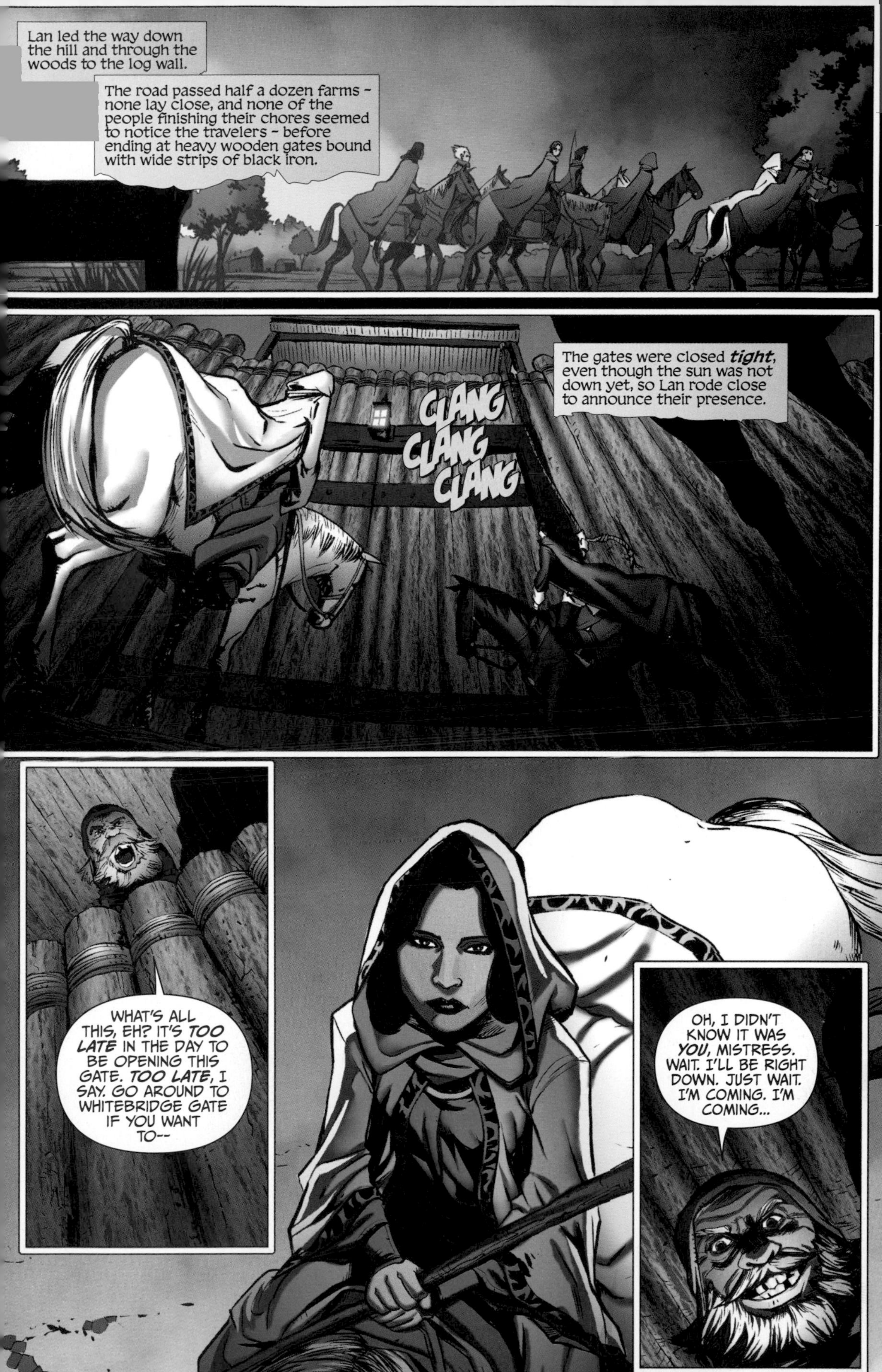

Lan led the way down the hill and through the woods to the log wall.
The road passed half a dozen farms - none lay close, and none of the people finishing their chores seemed to notice the travelers - before ending at heavy wooden gates bound with wide strips of black iron.
The gates were closed *tight*, even though the sun was not down yet, so Lan rode close to announce their presence.
CLANG
CLANG
CLANG
WHAT'S ALL THIS, EH? IT'S *TOO LATE* IN THE DAY TO BE OPENING THIS GATE. *TOO LATE*, I SAY. GO AROUND TO WHITEBRIDGE GATE IF YOU WANT TO--
OH, I DIDN'T KNOW IT WAS *YOU*, MISTRESS. WAIT. I'LL BE RIGHT DOWN. JUST WAIT. I'M COMING. I'M COMING...

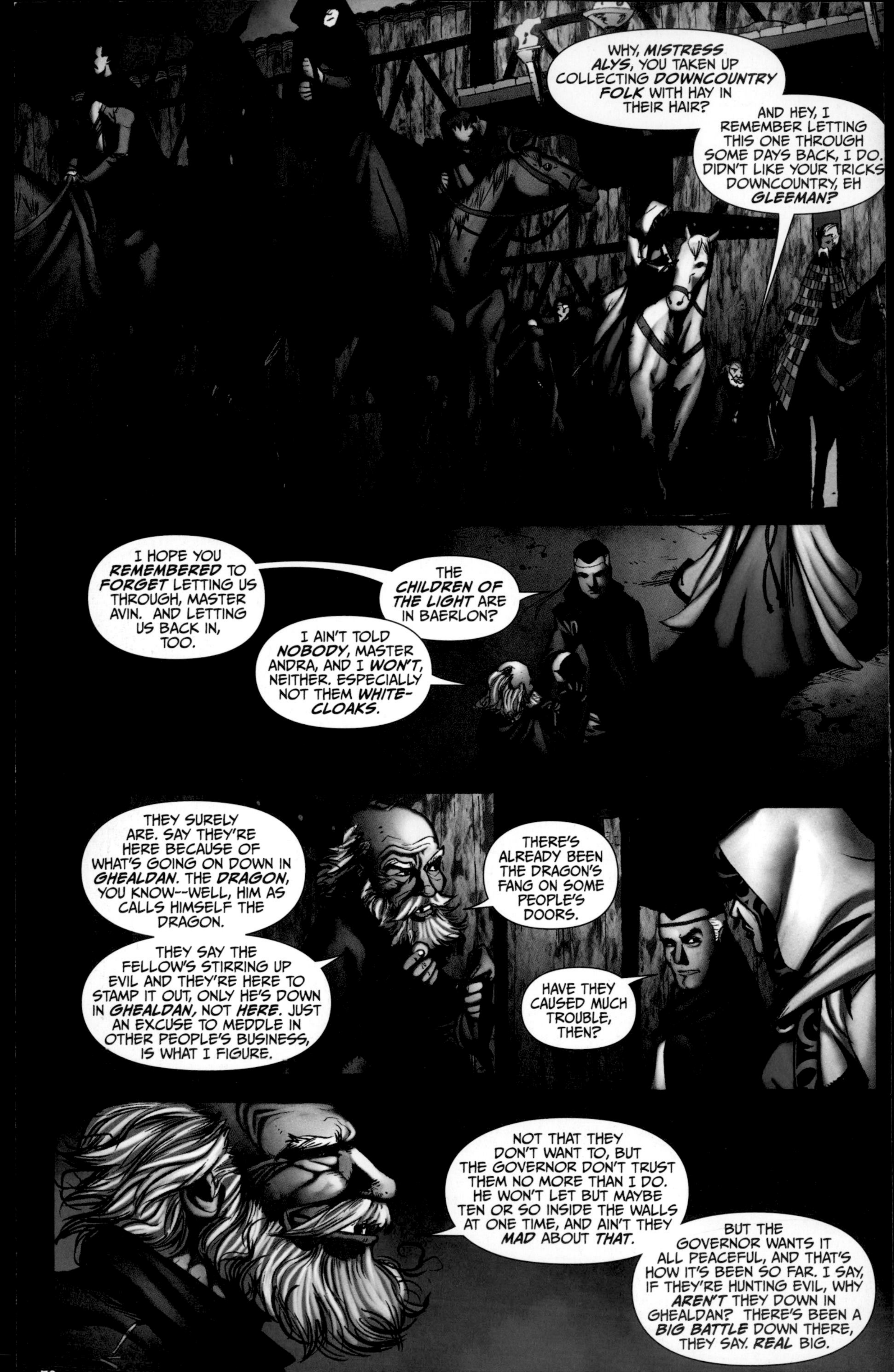
WHY, MISTRESS ALYS, YOU TAKEN UP COLLECTING DOWNCOUNTRY FOLK WITH HAY IN THEIR HAIR?
AND HEY, I REMEMBER LETTING THIS ONE THROUGH SOME DAYS BACK, I DO. DIDN'T LIKE YOUR TRICKS DOWNCOUNTRY, EH GLEEMAN?
I HOPE YOU REMEMBERED TO FORGET LETTING US THROUGH, MASTER AVIN. AND LETTING US BACK IN, TOO.
THE CHILDREN OF THE LIGHT ARE IN BAERLON?
I AIN'T TOLD NOBODY, MASTER ANDRA, AND I WON'T, NEITHER. ESPECIALLY NOT THEM WHITE-CLOAKS.
THEY SURELY ARE. SAY THEY'RE HERE BECAUSE OF WHAT'S GOING ON DOWN IN GHEALDAN. THE DRAGON, YOU KNOW--WELL, HIM AS CALLS HIMSELF THE DRAGON.
THEY SAY THE FELLOW'S STIRRING UP EVIL AND THEY'RE HERE TO STAMP IT OUT, ONLY HE'S DOWN IN GHEALDAN, NOT HERE. JUST AN EXCUSE TO MEDDLE IN OTHER PEOPLE'S BUSINESS, IS WHAT I FIGURE.
THERE'S ALREADY BEEN THE DRAGON'S FANG ON SOME PEOPLE'S DOORS.
HAVE THEY CAUSED MUCH TROUBLE, THEN?
NOT THAT THEY DON'T WANT TO, BUT THE GOVERNOR DON'T TRUST THEM NO MORE THAN I DO. HE WON'T LET BUT MAYBE TEN OR SO INSIDE THE WALLS AT ONE TIME, AND AIN'T THEY MAD ABOUT THAT.
BUT THE GOVERNOR WANTS IT ALL PEACEFUL, AND THAT'S HOW IT'S BEEN SO FAR. I SAY, IF THEY'RE HUNTING EVIL, WHY AREN'T THEY DOWN IN GHEALDAN? THERE'S BEEN A BIG BATTLE DOWN THERE, THEY SAY. REAL BIG.

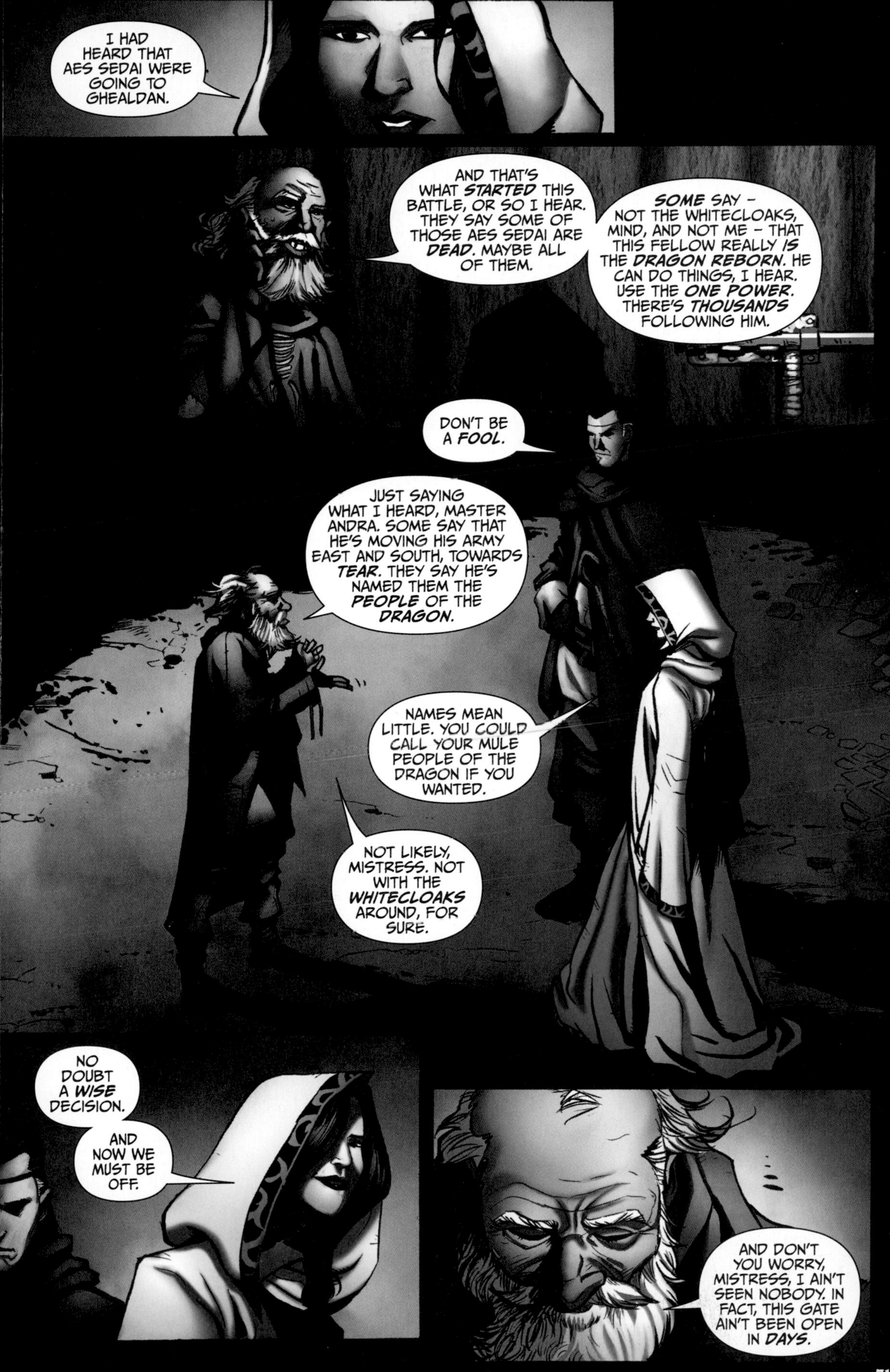
I HAD HEARD THAT AES SEDAI WERE GOING TO GHEALDAN.
AND THAT'S WHAT STARTED THIS BATTLE, OR SO I HEAR. THEY SAY SOME OF THOSE AES SEDAI ARE DEAD. MAYBE ALL OF THEM.
SOME SAY – NOT THE WHITECLOAKS, MIND, AND NOT ME – THAT THIS FELLOW REALLY IS THE DRAGON REBORN. HE CAN DO THINGS, I HEAR. USE THE ONE POWER. THERE'S THOUSANDS FOLLOWING HIM.
DON'T BE A FOOL.
JUST SAYING WHAT I HEARD, MASTER ANDRA. SOME SAY THAT HE'S MOVING HIS ARMY EAST AND SOUTH, TOWARDS TEAR. THEY SAY HE'S NAMED THEM THE PEOPLE OF THE DRAGON.
NAMES MEAN LITTLE. YOU COULD CALL YOUR MULE PEOPLE OF THE DRAGON IF YOU WANTED.
NOT LIKELY, MISTRESS. NOT WITH THE WHITECLOAKS AROUND, FOR SURE.
NO DOUBT A WISE DECISION.
AND NOW WE MUST BE OFF.
AND DON'T YOU WORRY, MISTRESS, I AIN'T SEEN NOBODY. IN FACT, THIS GATE AIN'T BEEN OPEN IN DAYS.

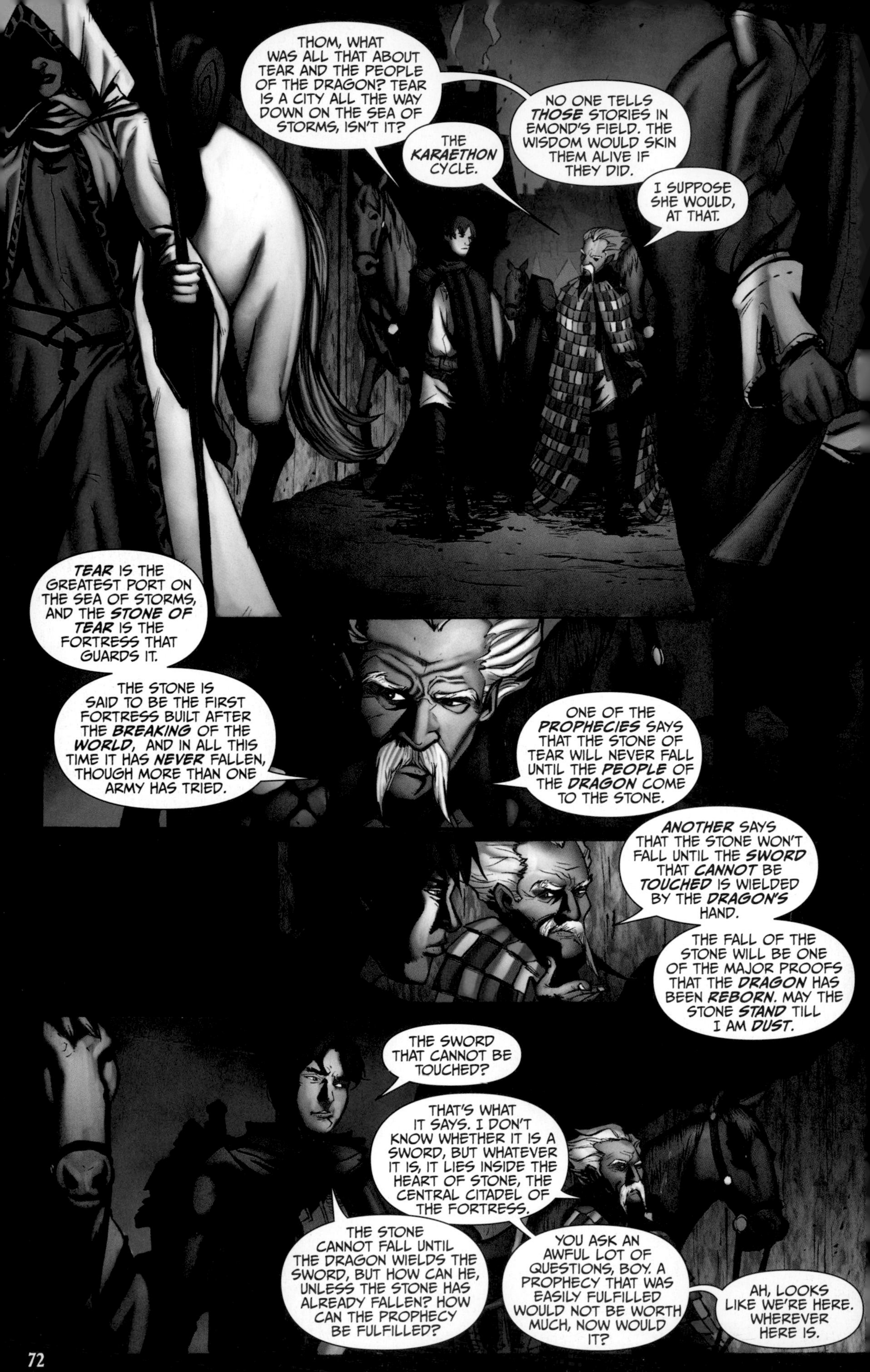
THOM, WHAT WAS ALL THAT ABOUT TEAR AND THE PEOPLE OF THE DRAGON? TEAR IS A CITY ALL THE WAY DOWN ON THE SEA OF STORMS, ISN'T IT?
THE KARAETHON CYCLE.
NO ONE TELLS THOSE STORIES IN EMOND'S FIELD. THE WISDOM WOULD SKIN THEM ALIVE IF THEY DID.
I SUPPOSE SHE WOULD, AT THAT.
TEAR IS THE GREATEST PORT ON THE SEA OF STORMS, AND THE STONE OF TEAR IS THE FORTRESS THAT GUARDS IT.
THE STONE IS SAID TO BE THE FIRST FORTRESS BUILT AFTER THE BREAKING OF THE WORLD, AND IN ALL THIS TIME IT HAS NEVER FALLEN, THOUGH MORE THAN ONE ARMY HAS TRIED.
ONE OF THE PROPHECIES SAYS THAT THE STONE OF TEAR WILL NEVER FALL UNTIL THE PEOPLE OF THE DRAGON COME TO THE STONE.
ANOTHER SAYS THAT THE STONE WON'T FALL UNTIL THE SWORD THAT CANNOT BE TOUCHED IS WIELDED BY THE DRAGON'S HAND.
THE FALL OF THE STONE WILL BE ONE OF THE MAJOR PROOFS THAT THE DRAGON HAS BEEN REBORN. MAY THE STONE STAND TILL I AM DUST.
THE SWORD THAT CANNOT BE TOUCHED?
THAT'S WHAT IT SAYS. I DON'T KNOW WHETHER IT IS A SWORD, BUT WHATEVER IT IS, IT LIES INSIDE THE HEART OF STONE, THE CENTRAL CITADEL OF THE FORTRESS.
THE STONE CANNOT FALL UNTIL THE DRAGON WIELDS THE SWORD, BUT HOW CAN HE, UNLESS THE STONE HAS ALREADY FALLEN? HOW CAN THE PROPHECY BE FULFILLED?
YOU ASK AN AWFUL LOT OF QUESTIONS, BOY. A PROPHECY THAT WAS EASILY FULFILLED WOULD NOT BE WORTH MUCH, NOW WOULD IT?
AH, LOOKS LIKE WE'RE HERE. WHEREVER HERE IS.

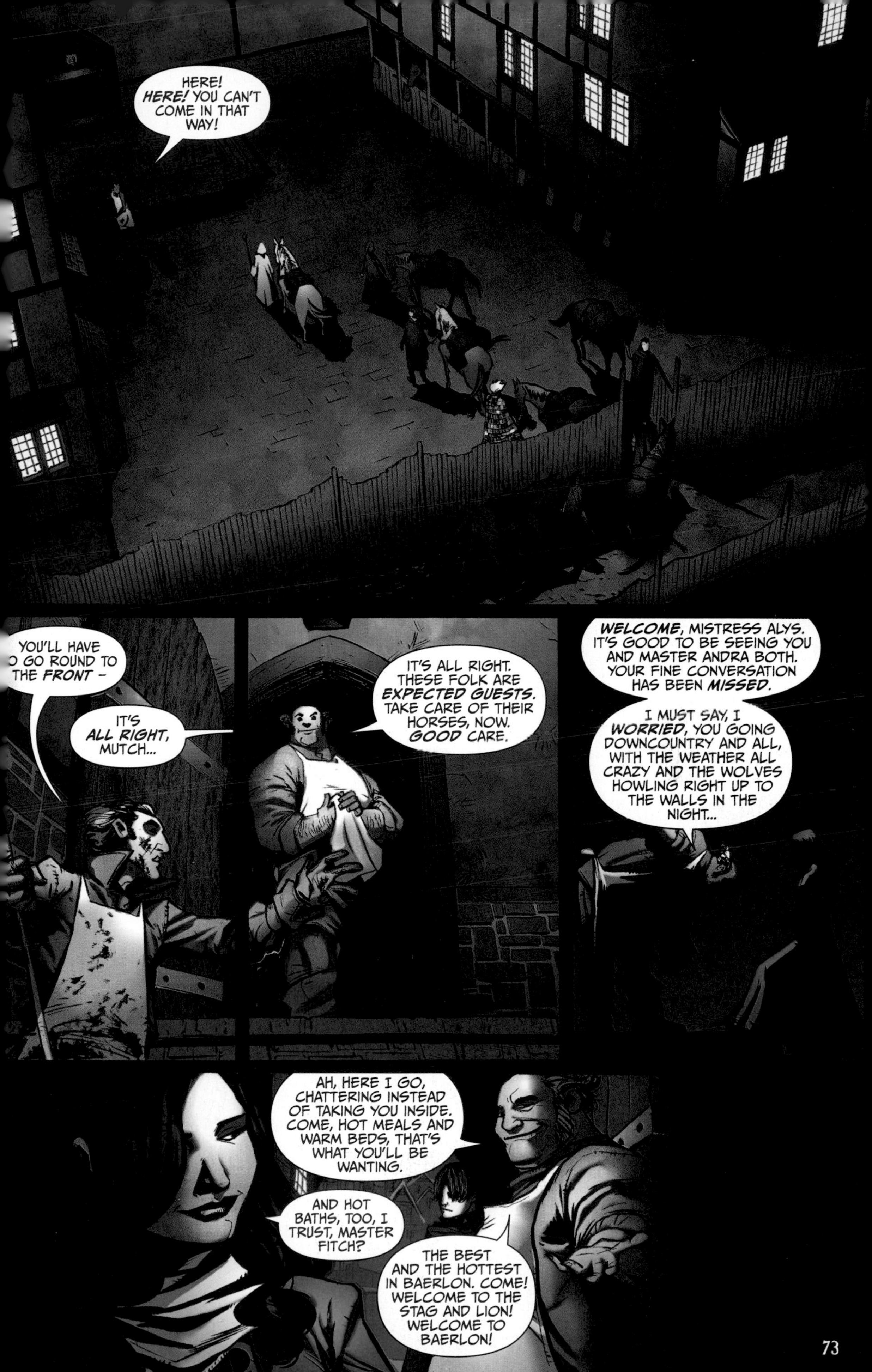
HERE! HERE! YOU CAN'T COME IN THAT WAY!
YOU'LL HAVE TO GO ROUND TO THE FRONT –
IT'S ALL RIGHT, MUTCH...
IT'S ALL RIGHT. THESE FOLK ARE EXPECTED GUESTS. TAKE CARE OF THEIR HORSES, NOW. GOOD CARE.
WELCOME, MISTRESS ALYS. IT'S GOOD TO BE SEEING YOU AND MASTER ANDRA BOTH. YOUR FINE CONVERSATION HAS BEEN MISSED.
I MUST SAY, I WORRIED, YOU GOING DOWNCOUNTRY AND ALL, WITH THE WEATHER ALL CRAZY AND THE WOLVES HOWLING RIGHT UP TO THE WALLS IN THE NIGHT...
AH, HERE I GO, CHATTERING INSTEAD OF TAKING YOU INSIDE. COME, HOT MEALS AND WARM BEDS, THAT'S WHAT YOU'LL BE WANTING.
AND HOT BATHS, TOO, I TRUST, MASTER FITCH?
THE BEST AND THE HOTTEST IN BAERLON. COME! WELCOME TO THE STAG AND LION! WELCOME TO BAERLON!

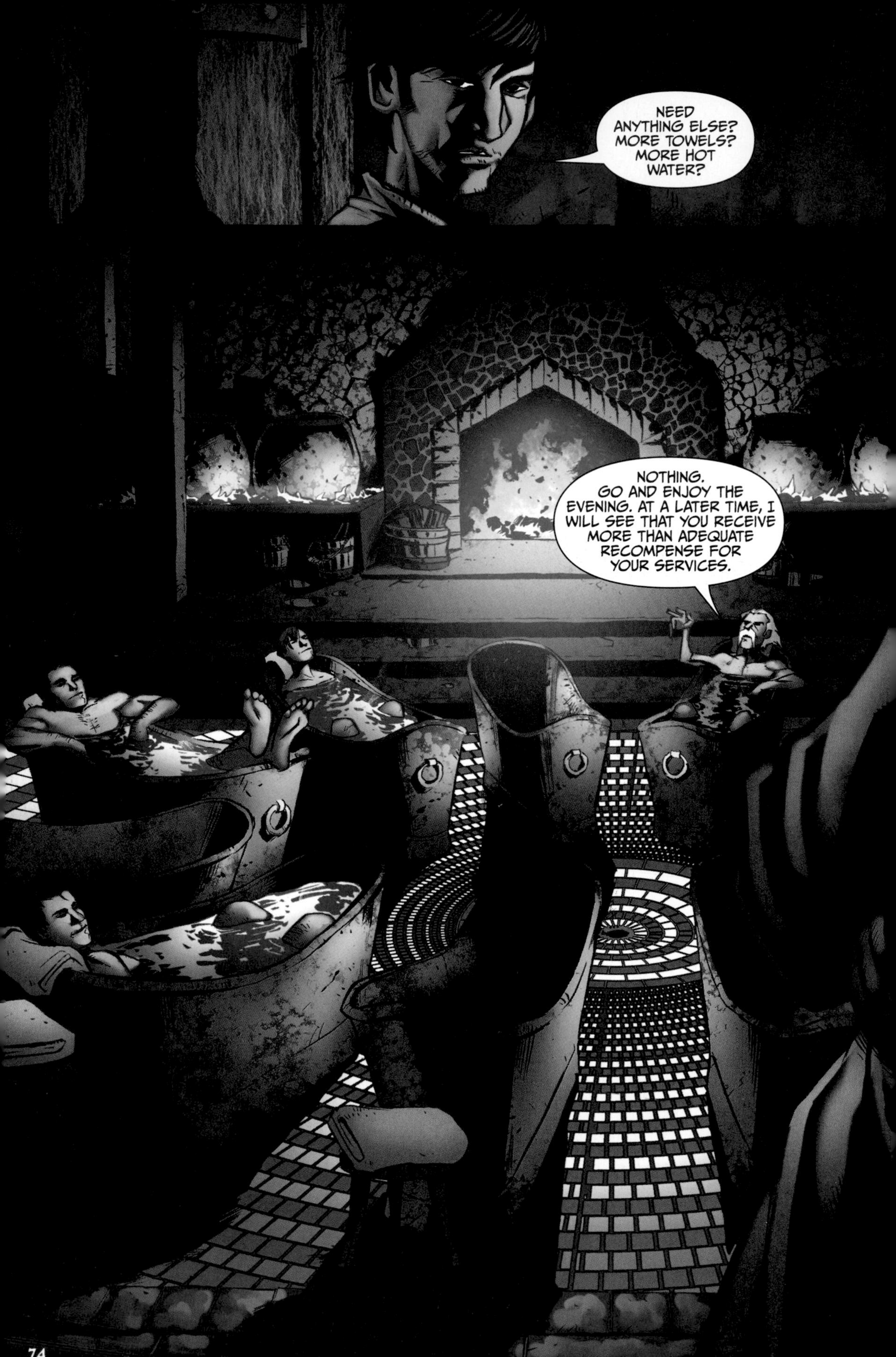
NEED ANYTHING ELSE? MORE TOWELS? MORE HOT WATER?
NOTHING. GO AND ENJOY THE EVENING. AT A LATER TIME, I WILL SEE THAT YOU RECEIVE MORE THAN ADEQUATE RECOMPENSE FOR YOUR SERVICES.

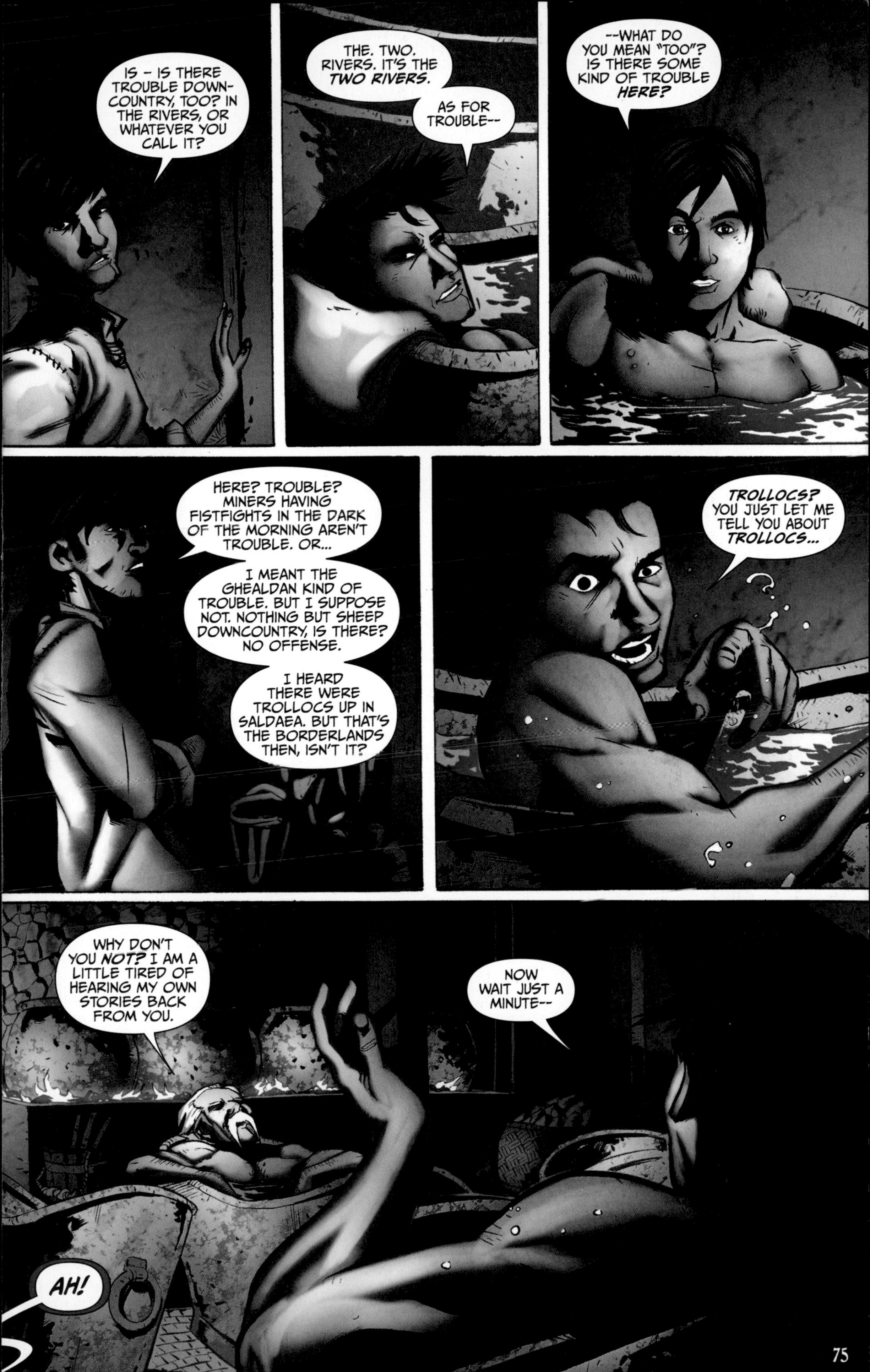
IS – IS THERE TROUBLE DOWN-COUNTRY, TOO? IN THE RIVERS, OR WHATEVER YOU CALL IT?
THE. TWO. RIVERS. IT'S THE *TWO RIVERS.*
AS FOR TROUBLE--
--WHAT DO YOU MEAN "TOO"? IS THERE SOME KIND OF TROUBLE *HERE?*
HERE? TROUBLE? MINERS HAVING FISTFIGHTS IN THE DARK OF THE MORNING AREN'T TROUBLE. OR...
I MEANT THE GHEALDAN KIND OF TROUBLE. BUT I SUPPOSE NOT. NOTHING BUT SHEEP DOWNCOUNTRY, IS THERE? NO OFFENSE.
I HEARD THERE WERE TROLLOCS UP IN SALDAEA. BUT THAT'S THE BORDERLANDS THEN, ISN'T IT?
TROLLOCS? YOU JUST LET ME TELL YOU ABOUT *TROLLOCS...*
WHY DON'T YOU *NOT?* I AM A LITTLE TIRED OF HEARING MY OWN STORIES BACK FROM YOU.
NOW WAIT JUST A MINUTE--
AH!

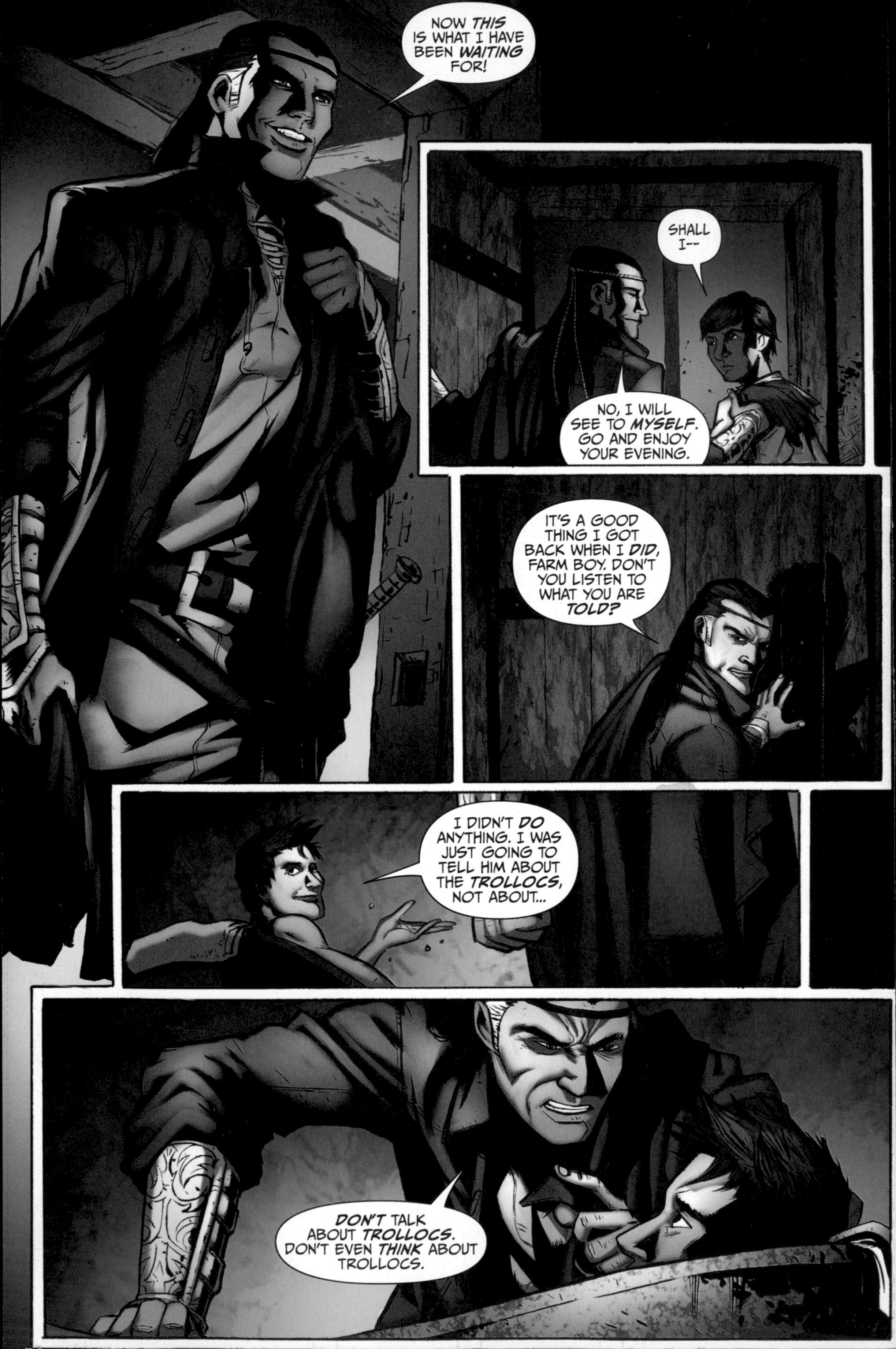
NOW THIS IS WHAT I HAVE BEEN WAITING FOR!
SHALL I--
NO, I WILL SEE TO MYSELF. GO AND ENJOY YOUR EVENING.
IT'S A GOOD THING I GOT BACK WHEN I DID, FARM BOY. DON'T YOU LISTEN TO WHAT YOU ARE TOLD?
I DIDN'T DO ANYTHING. I WAS JUST GOING TO TELL HIM ABOUT THE TROLLOCS, NOT ABOUT...
DON'T TALK ABOUT TROLLOCS. DON'T EVEN THINK ABOUT TROLLOCS.

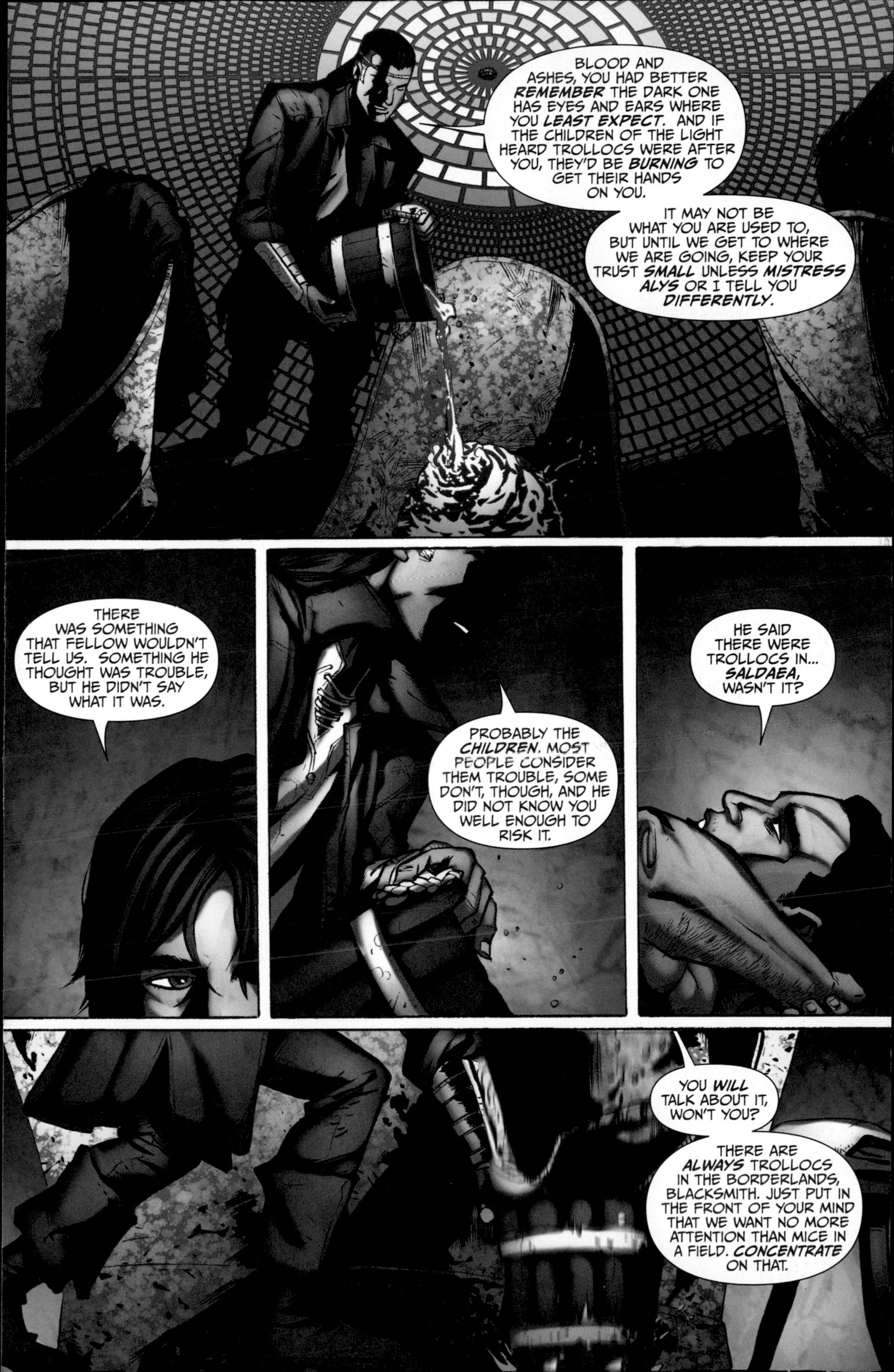
BLOOD AND ASHES, YOU HAD BETTER REMEMBER THE DARK ONE HAS EYES AND EARS WHERE YOU LEAST EXPECT. AND IF THE CHILDREN OF THE LIGHT HEARD TROLLOCS WERE AFTER YOU, THEY'D BE BURNING TO GET THEIR HANDS ON YOU.
IT MAY NOT BE WHAT YOU ARE USED TO, BUT UNTIL WE GET TO WHERE WE ARE GOING, KEEP YOUR TRUST SMALL UNLESS MISTRESS ALYS OR I TELL YOU DIFFERENTLY.
THERE WAS SOMETHING THAT FELLOW WOULDN'T TELL US. SOMETHING HE THOUGHT WAS TROUBLE, BUT HE DIDN'T SAY WHAT IT WAS.
PROBABLY THE CHILDREN. MOST PEOPLE CONSIDER THEM TROUBLE, SOME DON'T, THOUGH, AND HE DID NOT KNOW YOU WELL ENOUGH TO RISK IT.
HE SAID THERE WERE TROLLOCS IN... SALDAEA, WASN'T IT?
YOU WILL TALK ABOUT IT, WON'T YOU?
THERE ARE ALWAYS TROLLOCS IN THE BORDERLANDS, BLACKSMITH. JUST PUT IN THE FRONT OF YOUR MIND THAT WE WANT NO MORE ATTENTION THAN MICE IN A FIELD. CONCENTRATE ON THAT.

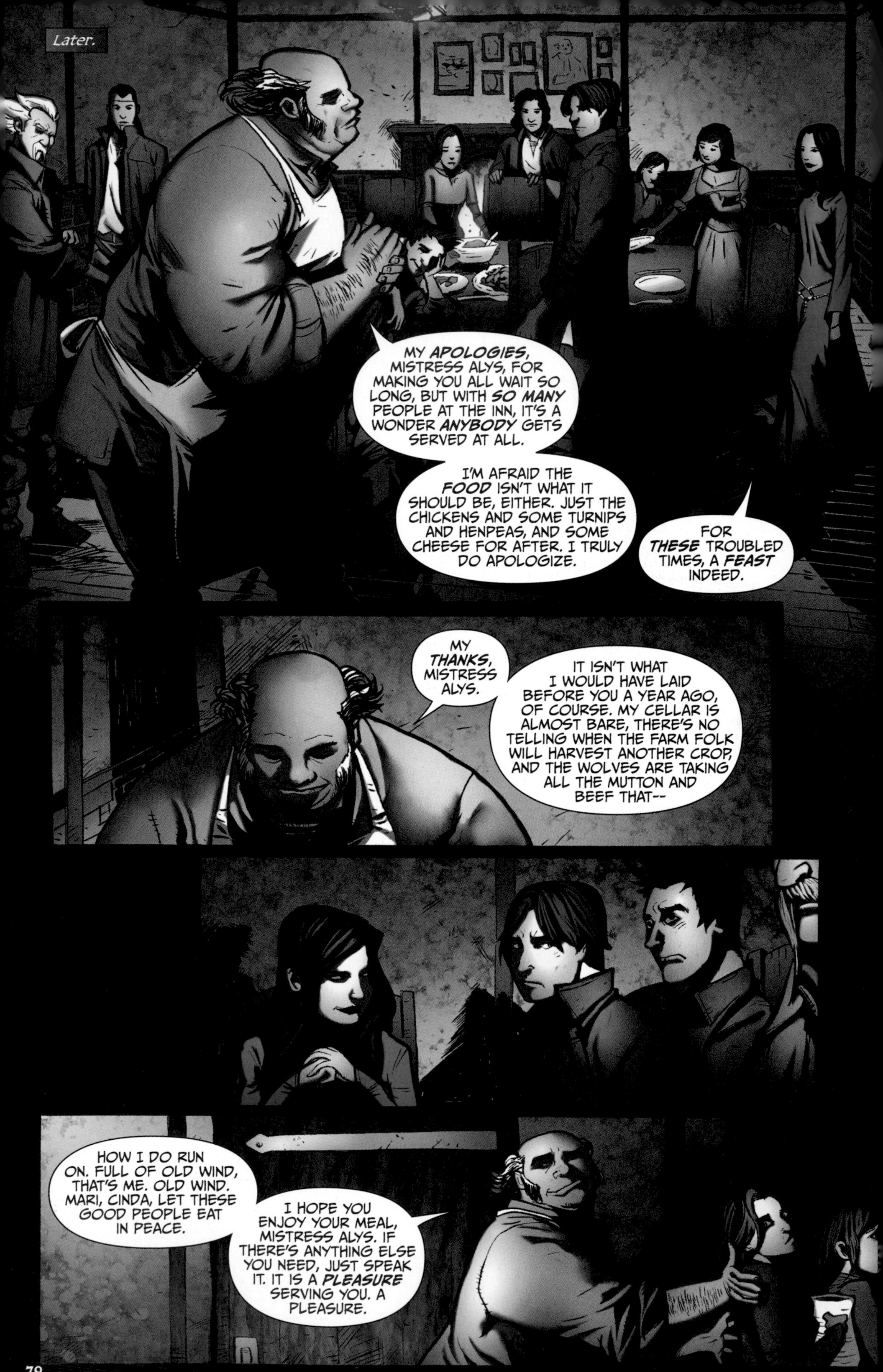
Later.
MY APOLOGIES, MISTRESS ALYS, FOR MAKING YOU ALL WAIT SO LONG, BUT WITH SO MANY PEOPLE AT THE INN, IT'S A WONDER ANYBODY GETS SERVED AT ALL.
I'M AFRAID THE FOOD ISN'T WHAT IT SHOULD BE, EITHER. JUST THE CHICKENS AND SOME TURNIPS AND HENPEAS, AND SOME CHEESE FOR AFTER. I TRULY DO APOLOGIZE.
FOR THESE TROUBLED TIMES, A FEAST INDEED.
MY THANKS, MISTRESS ALYS.
IT ISN'T WHAT I WOULD HAVE LAID BEFORE YOU A YEAR AGO, OF COURSE. MY CELLAR IS ALMOST BARE, THERE'S NO TELLING WHEN THE FARM FOLK WILL HARVEST ANOTHER CROP, AND THE WOLVES ARE TAKING ALL THE MUTTON AND BEEF THAT--
HOW I DO RUN ON. FULL OF OLD WIND, THAT'S ME. OLD WIND. MARI, CINDA, LET THESE GOOD PEOPLE EAT IN PEACE.
I HOPE YOU ENJOY YOUR MEAL, MISTRESS ALYS. IF THERE'S ANYTHING ELSE YOU NEED, JUST SPEAK IT. IT IS A PLEASURE SERVING YOU. A PLEASURE.

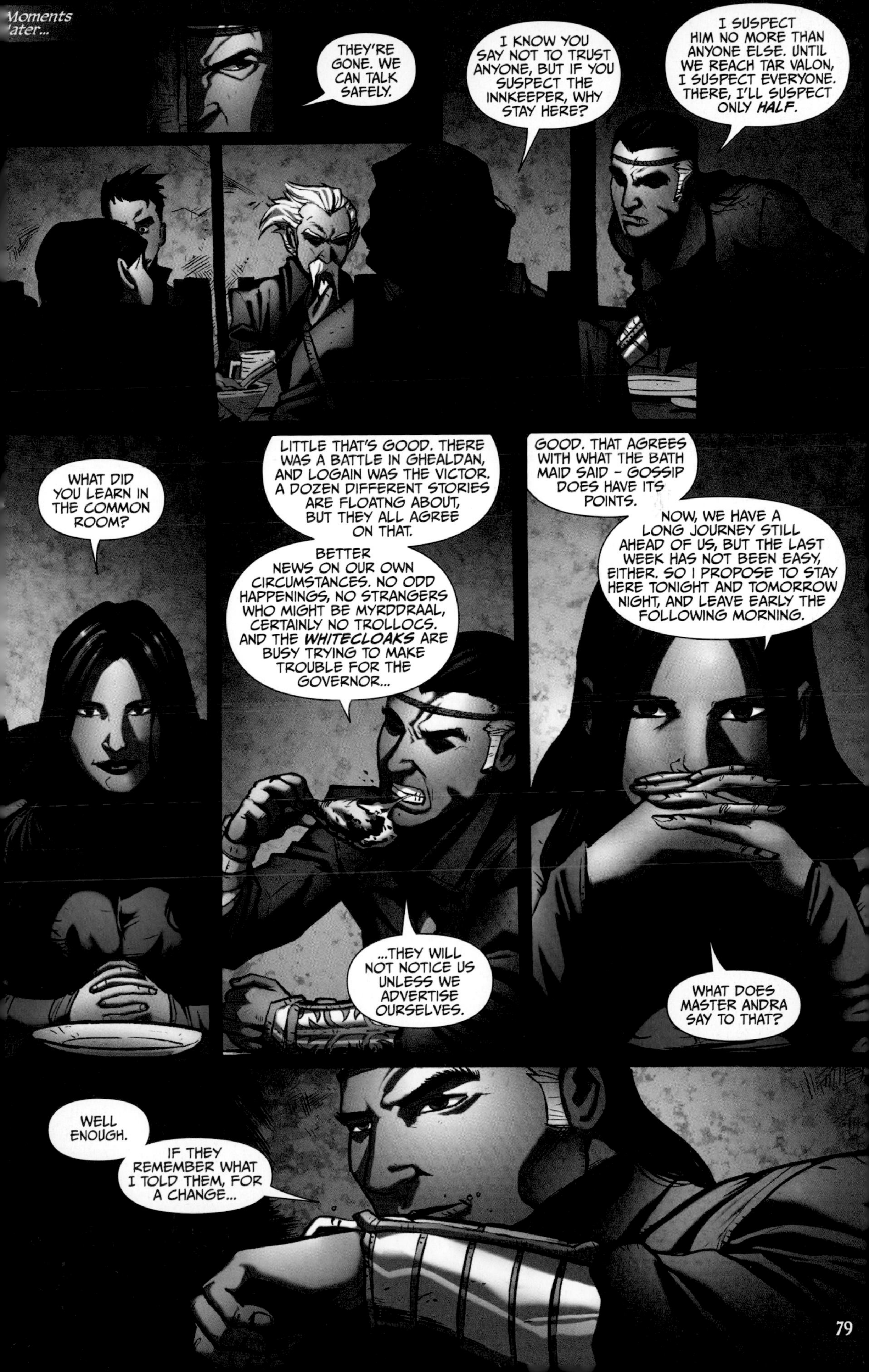
Moments later...
THEY'RE GONE. WE CAN TALK SAFELY.
I KNOW YOU SAY NOT TO TRUST ANYONE, BUT IF YOU SUSPECT THE INNKEEPER, WHY STAY HERE?
I SUSPECT HIM NO MORE THAN ANYONE ELSE. UNTIL WE REACH TAR VALON, I SUSPECT EVERYONE. THERE, I'LL SUSPECT ONLY HALF.
WHAT DID YOU LEARN IN THE COMMON ROOM?
LITTLE THAT'S GOOD. THERE WAS A BATTLE IN GHEALDAN, AND LOGAIN WAS THE VICTOR. A DOZEN DIFFERENT STORIES ARE FLOATNG ABOUT, BUT THEY ALL AGREE ON THAT.
BETTER NEWS ON OUR OWN CIRCUMSTANCES. NO ODD HAPPENINGS, NO STRANGERS WHO MIGHT BE MYRDDRAAL, CERTAINLY NO TROLLOCS. AND THE WHITECLOAKS ARE BUSY TRYING TO MAKE TROUBLE FOR THE GOVERNOR...
...THEY WILL NOT NOTICE US UNLESS WE ADVERTISE OURSELVES.
GOOD. THAT AGREES WITH WHAT THE BATH MAID SAID – GOSSIP DOES HAVE ITS POINTS.
NOW, WE HAVE A LONG JOURNEY STILL AHEAD OF US, BUT THE LAST WEEK HAS NOT BEEN EASY, EITHER. SO I PROPOSE TO STAY HERE TONIGHT AND TOMORROW NIGHT, AND LEAVE EARLY THE FOLLOWING MORNING.
WHAT DOES MASTER ANDRA SAY TO THAT?
WELL ENOUGH.
IF THEY REMEMBER WHAT I TOLD THEM, FOR A CHANGE...

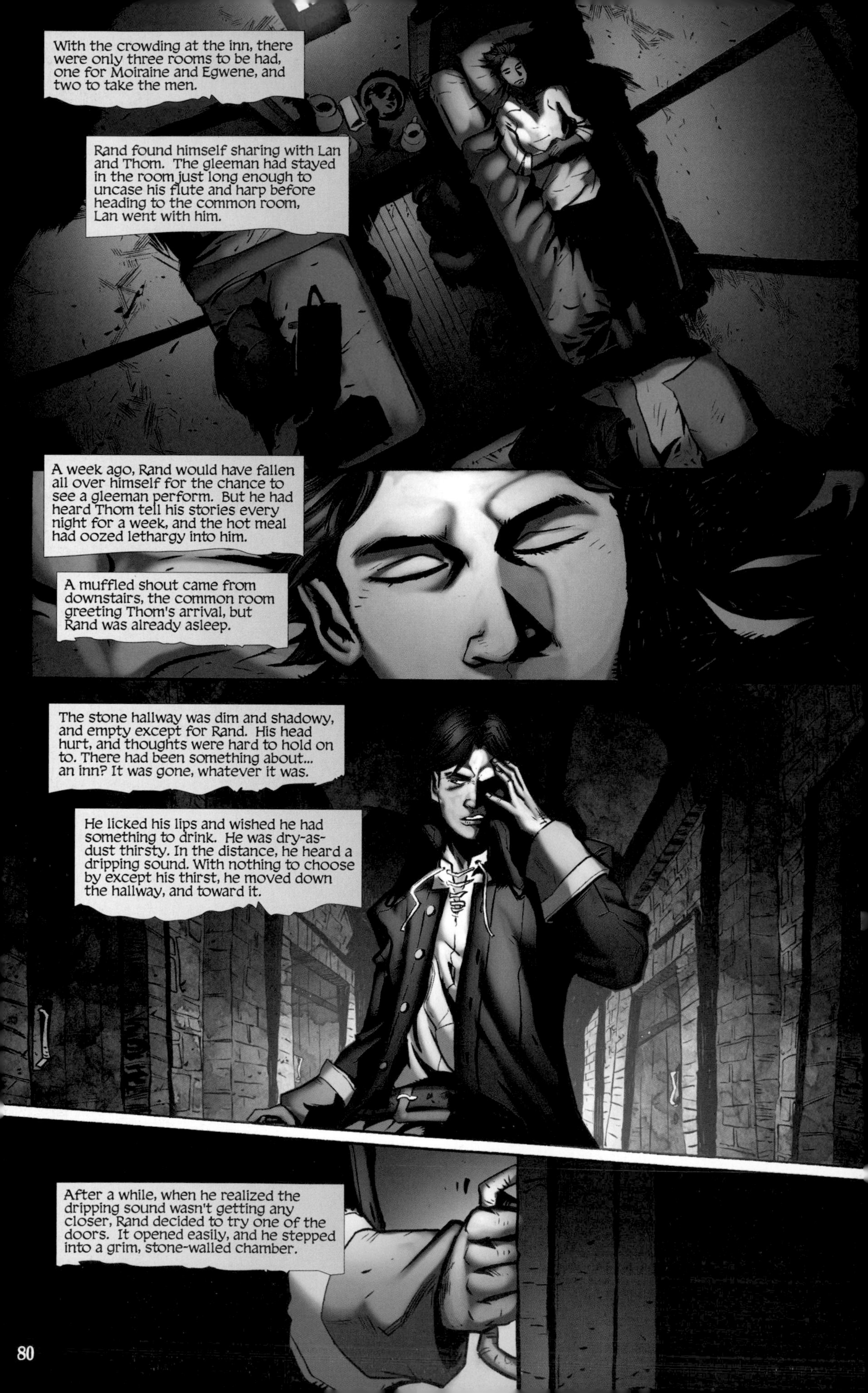
With the crowding at the inn, there were only three rooms to be had, one for Moiraine and Egwene, and two to take the men.
Rand found himself sharing with Lan and Thom. The gleeman had stayed in the room just long enough to uncase his flute and harp before heading to the common room, Lan went with him.
A week ago, Rand would have fallen all over himself for the chance to see a gleeman perform. But he had heard Thom tell his stories every night for a week, and the hot meal had oozed lethargy into him.
A muffled shout came from downstairs, the common room greeting Thom's arrival, but Rand was already asleep.
The stone hallway was dim and shadowy, and empty except for Rand. His head hurt, and thoughts were hard to hold on to. There had been something about... an inn? It was gone, whatever it was.
He licked his lips and wished he had something to drink. He was dry-as-dust thirsty. In the distance, he heard a dripping sound. With nothing to choose by except his thirst, he moved down the hallway, and toward it.
After a while, when he realized the dripping sound wasn't getting any closer, Rand decided to try one of the doors. It opened easily, and he stepped into a grim, stone-walled chamber.

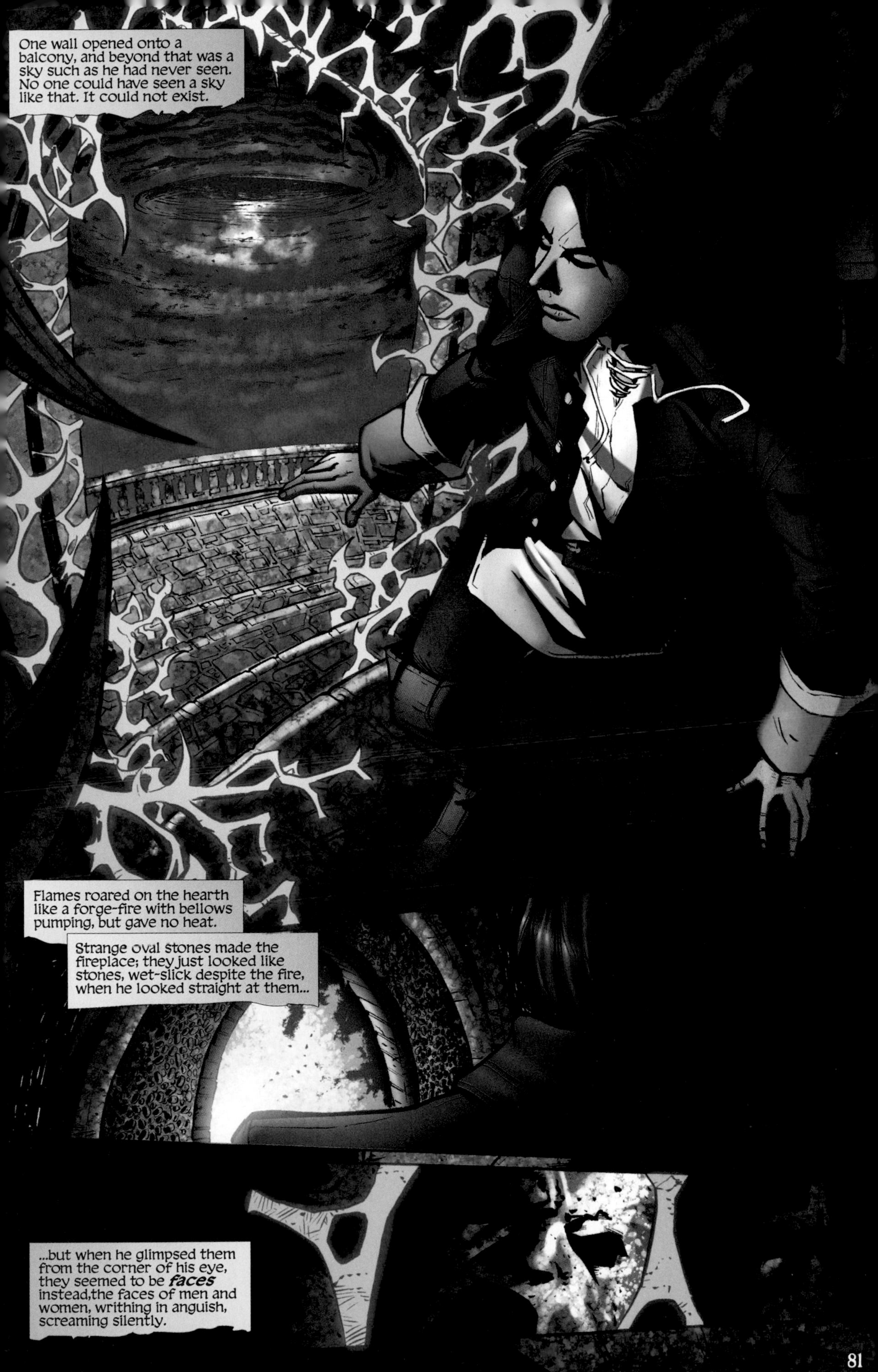
One wall opened onto a balcony, and beyond that was a sky such as he had never seen. No one could have seen a sky like that. It could not exist.
Flames roared on the hearth like a forge-fire with bellows pumping, but gave no heat.
Strange oval stones made the fireplace; they just looked like stones, wet-slick despite the fire, when he looked straight at them...
...but when he glimpsed them from the corner of his eye, they seemed to be *faces* instead,the faces of men and women, writhing in anguish, screaming silently.

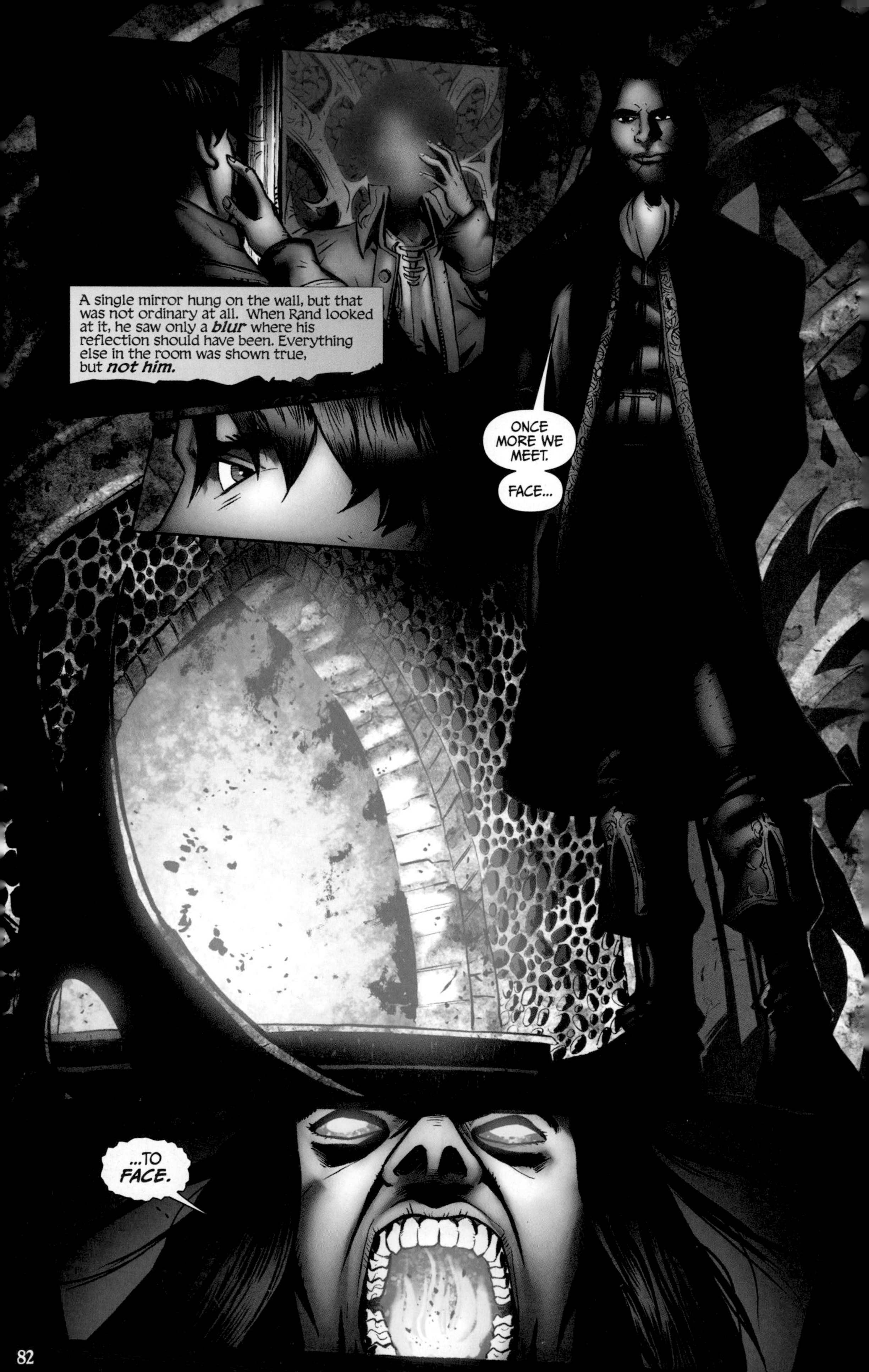
A single mirror hung on the wall, but that was not ordinary at all. When Rand looked at it, he saw only a *blur* where his reflection should have been. Everything else in the room was shown true, but ***not him.***
ONCE MORE WE MEET.
FACE...
...TO *FACE.*

chapter four

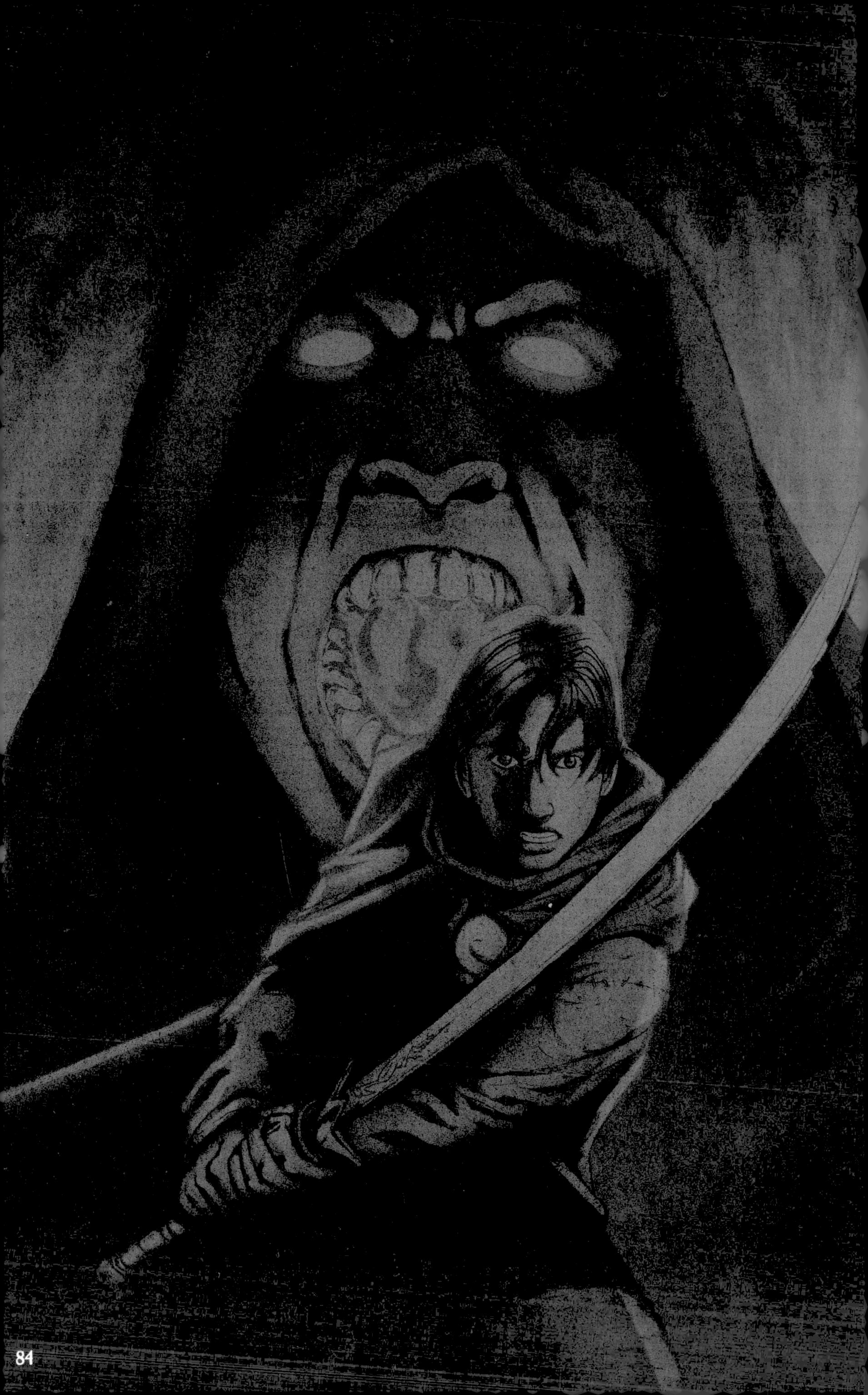

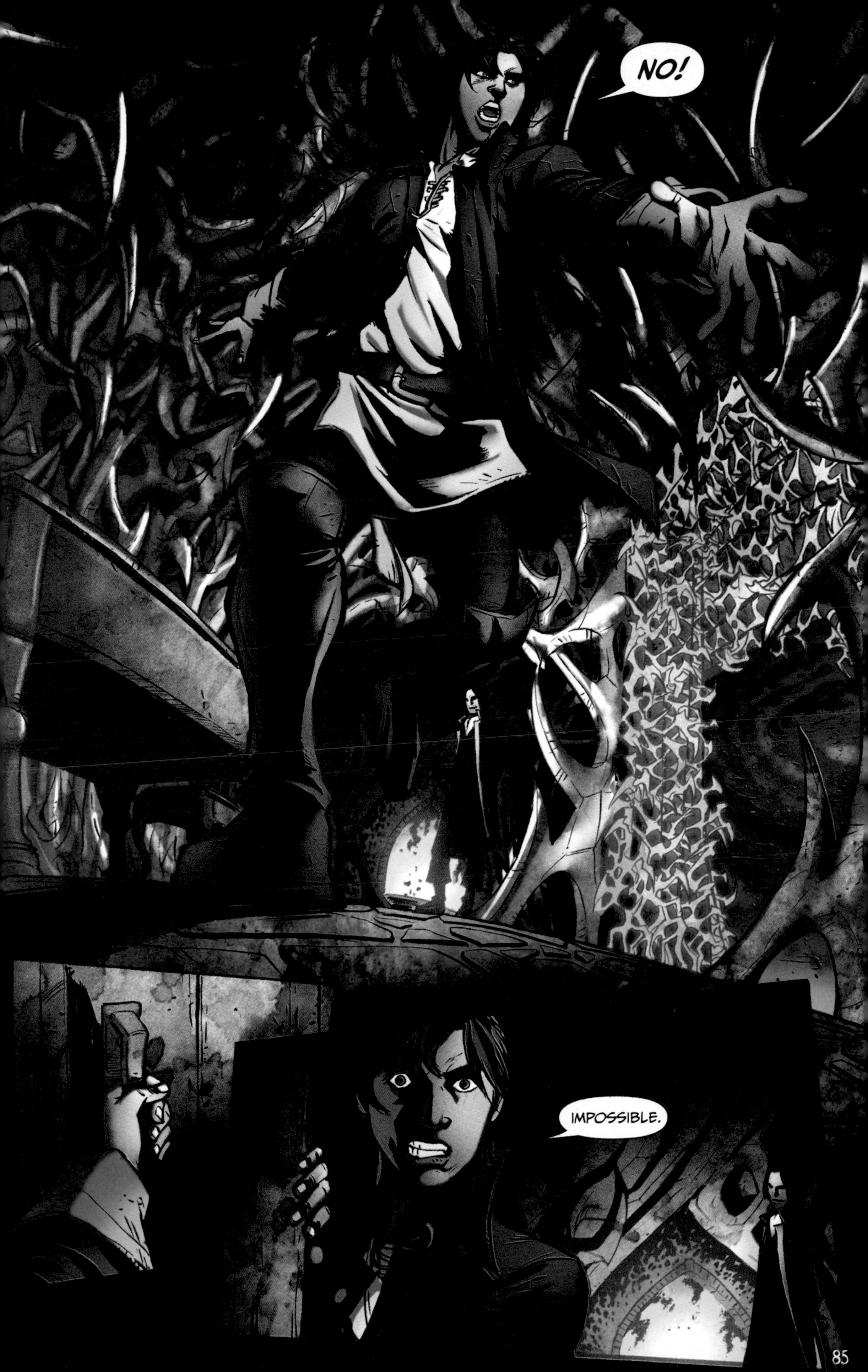
NO!
IMPOSSIBLE.

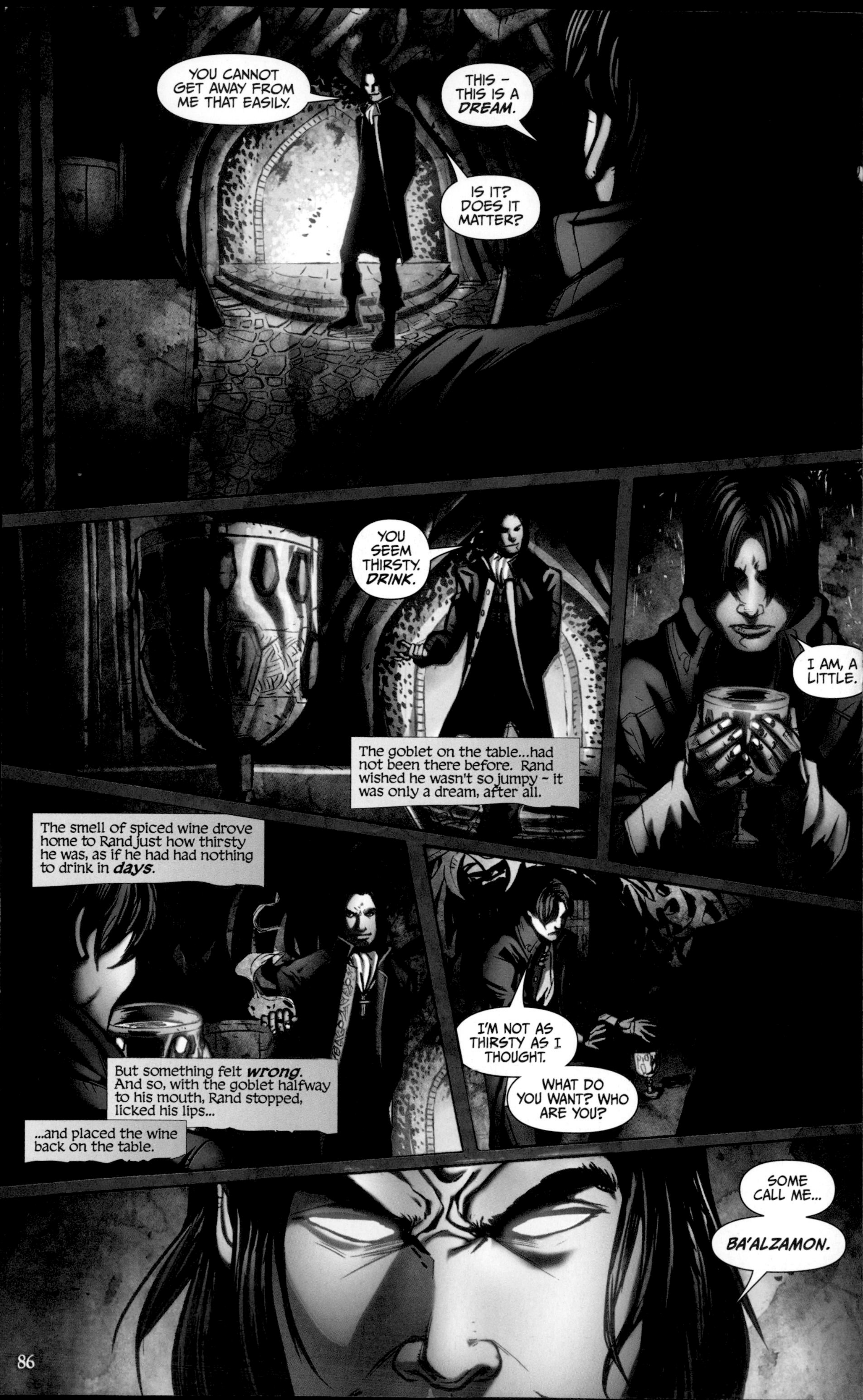
YOU CANNOT GET AWAY FROM ME THAT EASILY.
THIS – THIS IS A DREAM.
IS IT? DOES IT MATTER?
YOU SEEM THIRSTY. DRINK.
The goblet on the table...had not been there before. Rand wished he wasn't so jumpy – it was only a dream, after all.
I AM, A LITTLE.
The smell of spiced wine drove home to Rand just how thirsty he was, as if he had had nothing to drink in days.
But something felt wrong. And so, with the goblet halfway to his mouth, Rand stopped, licked his lips...
...and placed the wine back on the table.
I'M NOT AS THIRSTY AS I THOUGHT.
WHAT DO YOU WANT? WHO ARE YOU?
SOME CALL ME...
BA'ALZAMON.

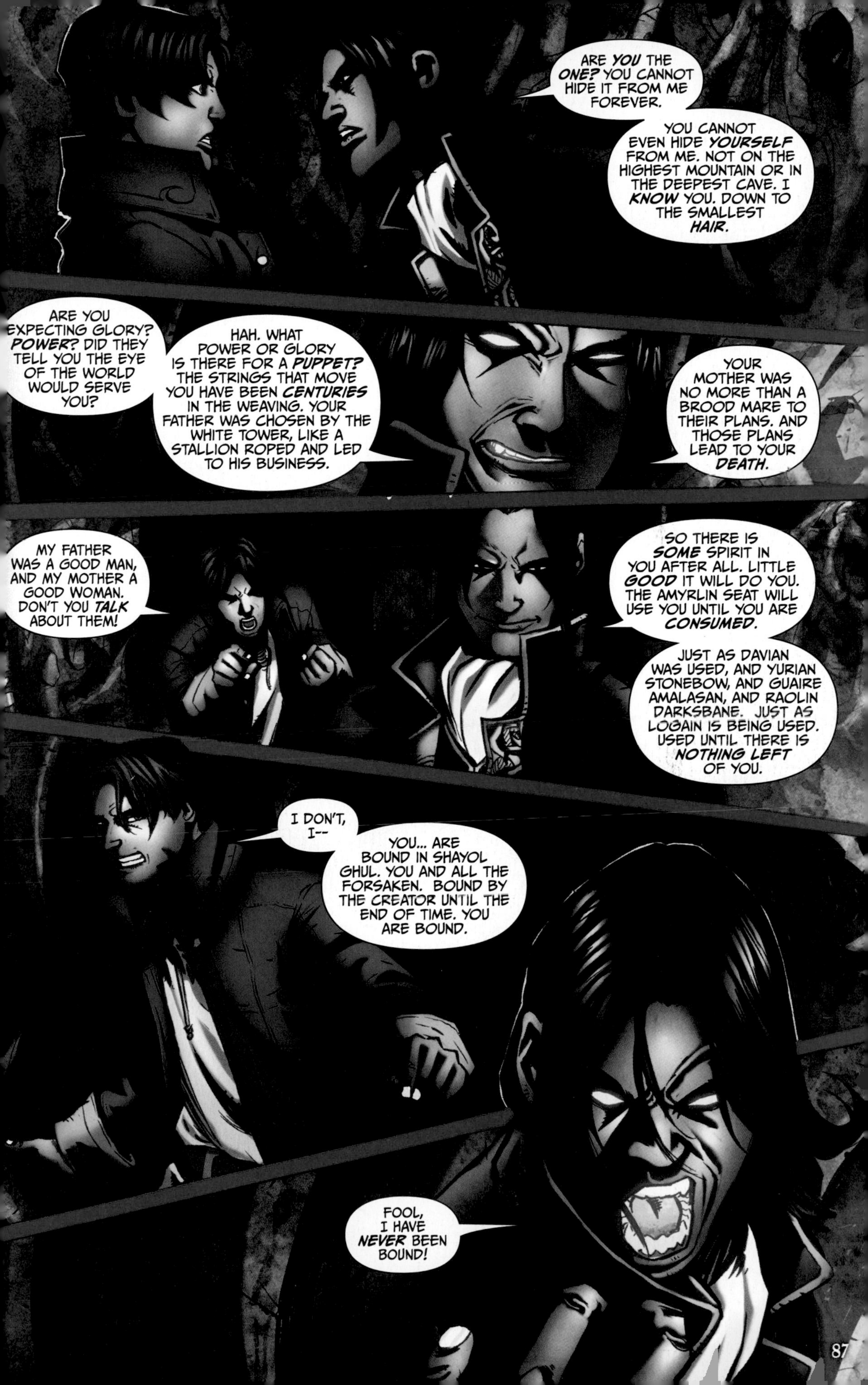

ARE *YOU* THE *ONE?* YOU CANNOT HIDE IT FROM ME FOREVER.
YOU CANNOT EVEN HIDE *YOURSELF* FROM ME. NOT ON THE HIGHEST MOUNTAIN OR IN THE DEEPEST CAVE. I *KNOW* YOU. DOWN TO THE SMALLEST *HAIR*.
ARE YOU EXPECTING GLORY? *POWER?* DID THEY TELL YOU THE EYE OF THE WORLD WOULD SERVE YOU?
HAH. WHAT POWER OR GLORY IS THERE FOR A *PUPPET?* THE STRINGS THAT MOVE YOU HAVE BEEN *CENTURIES* IN THE WEAVING. YOUR FATHER WAS CHOSEN BY THE WHITE TOWER, LIKE A STALLION ROPED AND LED TO HIS BUSINESS.
YOUR MOTHER WAS NO MORE THAN A BROOD MARE TO THEIR PLANS. AND THOSE PLANS LEAD TO YOUR *DEATH*.
MY FATHER WAS A GOOD MAN, AND MY MOTHER A GOOD WOMAN. DON'T YOU *TALK* ABOUT THEM!
SO THERE IS *SOME* SPIRIT IN YOU AFTER ALL. LITTLE *GOOD* IT WILL DO YOU. THE AMYRLIN SEAT WILL USE YOU UNTIL YOU ARE *CONSUMED*.
JUST AS DAVIAN WAS USED, AND YURIAN STONEBOW, AND GUAIRE AMALASAN, AND RAOLIN DARKSBANE. JUST AS LOGAIN IS BEING USED. USED UNTIL THERE IS *NOTHING LEFT* OF YOU.
I DON'T, I--
YOU... ARE BOUND IN SHAYOL GHUL. YOU AND ALL THE FORSAKEN. BOUND BY THE CREATOR UNTIL THE END OF TIME. YOU ARE BOUND.
FOOL, I HAVE *NEVER* BEEN BOUND!

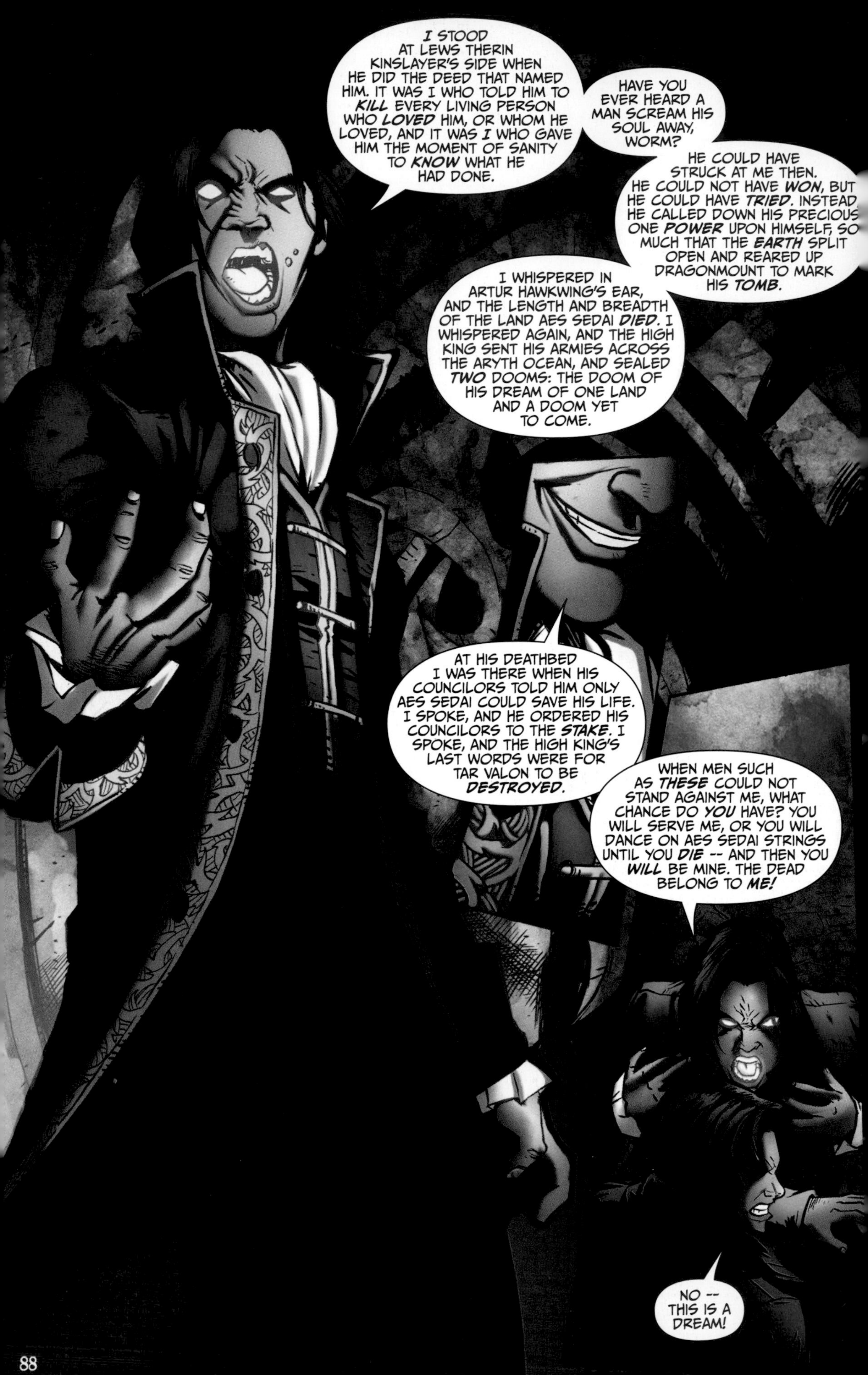
I STOOD AT LEWS THERIN KINSLAYER'S SIDE WHEN HE DID THE DEED THAT NAMED HIM. IT WAS I WHO TOLD HIM TO KILL EVERY LIVING PERSON WHO LOVED HIM, OR WHOM HE LOVED, AND IT WAS I WHO GAVE HIM THE MOMENT OF SANITY TO KNOW WHAT HE HAD DONE.
HAVE YOU EVER HEARD A MAN SCREAM HIS SOUL AWAY, WORM?
HE COULD HAVE STRUCK AT ME THEN. HE COULD NOT HAVE WON, BUT HE COULD HAVE TRIED. INSTEAD HE CALLED DOWN HIS PRECIOUS ONE POWER UPON HIMSELF, SO MUCH THAT THE EARTH SPLIT OPEN AND REARED UP DRAGONMOUNT TO MARK HIS TOMB.
I WHISPERED IN ARTUR HAWKWING'S EAR, AND THE LENGTH AND BREADTH OF THE LAND AES SEDAI DIED. I WHISPERED AGAIN, AND THE HIGH KING SENT HIS ARMIES ACROSS THE ARYTH OCEAN, AND SEALED TWO DOOMS: THE DOOM OF HIS DREAM OF ONE LAND AND A DOOM YET TO COME.
AT HIS DEATHBED I WAS THERE WHEN HIS COUNCILORS TOLD HIM ONLY AES SEDAI COULD SAVE HIS LIFE. I SPOKE, AND HE ORDERED HIS COUNCILORS TO THE STAKE. I SPOKE, AND THE HIGH KING'S LAST WORDS WERE FOR TAR VALON TO BE DESTROYED.
WHEN MEN SUCH AS THESE COULD NOT STAND AGAINST ME, WHAT CHANCE DO YOU HAVE? YOU WILL SERVE ME, OR YOU WILL DANCE ON AES SEDAI STRINGS UNTIL YOU DIE -- AND THEN YOU WILL BE MINE. THE DEAD BELONG TO ME!
NO -- THIS IS A DREAM!

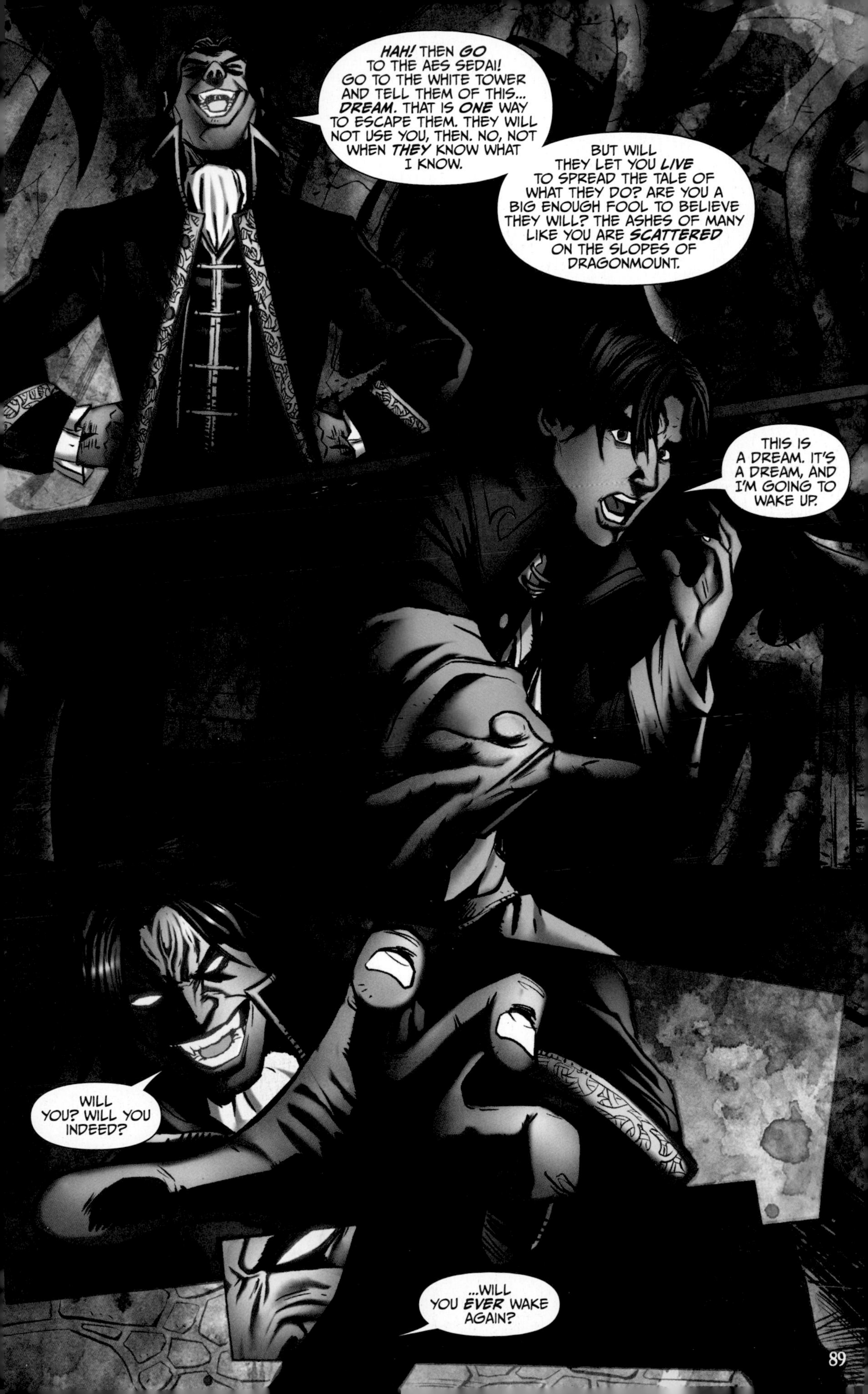
HAH! THEN GO TO THE AES SEDAI! GO TO THE WHITE TOWER AND TELL THEM OF THIS... DREAM. THAT IS ONE WAY TO ESCAPE THEM. THEY WILL NOT USE YOU, THEN. NO, NOT WHEN THEY KNOW WHAT I KNOW.
BUT WILL THEY LET YOU LIVE TO SPREAD THE TALE OF WHAT THEY DO? ARE YOU A BIG ENOUGH FOOL TO BELIEVE THEY WILL? THE ASHES OF MANY LIKE YOU ARE SCATTERED ON THE SLOPES OF DRAGONMOUNT.
THIS IS A DREAM. IT'S A DREAM, AND I'M GOING TO WAKE UP.
WILL YOU? WILL YOU INDEED?
...WILL YOU EVER WAKE AGAIN?

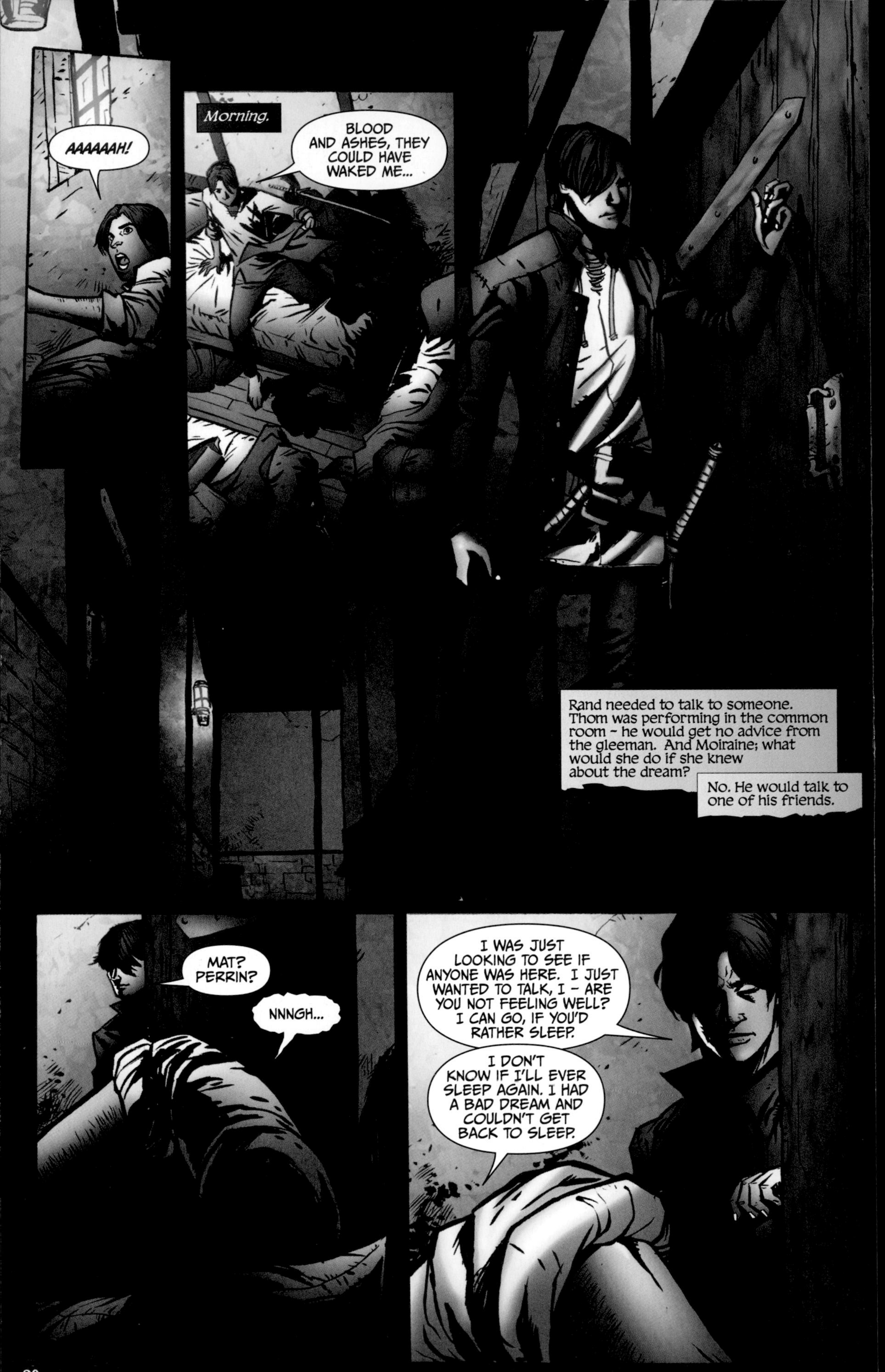
AAAAAAH!
Morning.
BLOOD AND ASHES, THEY COULD HAVE WAKED ME...
Rand needed to talk to someone. Thom was performing in the common room - he would get no advice from the gleeman. And Moiraine; what would she do if she knew about the dream?
No. He would talk to one of his friends.
MAT? PERRIN?
NNNGH...
I WAS JUST LOOKING TO SEE IF ANYONE WAS HERE. I JUST WANTED TO TALK, I - ARE YOU NOT FEELING WELL? I CAN GO, IF YOU'D RATHER SLEEP.
I DON'T KNOW IF I'LL EVER SLEEP AGAIN. I HAD A BAD DREAM AND COULDN'T GET BACK TO SLEEP.

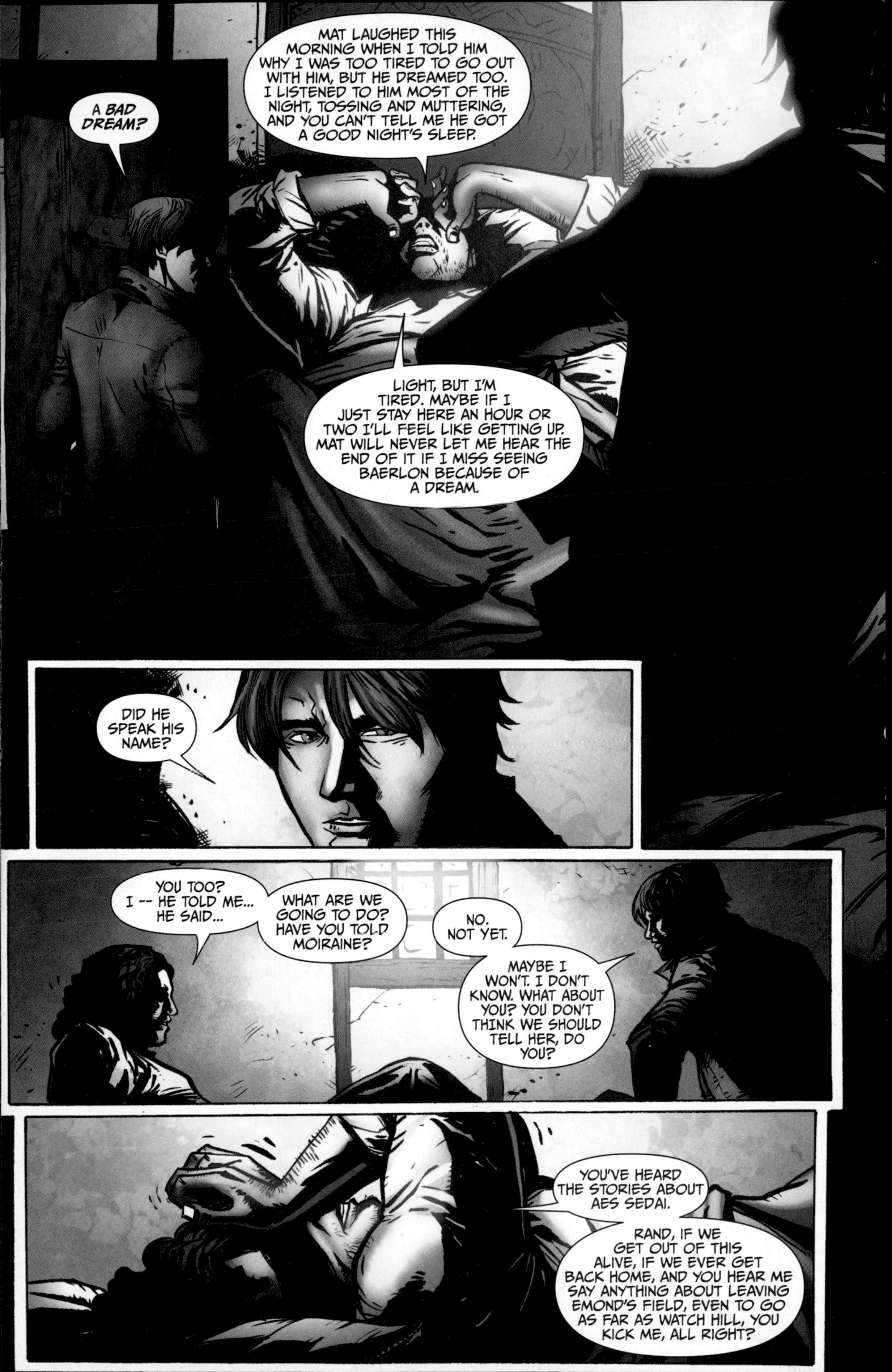
A BAD DREAM?
MAT LAUGHED THIS MORNING WHEN I TOLD HIM WHY I WAS TOO TIRED TO GO OUT WITH HIM, BUT HE DREAMED TOO. I LISTENED TO HIM MOST OF THE NIGHT, TOSSING AND MUTTERING, AND YOU CAN'T TELL ME HE GOT A GOOD NIGHT'S SLEEP.
LIGHT, BUT I'M TIRED. MAYBE IF I JUST STAY HERE AN HOUR OR TWO I'LL FEEL LIKE GETTING UP. MAT WILL NEVER LET ME HEAR THE END OF IT IF I MISS SEEING BAERLON BECAUSE OF A DREAM.
DID HE SPEAK HIS NAME?
YOU TOO? I -- HE TOLD ME... HE SAID...
WHAT ARE WE GOING TO DO? HAVE YOU TOLD MOIRAINE?
NO. NOT YET.
MAYBE I WON'T. I DON'T KNOW. WHAT ABOUT YOU? YOU DON'T THINK WE SHOULD TELL HER, DO YOU?
YOU'VE HEARD THE STORIES ABOUT AES SEDAI.
RAND, IF WE GET OUT OF THIS ALIVE, IF WE EVER GET BACK HOME, AND YOU HEAR ME SAY ANYTHING ABOUT LEAVING EMOND'S FIELD, EVEN TO GO AS FAR AS WATCH HILL, YOU KICK ME, ALL RIGHT?

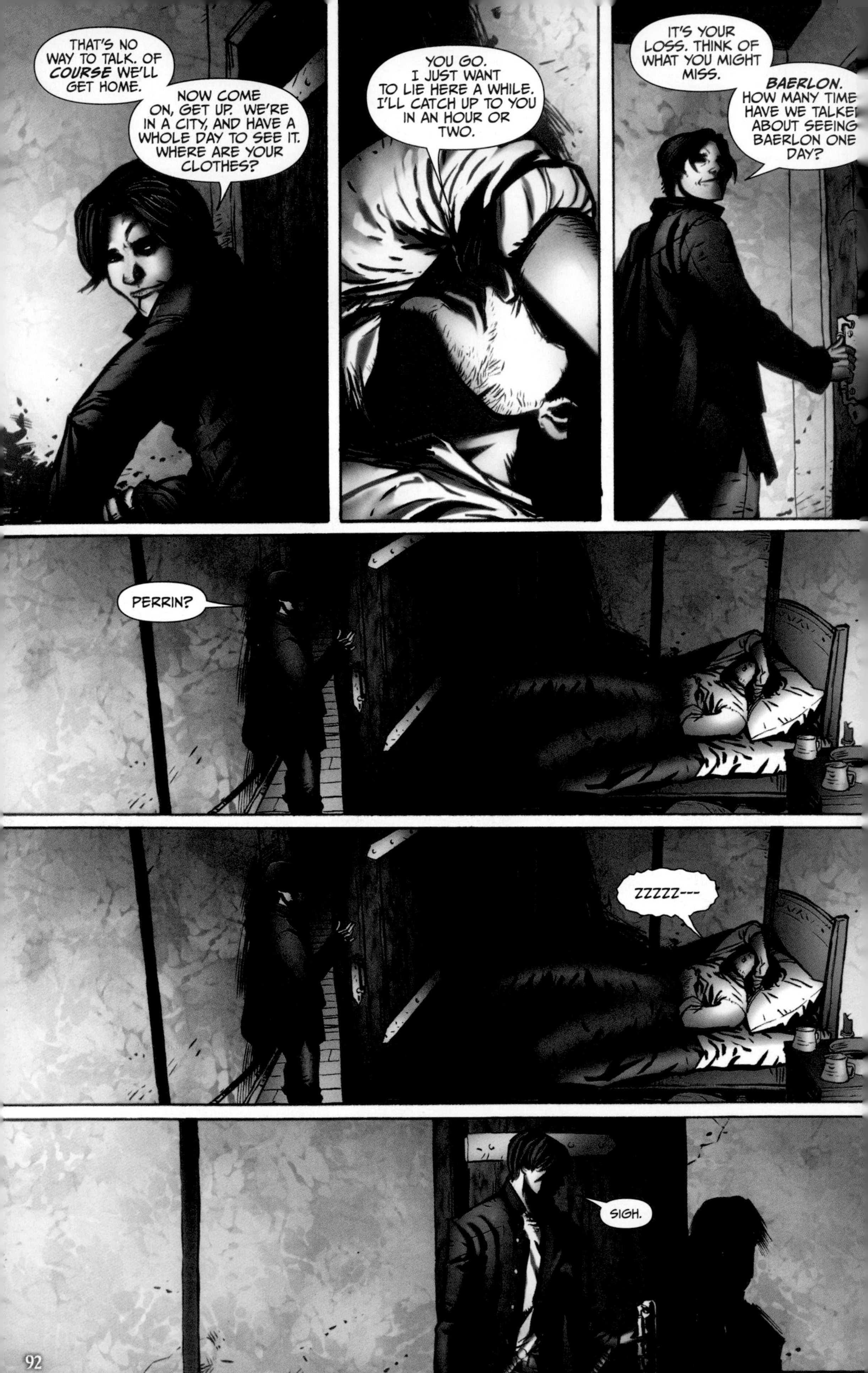
THAT'S NO WAY TO TALK. OF *COURSE* WE'LL GET HOME.
NOW COME ON, GET UP. WE'RE IN A CITY, AND HAVE A WHOLE DAY TO SEE IT. WHERE ARE YOUR CLOTHES?
YOU GO. I JUST WANT TO LIE HERE A WHILE. I'LL CATCH UP TO YOU IN AN HOUR OR TWO.
IT'S YOUR LOSS. THINK OF WHAT YOU MIGHT MISS.
BAERLON. HOW MANY TIME HAVE WE TALKE ABOUT SEEING BAERLON ONE DAY?
PERRIN?
ZZZZZ---
SIGH.

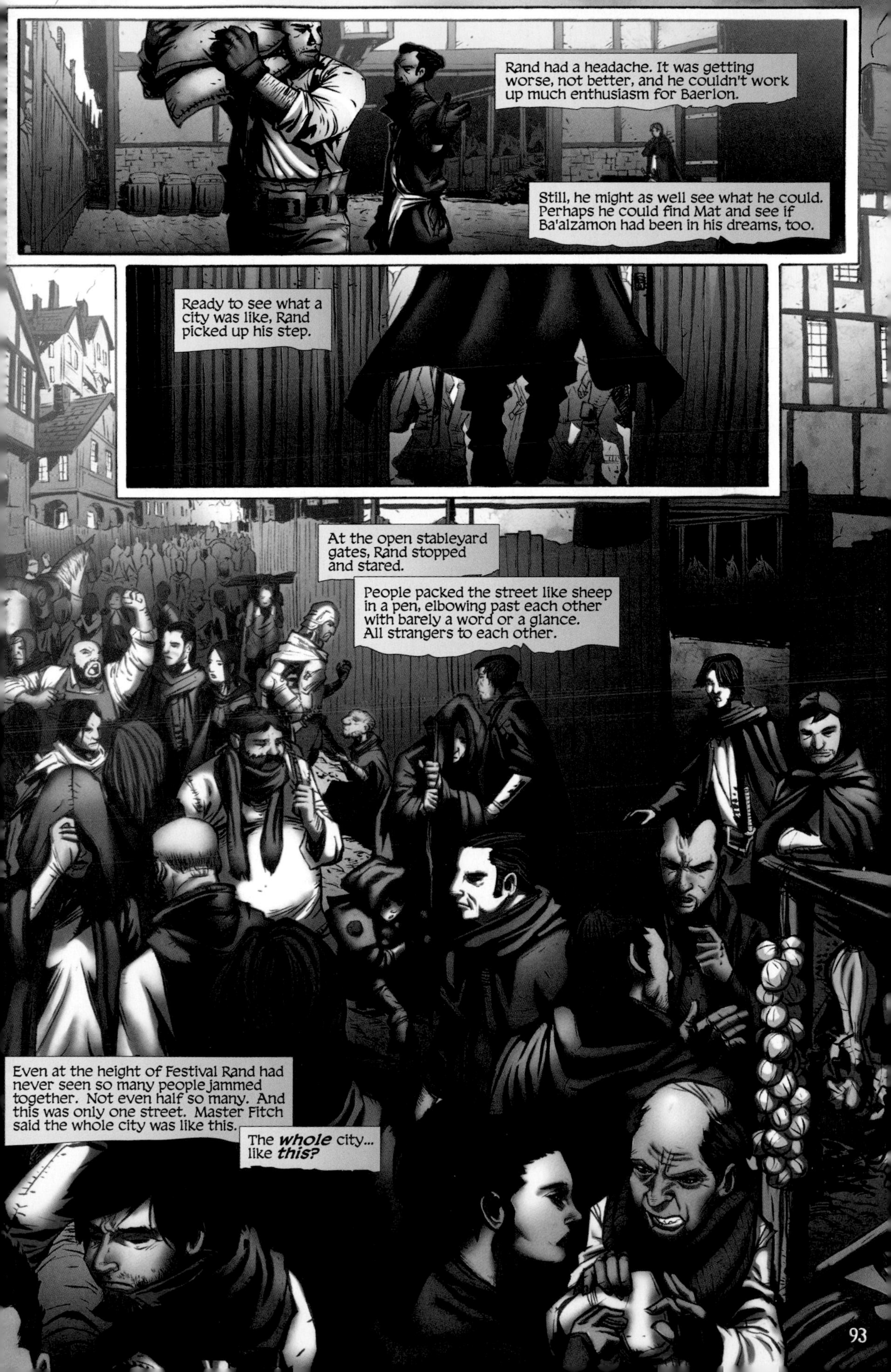
Rand had a headache. It was getting worse, not better, and he couldn't work up much enthusiasm for Baerlon.
Still, he might as well see what he could. Perhaps he could find Mat and see if Ba'alzamon had been in his dreams, too.
Ready to see what a city was like, Rand picked up his step.
At the open stableyard gates, Rand stopped and stared.
People packed the street like sheep in a pen, elbowing past each other with barely a word or a glance. All strangers to each other.
Even at the height of Festival Rand had never seen so many people jammed together. Not even half so many. And this was only one street. Master Fitch said the whole city was like this.
The *whole* city... like *this?*

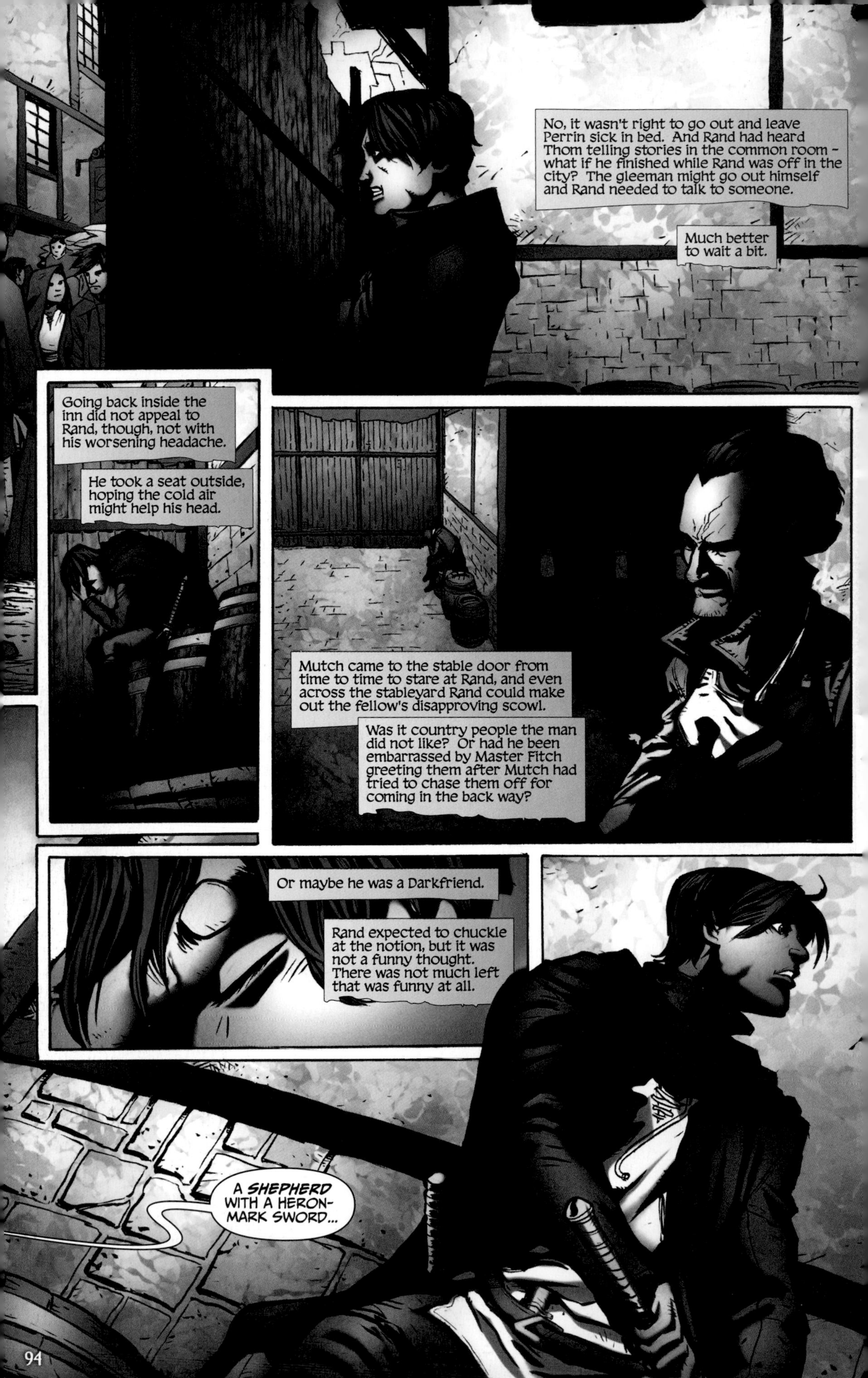

No, it wasn't right to go out and leave Perrin sick in bed. And Rand had heard Thom telling stories in the common room - what if he finished while Rand was off in the city? The gleeman might go out himself and Rand needed to talk to someone.
Much better to wait a bit.
Going back inside the inn did not appeal to Rand, though, not with his worsening headache.
He took a seat outside, hoping the cold air might help his head.
Mutch came to the stable door from time to time to stare at Rand, and even across the stableyard Rand could make out the fellow's disapproving scowl.
Was it country people the man did not like? Or had he been embarrassed by Master Fitch greeting them after Mutch had tried to chase them off for coming in the back way?
Or maybe he was a Darkfriend.
Rand expected to chuckle at the notion, but it was not a funny thought. There was not much left that was funny at all.
A *SHEPHERD* WITH A HERON-MARK SWORD...

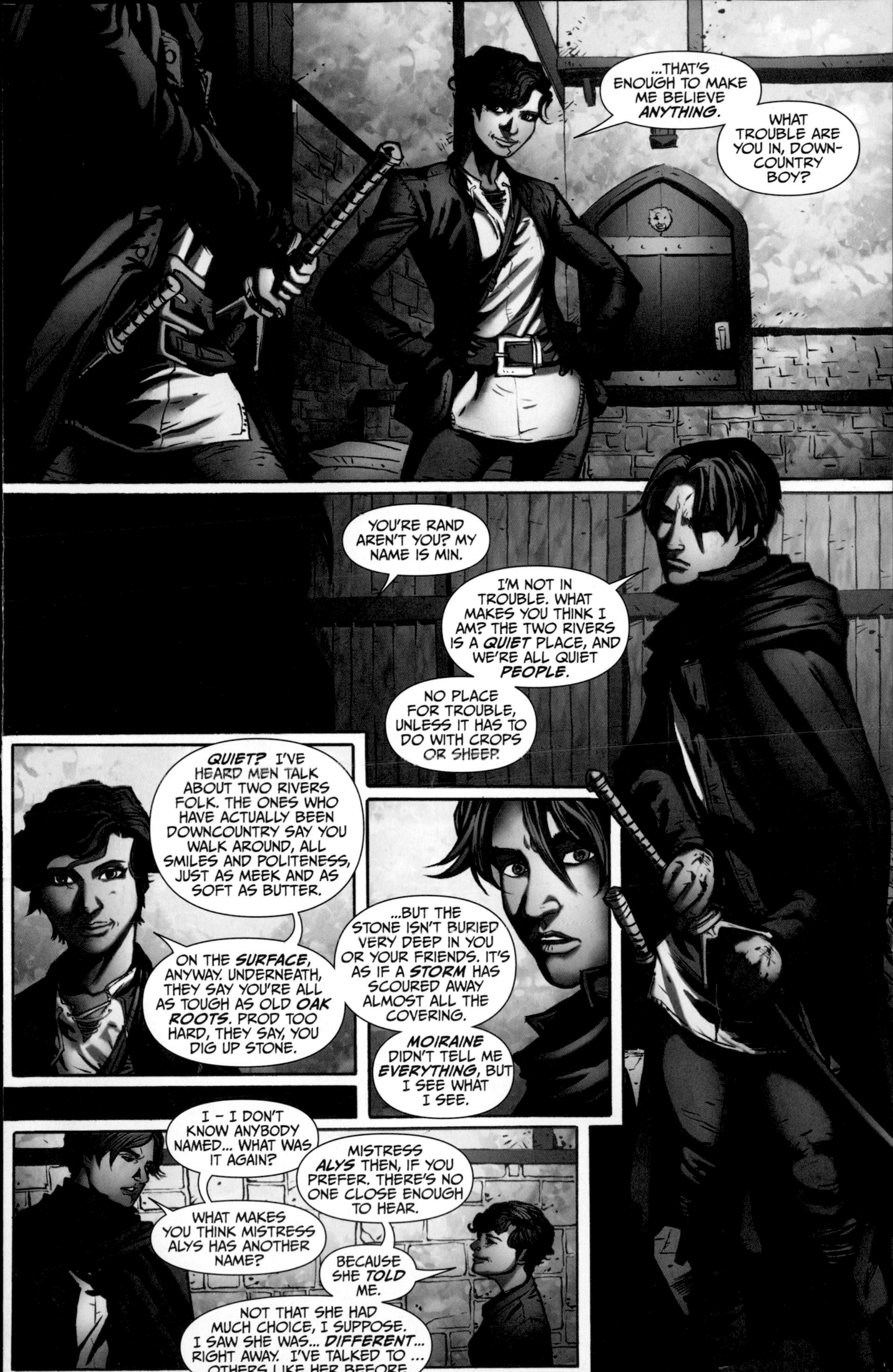
...THAT'S ENOUGH TO MAKE ME BELIEVE ANYTHING.
WHAT TROUBLE ARE YOU IN, DOWN-COUNTRY BOY?
YOU'RE RAND AREN'T YOU? MY NAME IS MIN.
I'M NOT IN TROUBLE. WHAT MAKES YOU THINK I AM? THE TWO RIVERS IS A QUIET PLACE, AND WE'RE ALL QUIET PEOPLE.
NO PLACE FOR TROUBLE, UNLESS IT HAS TO DO WITH CROPS OR SHEEP.
QUIET? I'VE HEARD MEN TALK ABOUT TWO RIVERS FOLK. THE ONES WHO HAVE ACTUALLY BEEN DOWNCOUNTRY SAY YOU WALK AROUND, ALL SMILES AND POLITENESS, JUST AS MEEK AND AS SOFT AS BUTTER.
ON THE SURFACE, ANYWAY. UNDERNEATH, THEY SAY YOU'RE ALL AS TOUGH AS OLD OAK ROOTS. PROD TOO HARD, THEY SAY, YOU DIG UP STONE.
...BUT THE STONE ISN'T BURIED VERY DEEP IN YOU OR YOUR FRIENDS. IT'S AS IF A STORM HAS SCOURED AWAY ALMOST ALL THE COVERING.
MOIRAINE DIDN'T TELL ME EVERYTHING, BUT I SEE WHAT I SEE.
I – I DON'T KNOW ANYBODY NAMED... WHAT WAS IT AGAIN?
WHAT MAKES YOU THINK MISTRESS ALYS HAS ANOTHER NAME?
MISTRESS ALYS THEN, IF YOU PREFER. THERE'S NO ONE CLOSE ENOUGH TO HEAR.
BECAUSE SHE TOLD ME.
NOT THAT SHE HAD MUCH CHOICE, I SUPPOSE. I SAW SHE WAS... DIFFERENT... RIGHT AWAY. I'VE TALKED TO ... OTHERS LIKE HER BEFORE.

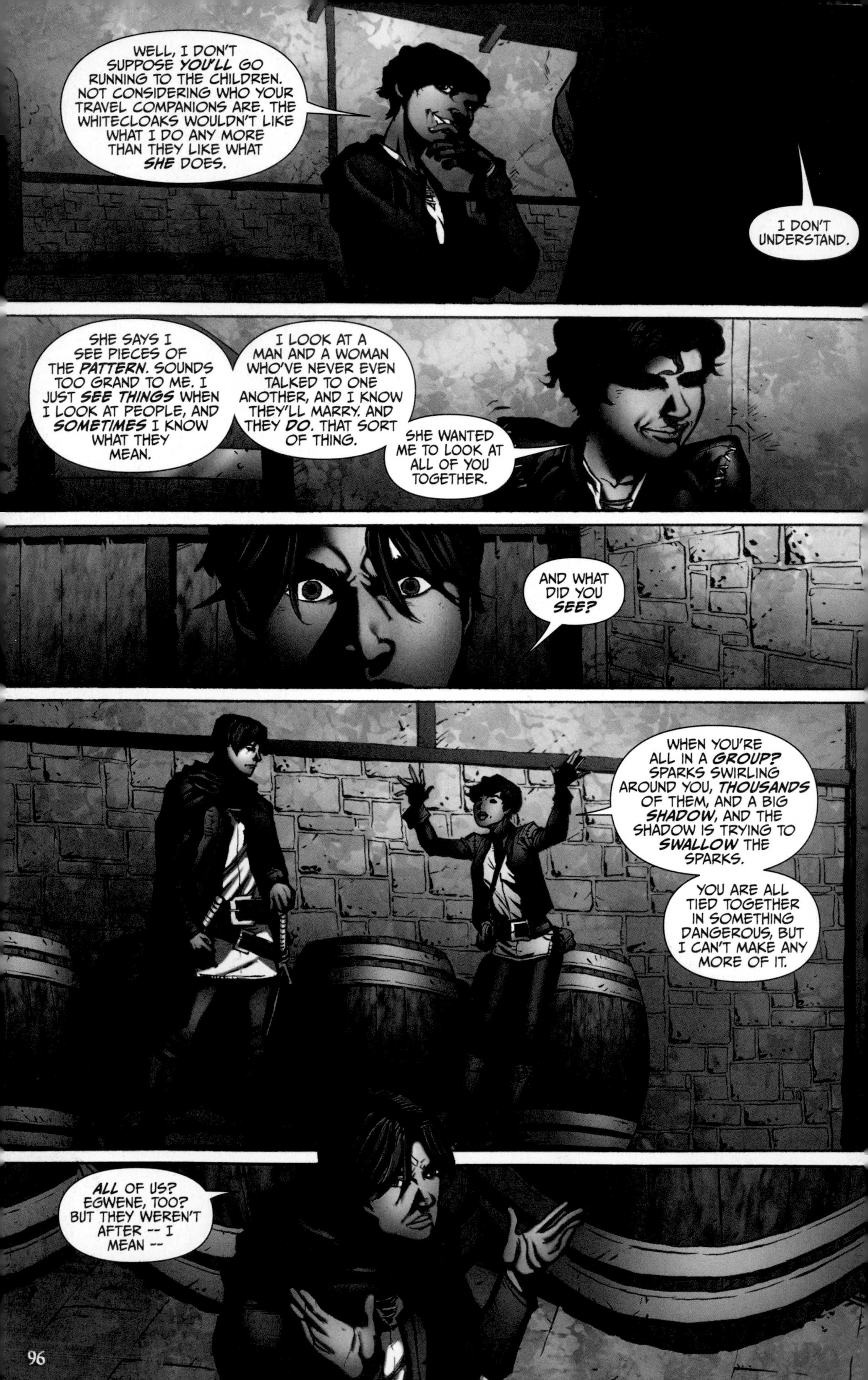
WELL, I DON'T SUPPOSE YOU'LL GO RUNNING TO THE CHILDREN. NOT CONSIDERING WHO YOUR TRAVEL COMPANIONS ARE. THE WHITECLOAKS WOULDN'T LIKE WHAT I DO ANY MORE THAN THEY LIKE WHAT SHE DOES.
I DON'T UNDERSTAND.
SHE SAYS I SEE PIECES OF THE PATTERN. SOUNDS TOO GRAND TO ME. I JUST SEE THINGS WHEN I LOOK AT PEOPLE, AND SOMETIMES I KNOW WHAT THEY MEAN.
I LOOK AT A MAN AND A WOMAN WHO'VE NEVER EVEN TALKED TO ONE ANOTHER, AND I KNOW THEY'LL MARRY. AND THEY DO. THAT SORT OF THING.
SHE WANTED ME TO LOOK AT ALL OF YOU TOGETHER.
AND WHAT DID YOU SEE?
WHEN YOU'RE ALL IN A GROUP? SPARKS SWIRLING AROUND YOU, THOUSANDS OF THEM, AND A BIG SHADOW, AND THE SHADOW IS TRYING TO SWALLOW THE SPARKS.
YOU ARE ALL TIED TOGETHER IN SOMETHING DANGEROUS, BUT I CAN'T MAKE ANY MORE OF IT.
ALL OF US? EGWENE, TOO? BUT THEY WEREN'T AFTER -- I MEAN --

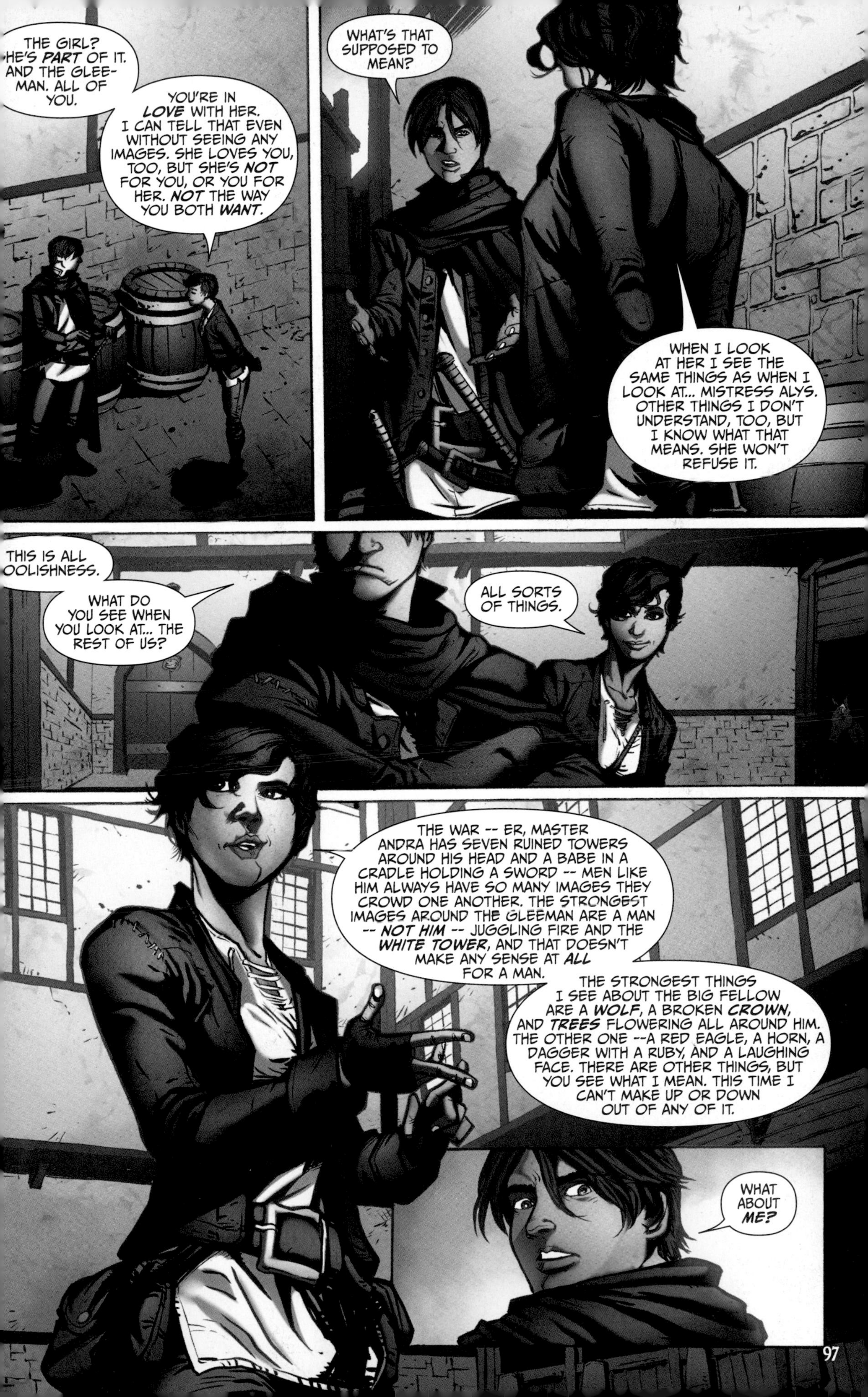

THE GIRL? HE'S PART OF IT. AND THE GLEE-MAN. ALL OF YOU.
YOU'RE IN LOVE WITH HER. I CAN TELL THAT EVEN WITHOUT SEEING ANY IMAGES. SHE LOVES YOU, TOO, BUT SHE'S NOT FOR YOU, OR YOU FOR HER. NOT THE WAY YOU BOTH WANT.
WHAT'S THAT SUPPOSED TO MEAN?
WHEN I LOOK AT HER I SEE THE SAME THINGS AS WHEN I LOOK AT... MISTRESS ALYS. OTHER THINGS I DON'T UNDERSTAND, TOO, BUT I KNOW WHAT THAT MEANS. SHE WON'T REFUSE IT.
THIS IS ALL OOLISHNESS.
WHAT DO YOU SEE WHEN YOU LOOK AT... THE REST OF US?
ALL SORTS OF THINGS.
THE WAR -- ER, MASTER ANDRA HAS SEVEN RUINED TOWERS AROUND HIS HEAD AND A BABE IN A CRADLE HOLDING A SWORD -- MEN LIKE HIM ALWAYS HAVE SO MANY IMAGES THEY CROWD ONE ANOTHER. THE STRONGEST IMAGES AROUND THE GLEEMAN ARE A MAN -- NOT HIM -- JUGGLING FIRE AND THE WHITE TOWER, AND THAT DOESN'T MAKE ANY SENSE AT ALL FOR A MAN.
THE STRONGEST THINGS I SEE ABOUT THE BIG FELLOW ARE A WOLF, A BROKEN CROWN, AND TREES FLOWERING ALL AROUND HIM. THE OTHER ONE --A RED EAGLE, A HORN, A DAGGER WITH A RUBY, AND A LAUGHING FACE. THERE ARE OTHER THINGS, BUT YOU SEE WHAT I MEAN. THIS TIME I CAN'T MAKE UP OR DOWN OUT OF ANY OF IT.
WHAT ABOUT ME?

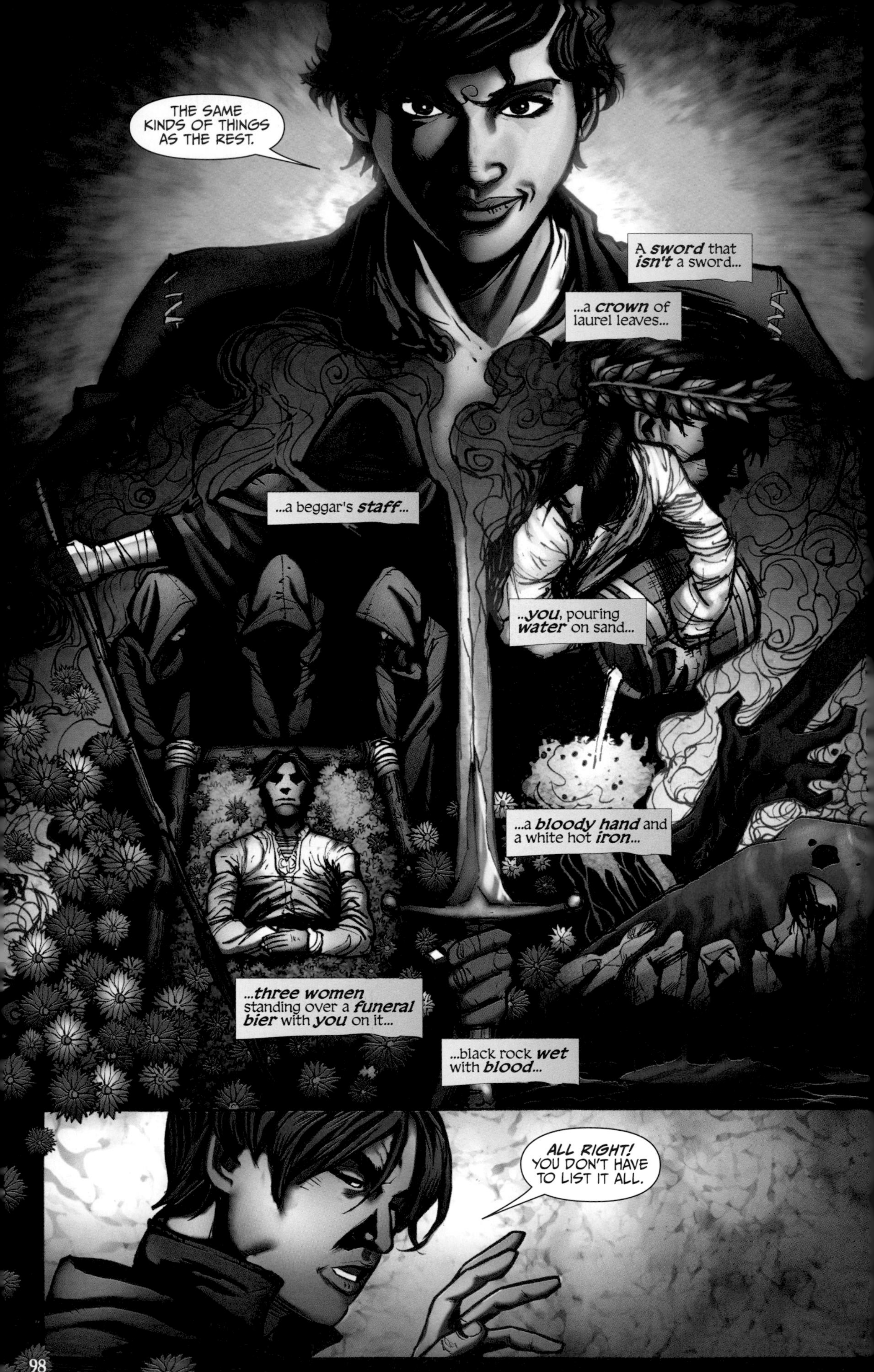
THE SAME KINDS OF THINGS AS THE REST.
A **sword** that **isn't** a sword...
...a **crown** of laurel leaves...
...a beggar's **staff**...
...**you**, pouring **water** on sand...
...a **bloody hand** and a white hot **iron**...
...**three women** standing over a **funeral bier** with **you** on it...
...black rock **wet** with **blood**...
ALL RIGHT! YOU DON'T HAVE TO LIST IT ALL.

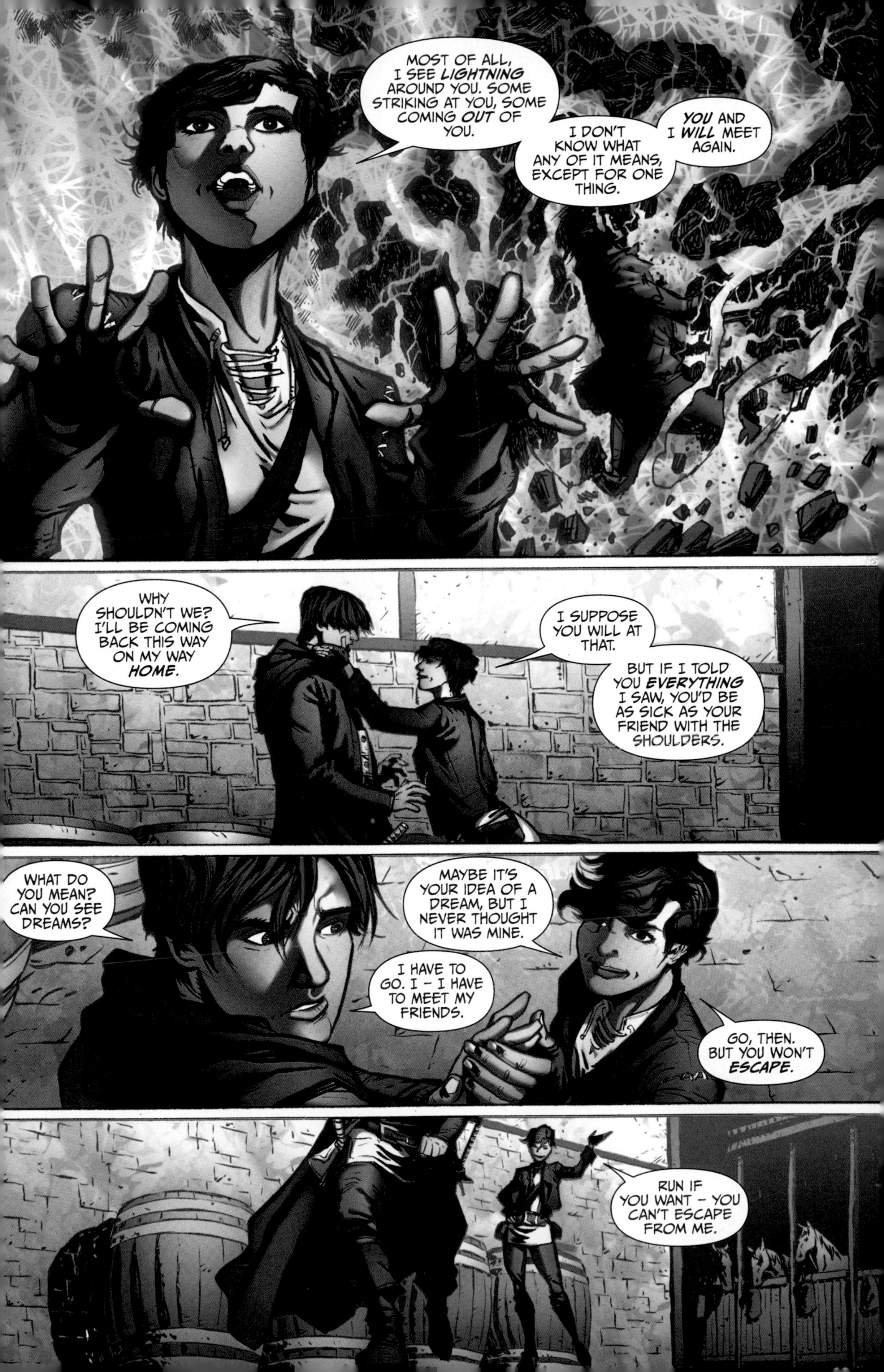
MOST OF ALL, I SEE LIGHTNING AROUND YOU. SOME STRIKING AT YOU, SOME COMING OUT OF YOU.
I DON'T KNOW WHAT ANY OF IT MEANS, EXCEPT FOR ONE THING.
YOU AND I WILL MEET AGAIN.
WHY SHOULDN'T WE? I'LL BE COMING BACK THIS WAY ON MY WAY HOME.
I SUPPOSE YOU WILL AT THAT.
BUT IF I TOLD YOU EVERYTHING I SAW, YOU'D BE AS SICK AS YOUR FRIEND WITH THE SHOULDERS.
WHAT DO YOU MEAN? CAN YOU SEE DREAMS?
MAYBE IT'S YOUR IDEA OF A DREAM, BUT I NEVER THOUGHT IT WAS MINE.
I HAVE TO GO. I – I HAVE TO MEET MY FRIENDS.
GO, THEN. BUT YOU WON'T ESCAPE.
RUN IF YOU WANT – YOU CAN'T ESCAPE FROM ME.

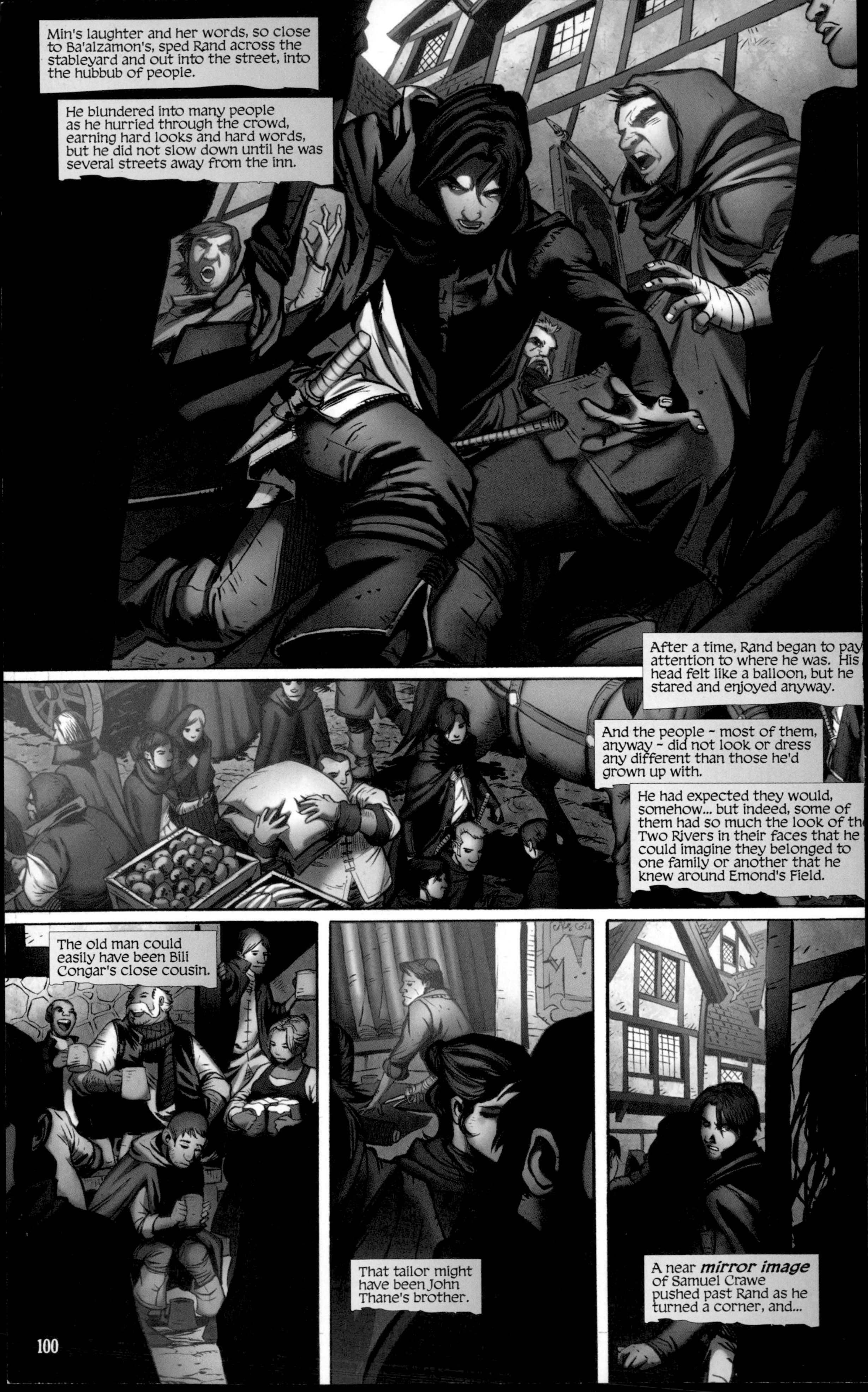
Min's laughter and her words, so close to Ba'alzamon's, sped Rand across the stableyard and out into the street, into the hubbub of people.
He blundered into many people as he hurried through the crowd, earning hard looks and hard words, but he did not slow down until he was several streets away from the inn.
After a time, Rand began to pay attention to where he was. His head felt like a balloon, but he stared and enjoyed anyway.
And the people - most of them, anyway - did not look or dress any different than those he'd grown up with.
He had expected they would, somehow... but indeed, some of them had so much the look of th Two Rivers in their faces that he could imagine they belonged to one family or another that he knew around Emond's Field.
The old man could easily have been Bili Congar's close cousin.
That tailor might have been John Thane's brother.
A near *mirror image* of Samuel Crawe pushed past Rand as he turned a corner, and...

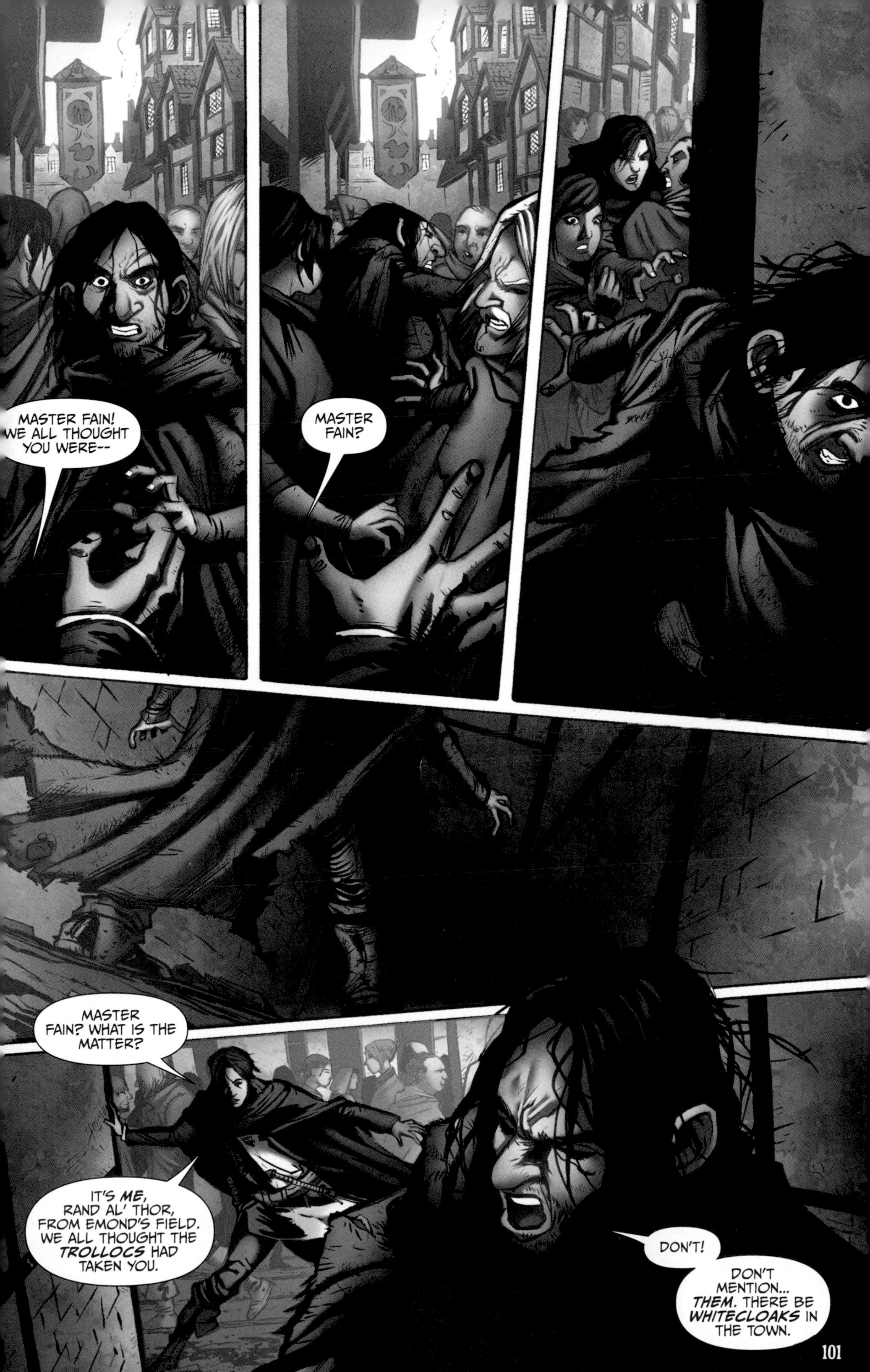
MASTER FAIN! WE ALL THOUGHT YOU WERE--
MASTER FAIN?
MASTER FAIN? WHAT IS THE MATTER?
IT'S ME, RAND AL' THOR, FROM EMOND'S FIELD. WE ALL THOUGHT THE TROLLOCS HAD TAKEN YOU.
DON'T!
DON'T MENTION... THEM. THERE BE WHITECLOAKS IN THE TOWN.

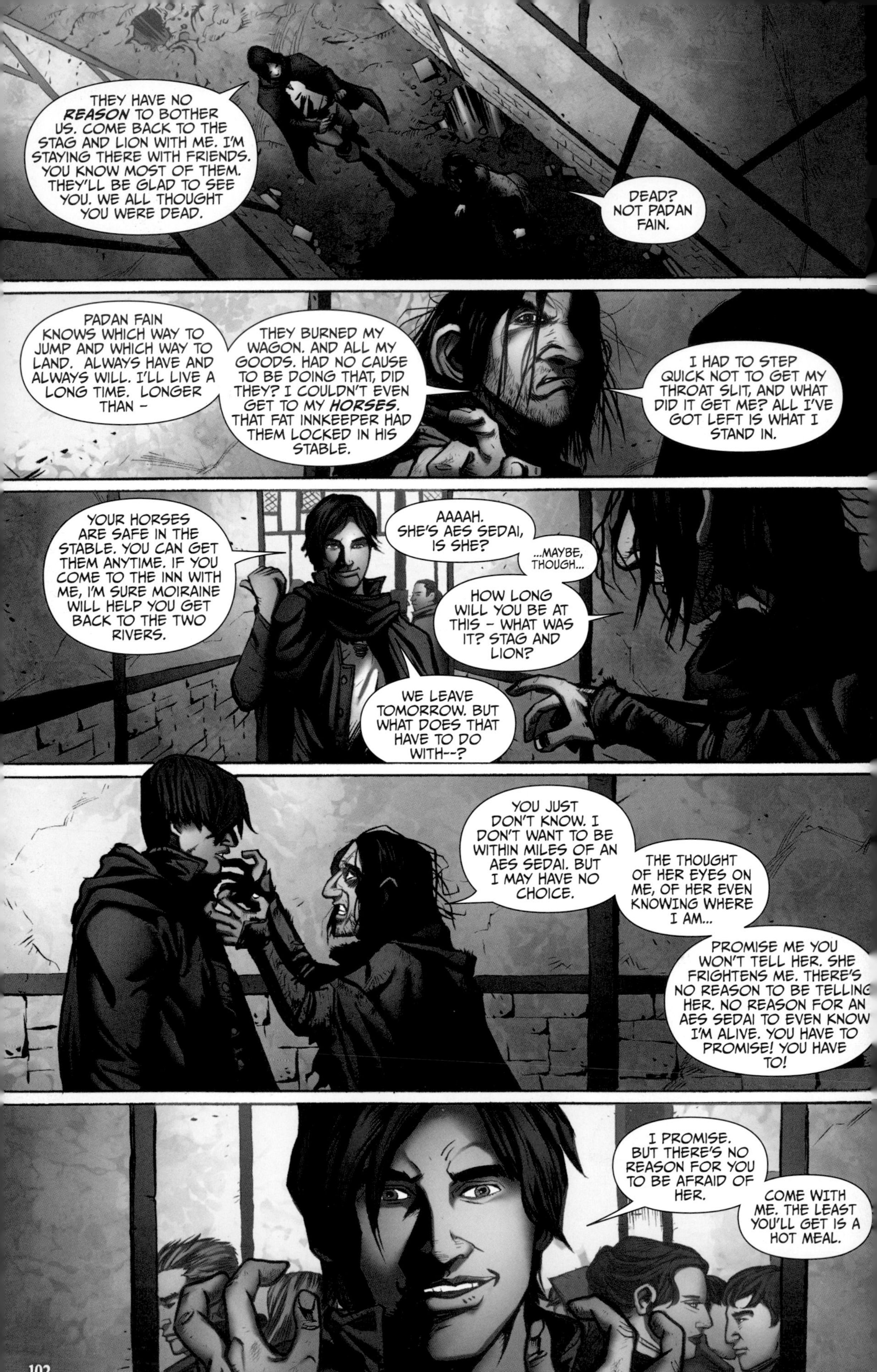
THEY HAVE NO REASON TO BOTHER US. COME BACK TO THE STAG AND LION WITH ME. I'M STAYING THERE WITH FRIENDS. YOU KNOW MOST OF THEM. THEY'LL BE GLAD TO SEE YOU. WE ALL THOUGHT YOU WERE DEAD.
DEAD? NOT PADAN FAIN.
PADAN FAIN KNOWS WHICH WAY TO JUMP AND WHICH WAY TO LAND. ALWAYS HAVE AND ALWAYS WILL. I'LL LIVE A LONG TIME. LONGER THAN –
THEY BURNED MY WAGON. AND ALL MY GOODS. HAD NO CAUSE TO BE DOING THAT, DID THEY? I COULDN'T EVEN GET TO MY HORSES. THAT FAT INNKEEPER HAD THEM LOCKED IN HIS STABLE.
I HAD TO STEP QUICK NOT TO GET MY THROAT SLIT, AND WHAT DID IT GET ME? ALL I'VE GOT LEFT IS WHAT I STAND IN.
YOUR HORSES ARE SAFE IN THE STABLE. YOU CAN GET THEM ANYTIME. IF YOU COME TO THE INN WITH ME, I'M SURE MOIRAINE WILL HELP YOU GET BACK TO THE TWO RIVERS.
AAAAH. SHE'S AES SEDAI, IS SHE?
...MAYBE, THOUGH...
HOW LONG WILL YOU BE AT THIS – WHAT WAS IT? STAG AND LION?
WE LEAVE TOMORROW. BUT WHAT DOES THAT HAVE TO DO WITH--?
YOU JUST DON'T KNOW. I DON'T WANT TO BE WITHIN MILES OF AN AES SEDAI. BUT I MAY HAVE NO CHOICE.
THE THOUGHT OF HER EYES ON ME, OF HER EVEN KNOWING WHERE I AM...
PROMISE ME YOU WON'T TELL HER. SHE FRIGHTENS ME. THERE'S NO REASON TO BE TELLING HER. NO REASON FOR AN AES SEDAI TO EVEN KNOW I'M ALIVE. YOU HAVE TO PROMISE! YOU HAVE TO!
I PROMISE. BUT THERE'S NO REASON FOR YOU TO BE AFRAID OF HER.
COME WITH ME. THE LEAST YOU'LL GET IS A HOT MEAL.

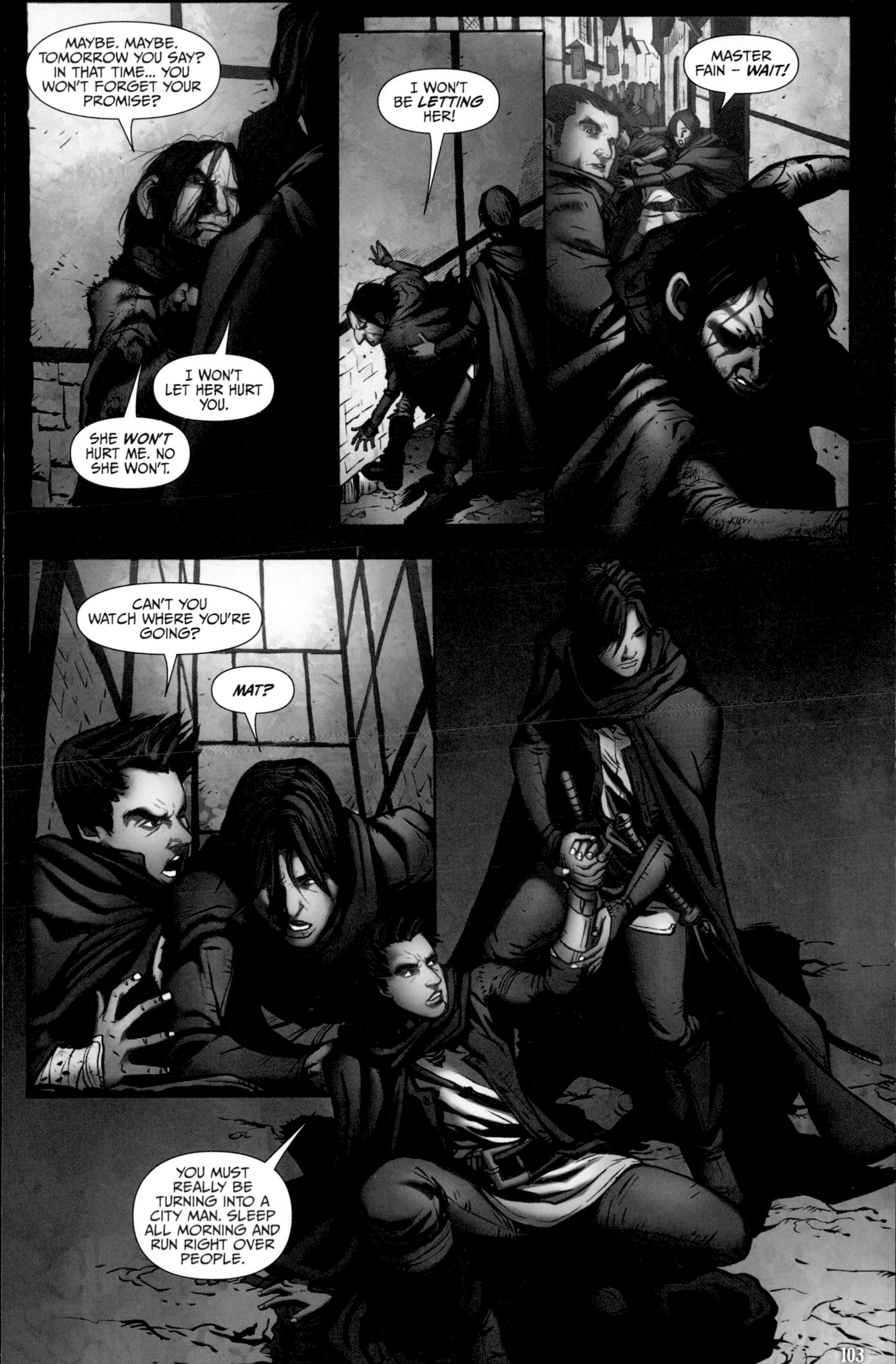

MAYBE. MAYBE. TOMORROW YOU SAY? IN THAT TIME... YOU WON'T FORGET YOUR PROMISE?
I WON'T LET HER HURT YOU.
SHE *WON'T* HURT ME. NO SHE WON'T.
I WON'T BE *LETTING* HER!
MASTER FAIN – *WAIT!*
CAN'T YOU WATCH WHERE YOU'RE GOING?
MAT?
YOU MUST REALLY BE TURNING INTO A CITY MAN. SLEEP ALL MORNING AND RUN RIGHT OVER PEOPLE.

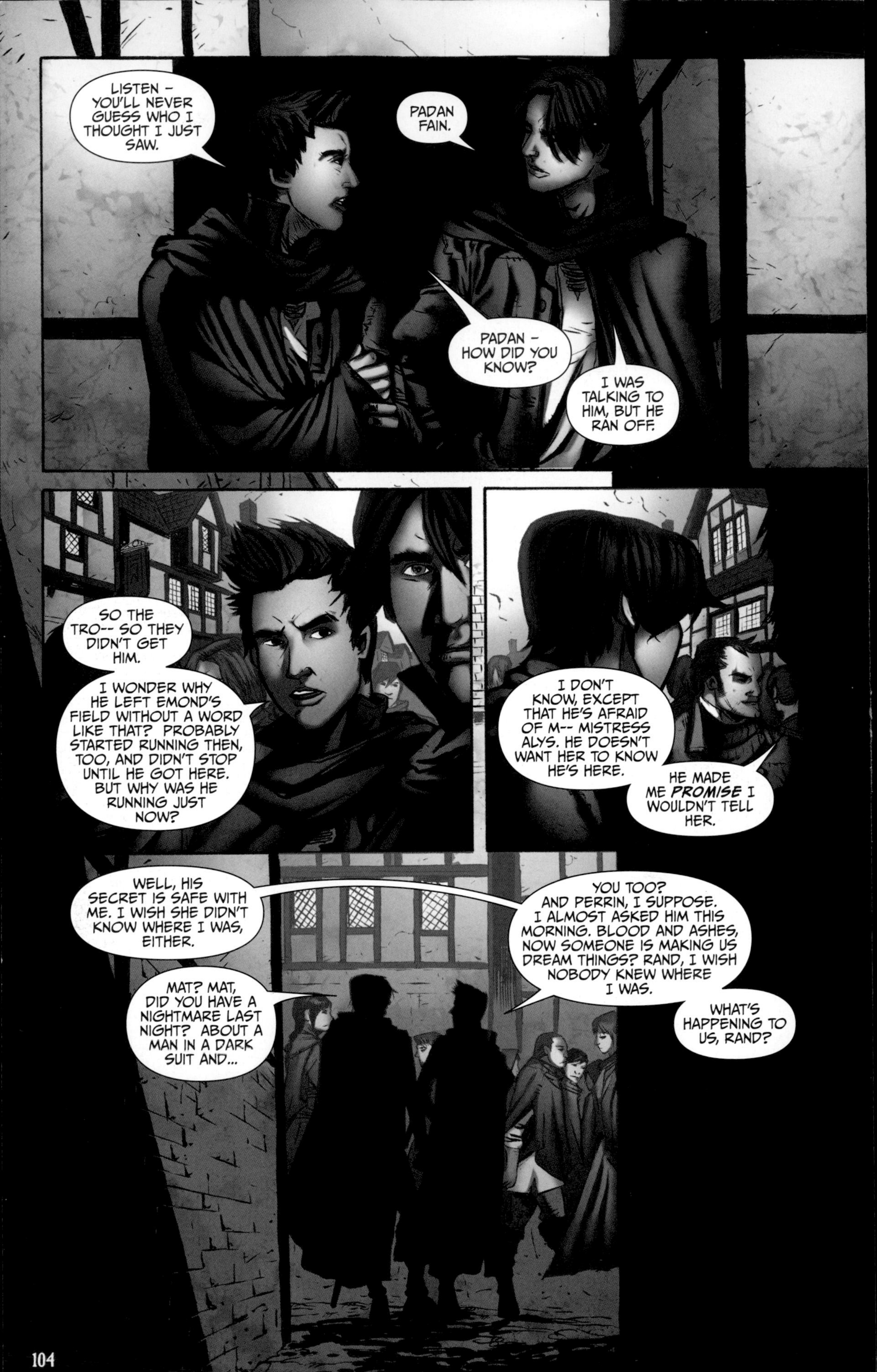
LISTEN – YOU'LL NEVER GUESS WHO I THOUGHT I JUST SAW.
PADAN FAIN.
PADAN – HOW DID YOU KNOW?
I WAS TALKING TO HIM, BUT HE RAN OFF.
SO THE TRO-- SO THEY DIDN'T GET HIM.
I WONDER WHY HE LEFT EMOND'S FIELD WITHOUT A WORD LIKE THAT? PROBABLY STARTED RUNNING THEN, TOO, AND DIDN'T STOP UNTIL HE GOT HERE. BUT WHY WAS HE RUNNING JUST NOW?
I DON'T KNOW, EXCEPT THAT HE'S AFRAID OF M-- MISTRESS ALYS. HE DOESN'T WANT HER TO KNOW HE'S HERE.
HE MADE ME *PROMISE* I WOULDN'T TELL HER.
WELL, HIS SECRET IS SAFE WITH ME. I WISH SHE DIDN'T KNOW WHERE I WAS, EITHER.
MAT? MAT, DID YOU HAVE A NIGHTMARE LAST NIGHT? ABOUT A MAN IN A DARK SUIT AND...
YOU TOO? AND PERRIN, I SUPPOSE. I ALMOST ASKED HIM THIS MORNING. BLOOD AND ASHES, NOW SOMEONE IS MAKING US DREAM THINGS? RAND, I WISH NOBODY KNEW WHERE I WAS.
WHAT'S HAPPENING TO US, RAND?

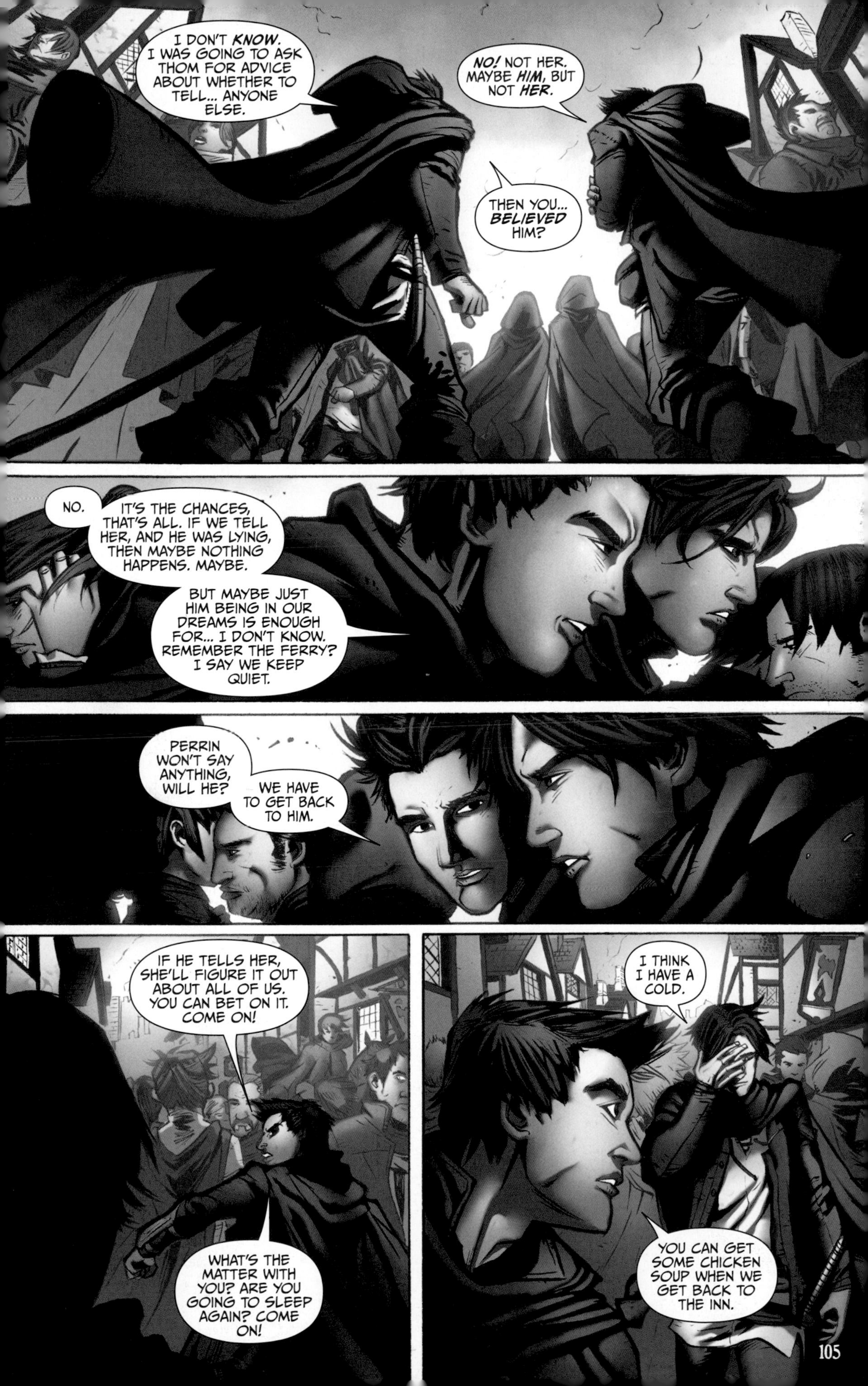
I DON'T KNOW. I WAS GOING TO ASK THOM FOR ADVICE ABOUT WHETHER TO TELL... ANYONE ELSE.
NO! NOT HER. MAYBE HIM, BUT NOT HER.
THEN YOU... BELIEVED HIM?
NO.
IT'S THE CHANCES, THAT'S ALL. IF WE TELL HER, AND HE WAS LYING, THEN MAYBE NOTHING HAPPENS. MAYBE.
BUT MAYBE JUST HIM BEING IN OUR DREAMS IS ENOUGH FOR... I DON'T KNOW. REMEMBER THE FERRY? I SAY WE KEEP QUIET.
PERRIN WON'T SAY ANYTHING, WILL HE?
WE HAVE TO GET BACK TO HIM.
IF HE TELLS HER, SHE'LL FIGURE IT OUT ABOUT ALL OF US. YOU CAN BET ON IT. COME ON!
WHAT'S THE MATTER WITH YOU? ARE YOU GOING TO SLEEP AGAIN? COME ON!
I THINK I HAVE A COLD.
YOU CAN GET SOME CHICKEN SOUP WHEN WE GET BACK TO THE INN.

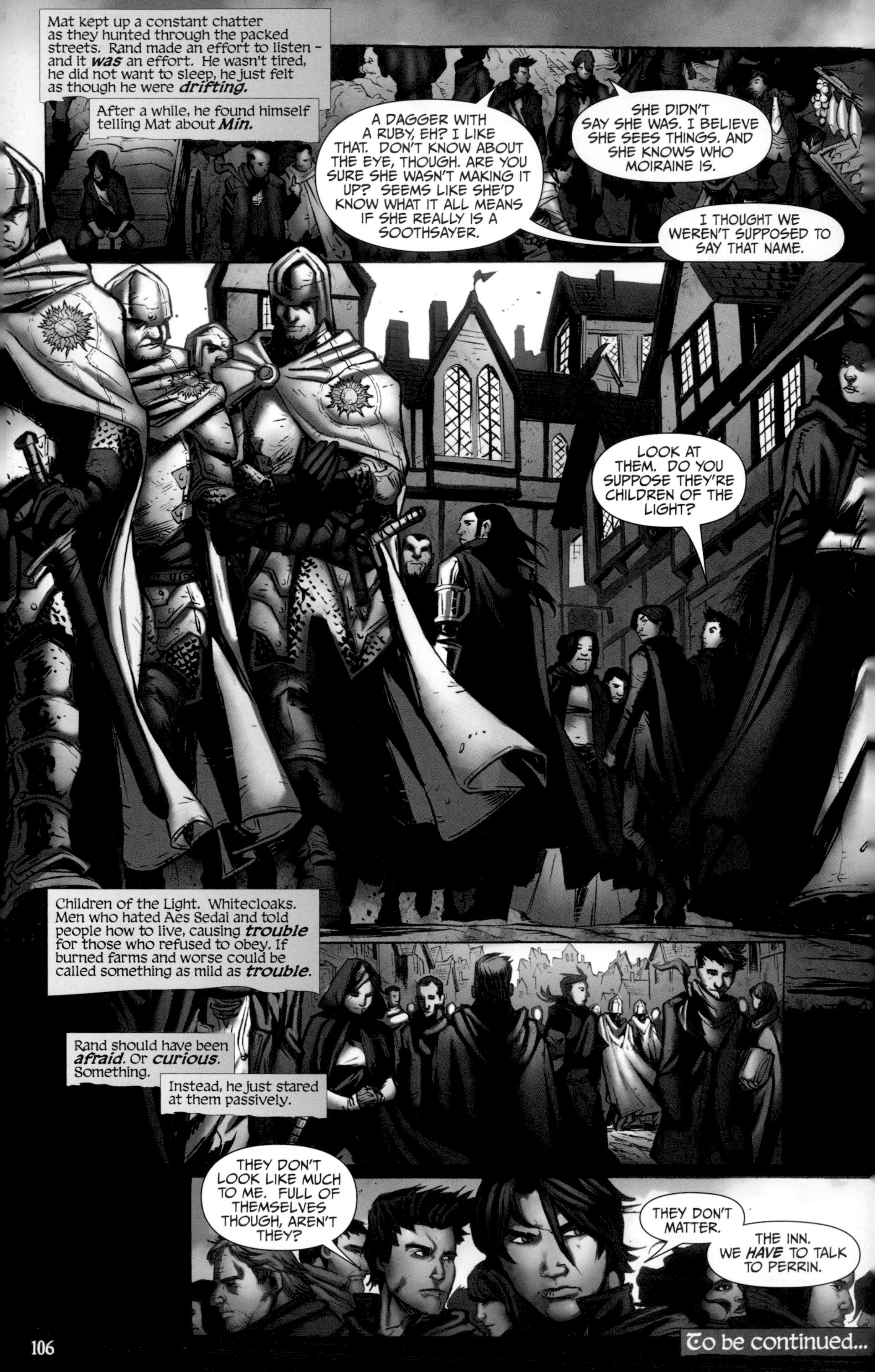
Mat kept up a constant chatter as they hunted through the packed streets. Rand made an effort to listen – and it *was* an effort. He wasn't tired, he did not want to sleep, he just felt as though he were *drifting.*
After a while, he found himself telling Mat about *Min.*
A DAGGER WITH A RUBY, EH? I LIKE THAT. DON'T KNOW ABOUT THE EYE, THOUGH. ARE YOU SURE SHE WASN'T MAKING IT UP? SEEMS LIKE SHE'D KNOW WHAT IT ALL MEANS IF SHE REALLY IS A SOOTHSAYER.
SHE DIDN'T SAY SHE WAS. I BELIEVE SHE SEES THINGS. AND SHE KNOWS WHO MOIRAINE IS.
I THOUGHT WE WEREN'T SUPPOSED TO SAY THAT NAME.
LOOK AT THEM. DO YOU SUPPOSE THEY'RE CHILDREN OF THE LIGHT?
Children of the Light. Whitecloaks. Men who hated Aes Sedai and told people how to live, causing *trouble* for those who refused to obey. If burned farms and worse could be called something as mild as *trouble.*
Rand should have been *afraid*. Or *curious*. Something.
Instead, he just stared at them passively.
THEY DON'T LOOK LIKE MUCH TO ME. FULL OF THEMSELVES THOUGH, AREN'T THEY?
THEY DON'T MATTER.
THE INN. WE *HAVE* TO TALK TO PERRIN.
To be continued...

chapter five

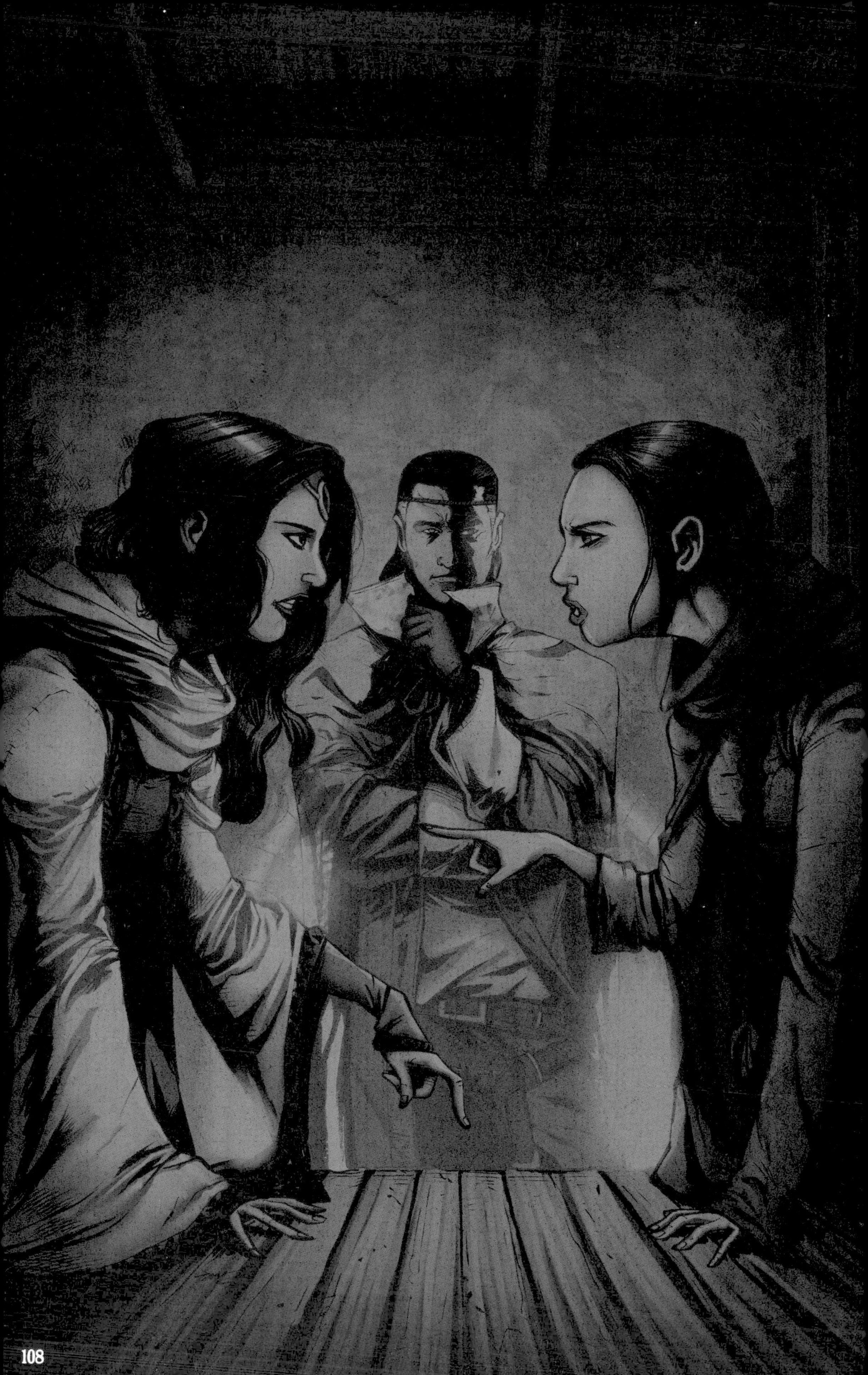

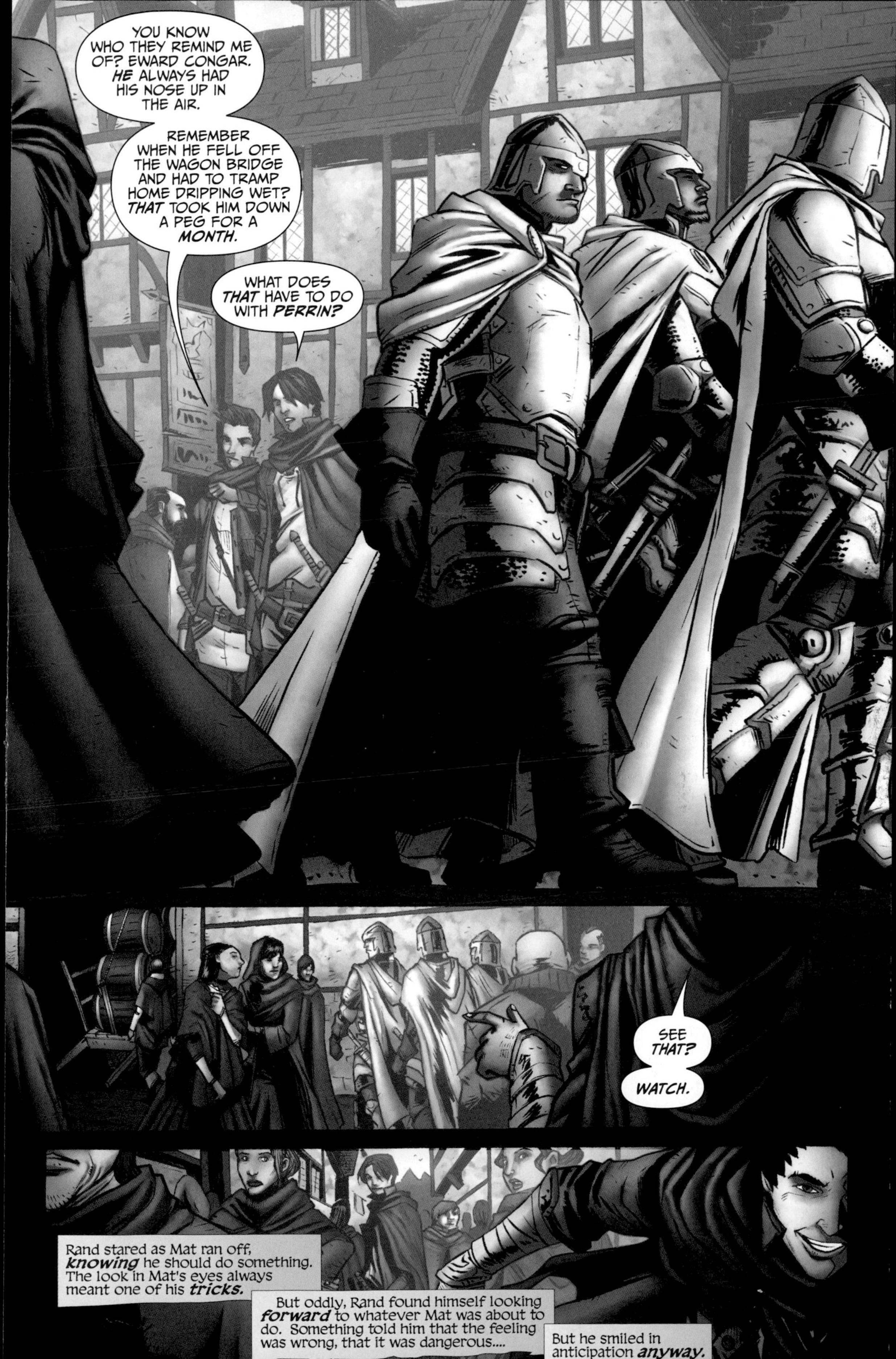
YOU KNOW WHO THEY REMIND ME OF? EWARD CONGAR. HE ALWAYS HAD HIS NOSE UP IN THE AIR.
REMEMBER WHEN HE FELL OFF THE WAGON BRIDGE AND HAD TO TRAMP HOME DRIPPING WET? THAT TOOK HIM DOWN A PEG FOR A MONTH.
WHAT DOES THAT HAVE TO DO WITH PERRIN?
SEE THAT?
WATCH.
Rand stared as Mat ran off, knowing he should do something. The look in Mat's eyes always meant one of his tricks.
But oddly, Rand found himself looking forward to whatever Mat was about to do. Something told him that the feeling was wrong, that it was dangerous....
But he smiled in anticipation anyway.

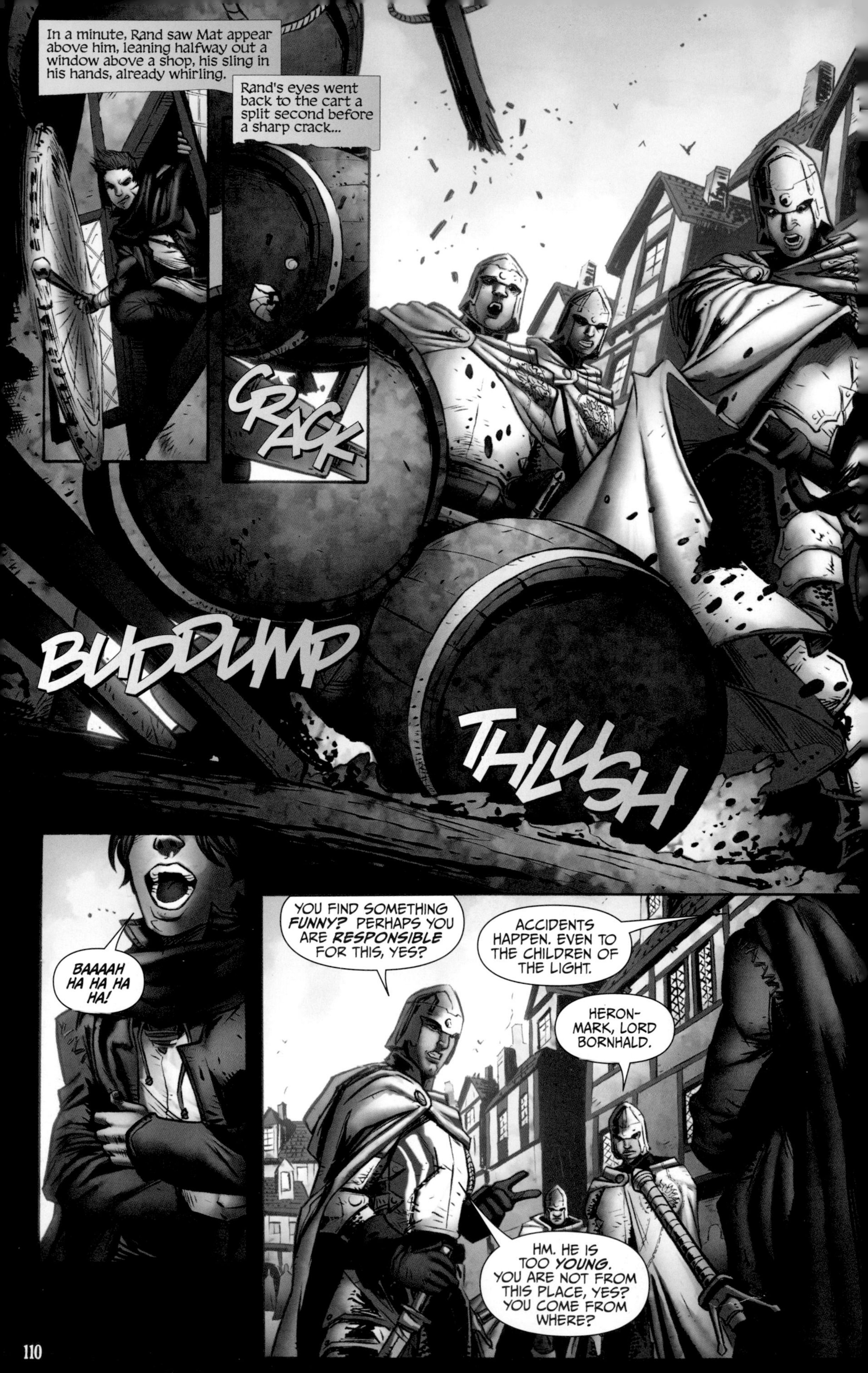
In a minute, Rand saw Mat appear above him, leaning halfway out a window above a shop, his sling in his hands, already whirling.
Rand's eyes went back to the cart a split second before a sharp crack...
CRACK
BUDDUMP
THLUSH
BAAAAH HA HA HA HA!
YOU FIND SOMETHING FUNNY? PERHAPS YOU ARE RESPONSIBLE FOR THIS, YES?
ACCIDENTS HAPPEN. EVEN TO THE CHILDREN OF THE LIGHT.
HERON-MARK, LORD BORNHALD.
HM. HE IS TOO YOUNG. YOU ARE NOT FROM THIS PLACE, YES? YOU COME FROM WHERE?

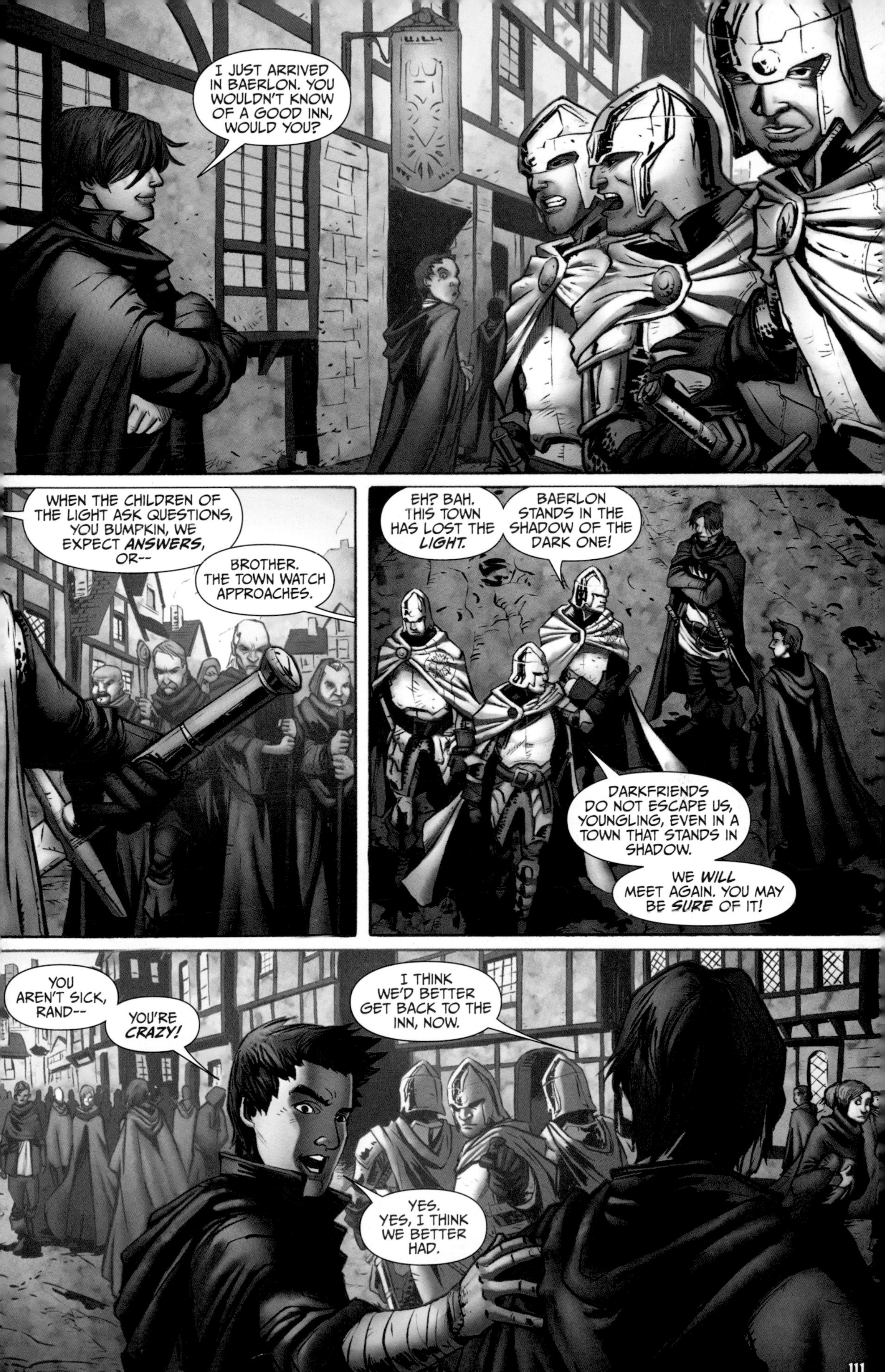
I JUST ARRIVED IN BAERLON. YOU WOULDN'T KNOW OF A GOOD INN, WOULD YOU?
WHEN THE CHILDREN OF THE LIGHT ASK QUESTIONS, YOU BUMPKIN, WE EXPECT ANSWERS, OR--
BROTHER. THE TOWN WATCH APPROACHES.
EH? BAH. THIS TOWN HAS LOST THE LIGHT.
BAERLON STANDS IN THE SHADOW OF THE DARK ONE!
DARKFRIENDS DO NOT ESCAPE US, YOUNGLING, EVEN IN A TOWN THAT STANDS IN SHADOW.
WE WILL MEET AGAIN. YOU MAY BE SURE OF IT!
YOU AREN'T SICK, RAND--
YOU'RE CRAZY!
I THINK WE'D BETTER GET BACK TO THE INN, NOW.
YES. YES, I THINK WE BETTER HAD.

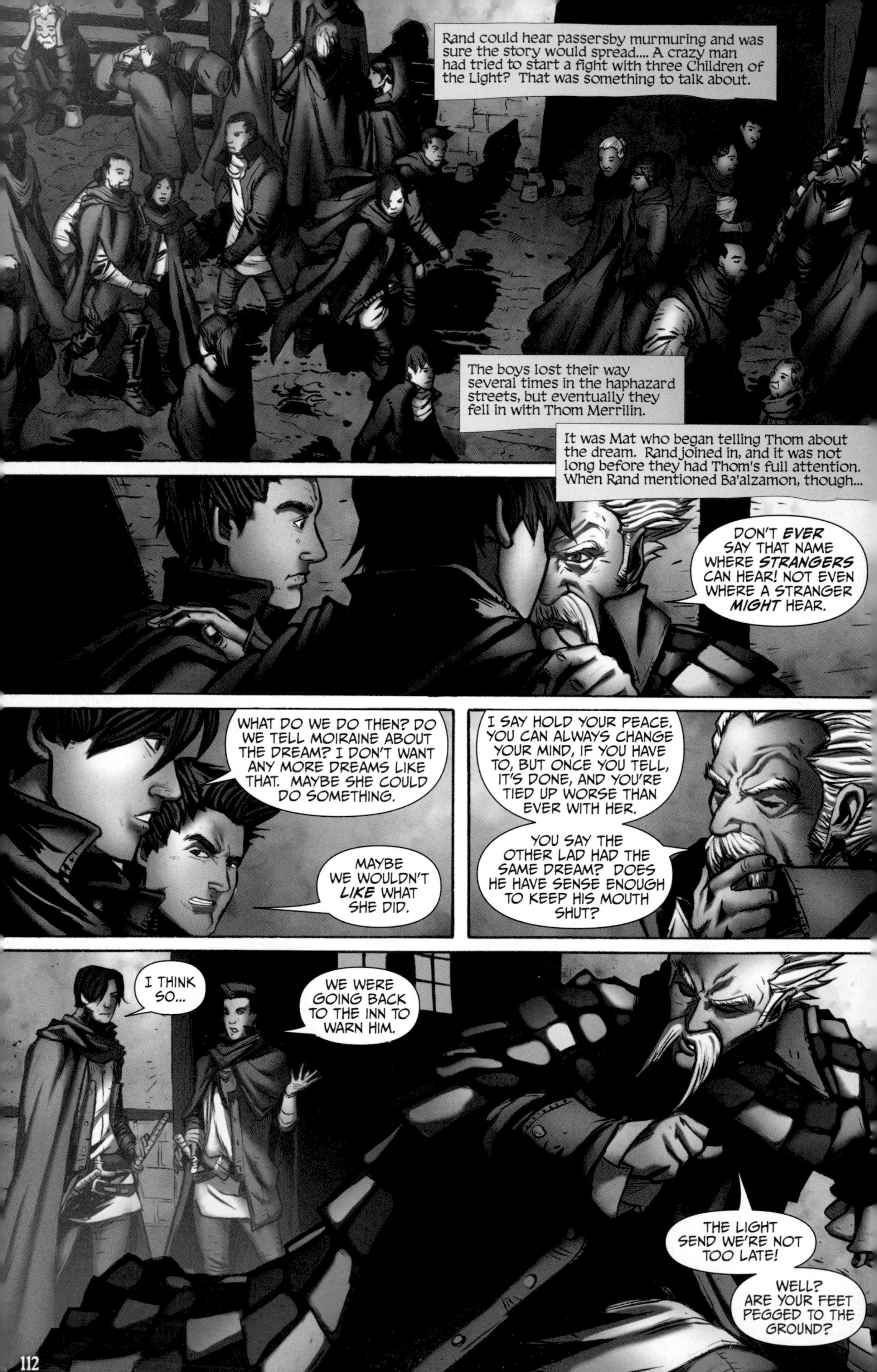
Rand could hear passersby murmuring and was sure the story would spread.... A crazy man had tried to start a fight with three Children of the Light? That was something to talk about.
The boys lost their way several times in the haphazard streets, but eventually they fell in with Thom Merrilin.
It was Mat who began telling Thom about the dream. Rand joined in, and it was not long before they had Thom's full attention. When Rand mentioned Ba'alzamon, though...
DON'T EVER SAY THAT NAME WHERE STRANGERS CAN HEAR! NOT EVEN WHERE A STRANGER MIGHT HEAR.
WHAT DO WE DO THEN? DO WE TELL MOIRAINE ABOUT THE DREAM? I DON'T WANT ANY MORE DREAMS LIKE THAT. MAYBE SHE COULD DO SOMETHING.
MAYBE WE WOULDN'T LIKE WHAT SHE DID.
I SAY HOLD YOUR PEACE. YOU CAN ALWAYS CHANGE YOUR MIND, IF YOU HAVE TO, BUT ONCE YOU TELL, IT'S DONE, AND YOU'RE TIED UP WORSE THAN EVER WITH HER.
YOU SAY THE OTHER LAD HAD THE SAME DREAM? DOES HE HAVE SENSE ENOUGH TO KEEP HIS MOUTH SHUT?
I THINK SO...
WE WERE GOING BACK TO THE INN TO WARN HIM.
THE LIGHT SEND WE'RE NOT TOO LATE!
WELL? ARE YOUR FEET PEGGED TO THE GROUND?

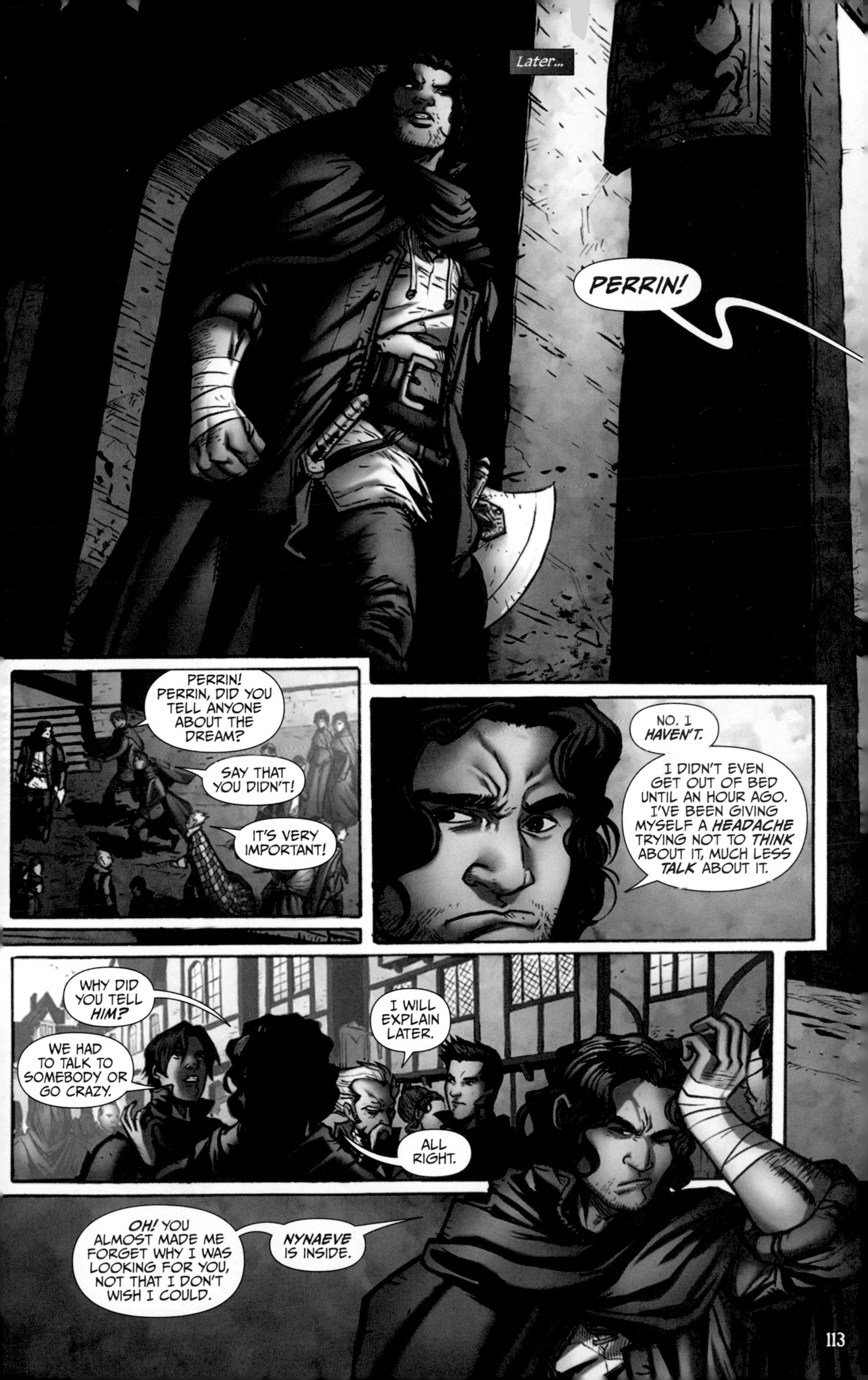

Later...
PERRIN!
PERRIN! PERRIN, DID YOU TELL ANYONE ABOUT THE DREAM?
SAY THAT YOU DIDN'T!
IT'S VERY IMPORTANT!
NO. I *HAVEN'T.*
I DIDN'T EVEN GET OUT OF BED UNTIL AN HOUR AGO. I'VE BEEN GIVING MYSELF A *HEADACHE* TRYING NOT TO *THINK* ABOUT IT, MUCH LESS *TALK* ABOUT IT.
WHY DID YOU TELL *HIM?*
WE HAD TO TALK TO SOMEBODY OR GO CRAZY.
I WILL EXPLAIN LATER.
ALL RIGHT.
OH! YOU ALMOST MADE ME FORGET WHY I WAS LOOKING FOR YOU, NOT THAT I DON'T WISH I COULD.
NYNAEVE IS INSIDE.

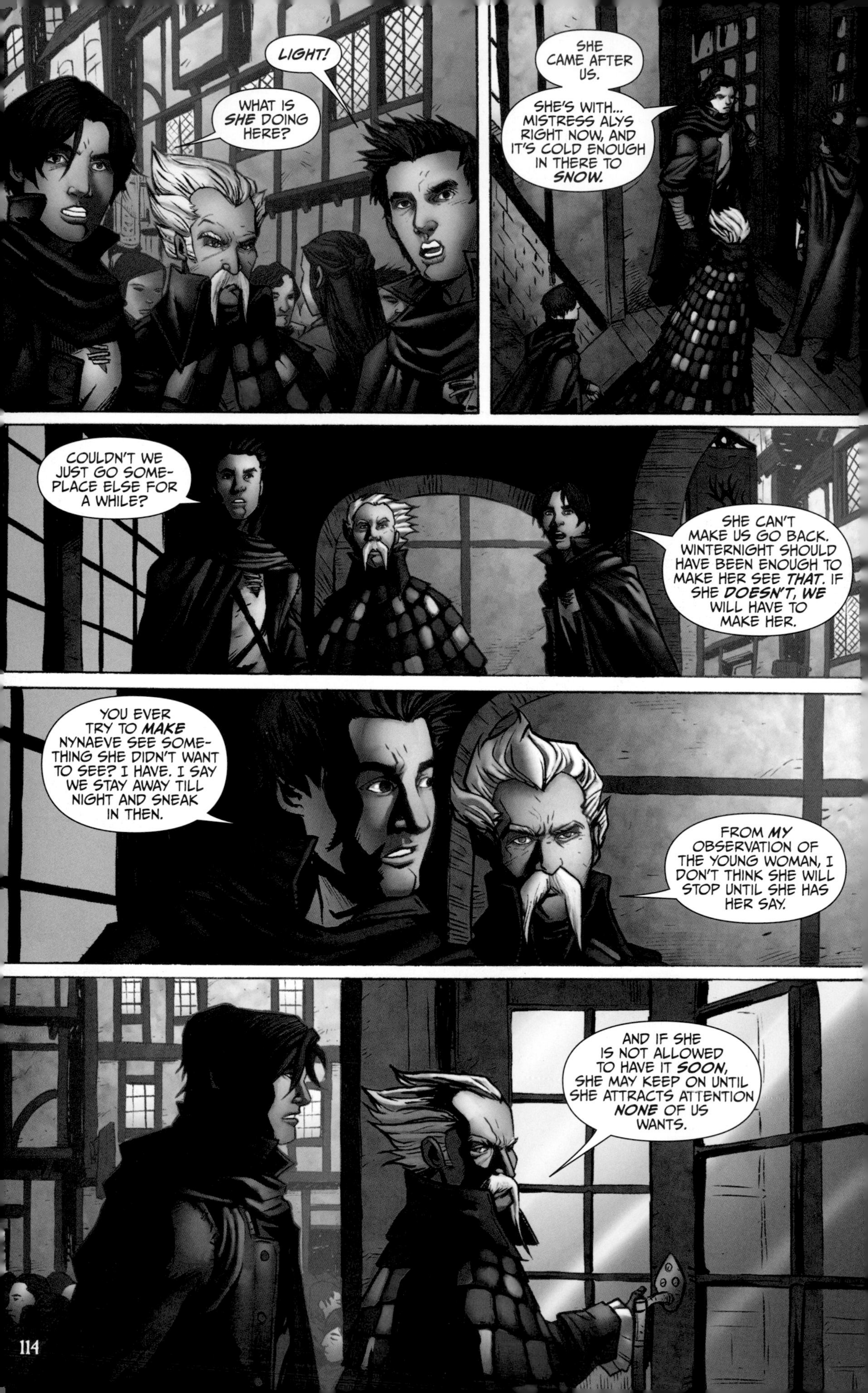
LIGHT!
WHAT IS SHE DOING HERE?
SHE CAME AFTER US.
SHE'S WITH... MISTRESS ALYS RIGHT NOW, AND IT'S COLD ENOUGH IN THERE TO SNOW.
COULDN'T WE JUST GO SOME-PLACE ELSE FOR A WHILE?
SHE CAN'T MAKE US GO BACK. WINTERNIGHT SHOULD HAVE BEEN ENOUGH TO MAKE HER SEE THAT. IF SHE DOESN'T, WE WILL HAVE TO MAKE HER.
YOU EVER TRY TO MAKE NYNAEVE SEE SOME-THING SHE DIDN'T WANT TO SEE? I HAVE. I SAY WE STAY AWAY TILL NIGHT AND SNEAK IN THEN.
FROM MY OBSERVATION OF THE YOUNG WOMAN, I DON'T THINK SHE WILL STOP UNTIL SHE HAS HER SAY.
AND IF SHE IS NOT ALLOWED TO HAVE IT SOON, SHE MAY KEEP ON UNTIL SHE ATTRACTS ATTENTION NONE OF US WANTS.

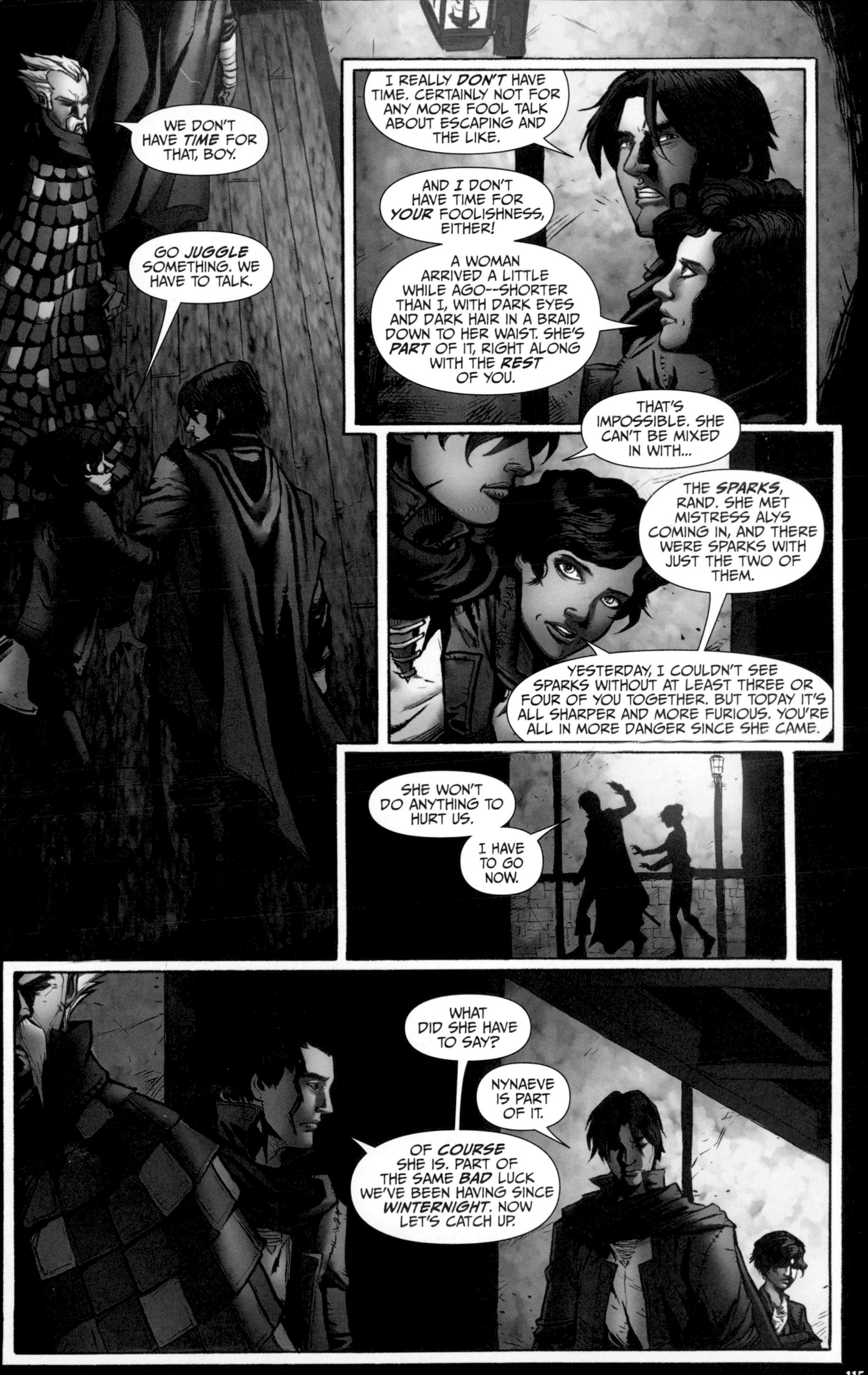
WE DON'T HAVE TIME FOR THAT, BOY.
GO JUGGLE SOMETHING. WE HAVE TO TALK.
I REALLY DON'T HAVE TIME. CERTAINLY NOT FOR ANY MORE FOOL TALK ABOUT ESCAPING AND THE LIKE.
AND I DON'T HAVE TIME FOR YOUR FOOLISHNESS, EITHER!
A WOMAN ARRIVED A LITTLE WHILE AGO--SHORTER THAN I, WITH DARK EYES AND DARK HAIR IN A BRAID DOWN TO HER WAIST. SHE'S PART OF IT, RIGHT ALONG WITH THE REST OF YOU.
THAT'S IMPOSSIBLE. SHE CAN'T BE MIXED IN WITH...
THE SPARKS, RAND. SHE MET MISTRESS ALYS COMING IN, AND THERE WERE SPARKS WITH JUST THE TWO OF THEM.
YESTERDAY, I COULDN'T SEE SPARKS WITHOUT AT LEAST THREE OR FOUR OF YOU TOGETHER. BUT TODAY IT'S ALL SHARPER AND MORE FURIOUS. YOU'RE ALL IN MORE DANGER SINCE SHE CAME.
SHE WON'T DO ANYTHING TO HURT US.
I HAVE TO GO NOW.
WHAT DID SHE HAVE TO SAY?
NYNAEVE IS PART OF IT.
OF COURSE SHE IS. PART OF THE SAME BAD LUCK WE'VE BEEN HAVING SINCE WINTERNIGHT. NOW LET'S CATCH UP.

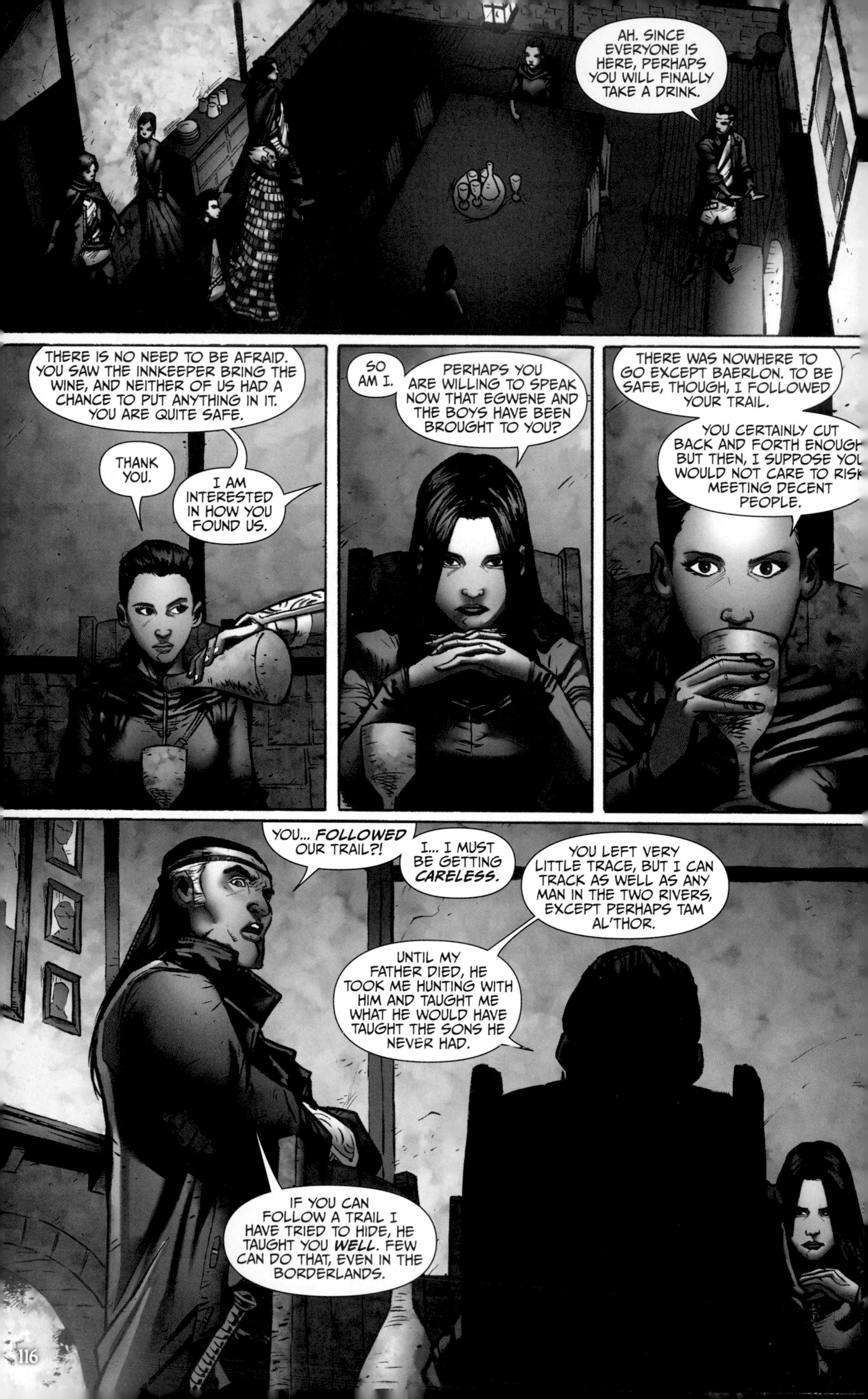
AH. SINCE EVERYONE IS HERE, PERHAPS YOU WILL FINALLY TAKE A DRINK.
THERE IS NO NEED TO BE AFRAID. YOU SAW THE INNKEEPER BRING THE WINE, AND NEITHER OF US HAD A CHANCE TO PUT ANYTHING IN IT. YOU ARE QUITE SAFE.
THANK YOU.
I AM INTERESTED IN HOW YOU FOUND US.
SO AM I.
PERHAPS YOU ARE WILLING TO SPEAK NOW THAT EGWENE AND THE BOYS HAVE BEEN BROUGHT TO YOU?
THERE WAS NOWHERE TO GO EXCEPT BAERLON. TO BE SAFE, THOUGH, I FOLLOWED YOUR TRAIL.
YOU CERTAINLY CUT BACK AND FORTH ENOUGH BUT THEN, I SUPPOSE YOU WOULD NOT CARE TO RISK MEETING DECENT PEOPLE.
YOU... FOLLOWED OUR TRAIL?!
I... I MUST BE GETTING CARELESS.
YOU LEFT VERY LITTLE TRACE, BUT I CAN TRACK AS WELL AS ANY MAN IN THE TWO RIVERS, EXCEPT PERHAPS TAM AL'THOR.
UNTIL MY FATHER DIED, HE TOOK ME HUNTING WITH HIM AND TAUGHT ME WHAT HE WOULD HAVE TAUGHT THE SONS HE NEVER HAD.
IF YOU CAN FOLLOW A TRAIL I HAVE TRIED TO HIDE, HE TAUGHT YOU WELL. FEW CAN DO THAT, EVEN IN THE BORDERLANDS.

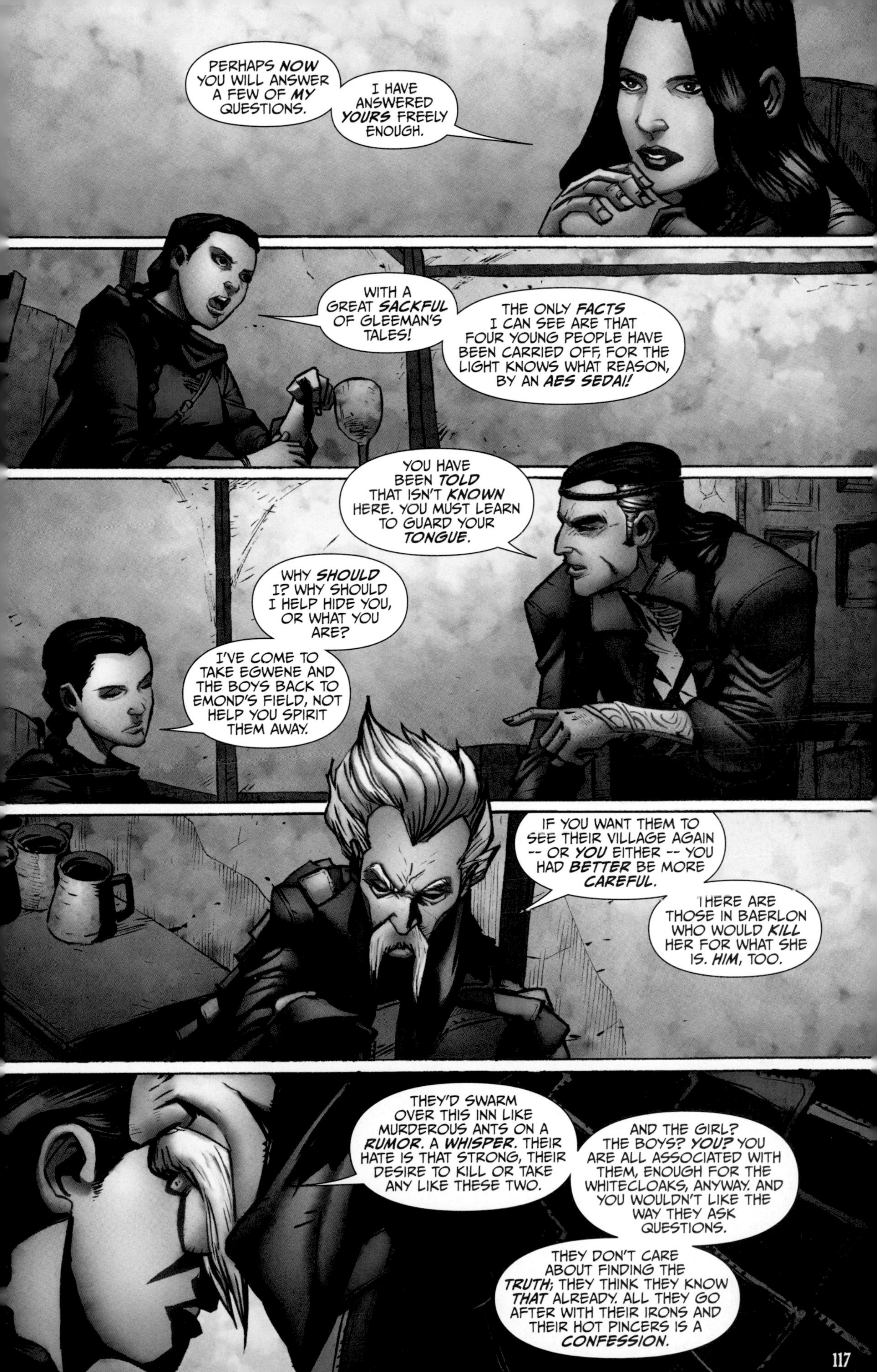
PERHAPS NOW YOU WILL ANSWER A FEW OF MY QUESTIONS.
I HAVE ANSWERED YOURS FREELY ENOUGH.
WITH A GREAT SACKFUL OF GLEEMAN'S TALES!
THE ONLY FACTS I CAN SEE ARE THAT FOUR YOUNG PEOPLE HAVE BEEN CARRIED OFF, FOR THE LIGHT KNOWS WHAT REASON, BY AN AES SEDAI!
YOU HAVE BEEN TOLD THAT ISN'T KNOWN HERE. YOU MUST LEARN TO GUARD YOUR TONGUE.
WHY SHOULD I? WHY SHOULD I HELP HIDE YOU, OR WHAT YOU ARE?
I'VE COME TO TAKE EGWENE AND THE BOYS BACK TO EMOND'S FIELD, NOT HELP YOU SPIRIT THEM AWAY.
IF YOU WANT THEM TO SEE THEIR VILLAGE AGAIN -- OR YOU EITHER -- YOU HAD BETTER BE MORE CAREFUL.
THERE ARE THOSE IN BAERLON WHO WOULD KILL HER FOR WHAT SHE IS. HIM, TOO.
THEY'D SWARM OVER THIS INN LIKE MURDEROUS ANTS ON A RUMOR. A WHISPER. THEIR HATE IS THAT STRONG, THEIR DESIRE TO KILL OR TAKE ANY LIKE THESE TWO.
AND THE GIRL? THE BOYS? YOU? YOU ARE ALL ASSOCIATED WITH THEM, ENOUGH FOR THE WHITECLOAKS, ANYWAY. AND YOU WOULDN'T LIKE THE WAY THEY ASK QUESTIONS.
THEY DON'T CARE ABOUT FINDING THE TRUTH; THEY THINK THEY KNOW THAT ALREADY. ALL THEY GO AFTER WITH THEIR IRONS AND THEIR HOT PINCERS IS A CONFESSION.

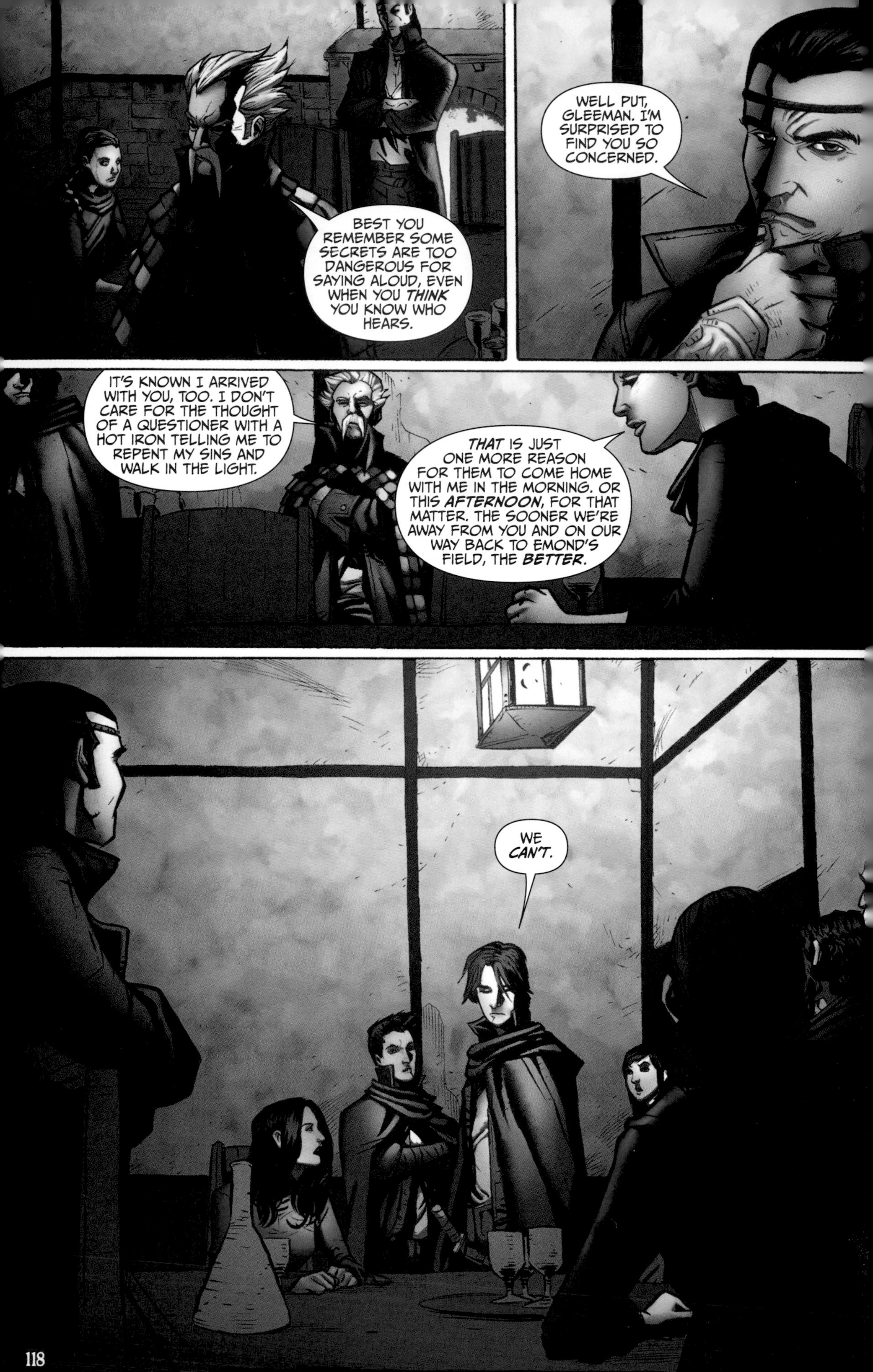
BEST YOU REMEMBER SOME SECRETS ARE TOO DANGEROUS FOR SAYING ALOUD, EVEN WHEN YOU *THINK* YOU KNOW WHO HEARS.
WELL PUT, GLEEMAN. I'M SURPRISED TO FIND YOU SO CONCERNED.
IT'S KNOWN I ARRIVED WITH YOU, TOO. I DON'T CARE FOR THE THOUGHT OF A QUESTIONER WITH A HOT IRON TELLING ME TO REPENT MY SINS AND WALK IN THE LIGHT.
THAT IS JUST ONE MORE REASON FOR THEM TO COME HOME WITH ME IN THE MORNING. OR THIS *AFTERNOON*, FOR THAT MATTER. THE SOONER WE'RE AWAY FROM YOU AND ON OUR WAY BACK TO EMOND'S FIELD, THE *BETTER*.
WE *CAN'T*.

IF WE GO BACK TO EMOND'S FIELD, THE TROLLOCS WILL COME BACK, TOO. THEY'RE...

THEY'RE *HUNTING* US. I DON'T KNOW *WHY*, BUT THEY ARE. MAYBE WE CAN FIND OUT IN TAR VALON. MAYBE WE CAN FIND OUT HOW TO STOP IT. IT'S THE *ONLY* WAY.

YOU SOUND JUST LIKE *TAM!* HE HAD HIMSELF *CARRIED* TO THE VILLAGE MEETING AND TRIED TO CONVINCE *EVERYBODY*.

LIGHT KNOWS HOW YOUR MISTRESS ALYS MANAGED TO MAKE HIM *BELIEVE*; HE HAS A MITE OF *SENSE* USUALLY. MORE THAN *MOST* MEN.

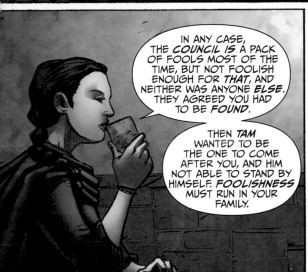

IN ANY CASE, THE *COUNCIL IS* A PACK OF FOOLS MOST OF THE TIME, BUT NOT FOOLISH ENOUGH FOR *THAT*, AND NEITHER WAS ANYONE *ELSE*. THEY AGREED YOU HAD TO BE *FOUND*.

THEN *TAM* WANTED TO BE THE ONE TO COME AFTER YOU, AND HIM NOT ABLE TO STAND BY HIMSELF. *FOOLISHNESS* MUST RUN IN YOUR FAMILY.

WISDOM. YOU MUST BELIEVE THAT THEY ARE SAFER WITH ME THAN THEY WOULD BE BACK IN THE TWO RIVERS.

SAFER! YOU ARE THE ONE WHO BROUGHT THEM HERE, WHERE THE *WHITECLOAKS* ARE! THE WHITECLOAKS WHO, IF THE GLEEMAN IS TELLING THE TRUTH, MAY HARM THEM BECAUSE OF YOU!

TELL ME *HOW* THEY ARE *SAFER*, AES SEDAI!

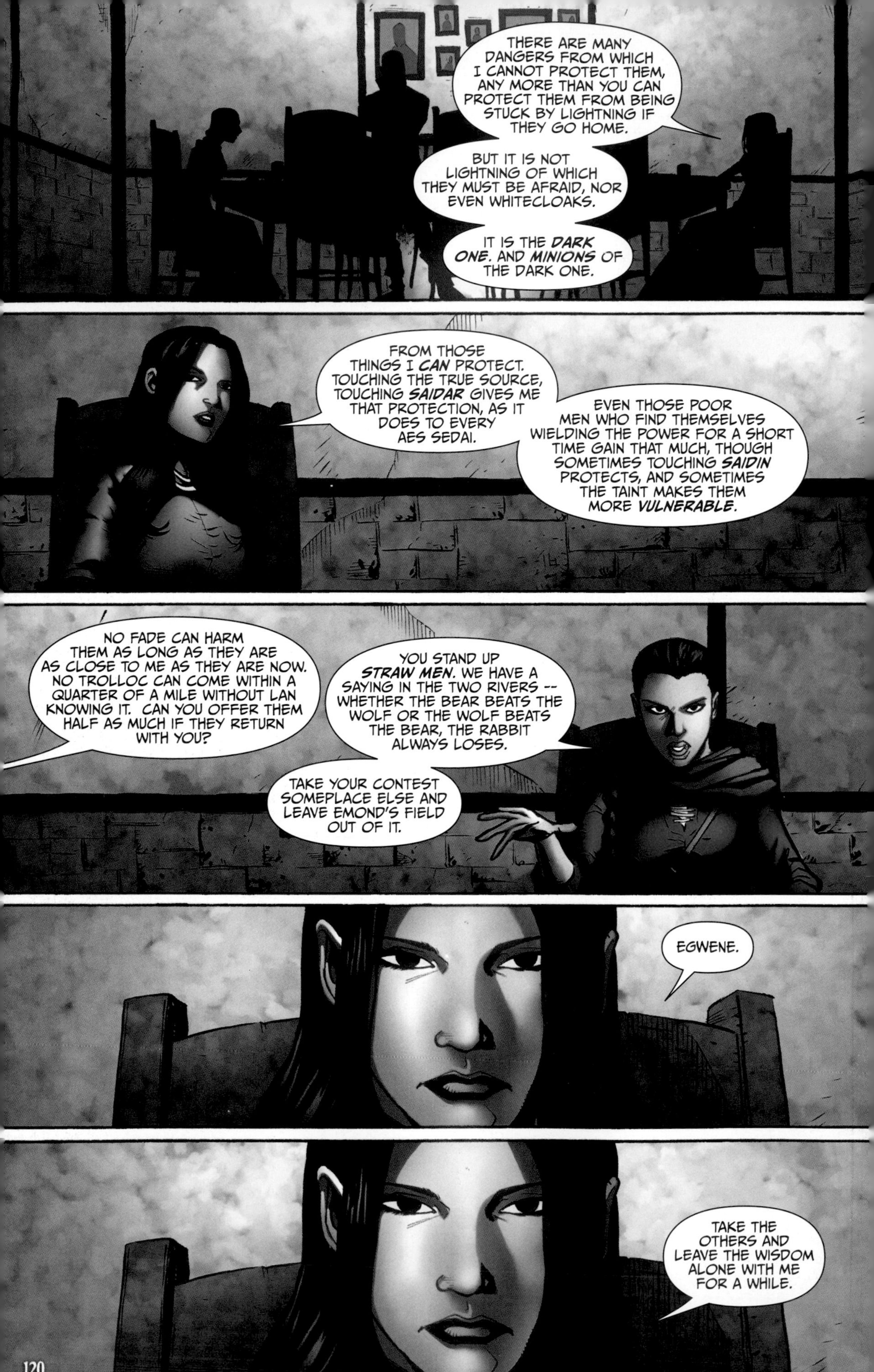
THERE ARE MANY DANGERS FROM WHICH I CANNOT PROTECT THEM, ANY MORE THAN YOU CAN PROTECT THEM FROM BEING STUCK BY LIGHTNING IF THEY GO HOME.
BUT IT IS NOT LIGHTNING OF WHICH THEY MUST BE AFRAID, NOR EVEN WHITECLOAKS.
IT IS THE DARK ONE. AND MINIONS OF THE DARK ONE.
FROM THOSE THINGS I CAN PROTECT. TOUCHING THE TRUE SOURCE, TOUCHING SAIDAR GIVES ME THAT PROTECTION, AS IT DOES TO EVERY AES SEDAI.
EVEN THOSE POOR MEN WHO FIND THEMSELVES WIELDING THE POWER FOR A SHORT TIME GAIN THAT MUCH, THOUGH SOMETIMES TOUCHING SAIDIN PROTECTS, AND SOMETIMES THE TAINT MAKES THEM MORE VULNERABLE.
NO FADE CAN HARM THEM AS LONG AS THEY ARE AS CLOSE TO ME AS THEY ARE NOW. NO TROLLOC CAN COME WITHIN A QUARTER OF A MILE WITHOUT LAN KNOWING IT. CAN YOU OFFER THEM HALF AS MUCH IF THEY RETURN WITH YOU?
YOU STAND UP STRAW MEN. WE HAVE A SAYING IN THE TWO RIVERS -- WHETHER THE BEAR BEATS THE WOLF OR THE WOLF BEATS THE BEAR, THE RABBIT ALWAYS LOSES.
TAKE YOUR CONTEST SOMEPLACE ELSE AND LEAVE EMOND'S FIELD OUT OF IT.
EGWENE.
TAKE THE OTHERS AND LEAVE THE WISDOM ALONE WITH ME FOR A WHILE.

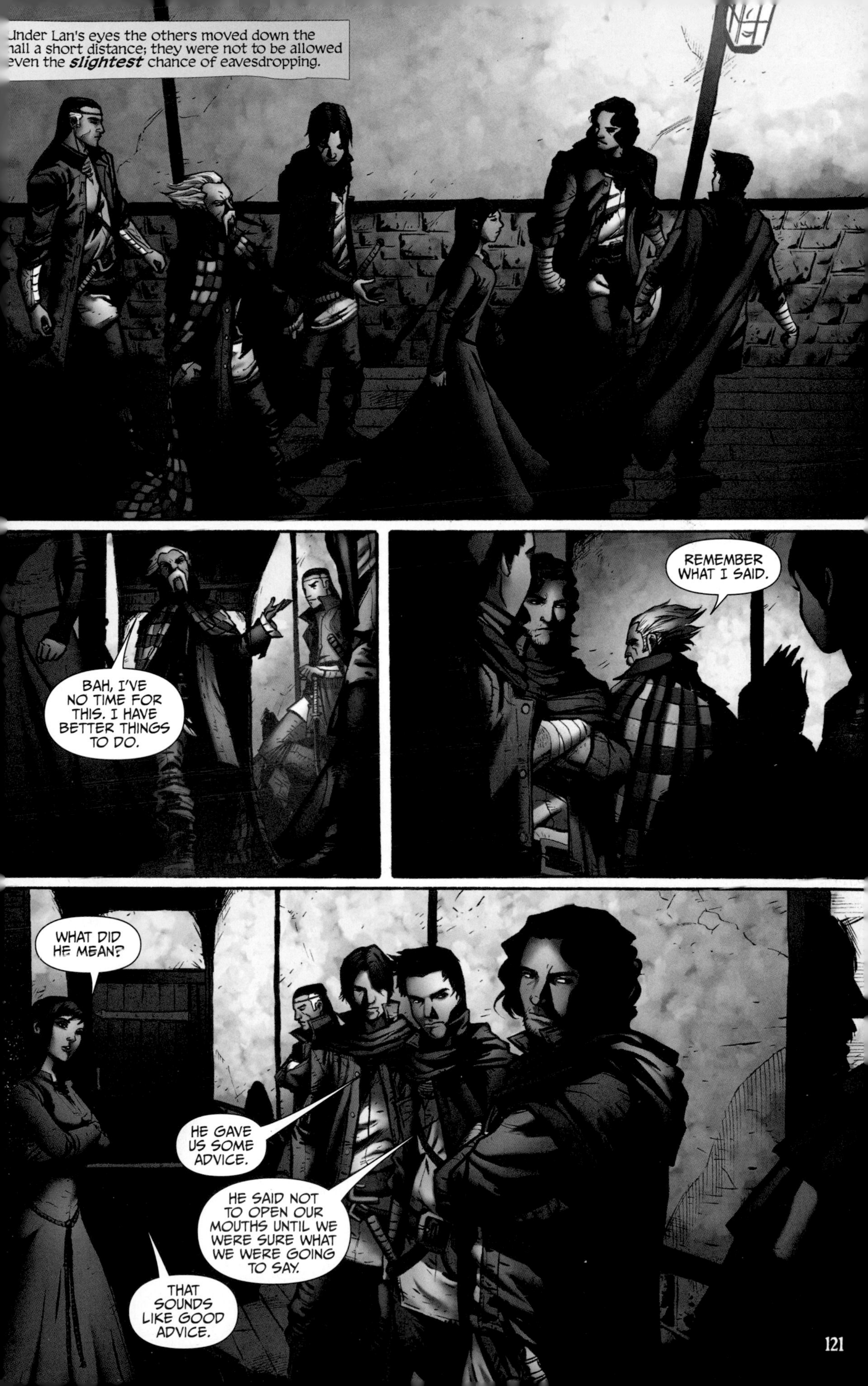
Under Lan's eyes the others moved down the hall a short distance; they were not to be allowed even the *slightest* chance of eavesdropping.
BAH, I'VE NO TIME FOR THIS. I HAVE BETTER THINGS TO DO.
REMEMBER WHAT I SAID.
WHAT DID HE MEAN?
HE GAVE US SOME ADVICE.
HE SAID NOT TO OPEN OUR MOUTHS UNTIL WE WERE SURE WHAT WE WERE GOING TO SAY.
THAT SOUNDS LIKE GOOD ADVICE.

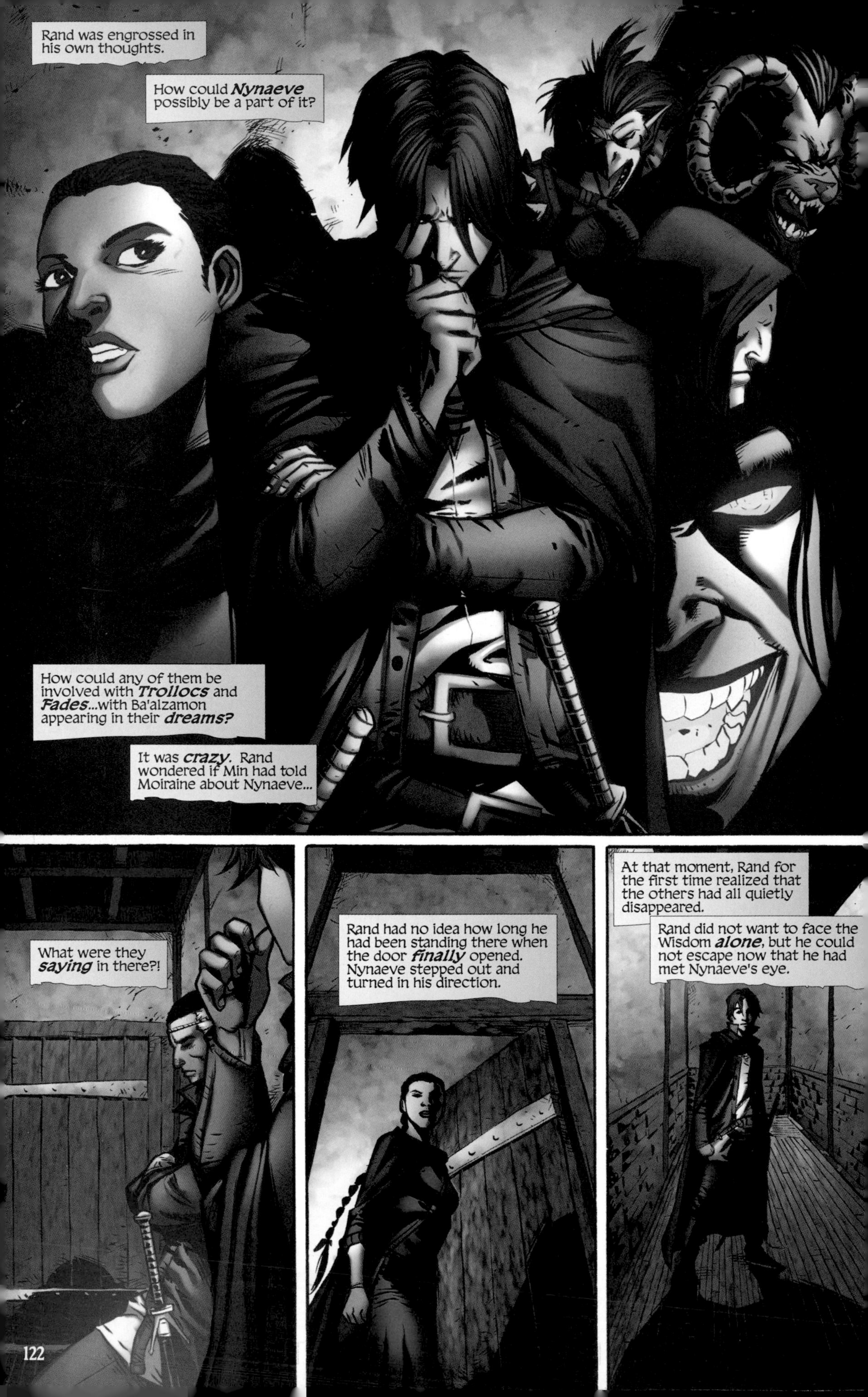
Rand was engrossed in his own thoughts.
How could Nynaeve possibly be a part of it?
How could any of them be involved with Trollocs and Fades...with Ba'alzamon appearing in their dreams?
It was crazy. Rand wondered if Min had told Moiraine about Nynaeve...
What were they saying in there?!
Rand had no idea how long he had been standing there when the door finally opened. Nynaeve stepped out and turned in his direction.
At that moment, Rand for the first time realized that the others had all quietly disappeared.
Rand did not want to face the Wisdom alone, but he could not escape now that he had met Nynaeve's eye.

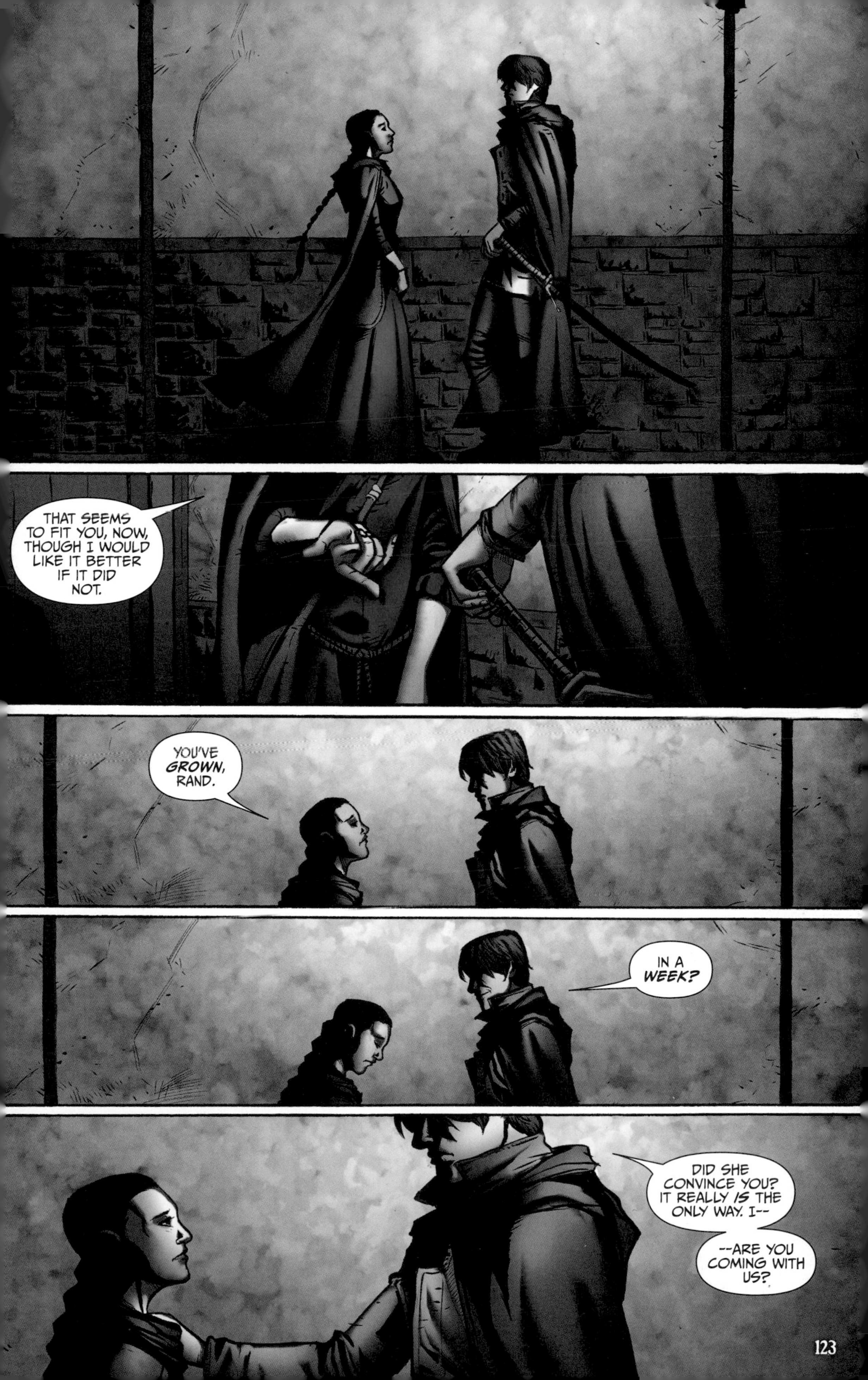
THAT SEEMS TO FIT YOU, NOW, THOUGH I WOULD LIKE IT BETTER IF IT DID NOT.
YOU'VE *GROWN*, RAND.
IN A *WEEK?*
DID SHE CONVINCE YOU? IT REALLY *IS* THE ONLY WAY. I--
--ARE YOU COMING WITH US?

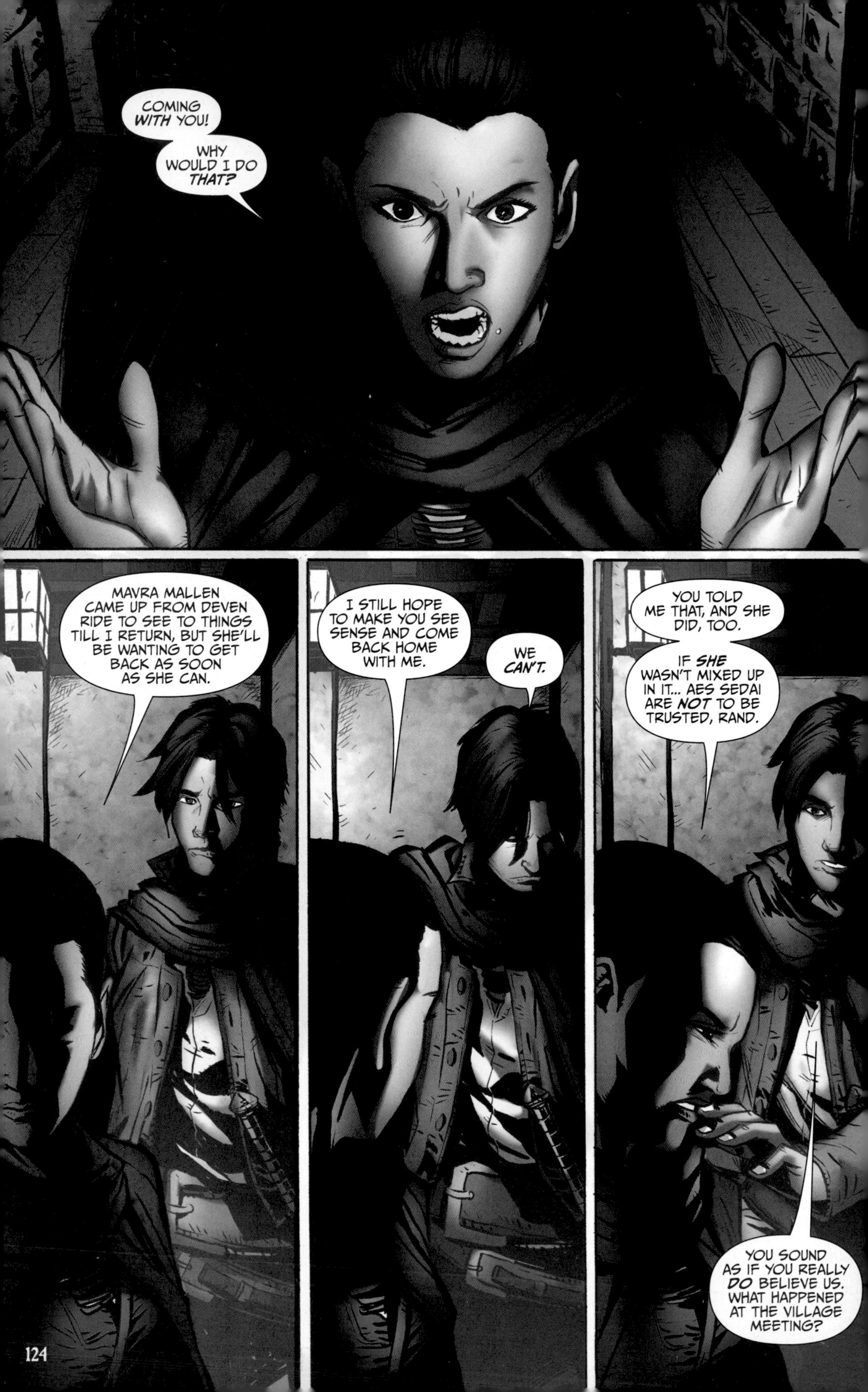
COMING WITH YOU!
WHY WOULD I DO THAT?
MAVRA MALLEN CAME UP FROM DEVEN RIDE TO SEE TO THINGS TILL I RETURN, BUT SHE'LL BE WANTING TO GET BACK AS SOON AS SHE CAN.
I STILL HOPE TO MAKE YOU SEE SENSE AND COME BACK HOME WITH ME.
WE CAN'T.
YOU TOLD ME THAT, AND SHE DID, TOO.
IF SHE WASN'T MIXED UP IN IT... AES SEDAI ARE NOT TO BE TRUSTED, RAND.
YOU SOUND AS IF YOU REALLY DO BELIEVE US. WHAT HAPPENED AT THE VILLAGE MEETING?

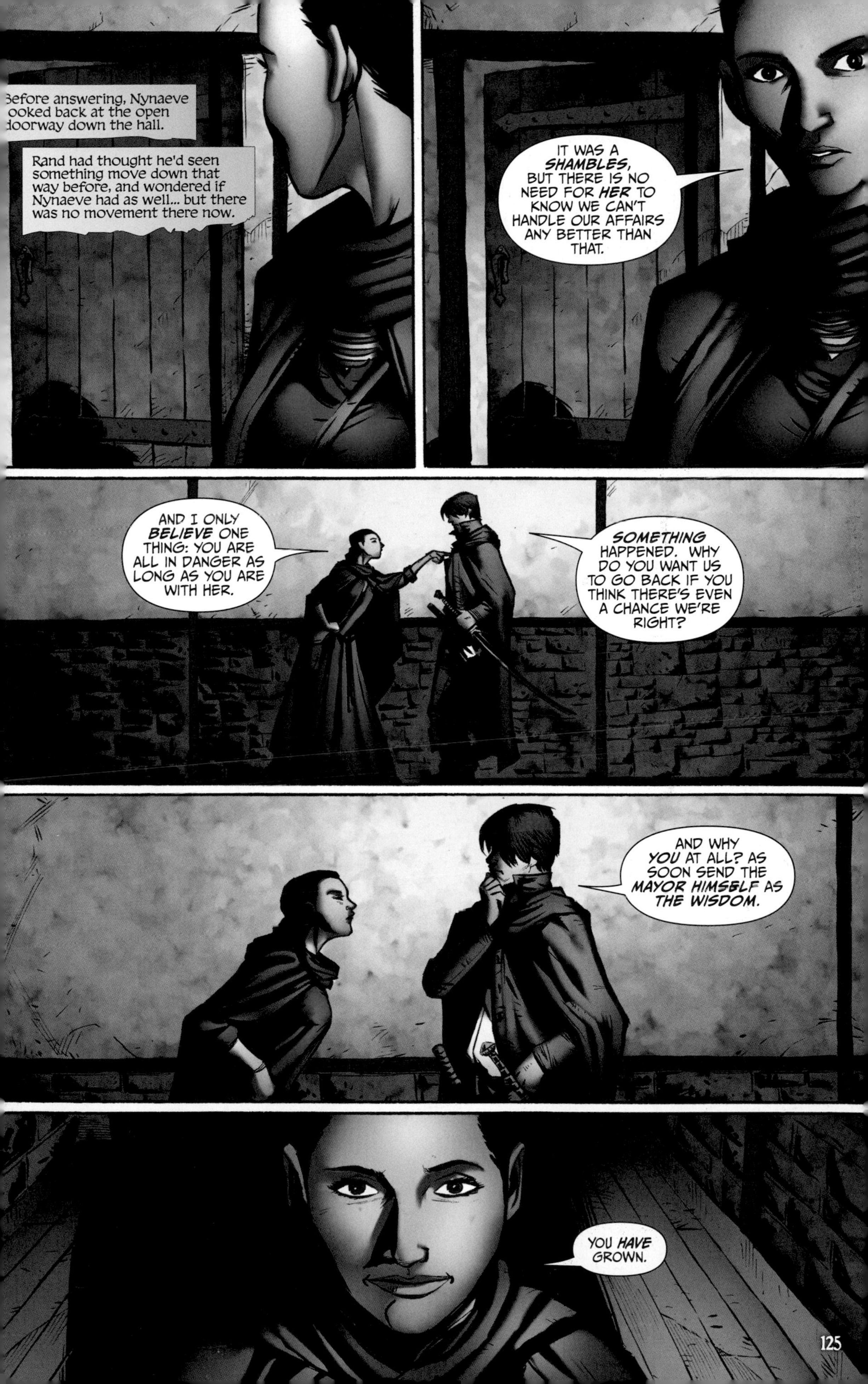
Before answering, Nynaeve looked back at the open doorway down the hall.
Rand had thought he'd seen something move down that way before, and wondered if Nynaeve had as well... but there was no movement there now.
IT WAS A SHAMBLES, BUT THERE IS NO NEED FOR HER TO KNOW WE CAN'T HANDLE OUR AFFAIRS ANY BETTER THAN THAT.
SOMETHING HAPPENED. WHY DO YOU WANT US TO GO BACK IF YOU THINK THERE'S EVEN A CHANCE WE'RE RIGHT?
AND I ONLY BELIEVE ONE THING: YOU ARE ALL IN DANGER AS LONG AS YOU ARE WITH HER.
AND WHY YOU AT ALL? AS SOON SEND THE MAYOR HIMSELF AS THE WISDOM.
YOU HAVE GROWN.

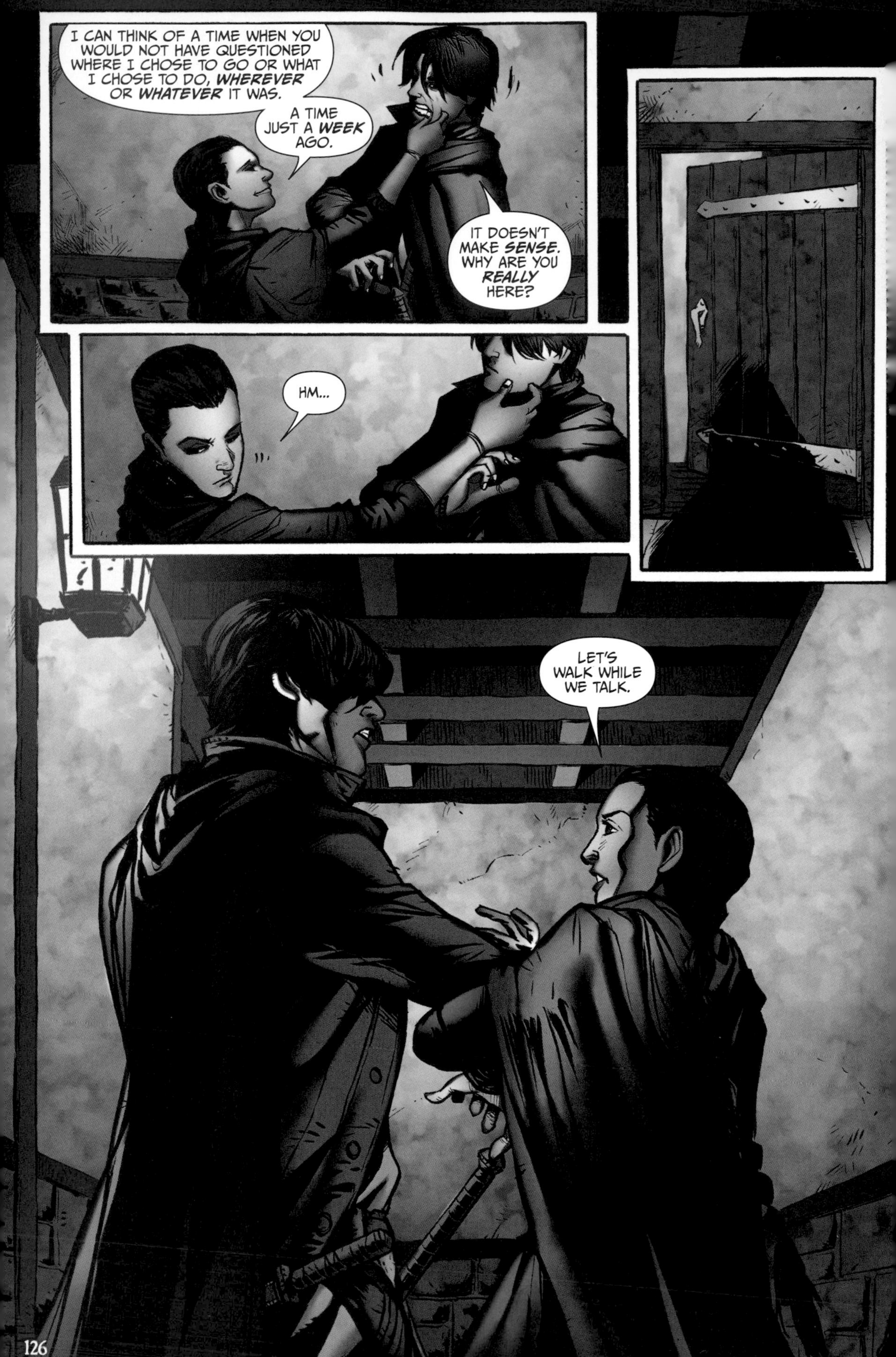
I CAN THINK OF A TIME WHEN YOU WOULD NOT HAVE QUESTIONED WHERE I CHOSE TO GO OR WHAT I CHOSE TO DO, WHEREVER OR WHATEVER IT WAS.
A TIME JUST A WEEK AGO.
IT DOESN'T MAKE SENSE. WHY ARE YOU REALLY HERE?
HM...
LET'S WALK WHILE WE TALK.

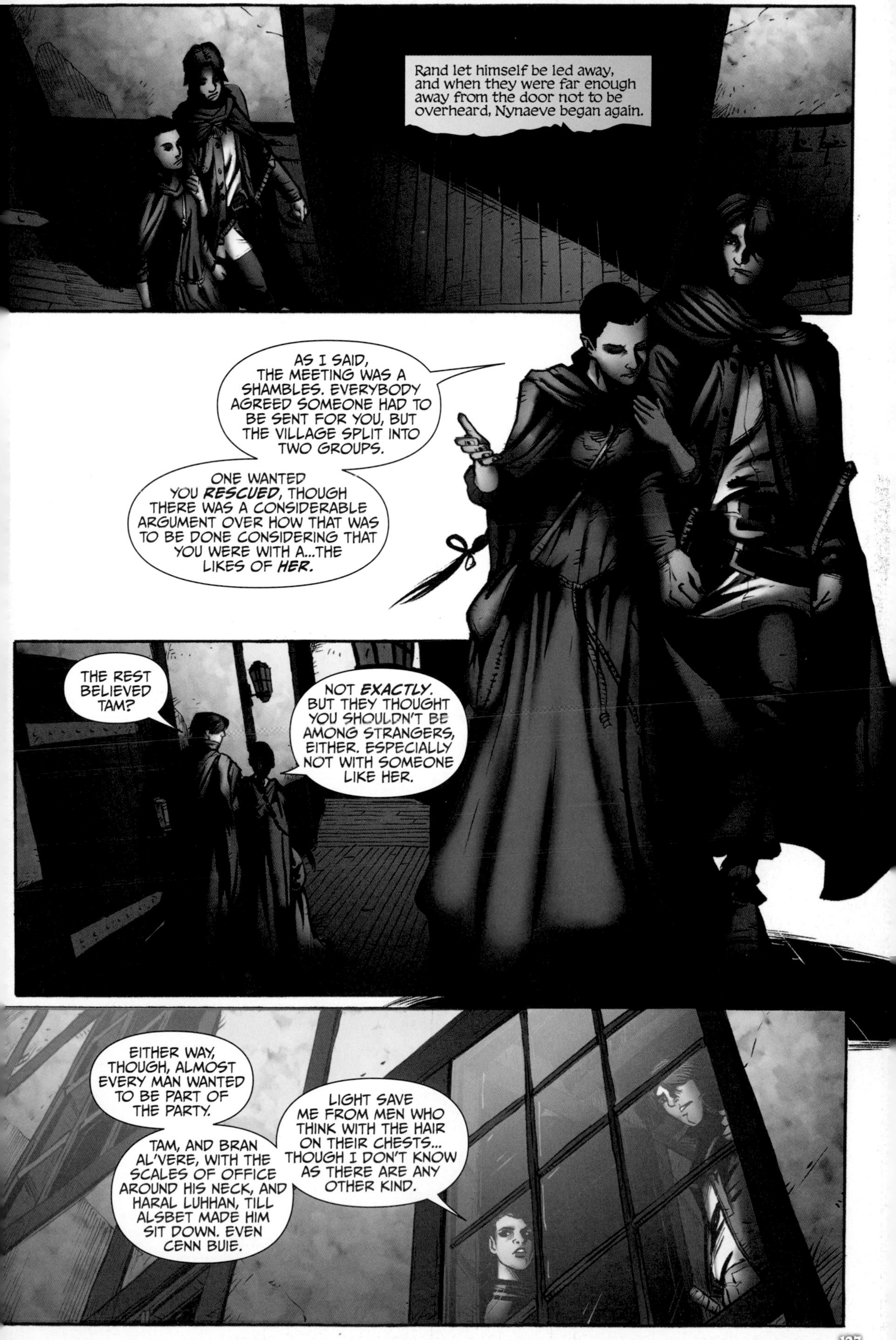
Rand let himself be led away, and when they were far enough away from the door not to be overheard, Nynaeve began again.
AS I SAID, THE MEETING WAS A SHAMBLES. EVERYBODY AGREED SOMEONE HAD TO BE SENT FOR YOU, BUT THE VILLAGE SPLIT INTO TWO GROUPS.
ONE WANTED YOU RESCUED, THOUGH THERE WAS A CONSIDERABLE ARGUMENT OVER HOW THAT WAS TO BE DONE CONSIDERING THAT YOU WERE WITH A...THE LIKES OF HER.
THE REST BELIEVED TAM?
NOT EXACTLY. BUT THEY THOUGHT YOU SHOULDN'T BE AMONG STRANGERS, EITHER. ESPECIALLY NOT WITH SOMEONE LIKE HER.
EITHER WAY, THOUGH, ALMOST EVERY MAN WANTED TO BE PART OF THE PARTY.
TAM, AND BRAN AL'VERE, WITH THE SCALES OF OFFICE AROUND HIS NECK, AND HARAL LUHHAN, TILL ALSBET MADE HIM SIT DOWN. EVEN CENN BUIE.
LIGHT SAVE ME FROM MEN WHO THINK WITH THE HAIR ON THEIR CHESTS... THOUGH I DON'T KNOW AS THERE ARE ANY OTHER KIND.

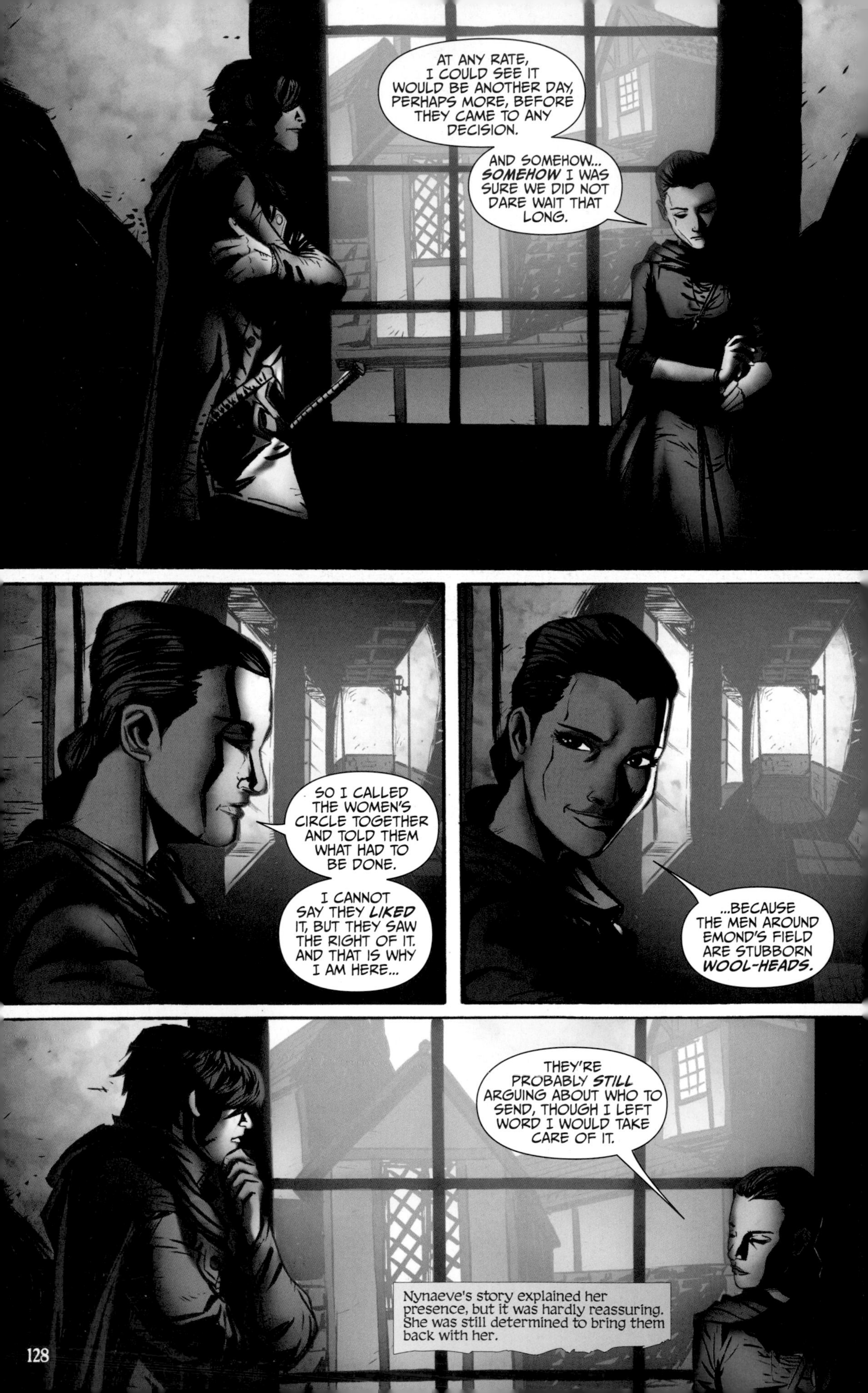
AT ANY RATE, I COULD SEE IT WOULD BE ANOTHER DAY, PERHAPS MORE, BEFORE THEY CAME TO ANY DECISION.
AND SOMEHOW... SOMEHOW I WAS SURE WE DID NOT DARE WAIT THAT LONG.
SO I CALLED THE WOMEN'S CIRCLE TOGETHER AND TOLD THEM WHAT HAD TO BE DONE.
I CANNOT SAY THEY LIKED IT, BUT THEY SAW THE RIGHT OF IT. AND THAT IS WHY I AM HERE...
...BECAUSE THE MEN AROUND EMOND'S FIELD ARE STUBBORN WOOL-HEADS.
THEY'RE PROBABLY STILL ARGUING ABOUT WHO TO SEND, THOUGH I LEFT WORD I WOULD TAKE CARE OF IT.
Nynaeve's story explained her presence, but it was hardly reassuring. She was still determined to bring them back with her.

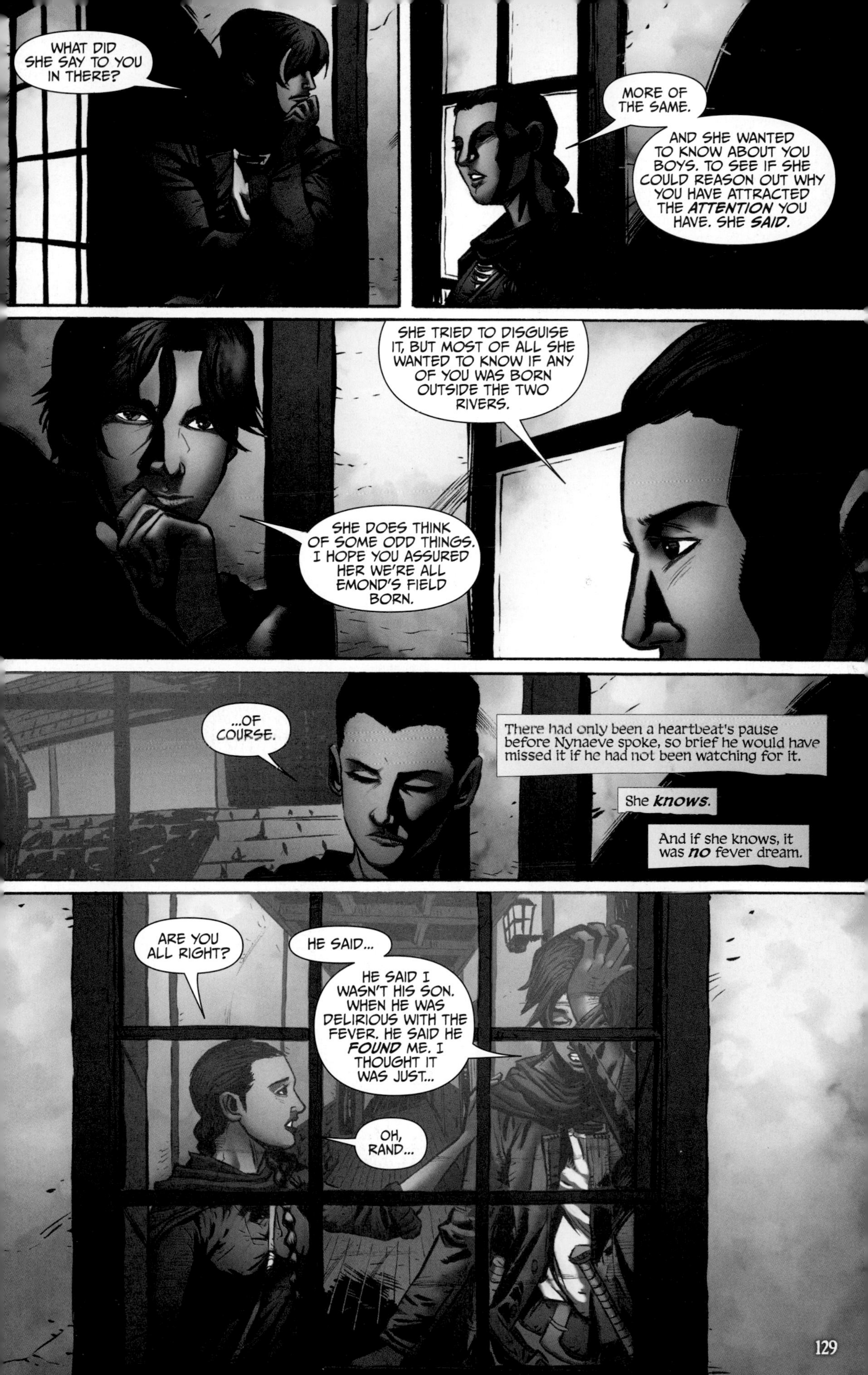
WHAT DID SHE SAY TO YOU IN THERE?
MORE OF THE SAME.
AND SHE WANTED TO KNOW ABOUT YOU BOYS. TO SEE IF SHE COULD REASON OUT WHY YOU HAVE ATTRACTED THE *ATTENTION* YOU HAVE. SHE *SAID*.
SHE TRIED TO DISGUISE IT, BUT MOST OF ALL SHE WANTED TO KNOW IF ANY OF YOU WAS BORN OUTSIDE THE TWO RIVERS.
SHE DOES THINK OF SOME ODD THINGS. I HOPE YOU ASSURED HER WE'RE ALL EMOND'S FIELD BORN.
...OF COURSE.
There had only been a heartbeat's pause before Nynaeve spoke, so brief he would have missed it if he had not been watching for it.
She ***knows***.
And if she knows, it was ***no*** fever dream.
ARE YOU ALL RIGHT?
HE SAID...
HE SAID I WASN'T HIS SON. WHEN HE WAS DELIRIOUS WITH THE FEVER. HE SAID HE *FOUND* ME. I THOUGHT IT WAS JUST...
OH, RAND...

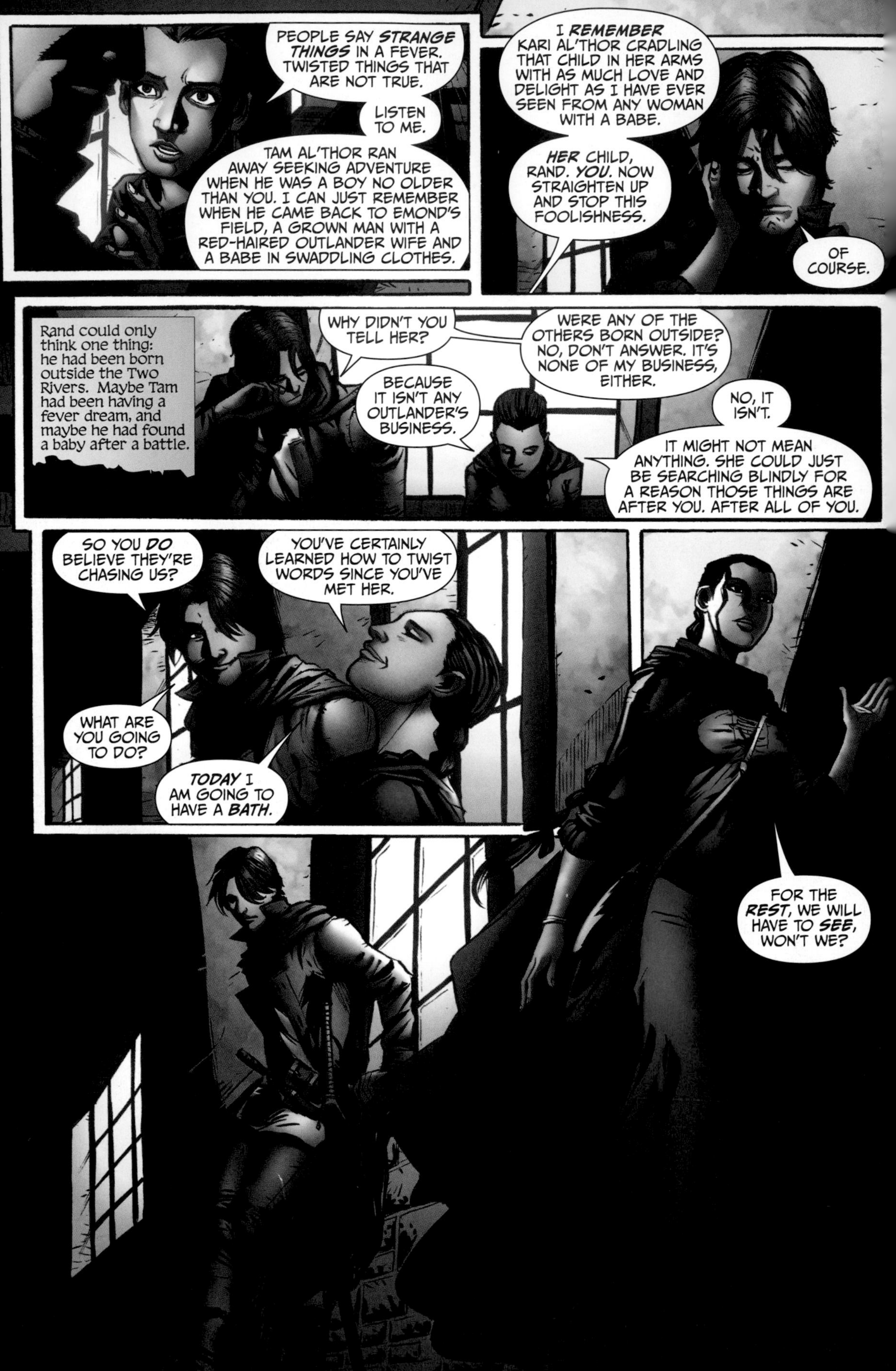
PEOPLE SAY STRANGE THINGS IN A FEVER. TWISTED THINGS THAT ARE NOT TRUE.
LISTEN TO ME.
TAM AL'THOR RAN AWAY SEEKING ADVENTURE WHEN HE WAS A BOY NO OLDER THAN YOU. I CAN JUST REMEMBER WHEN HE CAME BACK TO EMOND'S FIELD, A GROWN MAN WITH A RED-HAIRED OUTLANDER WIFE AND A BABE IN SWADDLING CLOTHES.
I REMEMBER KARI AL'THOR CRADLING THAT CHILD IN HER ARMS WITH AS MUCH LOVE AND DELIGHT AS I HAVE EVER SEEN FROM ANY WOMAN WITH A BABE.
HER CHILD, RAND. YOU. NOW STRAIGHTEN UP AND STOP THIS FOOLISHNESS.
OF COURSE.
Rand could only think one thing: he had been born outside the Two Rivers. Maybe Tam had been having a fever dream, and maybe he had found a baby after a battle.
WHY DIDN'T YOU TELL HER?
BECAUSE IT ISN'T ANY OUTLANDER'S BUSINESS.
WERE ANY OF THE OTHERS BORN OUTSIDE? NO, DON'T ANSWER. IT'S NONE OF MY BUSINESS, EITHER.
NO, IT ISN'T.
IT MIGHT NOT MEAN ANYTHING. SHE COULD JUST BE SEARCHING BLINDLY FOR A REASON THOSE THINGS ARE AFTER YOU. AFTER ALL OF YOU.
SO YOU DO BELIEVE THEY'RE CHASING US?
YOU'VE CERTAINLY LEARNED HOW TO TWIST WORDS SINCE YOU'VE MET HER.
WHAT ARE YOU GOING TO DO?
TODAY I AM GOING TO HAVE A BATH.
FOR THE REST, WE WILL HAVE TO SEE, WON'T WE?

chapter six

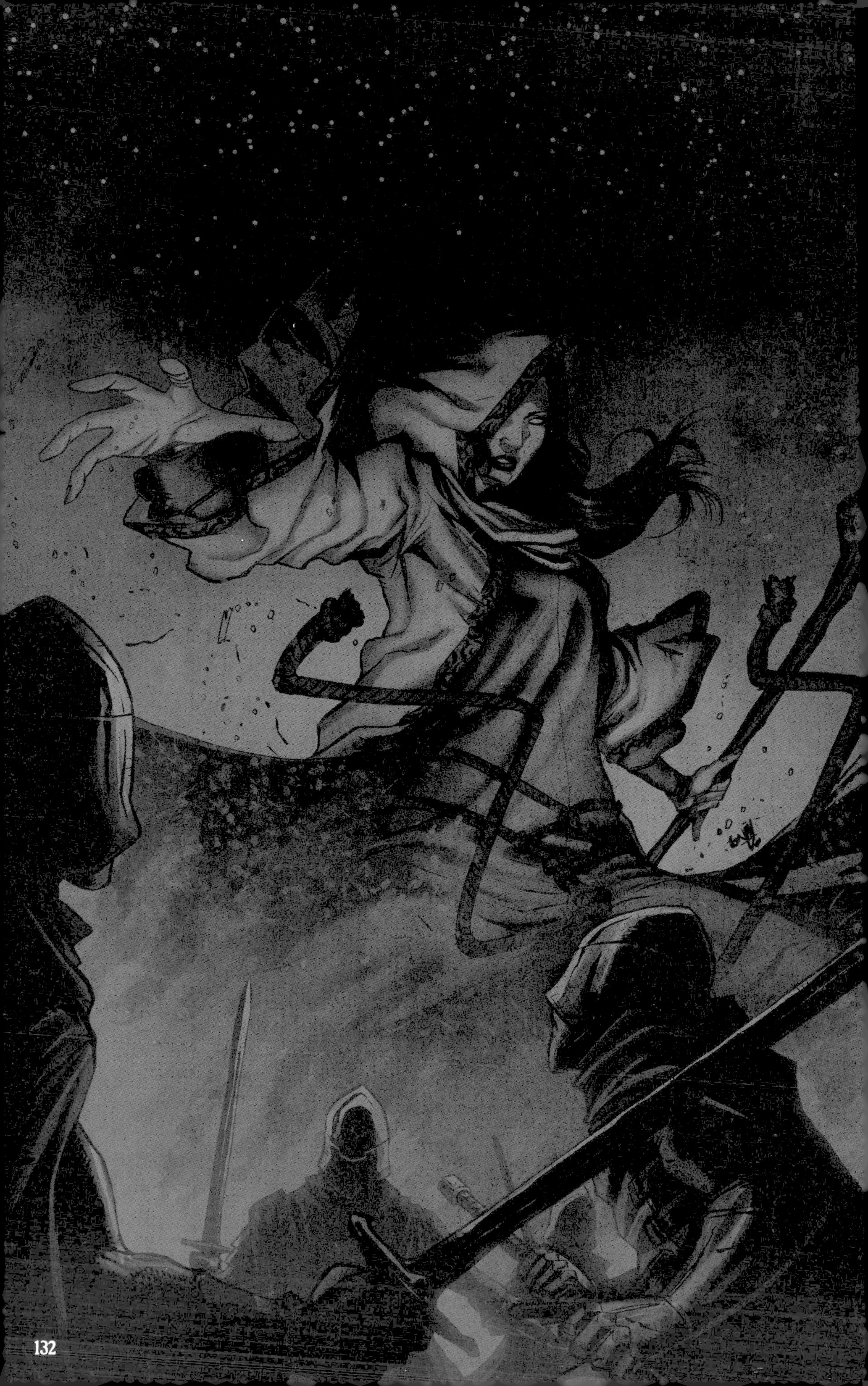

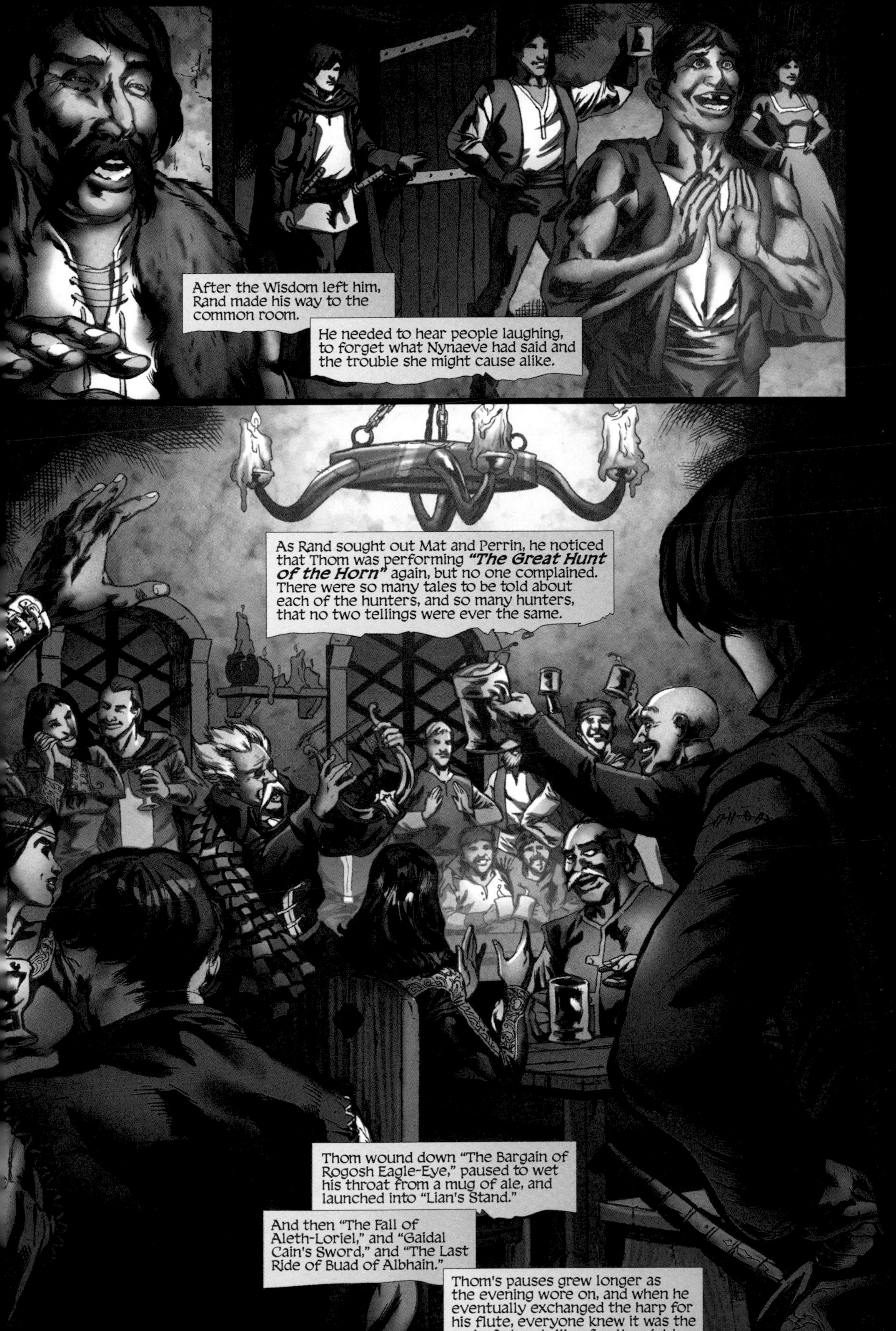
After the Wisdom left him, Rand made his way to the common room.
He needed to hear people laughing, to forget what Nynaeve had said and the trouble she might cause alike.
As Rand sought out Mat and Perrin, he noticed that Thom was performing ***"The Great Hunt of the Horn"*** again, but no one complained. There were so many tales to be told about each of the hunters, and so many hunters, that no two tellings were ever the same.
Thom wound down "The Bargain of Rogosh Eagle-Eye," paused to wet his throat from a mug of ale, and launched into "Lian's Stand."
And then "The Fall of Aleth-Loriel," and "Gaidal Cain's Sword," and "The Last Ride of Buad of Albhain."
Thom's pauses grew longer as the evening wore on, and when he eventually exchanged the harp for his flute, everyone knew it was the end of storytelling for the night.

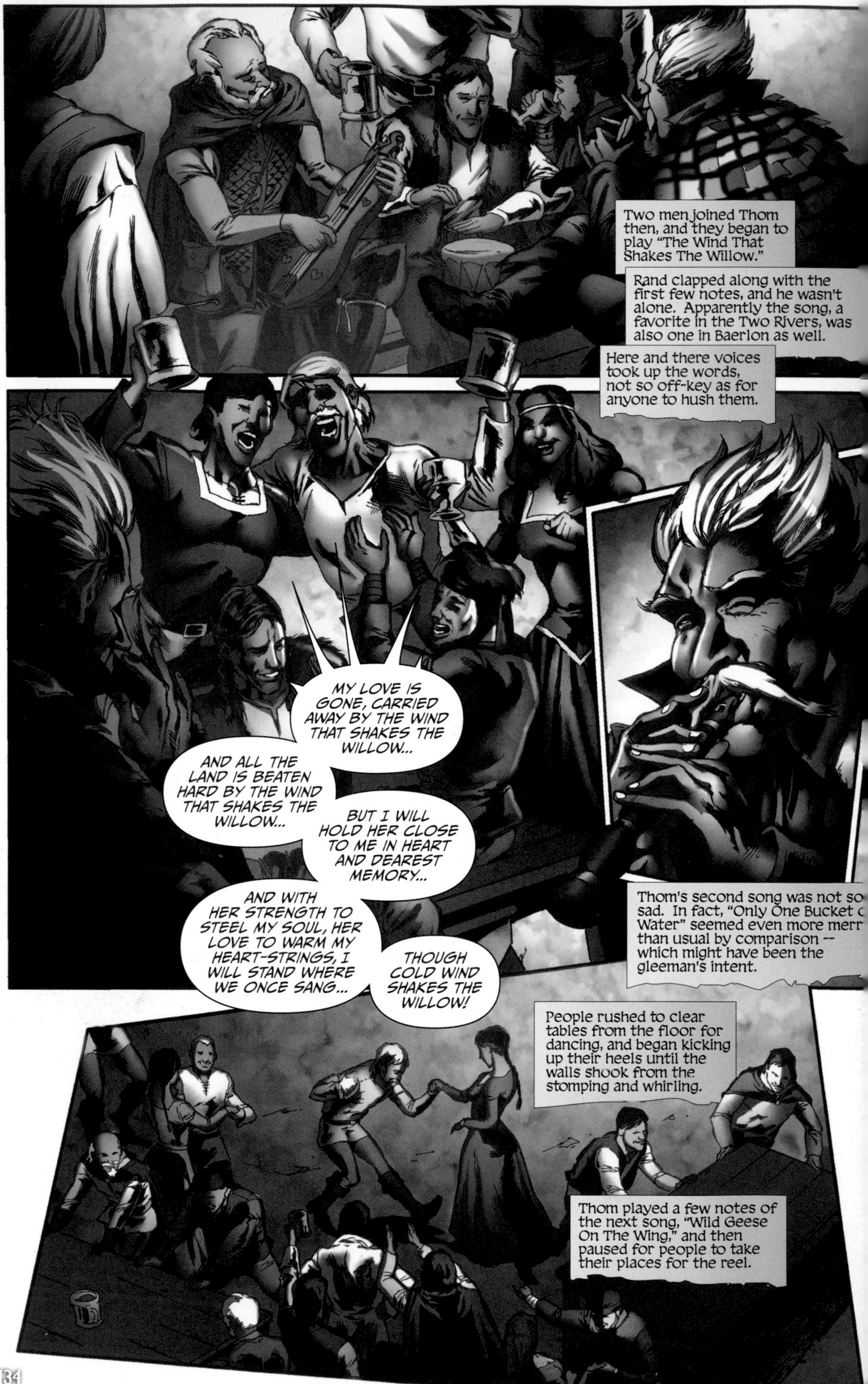

Two men joined Thom then, and they began to play “The Wind That Shakes The Willow.”
Rand clapped along with the first few notes, and he wasn't alone. Apparently the song, a favorite in the Two Rivers, was also one in Baerlon as well.
Here and there voices took up the words, not so off-key as for anyone to hush them.
MY LOVE IS GONE, CARRIED AWAY BY THE WIND THAT SHAKES THE WILLOW...
AND ALL THE LAND IS BEATEN HARD BY THE WIND THAT SHAKES THE WILLOW...
BUT I WILL HOLD HER CLOSE TO ME IN HEART AND DEAREST MEMORY...
AND WITH HER STRENGTH TO STEEL MY SOUL, HER LOVE TO WARM MY HEART-STRINGS, I WILL STAND WHERE WE ONCE SANG...
THOUGH COLD WIND SHAKES THE WILLOW!
Thom's second song was not so sad. In fact, “Only One Bucket o Water” seemed even more merr than usual by comparison -- which might have been the gleeman's intent.
People rushed to clear tables from the floor for dancing, and began kicking up their heels until the walls shook from the stomping and whirling.
Thom played a few notes of the next song, “Wild Geese On The Wing,” and then paused for people to take their places for the reel.

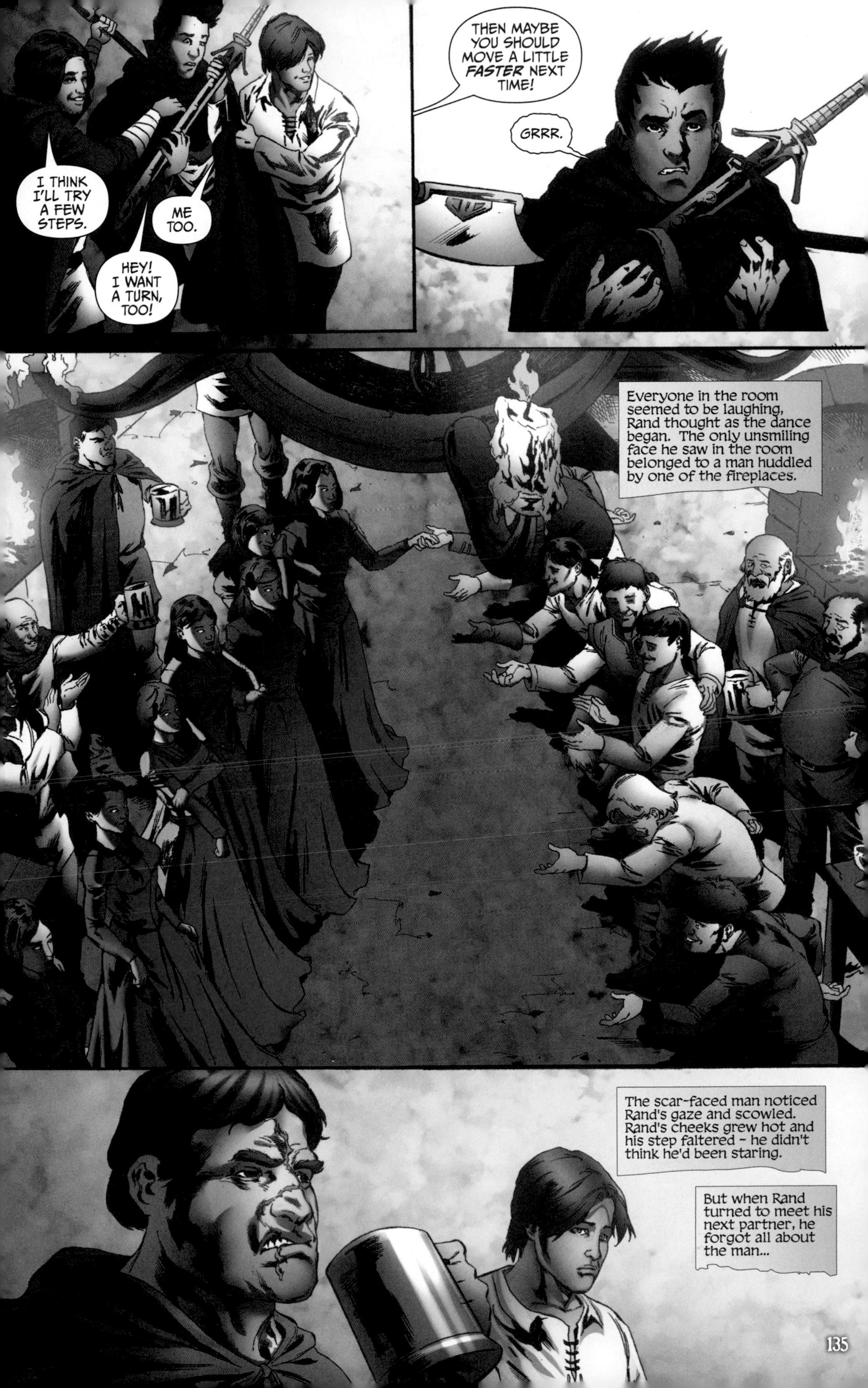
I THINK I'LL TRY A FEW STEPS.
ME TOO.
HEY! I WANT A TURN, TOO!
THEN MAYBE YOU SHOULD MOVE A LITTLE FASTER NEXT TIME!
GRRR.
Everyone in the room seemed to be laughing, Rand thought as the dance began. The only unsmiling face he saw in the room belonged to a man huddled by one of the fireplaces.
The scar-faced man noticed Rand's gaze and scowled. Rand's cheeks grew hot and his step faltered – he didn't think he'd been staring.
But when Rand turned to meet his next partner, he forgot all about the man...

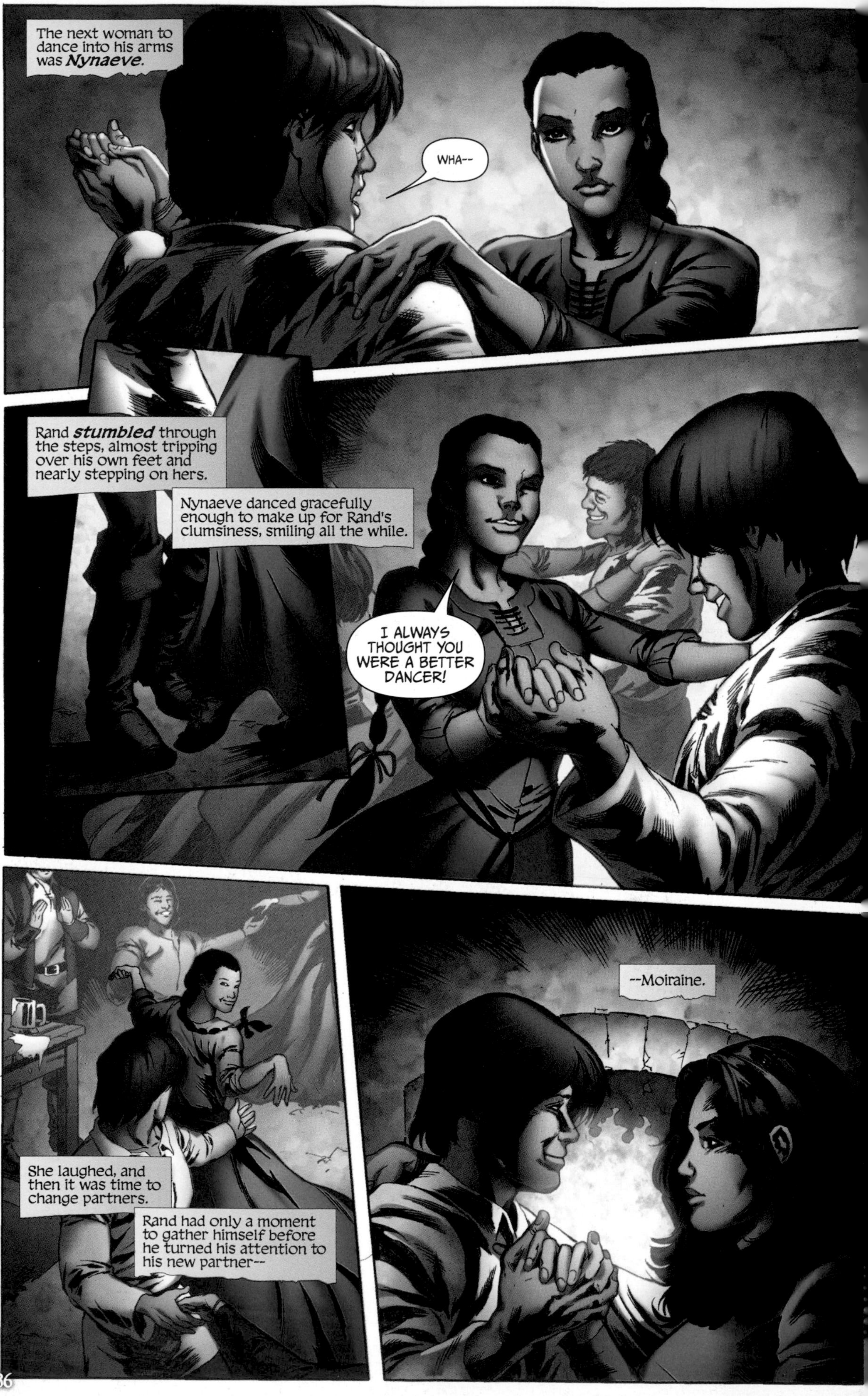

The next woman to dance into his arms was *Nynaeve*.
WHA--
Rand *stumbled* through the steps, almost tripping over his own feet and nearly stepping on hers.
Nynaeve danced gracefully enough to make up for Rand's clumsiness, smiling all the while.
I ALWAYS THOUGHT YOU WERE A BETTER DANCER!
She laughed, and then it was time to change partners.
Rand had only a moment to gather himself before he turned his attention to his new partner--
--Moiraine.

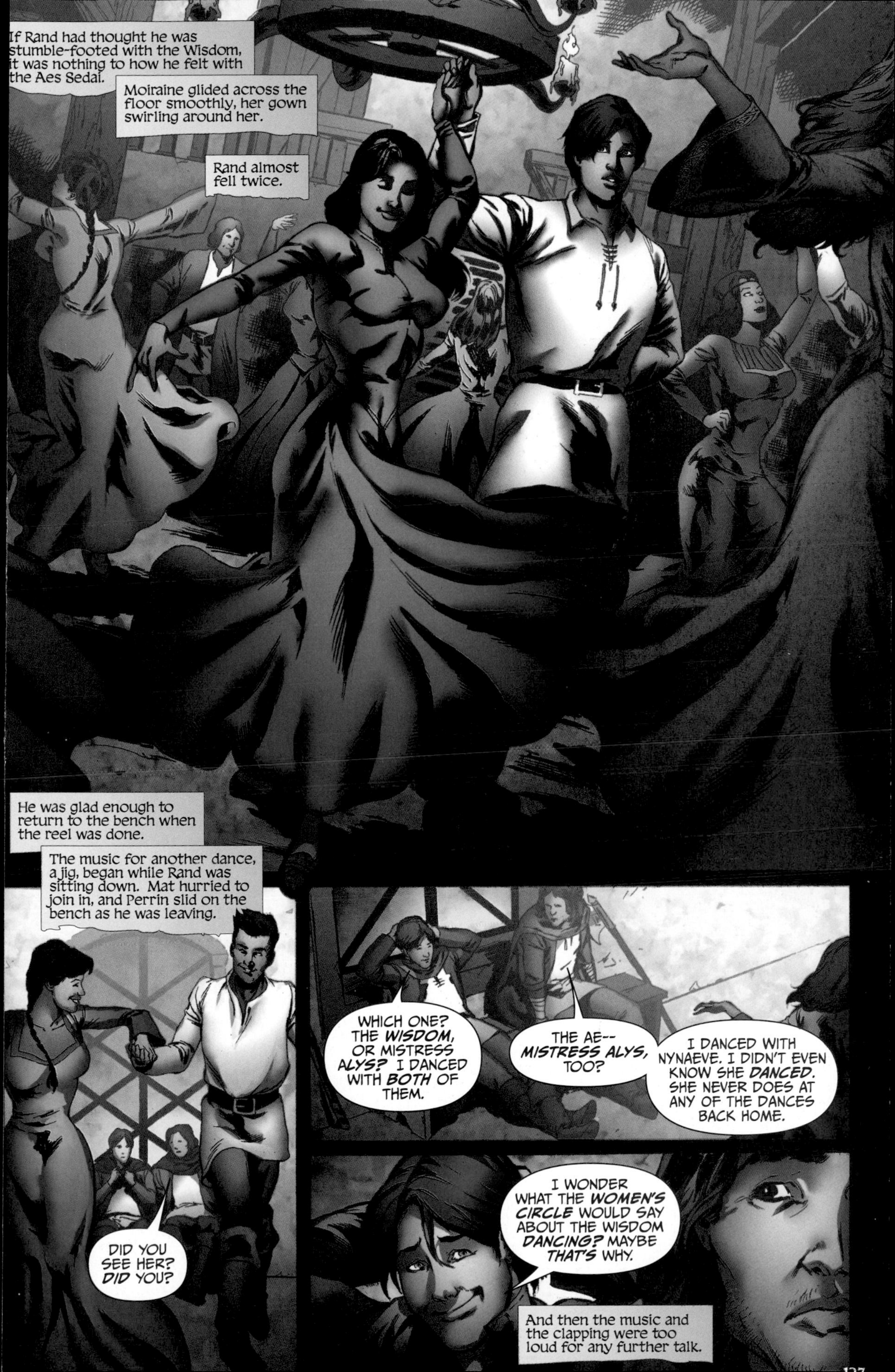

If Rand had thought he was stumble-footed with the Wisdom, it was nothing to how he felt with the Aes Sedai.
Moiraine glided across the floor smoothly, her gown swirling around her.
Rand almost fell twice.
He was glad enough to return to the bench when the reel was done.
The music for another dance, a jig, began while Rand was sitting down. Mat hurried to join in, and Perrin slid on the bench as he was leaving.
DID YOU SEE HER? DID YOU?
WHICH ONE? THE WISDOM, OR MISTRESS ALYS? I DANCED WITH BOTH OF THEM.
THE AE-- MISTRESS ALYS, TOO?
I DANCED WITH NYNAEVE. I DIDN'T EVEN KNOW SHE DANCED. SHE NEVER DOES AT ANY OF THE DANCES BACK HOME.
I WONDER WHAT THE WOMEN'S CIRCLE WOULD SAY ABOUT THE WISDOM DANCING? MAYBE THAT'S WHY.
And then the music and the clapping were too loud for any further talk.

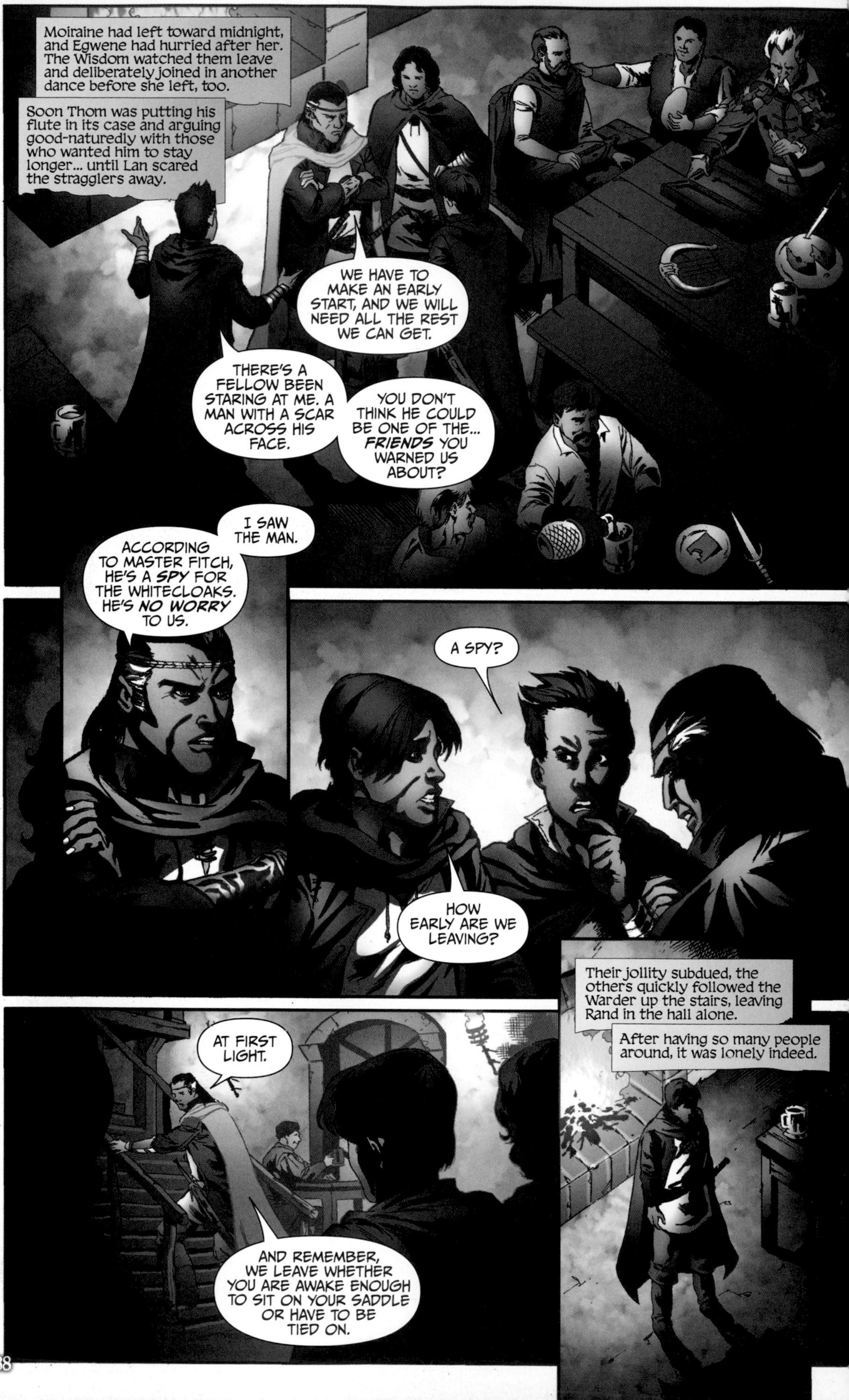
Moiraine had left toward midnight, and Egwene had hurried after her. The Wisdom watched them leave and deliberately joined in another dance before she left, too.
Soon Thom was putting his flute in its case and arguing good-naturedly with those who wanted him to stay longer... until Lan scared the stragglers away.
WE HAVE TO MAKE AN EARLY START, AND WE WILL NEED ALL THE REST WE CAN GET.
THERE'S A FELLOW BEEN STARING AT ME. A MAN WITH A SCAR ACROSS HIS FACE.
YOU DON'T THINK HE COULD BE ONE OF THE... FRIENDS YOU WARNED US ABOUT?
I SAW THE MAN.
ACCORDING TO MASTER FITCH, HE'S A SPY FOR THE WHITECLOAKS. HE'S NO WORRY TO US.
A SPY?
HOW EARLY ARE WE LEAVING?
AT FIRST LIGHT.
AND REMEMBER, WE LEAVE WHETHER YOU ARE AWAKE ENOUGH TO SIT ON YOUR SADDLE OR HAVE TO BE TIED ON.
Their jollity subdued, the others quickly followed the Warder up the stairs, leaving Rand in the hall alone.
After having so many people around, it was lonely indeed.

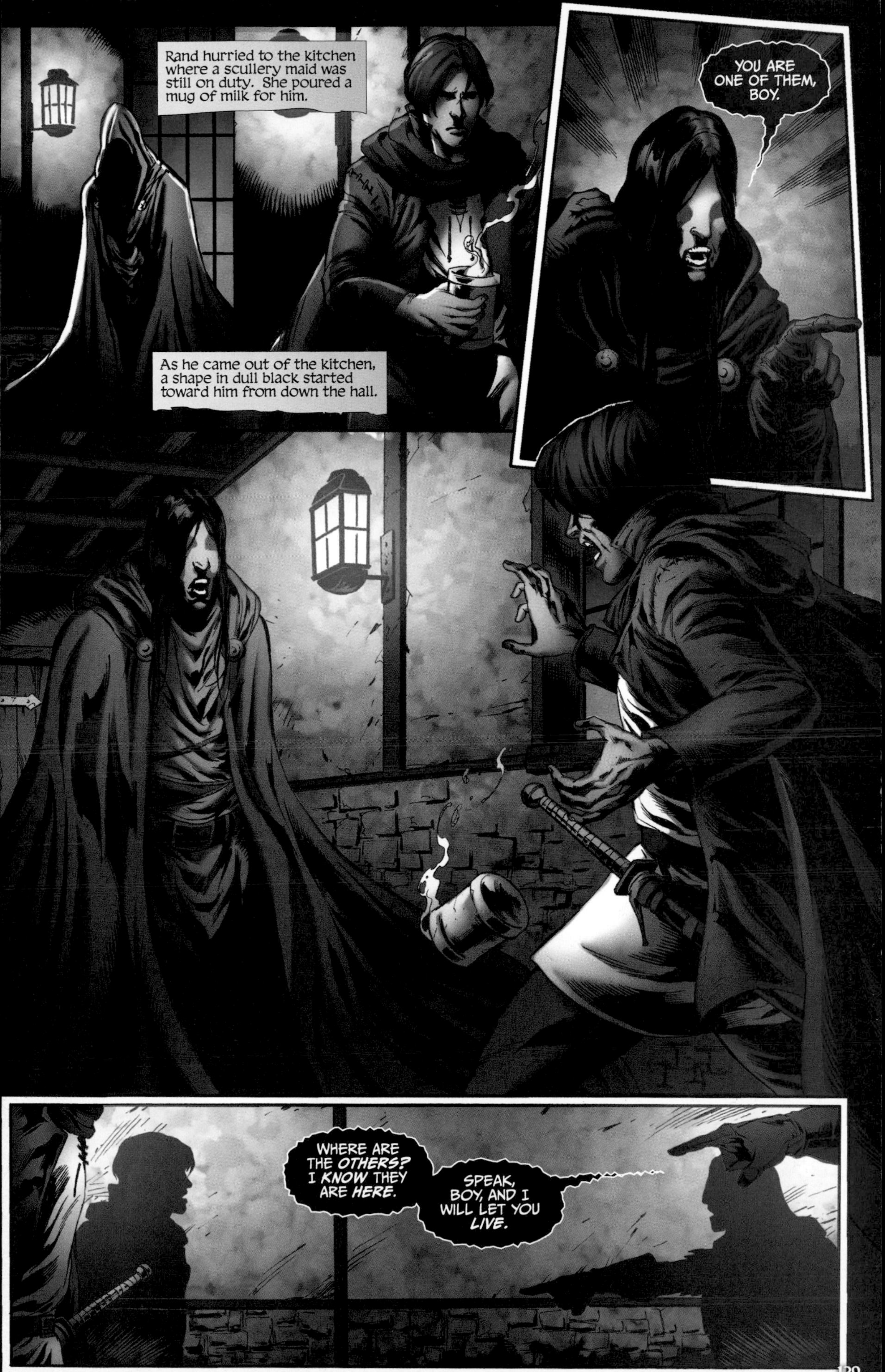
Rand hurried to the kitchen where a scullery maid was still on duty. She poured a mug of milk for him.
As he came out of the kitchen, a shape in dull black started toward him from down the hall.
YOU ARE ONE OF THEM, BOY.
WHERE ARE THE *OTHERS?* I *KNOW* THEY ARE *HERE*.
SPEAK, BOY, AND I WILL LET YOU *LIVE*.

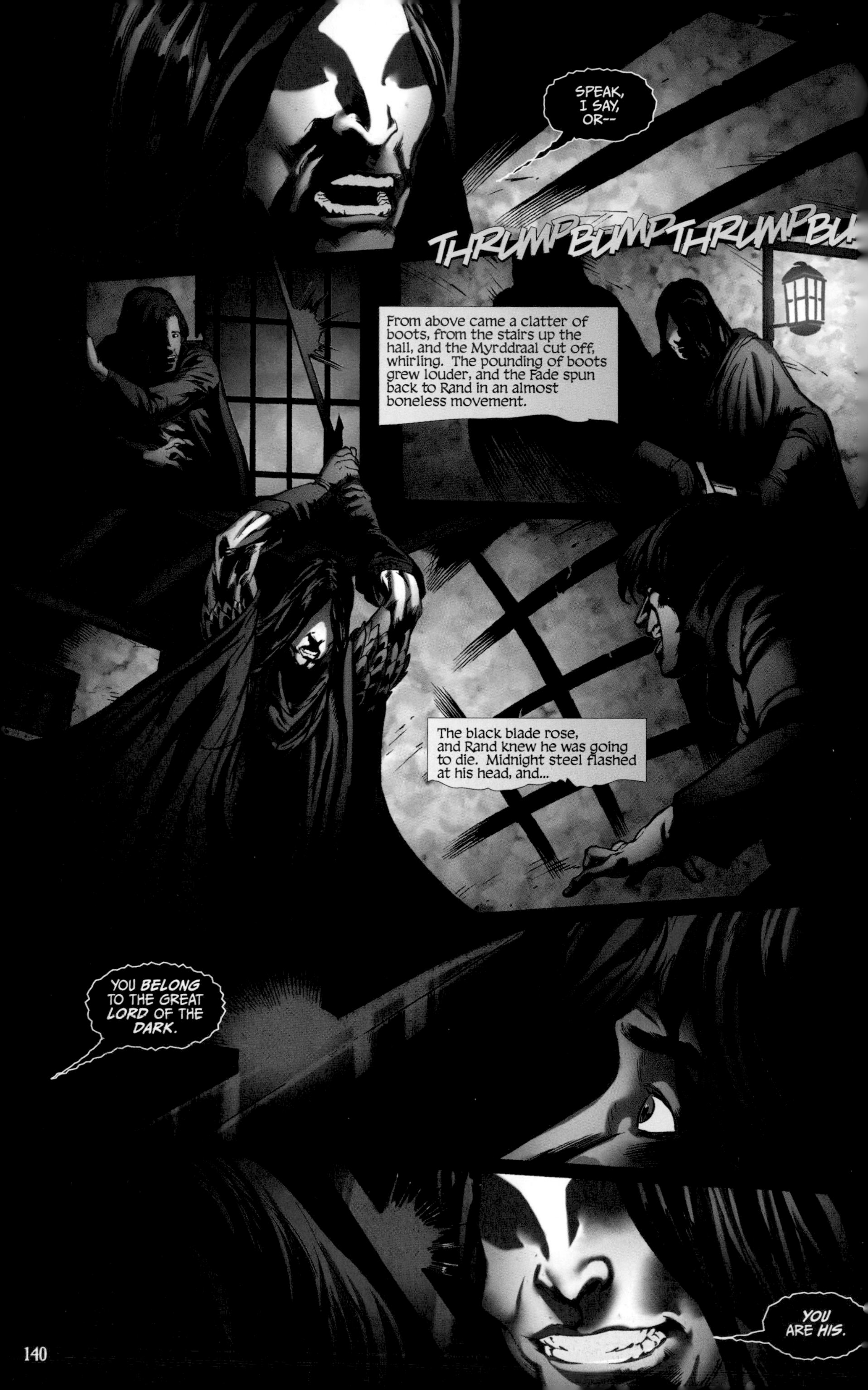

SPEAK, I SAY, OR--
THRUMPBUMPTHRUMPBU
From above came a clatter of boots, from the stairs up the hall, and the Myrddraal cut off, whirling. The pounding of boots grew louder, and the Fade spun back to Rand in an almost boneless movement.
The black blade rose, and Rand knew he was going to die. Midnight steel flashed at his head, and...
YOU BELONG TO THE GREAT LORD OF THE DARK.
YOU ARE HIS.

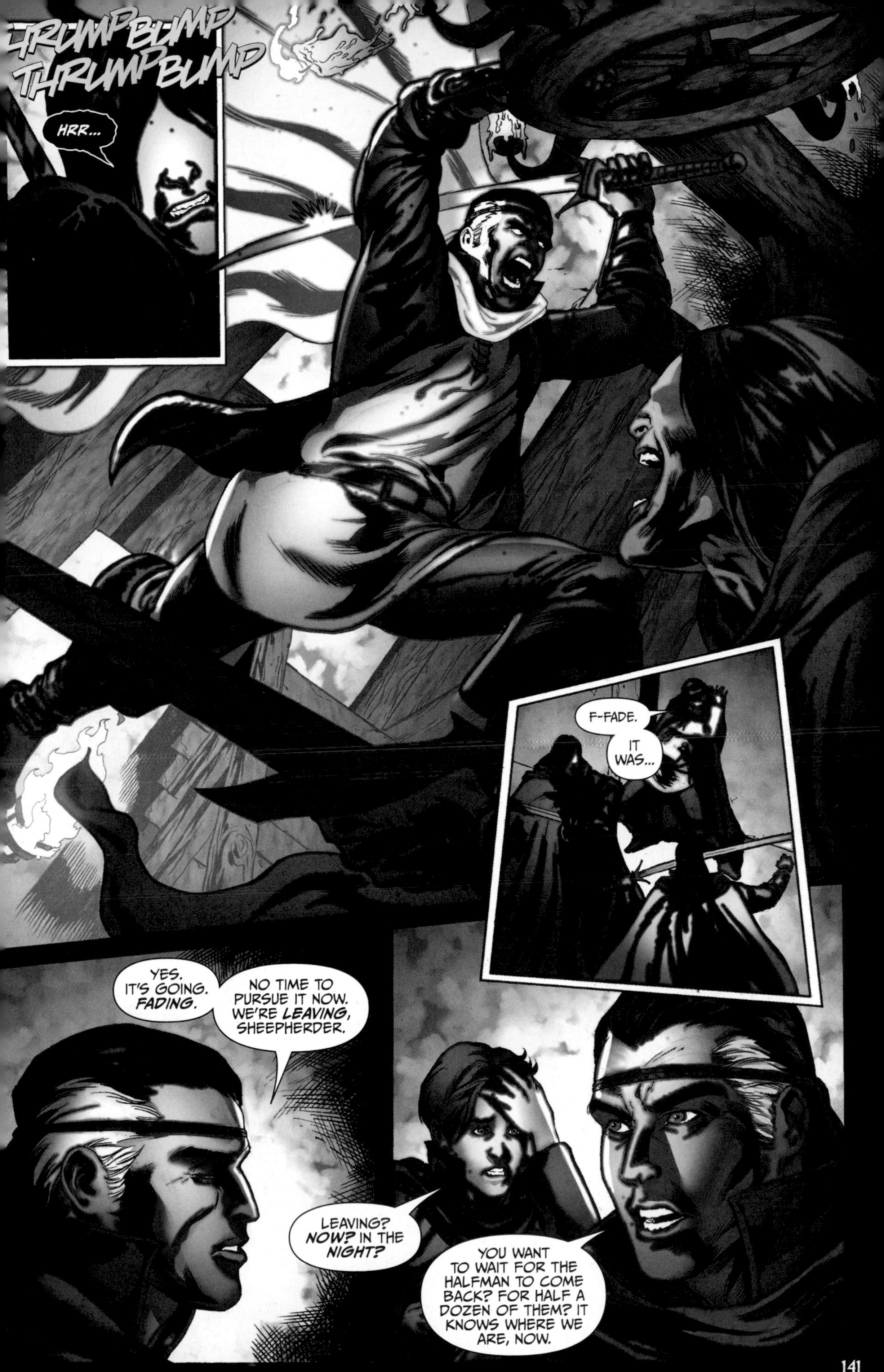
THRUMP BUMP
THRUMP BUMP
HRR...
F-FADE.
IT WAS...
YES. IT'S GOING. FADING.
NO TIME TO PURSUE IT NOW. WE'RE LEAVING, SHEEPHERDER.
LEAVING? NOW? IN THE NIGHT?
YOU WANT TO WAIT FOR THE HALFMAN TO COME BACK? FOR HALF A DOZEN OF THEM? IT KNOWS WHERE WE ARE, NOW.

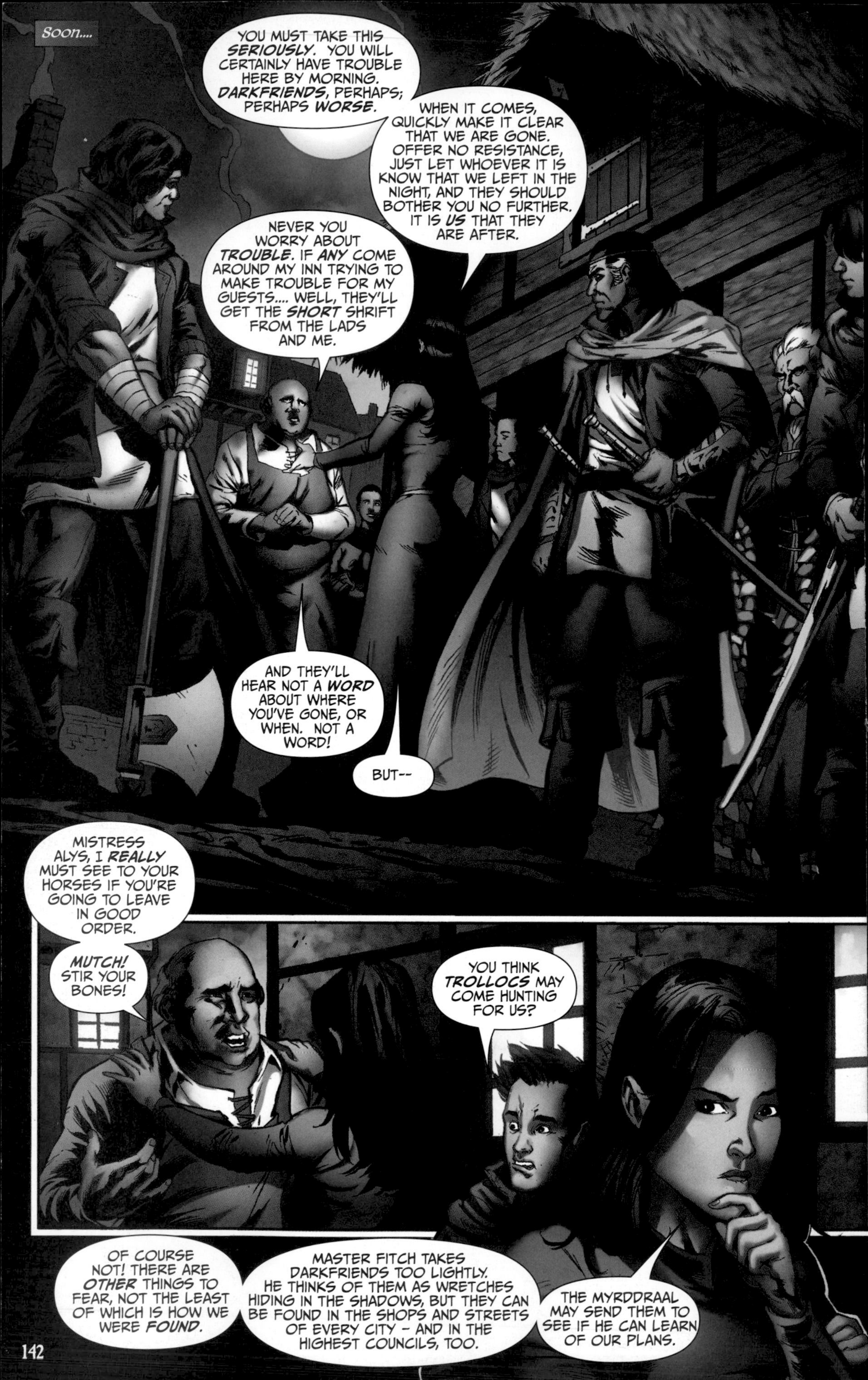

Soon....
YOU MUST TAKE THIS SERIOUSLY. YOU WILL CERTAINLY HAVE TROUBLE HERE BY MORNING. DARKFRIENDS, PERHAPS; PERHAPS WORSE.
WHEN IT COMES, QUICKLY MAKE IT CLEAR THAT WE ARE GONE. OFFER NO RESISTANCE, JUST LET WHOEVER IT IS KNOW THAT WE LEFT IN THE NIGHT, AND THEY SHOULD BOTHER YOU NO FURTHER. IT IS US THAT THEY ARE AFTER.
NEVER YOU WORRY ABOUT TROUBLE. IF ANY COME AROUND MY INN TRYING TO MAKE TROUBLE FOR MY GUESTS.... WELL, THEY'LL GET THE SHORT SHRIFT FROM THE LADS AND ME.
AND THEY'LL HEAR NOT A WORD ABOUT WHERE YOU'VE GONE, OR WHEN. NOT A WORD!
BUT--
MISTRESS ALYS, I REALLY MUST SEE TO YOUR HORSES IF YOU'RE GOING TO LEAVE IN GOOD ORDER.
MUTCH! STIR YOUR BONES!
YOU THINK TROLLOCS MAY COME HUNTING FOR US?
OF COURSE NOT! THERE ARE OTHER THINGS TO FEAR, NOT THE LEAST OF WHICH IS HOW WE WERE FOUND.
MASTER FITCH TAKES DARKFRIENDS TOO LIGHTLY. HE THINKS OF THEM AS WRETCHES HIDING IN THE SHADOWS, BUT THEY CAN BE FOUND IN THE SHOPS AND STREETS OF EVERY CITY – AND IN THE HIGHEST COUNCILS, TOO.
THE MYRDDRAAL MAY SEND THEM TO SEE IF HE CAN LEARN OF OUR PLANS.

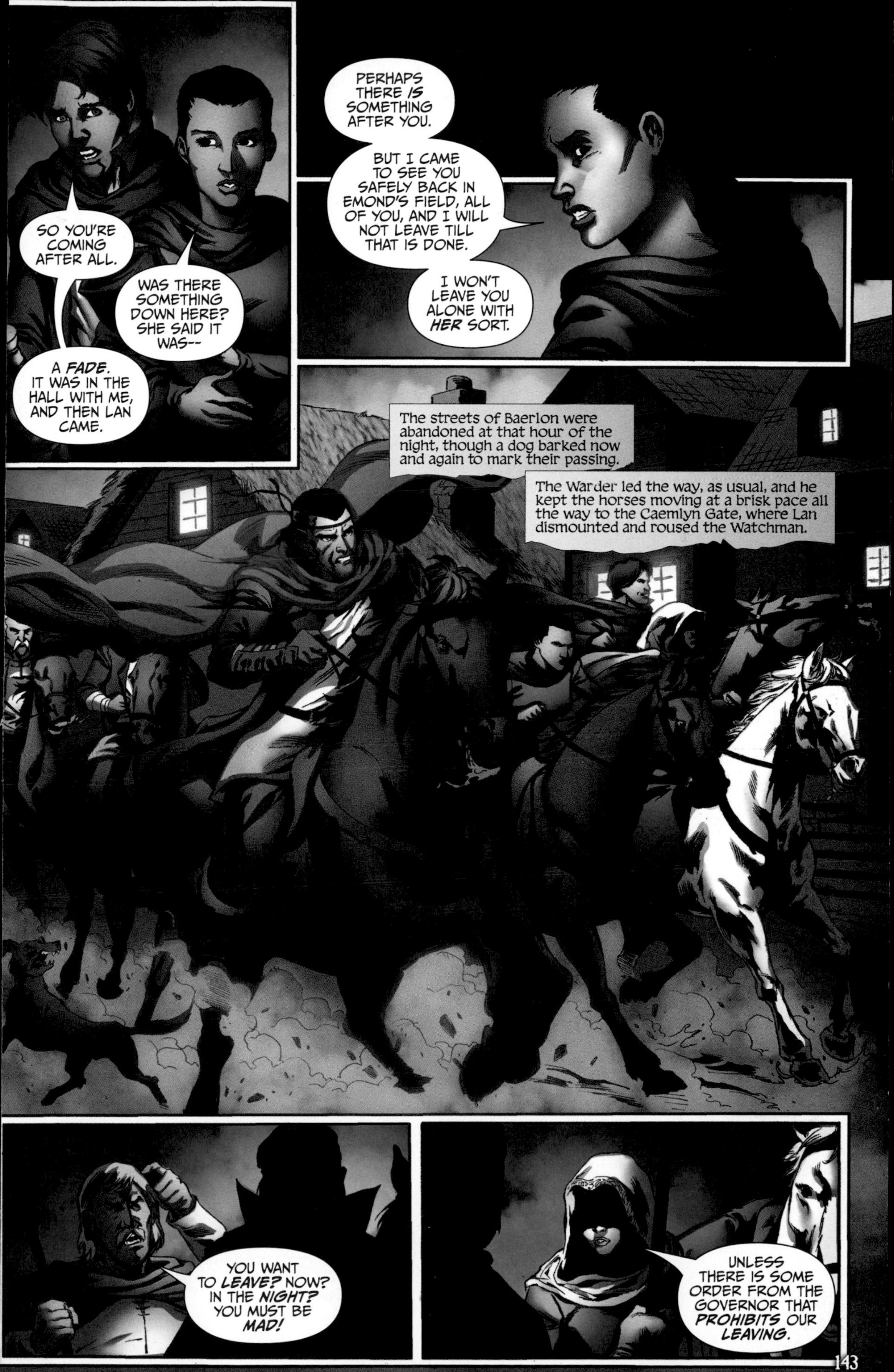
SO YOU'RE COMING AFTER ALL.
WAS THERE SOMETHING DOWN HERE? SHE SAID IT WAS--
A *FADE*. IT WAS IN THE HALL WITH ME, AND THEN LAN CAME.
PERHAPS THERE *IS* SOMETHING AFTER YOU.
BUT I CAME TO SEE YOU SAFELY BACK IN EMOND'S FIELD, ALL OF YOU, AND I WILL NOT LEAVE TILL THAT IS DONE.
I WON'T LEAVE YOU ALONE WITH *HER* SORT.
The streets of Baerlon were abandoned at that hour of the night, though a dog barked now and again to mark their passing.
The Warder led the way, as usual, and he kept the horses moving at a brisk pace all the way to the Caemlyn Gate, where Lan dismounted and roused the Watchman.
YOU WANT TO *LEAVE?* NOW? IN THE *NIGHT?* YOU MUST BE *MAD!*
UNLESS THERE IS SOME ORDER FROM THE GOVERNOR THAT *PROHIBITS* OUR *LEAVING*.

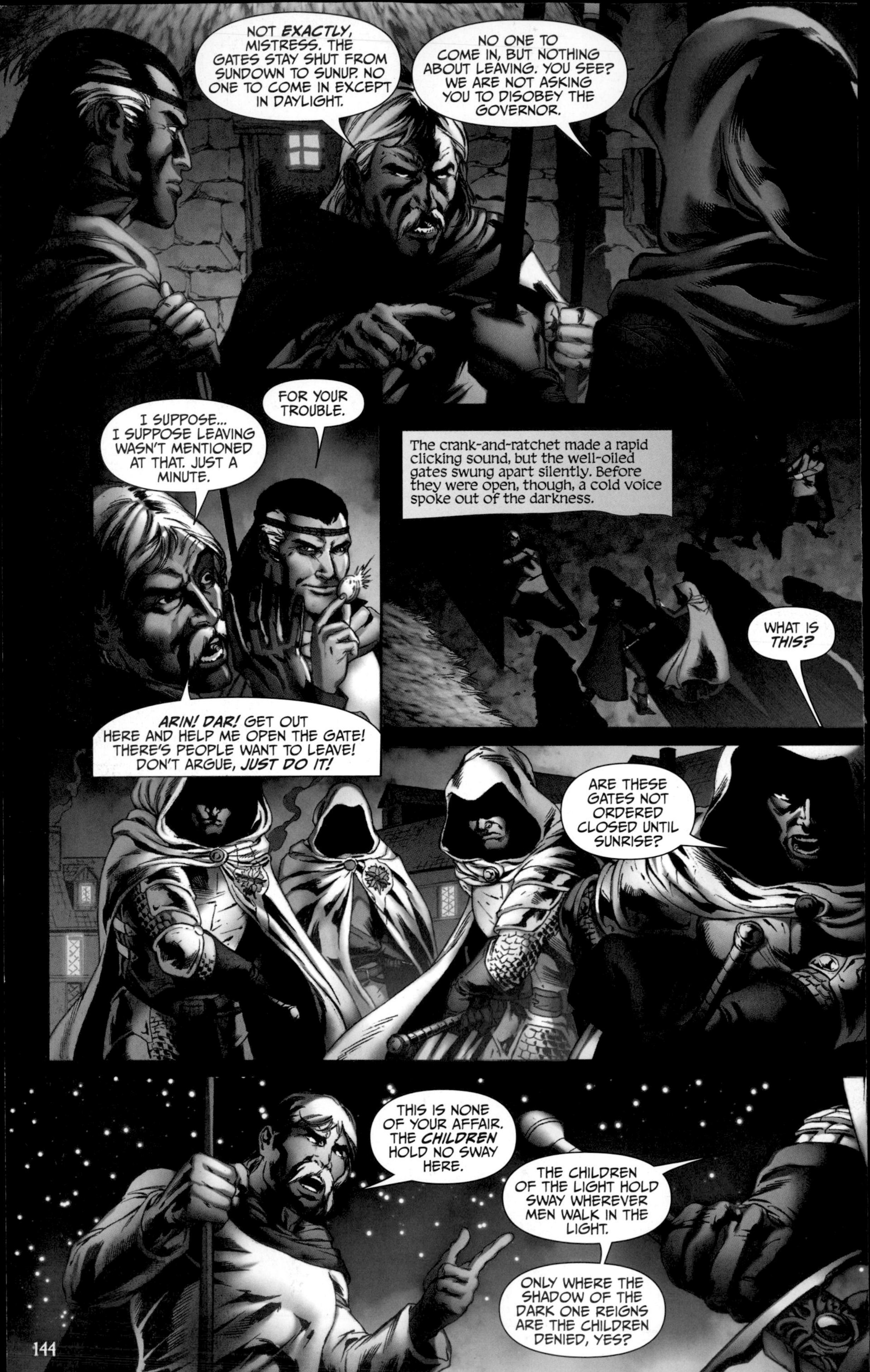
NOT *EXACTLY*, MISTRESS. THE GATES STAY SHUT FROM SUNDOWN TO SUNUP. NO ONE TO COME IN EXCEPT IN DAYLIGHT.
NO ONE TO COME IN, BUT NOTHING ABOUT LEAVING. YOU SEE? WE ARE NOT ASKING YOU TO DISOBEY THE GOVERNOR.
FOR YOUR TROUBLE.
I SUPPOSE... I SUPPOSE LEAVING WASN'T MENTIONED AT THAT. JUST A MINUTE.
ARIN! DAR! GET OUT HERE AND HELP ME OPEN THE GATE! THERE'S PEOPLE WANT TO LEAVE! DON'T ARGUE, *JUST DO IT!*
The crank-and-ratchet made a rapid clicking sound, but the well-oiled gates swung apart silently. Before they were open, though, a cold voice spoke out of the darkness.
WHAT IS *THIS?*
ARE THESE GATES NOT ORDERED CLOSED UNTIL SUNRISE?
THIS IS NONE OF YOUR AFFAIR. THE *CHILDREN* HOLD NO SWAY HERE.
THE CHILDREN OF THE LIGHT HOLD SWAY WHEREVER MEN WALK IN THE LIGHT.
ONLY WHERE THE SHADOW OF THE DARK ONE REIGNS ARE THE CHILDREN DENIED, YES?

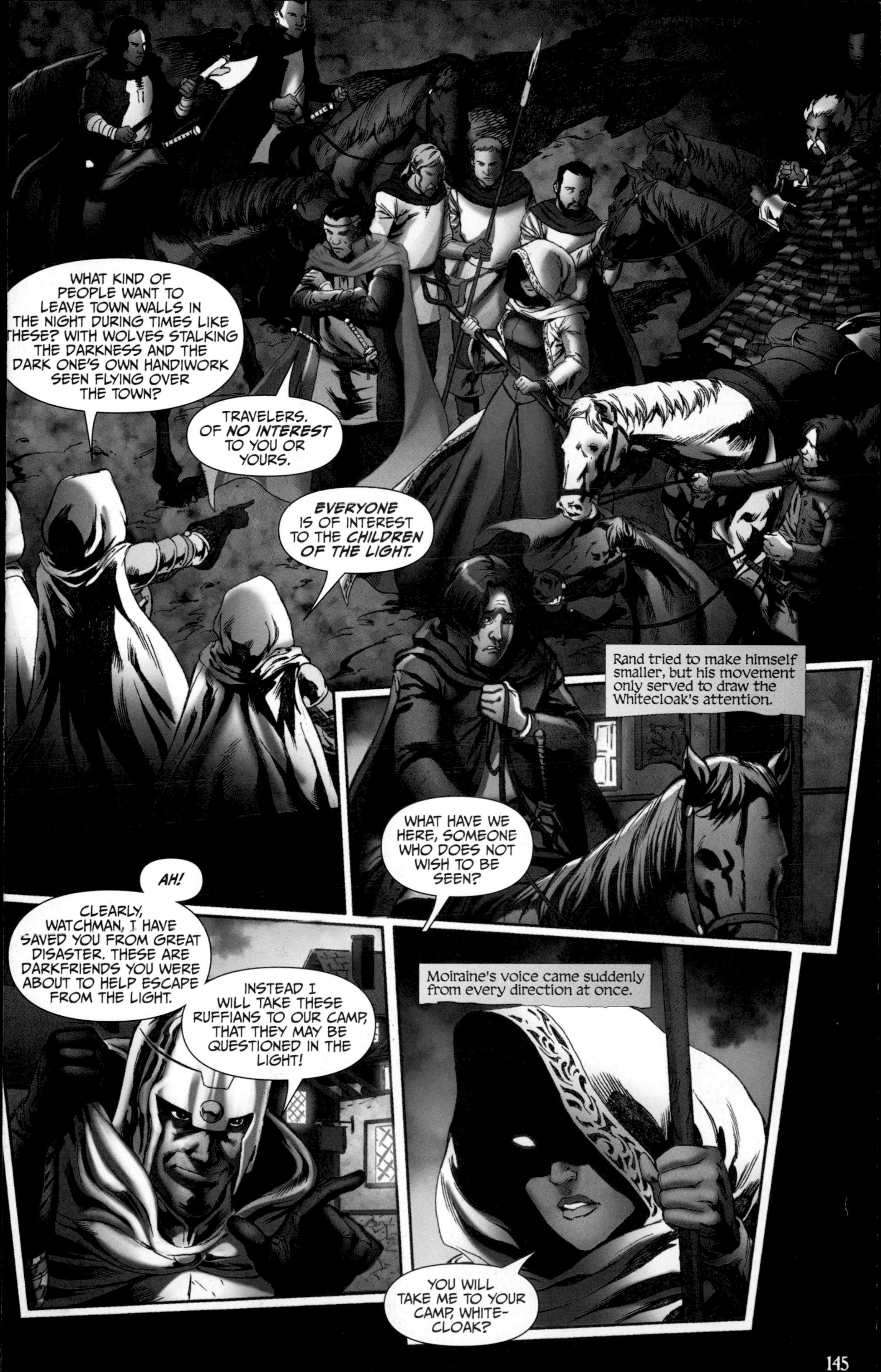
WHAT KIND OF PEOPLE WANT TO LEAVE TOWN WALLS IN THE NIGHT DURING TIMES LIKE THESE? WITH WOLVES STALKING THE DARKNESS AND THE DARK ONE'S OWN HANDIWORK SEEN FLYING OVER THE TOWN?
TRAVELERS. OF NO INTEREST TO YOU OR YOURS.
EVERYONE IS OF INTEREST TO THE CHILDREN OF THE LIGHT.
Rand tried to make himself smaller, but his movement only served to draw the Whitecloak's attention.
WHAT HAVE WE HERE, SOMEONE WHO DOES NOT WISH TO BE SEEN?
AH!
CLEARLY, WATCHMAN, I HAVE SAVED YOU FROM GREAT DISASTER. THESE ARE DARKFRIENDS YOU WERE ABOUT TO HELP ESCAPE FROM THE LIGHT.
INSTEAD I WILL TAKE THESE RUFFIANS TO OUR CAMP, THAT THEY MAY BE QUESTIONED IN THE LIGHT!
Moiraine's voice came suddenly from every direction at once.
YOU WILL TAKE ME TO YOUR CAMP, WHITE-CLOAK?

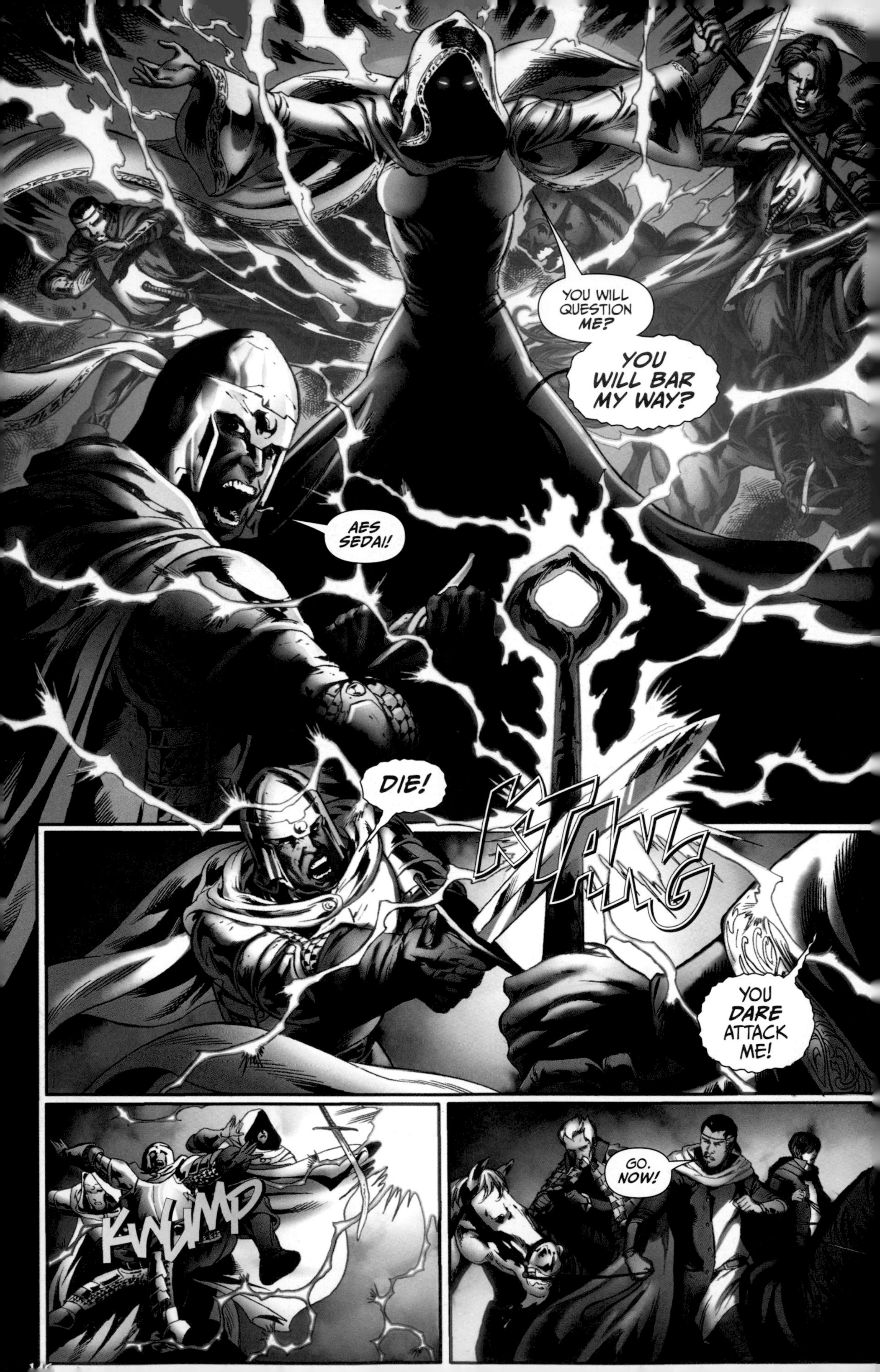
YOU WILL QUESTION ME?
YOU WILL BAR MY WAY?
AES SEDAI!
DIE!
KTANG
YOU DARE ATTACK ME!
KWUMP
GO. NOW!

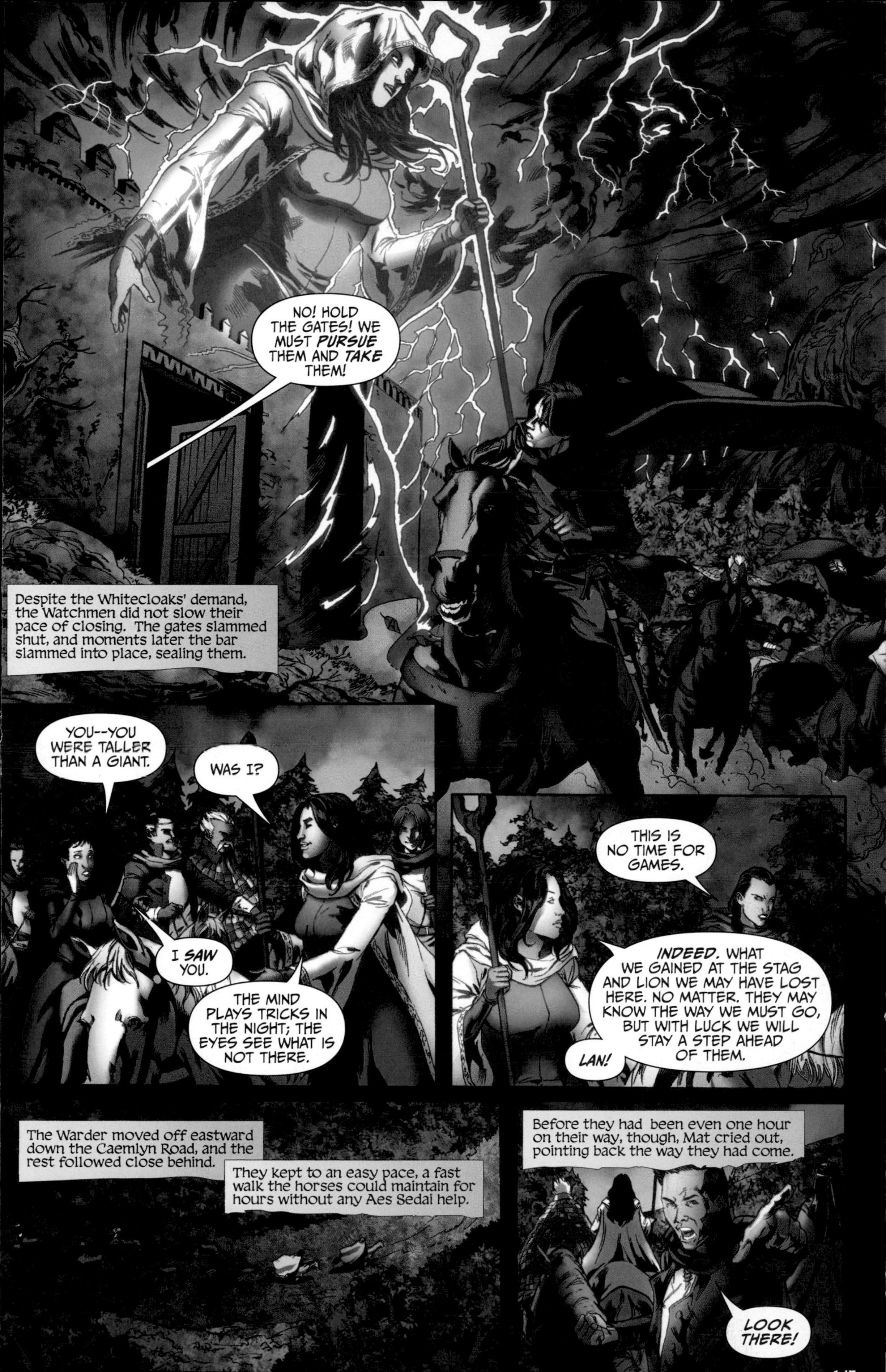
NO! HOLD THE GATES! WE MUST PURSUE THEM AND TAKE THEM!
Despite the Whitecloaks' demand, the Watchmen did not slow their pace of closing. The gates slammed shut, and moments later the bar slammed into place, sealing them.
YOU--YOU WERE TALLER THAN A GIANT.
WAS I?
I SAW YOU.
THE MIND PLAYS TRICKS IN THE NIGHT; THE EYES SEE WHAT IS NOT THERE.
THIS IS NO TIME FOR GAMES.
INDEED. WHAT WE GAINED AT THE STAG AND LION WE MAY HAVE LOST HERE. NO MATTER. THEY MAY KNOW THE WAY WE MUST GO, BUT WITH LUCK WE WILL STAY A STEP AHEAD OF THEM.
LAN!
The Warder moved off eastward down the Caemlyn Road, and the rest followed close behind.
They kept to an easy pace, a fast walk the horses could maintain for hours without any Aes Sedai help.
Before they had been even one hour on their way, though, Mat cried out, pointing back the way they had come.
LOOK THERE!

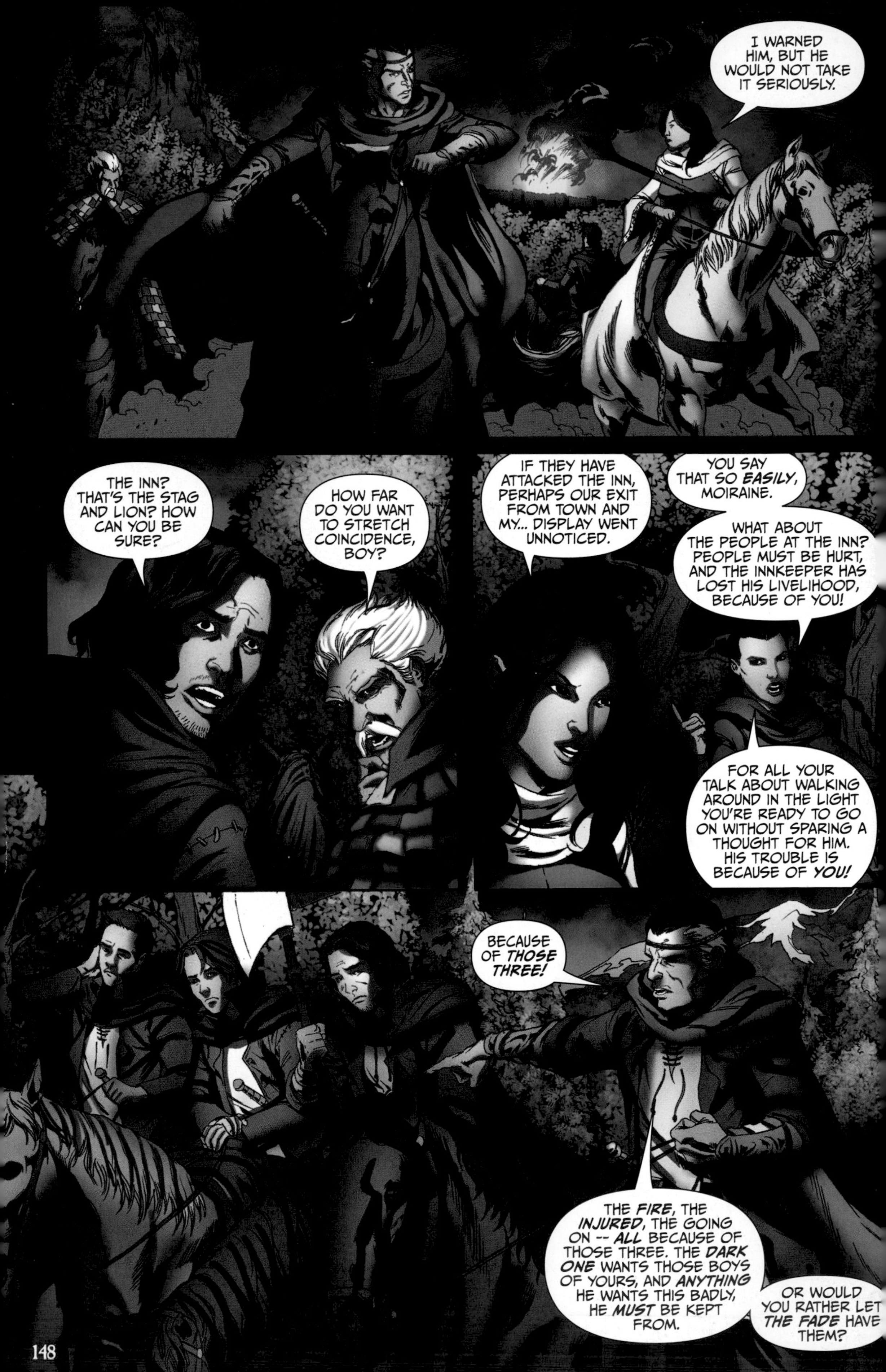

I WARNED HIM, BUT HE WOULD NOT TAKE IT SERIOUSLY.
THE INN? THAT'S THE STAG AND LION? HOW CAN YOU BE SURE?
HOW FAR DO YOU WANT TO STRETCH COINCIDENCE, BOY?
IF THEY HAVE ATTACKED THE INN, PERHAPS OUR EXIT FROM TOWN AND MY... DISPLAY WENT UNNOTICED.
YOU SAY THAT SO *EASILY*, MOIRAINE.
WHAT ABOUT THE PEOPLE AT THE INN? PEOPLE MUST BE HURT, AND THE INNKEEPER HAS LOST HIS LIVELIHOOD, BECAUSE OF YOU!
FOR ALL YOUR TALK ABOUT WALKING AROUND IN THE LIGHT YOU'RE READY TO GO ON WITHOUT SPARING A THOUGHT FOR HIM. HIS TROUBLE IS BECAUSE OF *YOU!*
BECAUSE OF *THOSE THREE!*
THE *FIRE*, THE *INJURED*, THE GOING ON -- *ALL* BECAUSE OF THOSE THREE. THE *DARK ONE* WANTS THOSE BOYS OF YOURS, AND *ANYTHING* HE WANTS THIS BADLY, HE *MUST* BE KEPT FROM.
OR WOULD YOU RATHER LET *THE FADE* HAVE THEM?

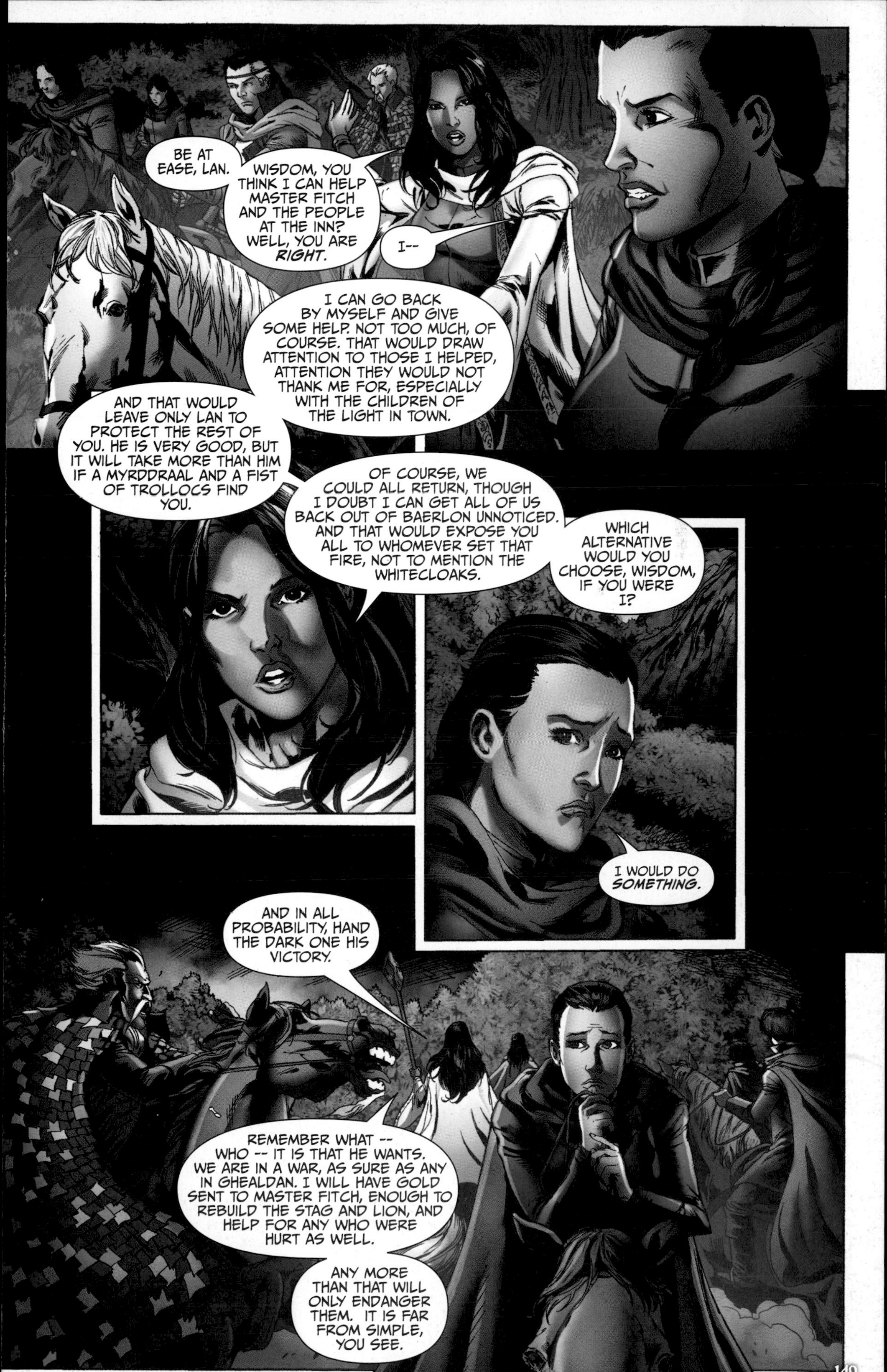
BE AT EASE, LAN.
WISDOM, YOU THINK I CAN HELP MASTER FITCH AND THE PEOPLE AT THE INN? WELL, YOU ARE *RIGHT.*
I--
I CAN GO BACK BY MYSELF AND GIVE SOME HELP. NOT TOO MUCH, OF COURSE. THAT WOULD DRAW ATTENTION TO THOSE I HELPED, ATTENTION THEY WOULD NOT THANK ME FOR, ESPECIALLY WITH THE CHILDREN OF THE LIGHT IN TOWN.
AND THAT WOULD LEAVE ONLY LAN TO PROTECT THE REST OF YOU. HE IS VERY GOOD, BUT IT WILL TAKE MORE THAN HIM IF A MYRDDRAAL AND A FIST OF TROLLOCS FIND YOU.
OF COURSE, WE COULD ALL RETURN, THOUGH I DOUBT I CAN GET ALL OF US BACK OUT OF BAERLON UNNOTICED. AND THAT WOULD EXPOSE YOU ALL TO WHOMEVER SET THAT FIRE, NOT TO MENTION THE WHITECLOAKS.
WHICH ALTERNATIVE WOULD YOU CHOOSE, WISDOM, IF YOU WERE I?
I WOULD DO *SOMETHING.*
AND IN ALL PROBABILITY, HAND THE DARK ONE HIS VICTORY.
REMEMBER WHAT -- WHO -- IT IS THAT HE WANTS. WE ARE IN A WAR, AS SURE AS ANY IN GHEALDAN. I WILL HAVE GOLD SENT TO MASTER FITCH, ENOUGH TO REBUILD THE STAG AND LION, AND HELP FOR ANY WHO WERE HURT AS WELL.
ANY MORE THAN THAT WILL ONLY ENDANGER THEM. IT IS FAR FROM SIMPLE, YOU SEE.

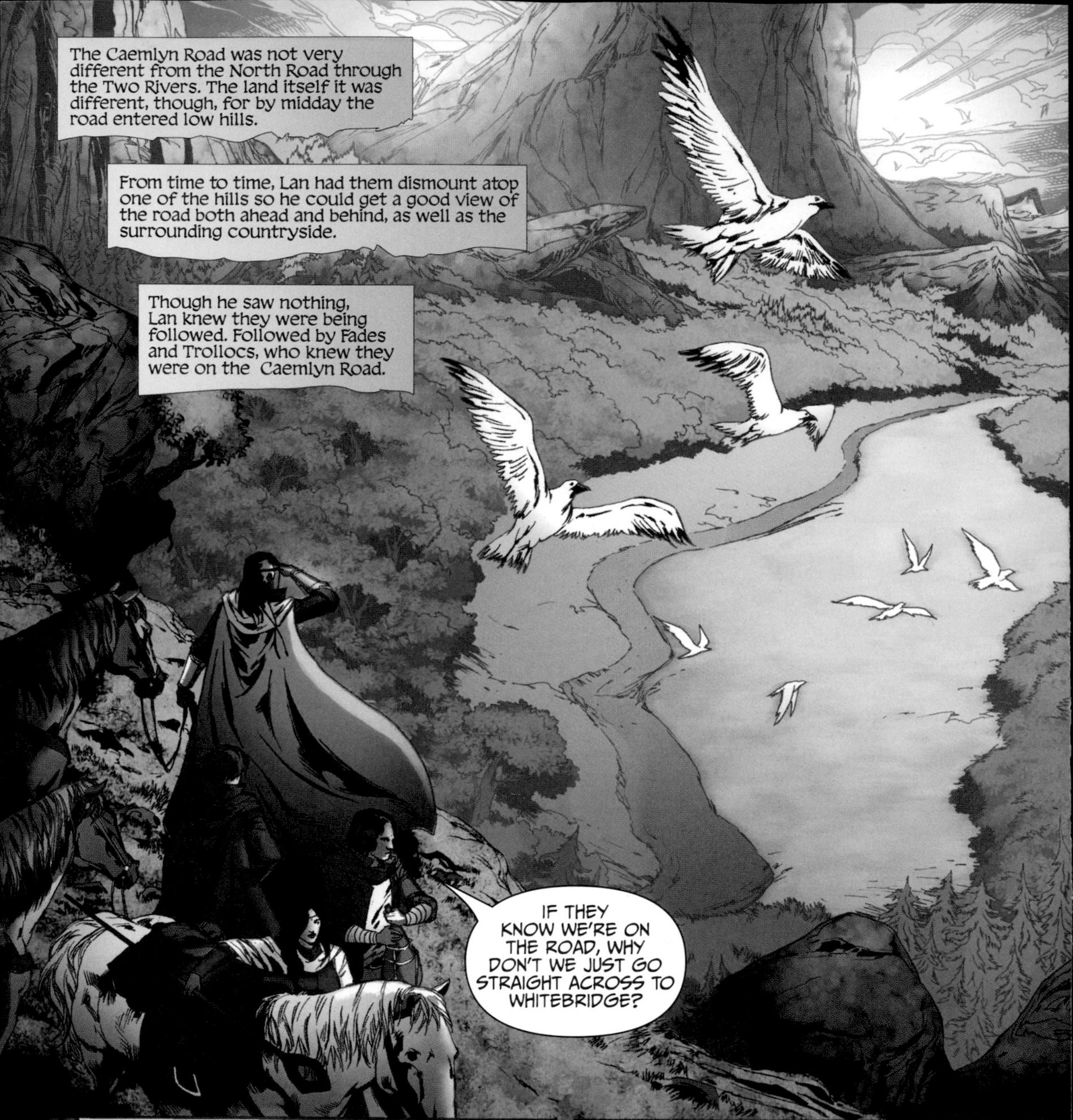
The Caemlyn Road was not very different from the North Road through the Two Rivers. The land itself it was different, though, for by midday the road entered low hills.
From time to time, Lan had them dismount atop one of the hills so he could get a good view of the road both ahead and behind, as well as the surrounding countryside.
Though he saw nothing, Lan knew they were being followed. Followed by Fades and Trollocs, who knew they were on the Caemlyn Road.
IF THEY KNOW WE'RE ON THE ROAD, WHY DON'T WE JUST GO STRAIGHT ACROSS TO WHITEBRIDGE?

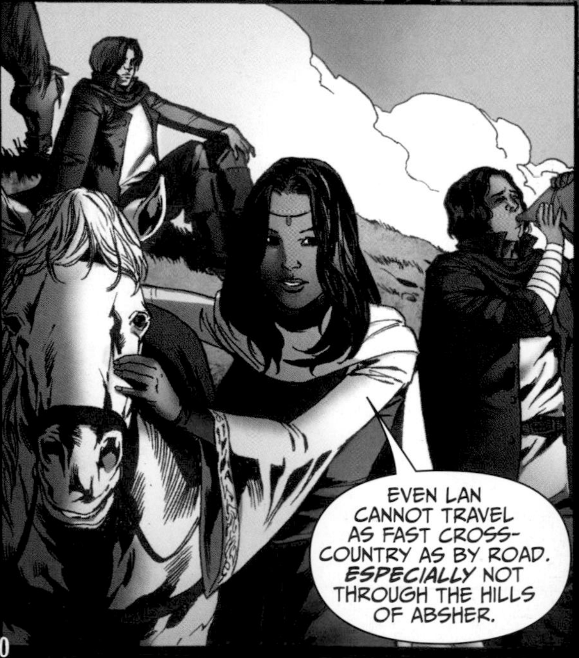
EVEN LAN CANNOT TRAVEL AS FAST CROSS-COUNTRY AS BY ROAD. *ESPECIALLY* NOT THROUGH THE HILLS OF ABSHER.

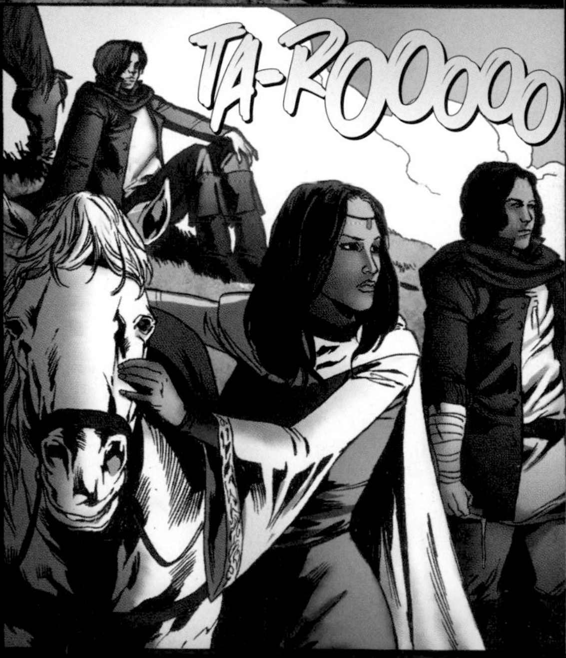
TA-ROOOOO

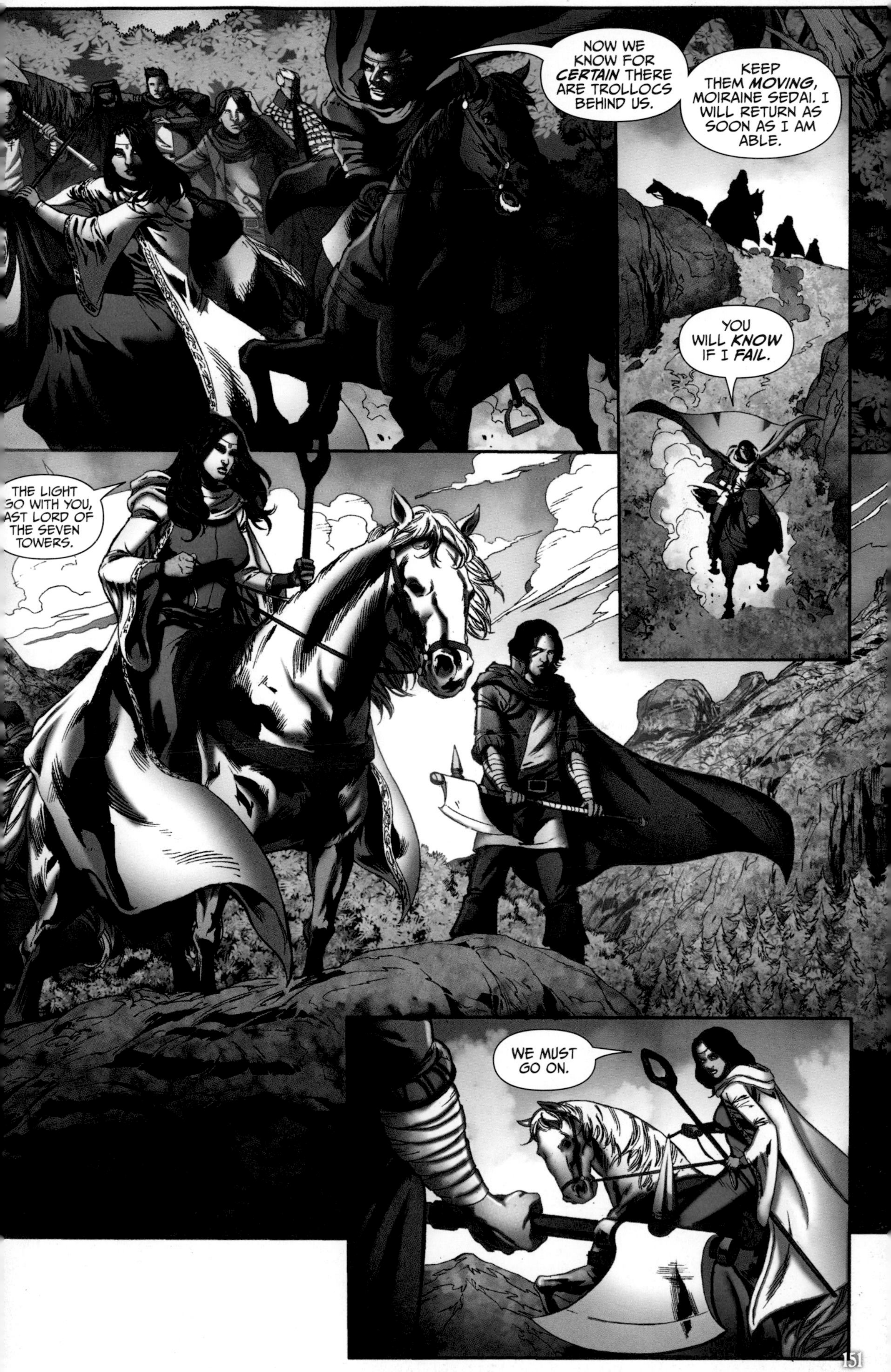
NOW WE KNOW FOR CERTAIN THERE ARE TROLLOCS BEHIND US.
KEEP THEM MOVING, MOIRAINE SEDAI. I WILL RETURN AS SOON AS I AM ABLE.
YOU WILL KNOW IF I FAIL.
THE LIGHT GO WITH YOU, LAST LORD OF THE SEVEN TOWERS.
WE MUST GO ON.

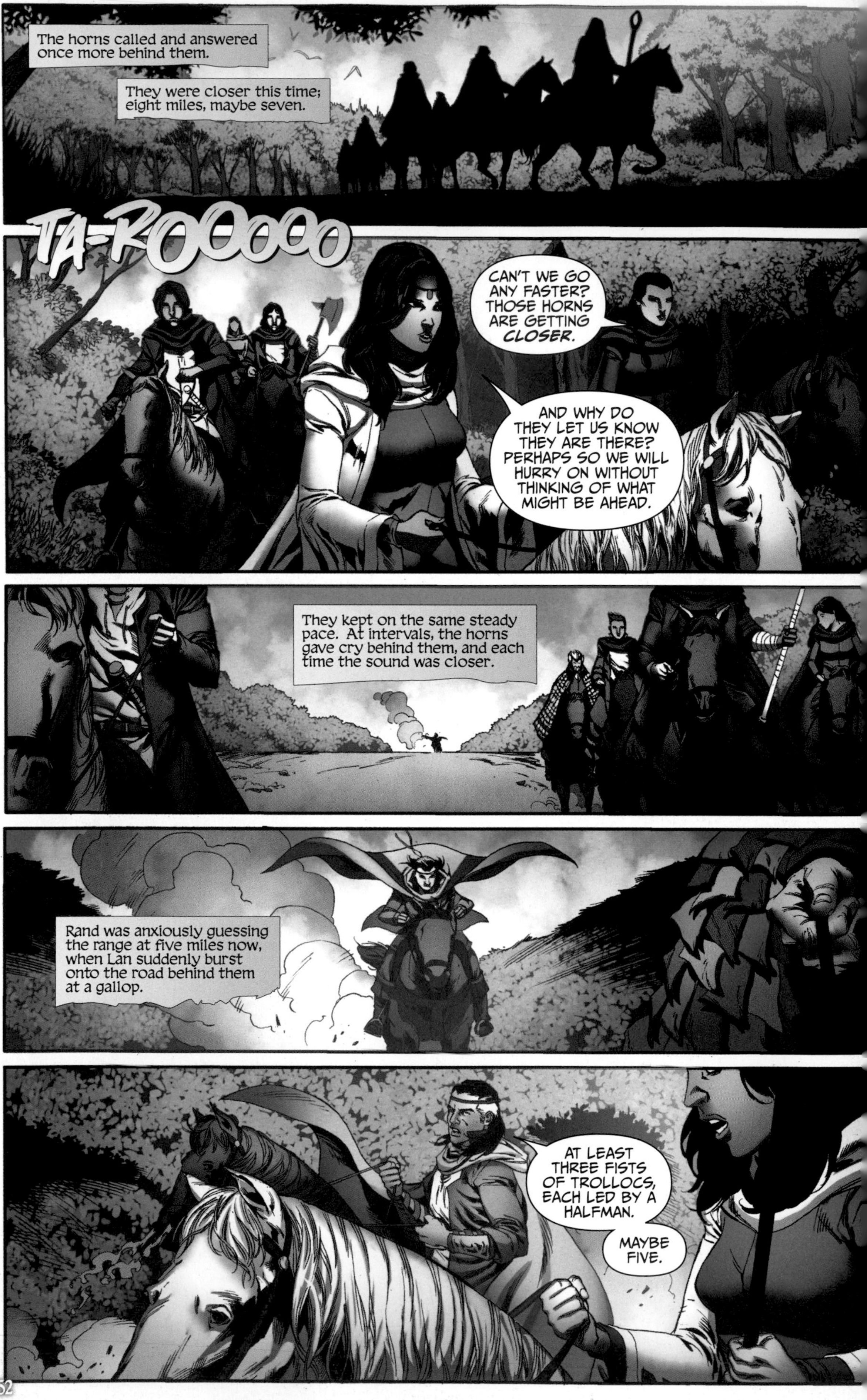

The horns called and answered once more behind them.
They were closer this time; eight miles, maybe seven.
TA-ROOOOO
CAN'T WE GO ANY FASTER? THOSE HORNS ARE GETTING CLOSER.
AND WHY DO THEY LET US KNOW THEY ARE THERE? PERHAPS SO WE WILL HURRY ON WITHOUT THINKING OF WHAT MIGHT BE AHEAD.
They kept on the same steady pace. At intervals, the horns gave cry behind them, and each time the sound was closer.
Rand was anxiously guessing the range at five miles now, when Lan suddenly burst onto the road behind them at a gallop.
AT LEAST THREE FISTS OF TROLLOCS, EACH LED BY A HALFMAN.
MAYBE FIVE.

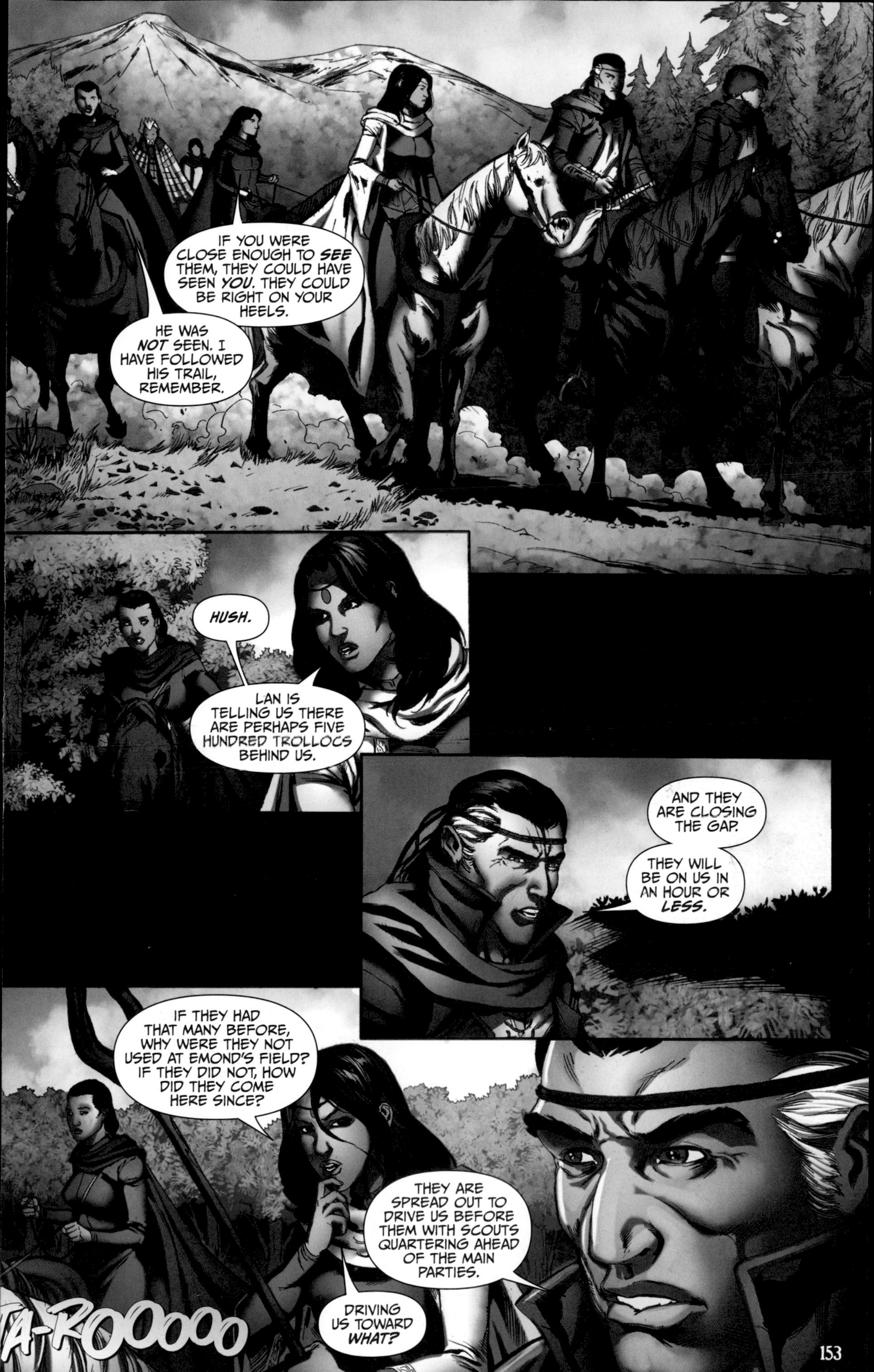
IF YOU WERE CLOSE ENOUGH TO SEE THEM, THEY COULD HAVE SEEN YOU. THEY COULD BE RIGHT ON YOUR HEELS.
HE WAS NOT SEEN. I HAVE FOLLOWED HIS TRAIL, REMEMBER.
HUSH.
LAN IS TELLING US THERE ARE PERHAPS FIVE HUNDRED TROLLOCS BEHIND US.
AND THEY ARE CLOSING THE GAP.
THEY WILL BE ON US IN AN HOUR OR LESS.
IF THEY HAD THAT MANY BEFORE, WHY WERE THEY NOT USED AT EMOND'S FIELD? IF THEY DID NOT, HOW DID THEY COME HERE SINCE?
THEY ARE SPREAD OUT TO DRIVE US BEFORE THEM WITH SCOUTS QUARTERING AHEAD OF THE MAIN PARTIES.
DRIVING US TOWARD WHAT?
TA-ROOOOO

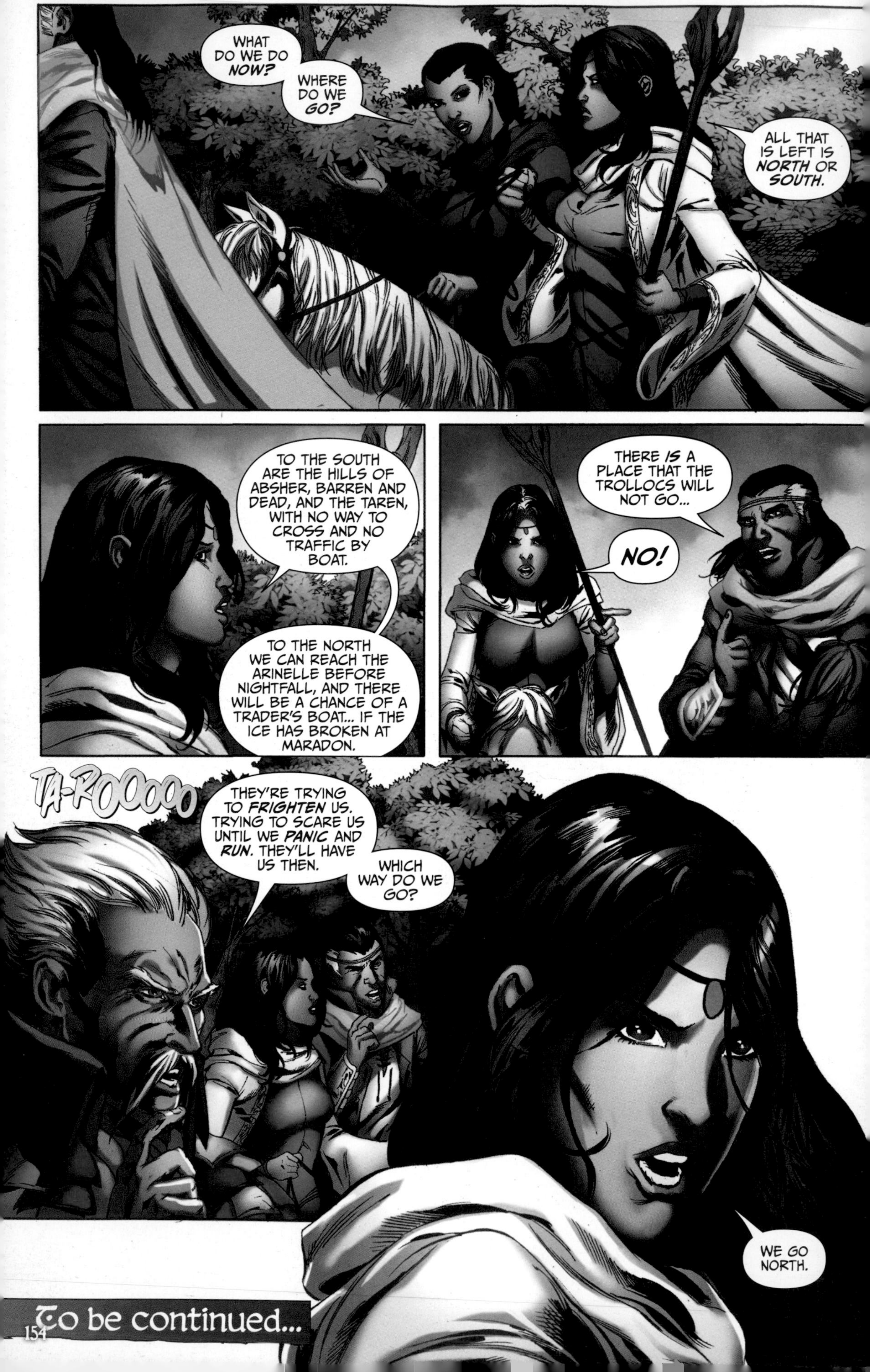
WHAT DO WE DO NOW?
WHERE DO WE GO?
ALL THAT IS LEFT IS NORTH OR SOUTH.
TO THE SOUTH ARE THE HILLS OF ABSHER, BARREN AND DEAD, AND THE TAREN, WITH NO WAY TO CROSS AND NO TRAFFIC BY BOAT.
TO THE NORTH WE CAN REACH THE ARINELLE BEFORE NIGHTFALL, AND THERE WILL BE A CHANCE OF A TRADER'S BOAT... IF THE ICE HAS BROKEN AT MARADON.
THERE IS A PLACE THAT THE TROLLOCS WILL NOT GO...
NO!
TA-ROOOOO
THEY'RE TRYING TO FRIGHTEN US. TRYING TO SCARE US UNTIL WE PANIC AND RUN. THEY'LL HAVE US THEN.
WHICH WAY DO WE GO?
WE GO NORTH.
To be continued...

cover gallery

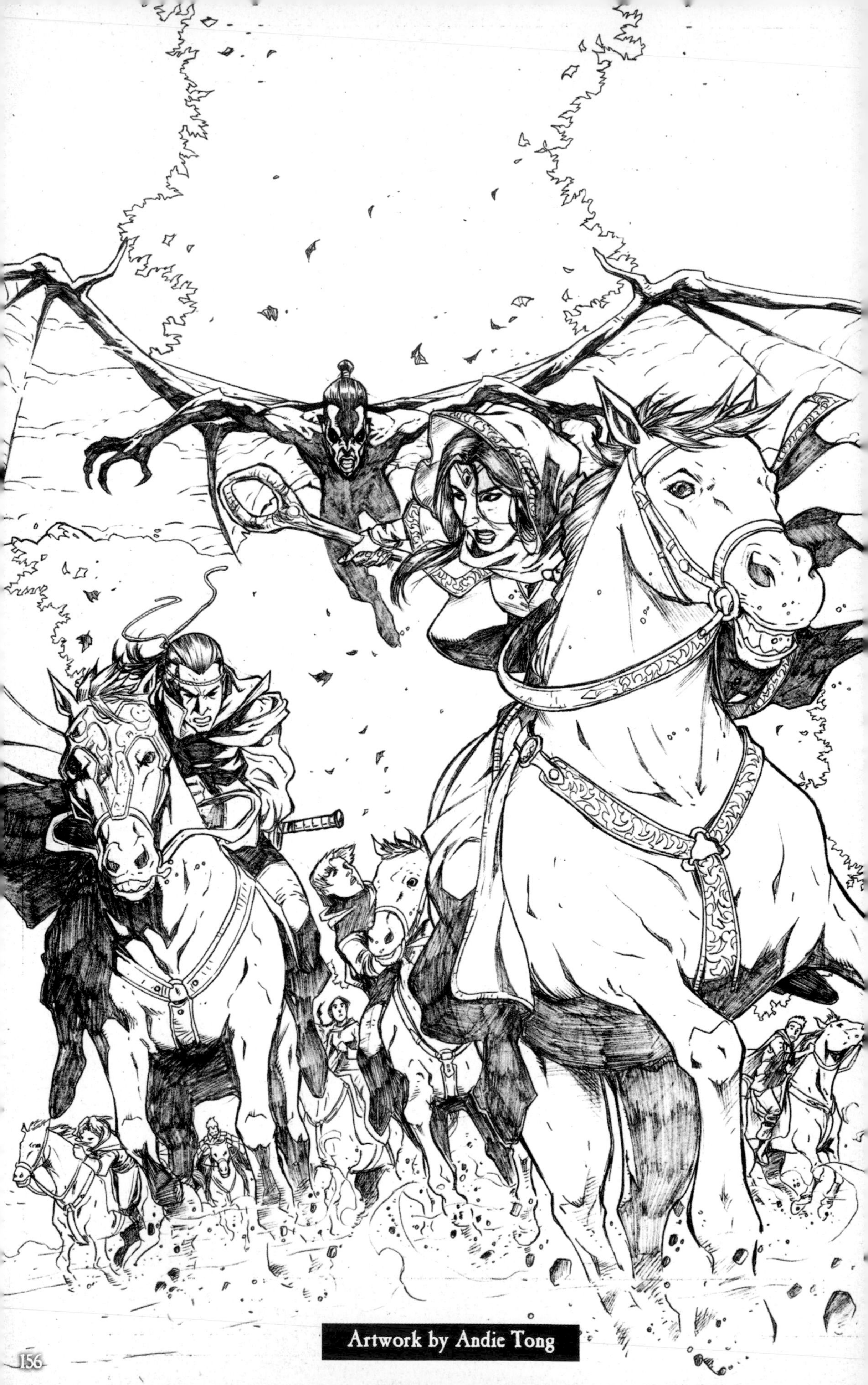

Artwork by Andie Tong

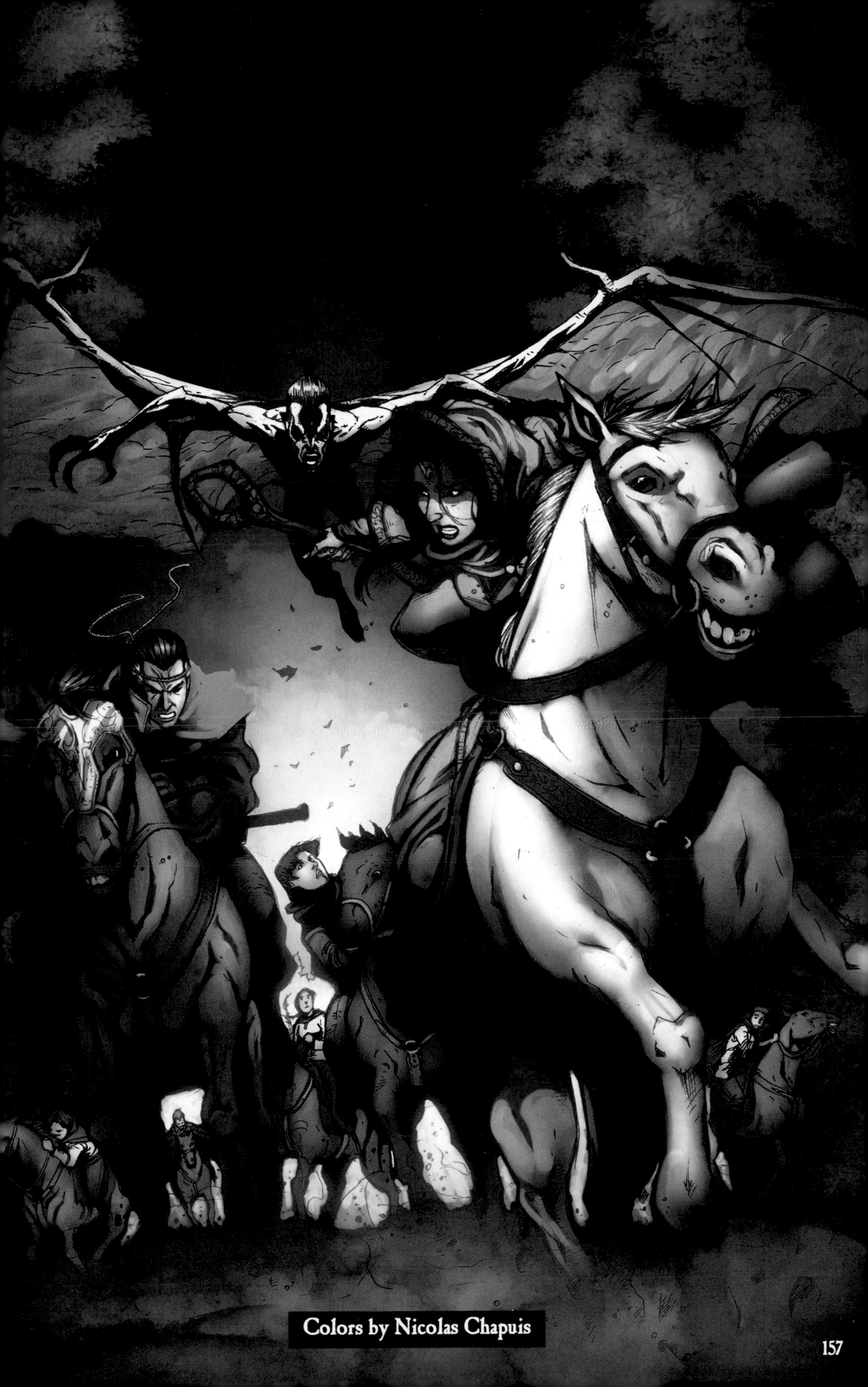

Colors by Nicolas Chapuis

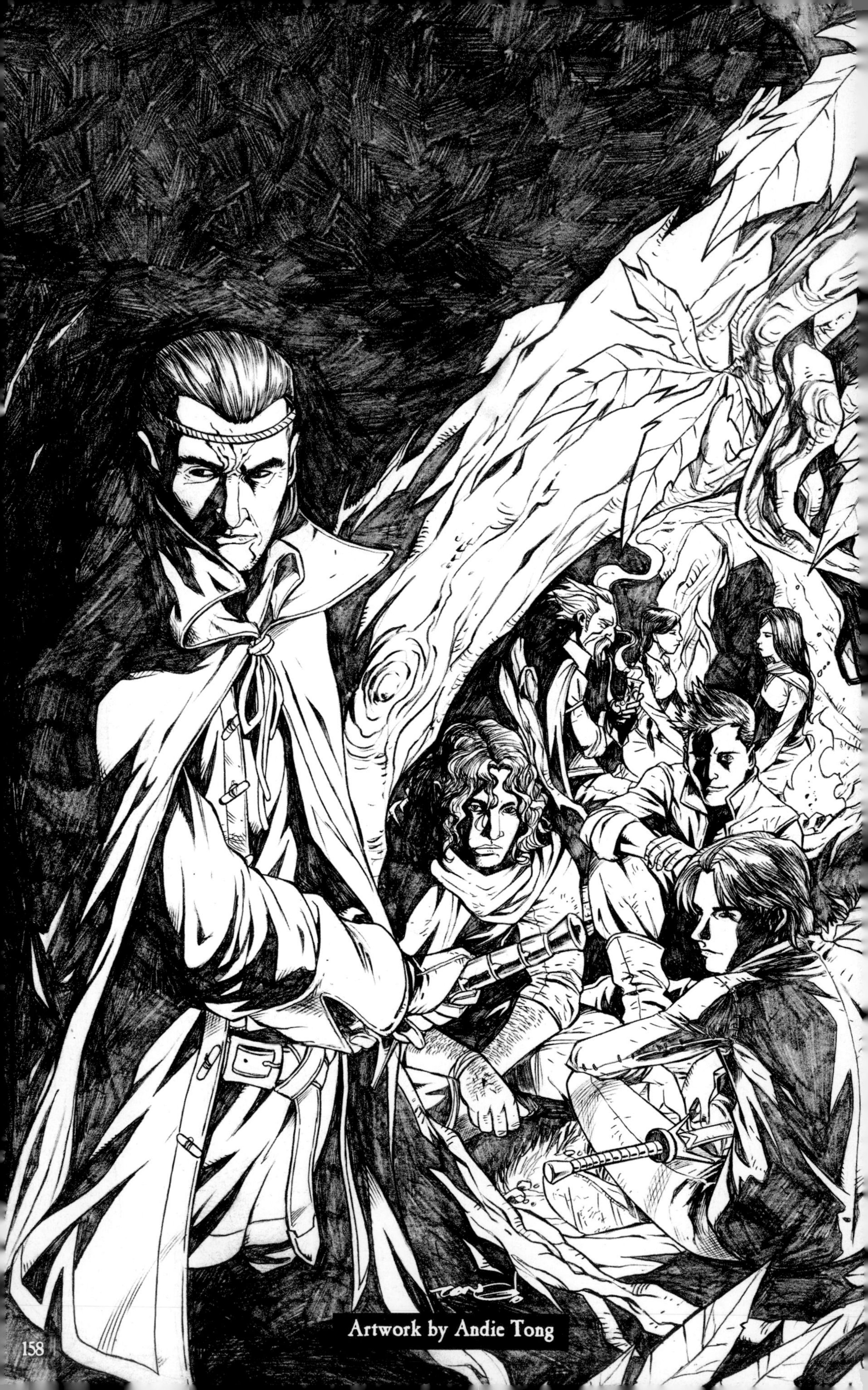

Artwork by Andie Tong

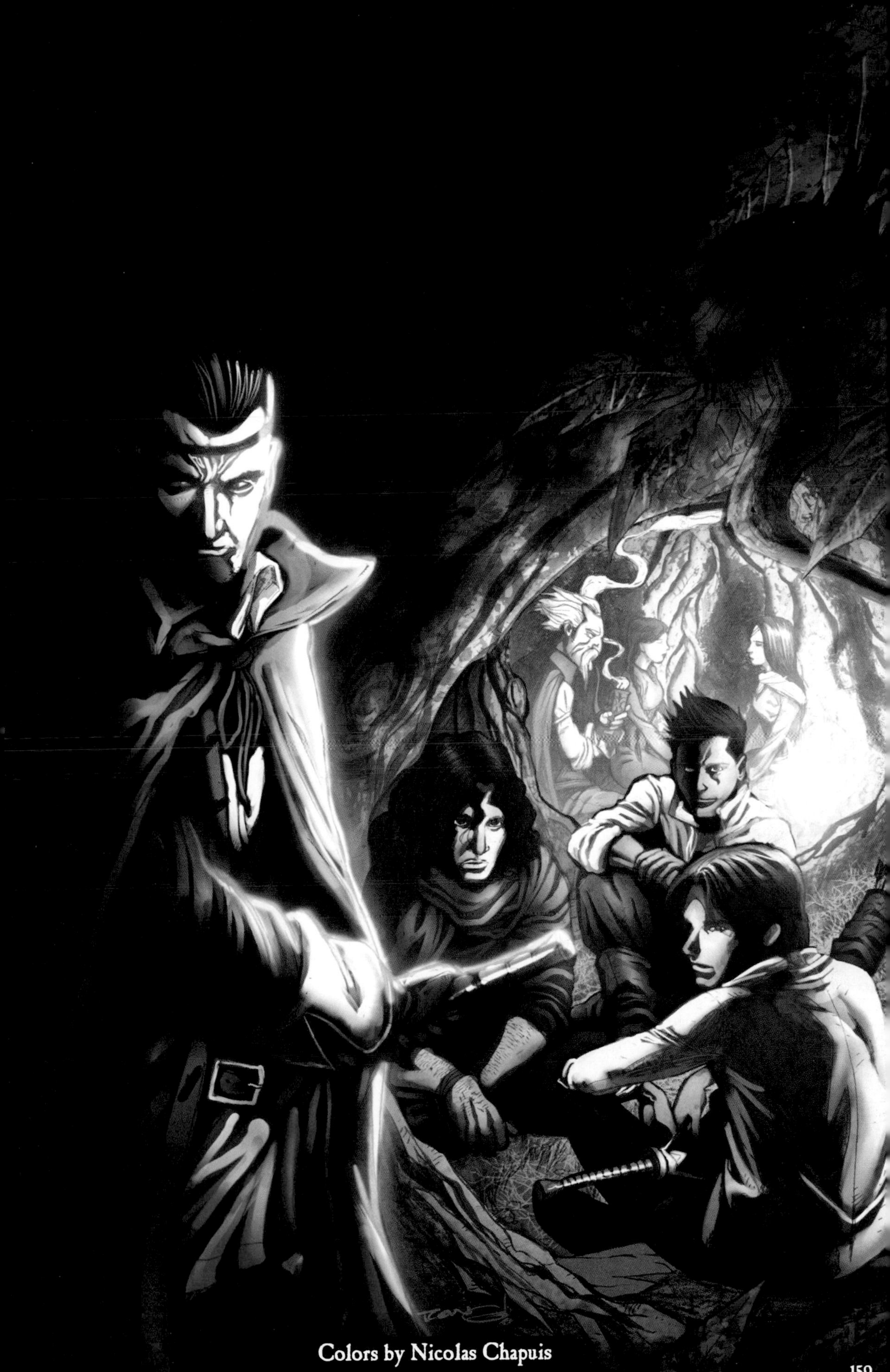

Colors by Nicolas Chapuis

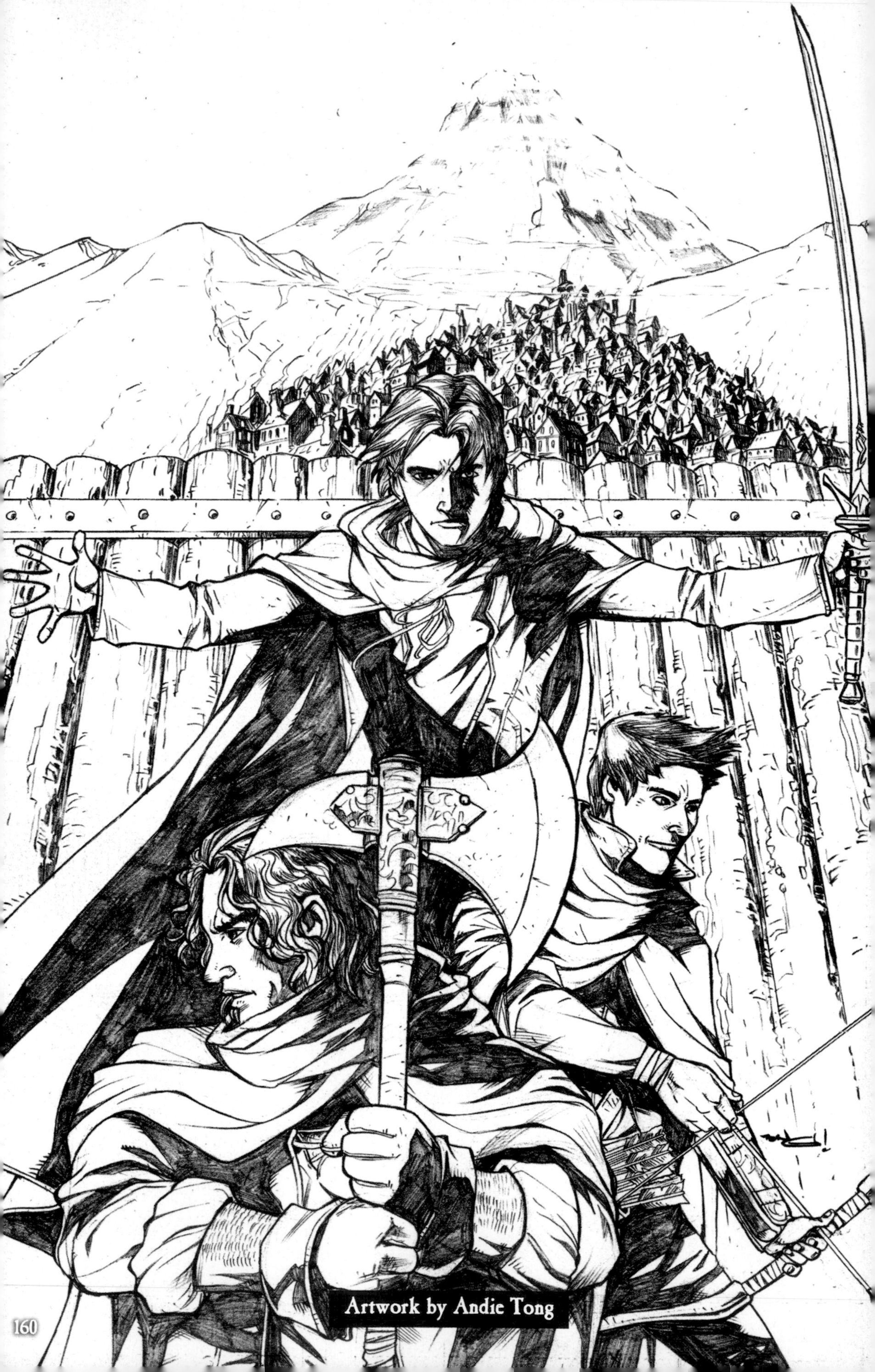

Artwork by Andie Tong

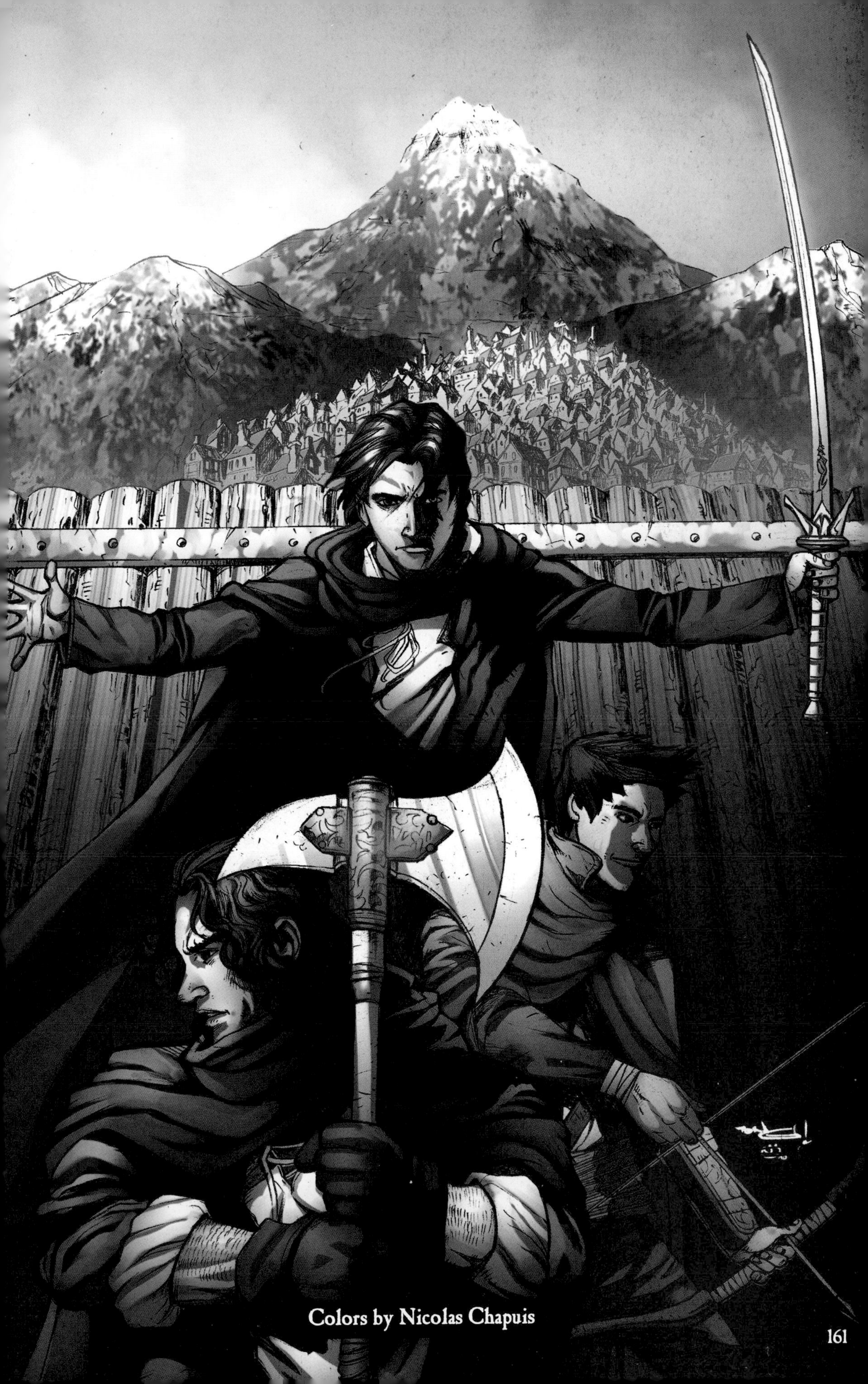

Colors by Nicolas Chapuis

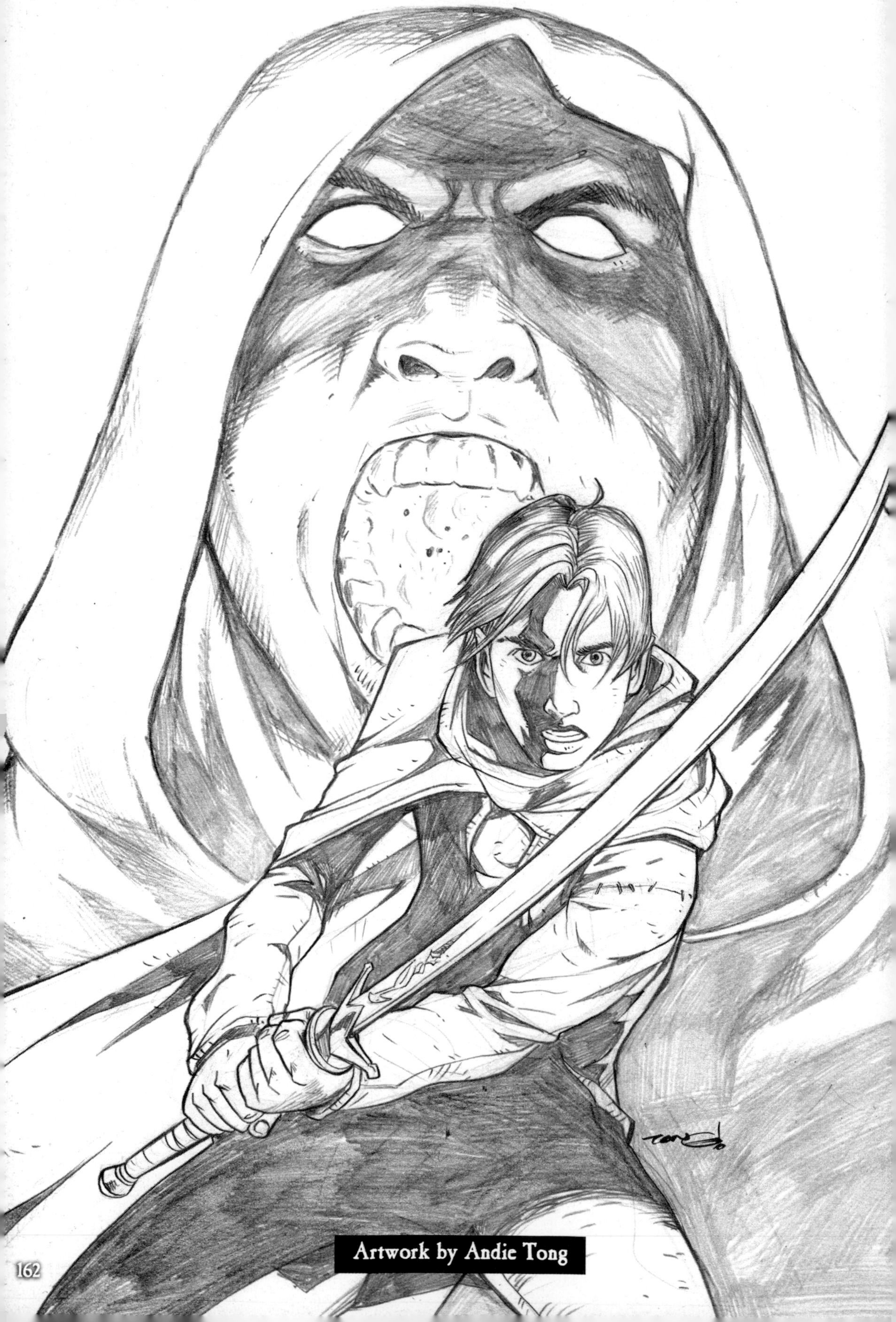

Artwork by Andie Tong

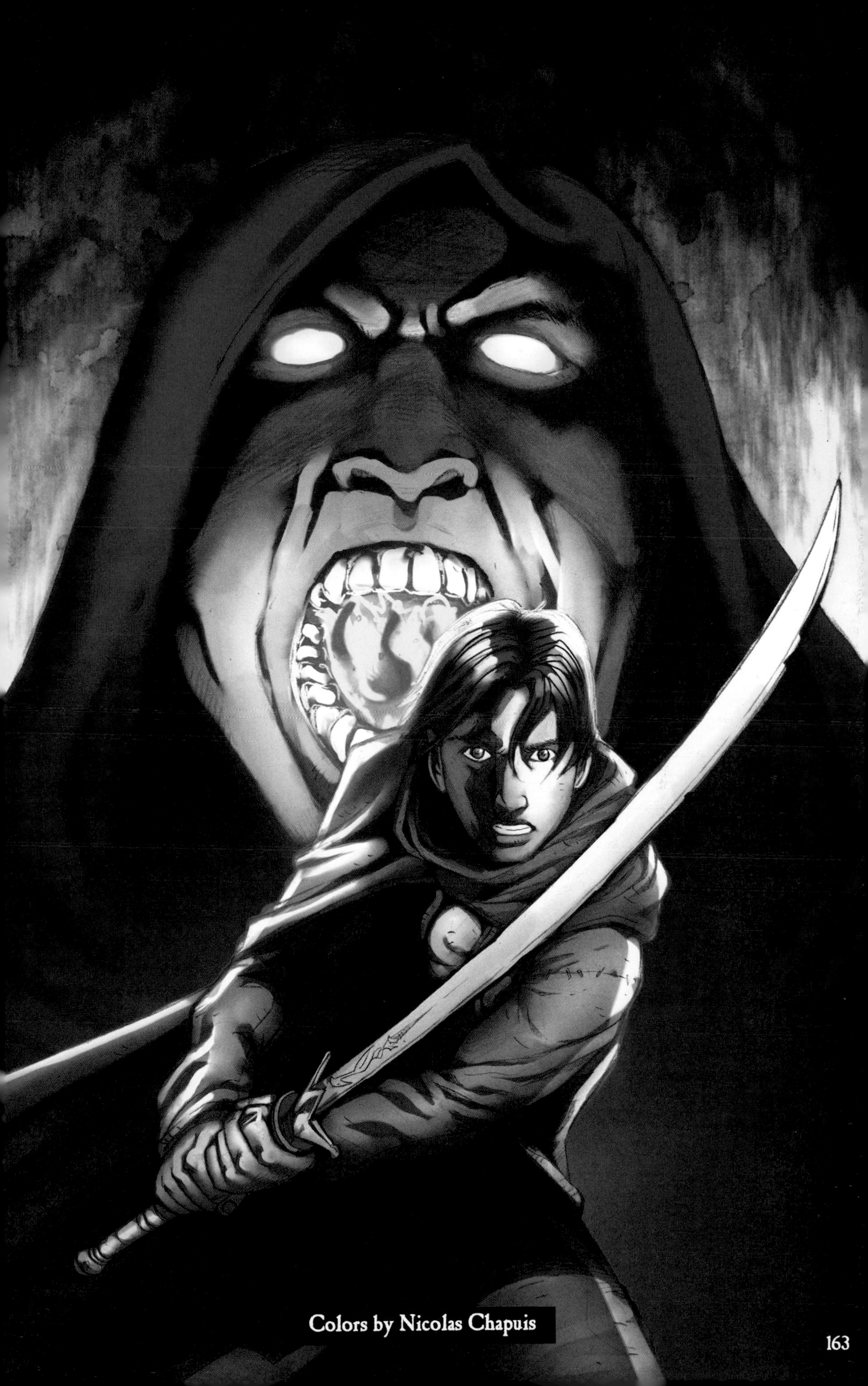

Colors by Nicolas Chapuis

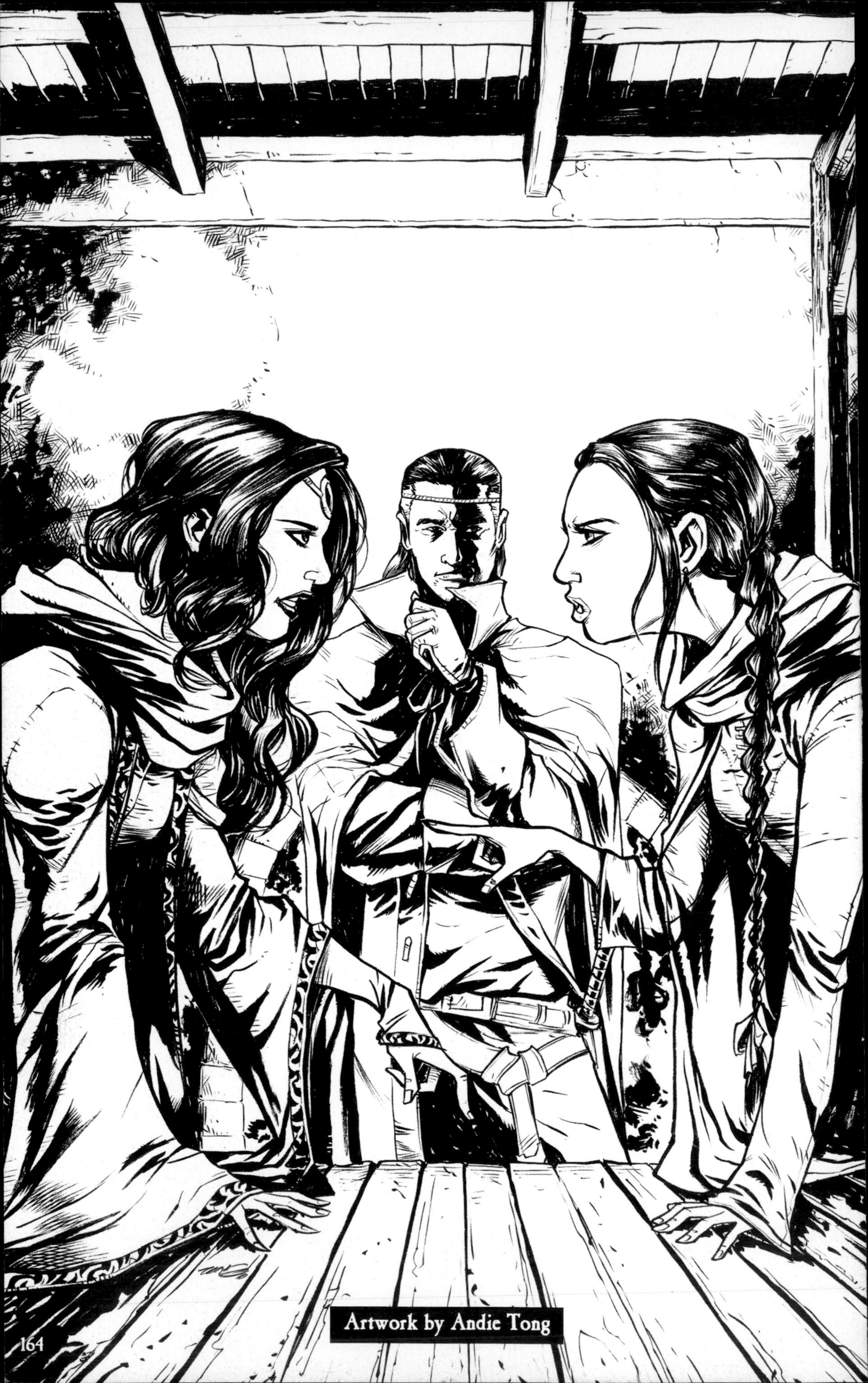

Artwork by Andie Tong

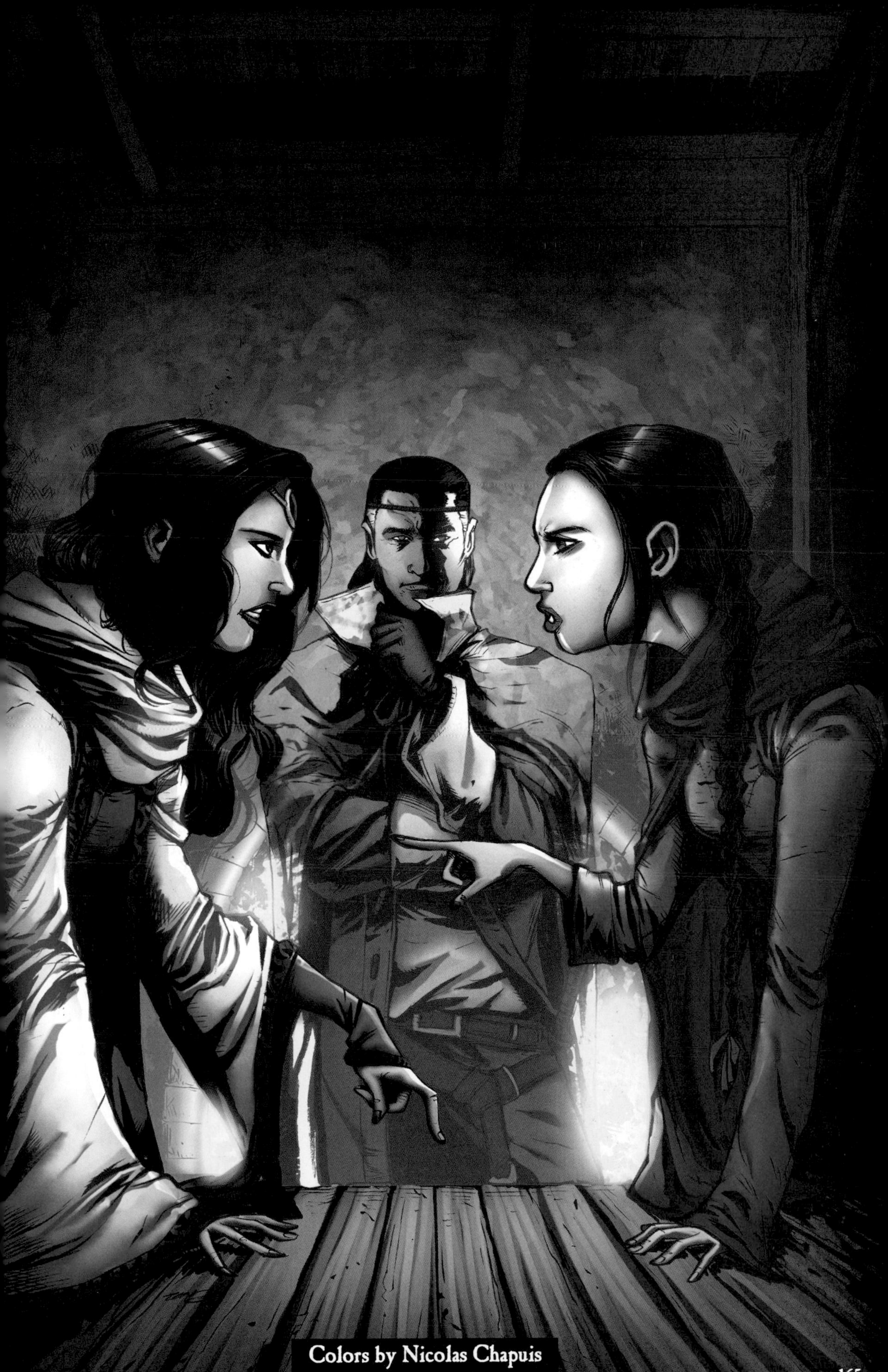

Colors by Nicolas Chapuis

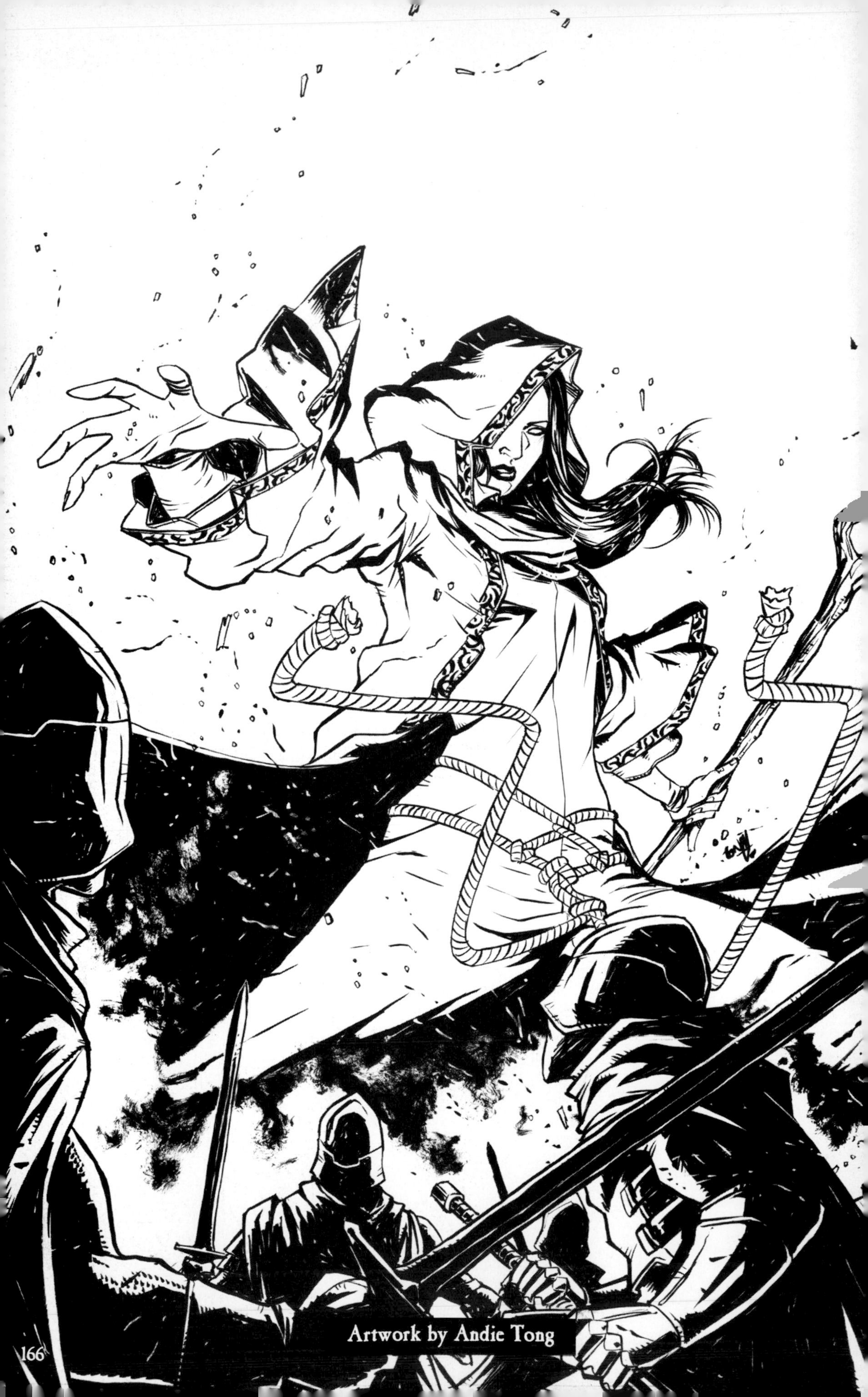

Artwork by Andie Tong

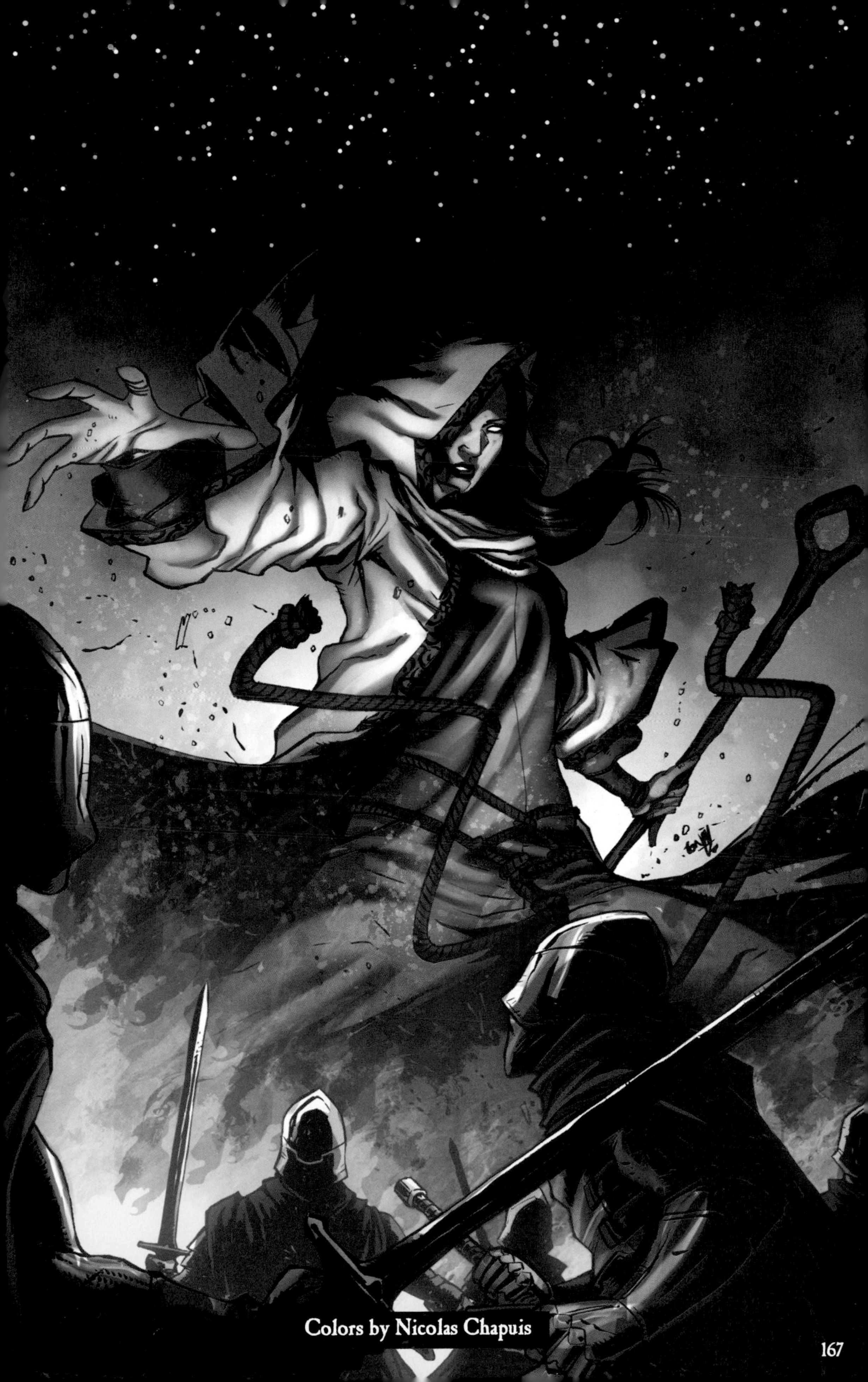

Colors by Nicolas Chapuis

biographies

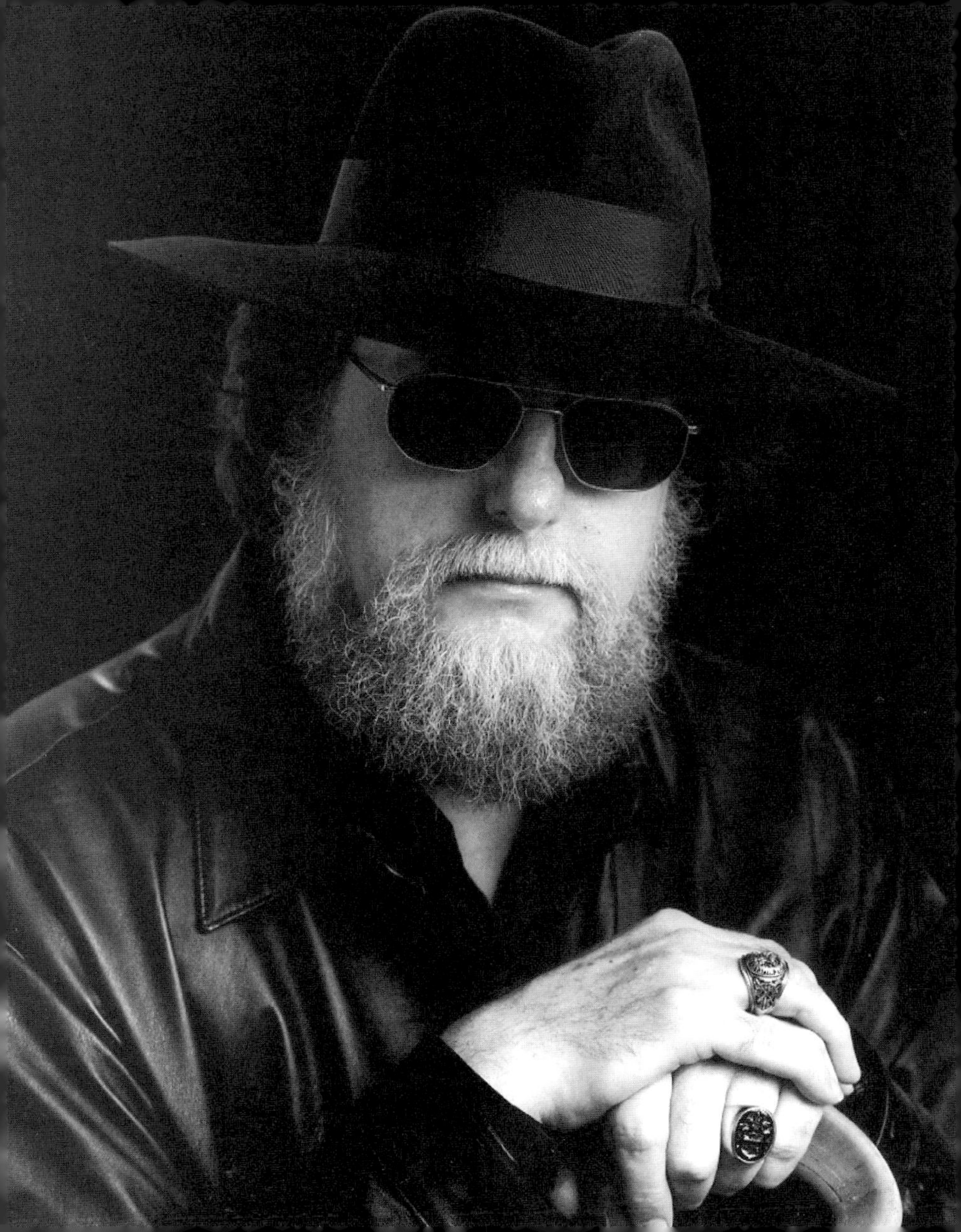

ROBERT JORDAN

Mr. Jordan was born in 1948 in Charleston, South Carolina. He taught himself to read when he was four with the incidental aid of a twelve-years-older brother, and was tackling Mark Twain and Jules Verne by five. He was a graduate of The Citadel, the Military College of South Carolina, with a degree in physics. He served two tours in Vietnam with the U. S. Army; among his decorations are the Distinguished Flying Cross with bronze oak leaf cluster, the Bronze Star with "V" and bronze oak leaf cluster, and two Vietnamese Gallantry Crosses with palm. A history buff, he also wrote dance and theater criticism and enjoyed the outdoor sports of hunting, fishing, and sailing, and the indoor sports of poker, chess, pool, and pipe collecting. He began writing in 1977 and went on to write The Wheel of Time®, one of the most important and bestselling series in the history of fantasy publishing with more than 14 million copies sold in North America, and countless more sold abroad. Robert Jordan died on September 16, 2007, after a courageous battle with the rare blood disease amyloidosis.

CHUCK DIXON

Mr. Dixon has worked for every major comic book publisher as a professional comic book writer. His credits include *The Hobbit* graphic novel, *The Punisher, Birds of Prey, Batman, Catwoman, Green Arrow, Green Lantern, Star Wars, Simpson* comics and the comic adaptation of *Dean Koontz's Frankenstein.*

Chuck currently resides in Florida.

ANDIE TONG

Andie Tong started off as a multimedia designer in 1997 and eventually migrated full time to comics in 2006. Since then he has worked on titles such as *Tron: Betrayal, Spectacular Spider-Man UK, Batman Strikes, Smallville, TMNT, Masters of the Universe,* and *Starship Troopers,* working for companies such as Disney, Marvel, DC, Panini, Darkhorse, as well as commercial illustration for Nike, Universal, CBS, Mattel, and Hasbro. Since 2008 he has also juggled illustration duties on a range of children's picture stories for HarperCollins.

Andie resides in London, United Kingdom.

NICOLAS CHAPUIS

Nicolas Chapuis was born in 1985 and decided to freelance as a comic book colorist after earning a degree in graphic design. His work includes Robert Jordan's *The Wheel of Time*, Jonathan Stroud's *Bartimaeus The Amulet of Samarkand*, and Richard Starking's *Elephantmen*.

He resides in Freiburg, Germany.

BILL TORTOLINI

Already an accomplished art director and graphic designer, Bill began lettering comics more than a decade ago and has worked with many of the comics industry's top creators and publishers.

Current and past projects include: *Stephen King's Talisman*, *Anita Blake: Vampire Hunter*, *Army of Darkness*, *Random Acts of Violence*, *Wolverine*, *Back to Brooklyn*, *The Hedge Knight*, *Archie Comics*, *Riftwar*, *Battlestar Galactica*, *The Warriors*, *The Wheel of Time*, *The Dresden Files*, *Transformers*, *Star Trek: The Next Generation*, *G.I. Joe*, *The Last Resort*, and many others.

Bill resides in Billerica, Massachusetts, with his wife and three children.

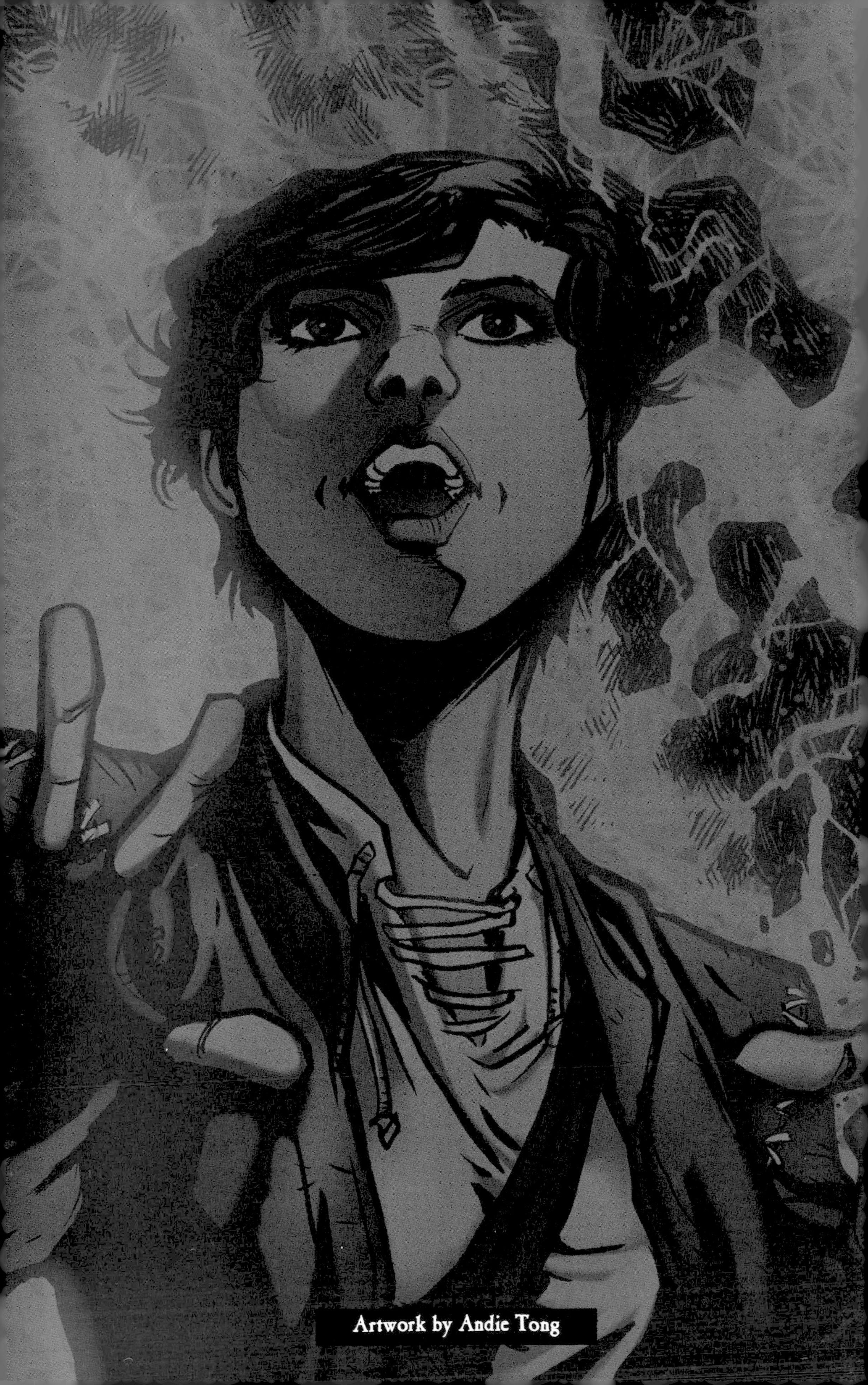

Artwork by Andie Tong

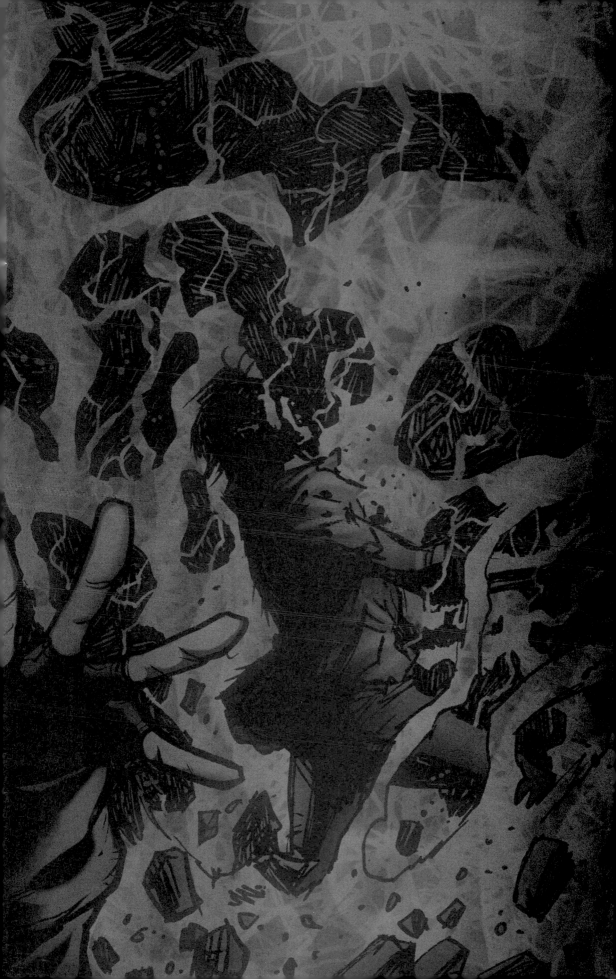